Workshop Manual
1975-1979

Leyland Cars
Service & Parts Division
Cowley, Oxford OX4 2PG, England

British Leyland Motors Inc.
600 Willow Tree Road, Leonia
New Jersey 07605

British Leyland Motors Canada Limited
4445 Fairview Street, P.O. Box 5033
Burlington, Ontario, Canada

Publication Part No. AKM 4071 / B

This manual is an enlarged edition of AKM 4071 and includes material from the following earlier MG Midget 1500 Workshop Manuals and Supplements, AKM 3267, AKM 3327, AKM3438 and AKM4071/1. All 1500 models are covered in this edition including those with US (including Californian), Canadian and UK specifications.

SPECIFICATION

Purchasers are advised that the specification details set out in this Manual apply to a range of vehicles and not to any particular vehicle. For the specification of any particular vehicle Purchasers should consult their authorised MG Dealer.

The Manufacturers reserve the right to vary their specifications with or without notice, and at such times and in such manner as they think fit. Major as well as minor changes may be involved in accordance with the Manufacturer's policy of constant product improvement.

Whilst every effort is made to ensure the accuracy of the particulars contained in this Manual, neither the Manufacturer nor the authorised Austin MG Dealer, by whom this Manual is supplied, shall in any circumstances be held liable for any inaccuracy or the consequences thereof.

NOTE: Each topic in this *Workshop Manual* is given a 6-digit number.
Topics are in numerical order throughout the *Workshop Manual*.
All references in the text are made using the 6-digit topic numbers.

© Copyright British Leyland Motors Inc. 1975, 1979, 1992
and Brooklands Books Limited 1994 and 2012

This book is published by Brooklands Books Limited and based upon text
and illustrations protected by copyright and first published in 1976 by
British Leyland Motors Inc. and may not be
reproduced transmitted or copied by any means without the
prior written permission of Rover Group Limited and
Brooklands Books Limited.

Printed and distributed by Brooklands Books Ltd., PO Box 146, Cobham,
Surrey KT11 1LG, England Phone: 01932 865051 Fax: 01932 868803
E-mail: sales@brooklands-books.com www.brooklands-books.com

Part Number: AKM4071/B

ISBN 9781855201699   Ref: MG49WH   2258

MG MIDGET 1500 WORKSHOP MANUAL
CONTENTS

system, Pressure differential warning actuator (P.D.W.A.) valve, Pressure differential warning actuator (P.D.W.A.), Master cylinder — tandem, Brake pedal assembly, Pedal box, Hand brake lever assembly, Hand brake lever, pawl and ratchet, 1975–1976 hand brake cable, 1977 and later hand brake cable, Hand brake compensator — 1975–1976 only, 1975–1976 hand brake cable assembly, 1977 and later hand brake assembly, Rear brake shoes, Front brake caliper, Rear wheel cylinder

CONTENTS

continued

continued

7

INSTRUMENTS

SERVICE TOOLS — All models, page 236

ADSORPTION CANISTER SPECIAL MAINTENANCE

INTRODUCTION

The purpose of this manual is to assist skilled mechanics in the efficient repair and maintenance of British Leyland vehicles.

Indexing
For convenience, this manual is divided into a number of divisions. A contents page listing the titles and reference numbers of the various divisions is provided.

Operating Numbering (where applicable)
Each operation is followed by the number allocated to it in a master index. The number consists of six digits arranged in three pairs.

The master index of operations has been compiled for universal application to vehicles manufactured by British Leyland Motor Corporation and therefore continuity of the numbering sequence is not maintained throughout the manual.

Each instruction within an operation has a sequence number, and to complete the operation in the minimum time it is essential that these instructions are performed in numerical sequence commencing at 1 unless otherwise stated. Where applicable, the sequence numbers identify the components in the appropriate illustration.

Where performance of an operation requires the use of a service tool, the tool number is quoted under the operation heading and is repeated in, or following, the instruction involving its use.

An illustrated list of all service tools necessary to complete the operations described in the manual is also included.

References
References to the left- or right-hand side in the manual are made when viewing the vehicle from the rear. With the engine and gearbox assembly removed, the water pump end of the engine is referred to as the front.

To reduce repetition, operations covered in this manual do not include reference to testing the vehicle after repair. It is essential that work is inspected and tested after completion and if necessary a road test of the vehicle is carried out particularly where safety related items are concerned.

Dimensions
The dimensions quoted are to design engineering specification. Alternative unit equivalents, shown in brackets following the dimensions, have been converted from the original specification.

REPAIRS AND REPLACEMENTS
When service parts are required it is essential that only genuine British Leyland or Unipart replacements are used.

Attention is particularly drawn to the following points concerning repairs and the fitting of replacement parts and accessories:

Safety features embodied in the car may be impaired if other than genuine parts are fitted.

In certain territories, legislation prohibits the fitting of parts not to the vehicle manufacturer's specification.

Torque wrench setting figures given in the Manual must be strictly adhered to. Locking devices, where specified, must be fitted. If the efficiency of a locking device is impaired during removal it must be renewed.

Owners purchasing accessories while travelling abroad should ensure that the accessory and its fitted location on the car conform to mandatory requirements existing in their country of origin.

The car warranty may be invalidated by the fitting of other than genuine British Leyland parts.

All British Leyland or Unipart replacements have the full backing of the factory warranty.

ABBREVIATIONS AND SYMBOLS IN THIS MANUAL

Across flats (bolt size)	A.F.
After bottom dead centre	A.B.D.C.
After top dead centre	A.T.D.C.
Alternating current	a.c.
Amperes	A
Ampere-hour	Ah
Before bottom dead centre	B.B.D.C.
Before top dead centre	B.T.D.C.
Bottom dead centre	B.D.C.
Brake horse-power	b.h.p.
Brake mean effective pressure	b.m.e.p.
British Standards	B.S.
Carbon monoxide	CO
Centigrade (Celsius)	C
Centimetres	cm
Cubic centimetres	cm³
Cubic inches	in³
Cycles per minute	c/min
Degree (angle)	deg. or °
Degree (temperature)	deg. or °
Diameter	dia.
Direct current	d.c.
Fahrenheit	F
Feet	ft
Feet per minute	ft/min
Fifth	5th
Figure (illustration)	Fig.
First	1st
Fourth	4th
Gallons (Imperial)	gal
Gallons (U.S.)	U.S. gal
Grammes (force)	gf
Grammes	g
High compression	h.c.
High tension (electrical)	h.t.
Horse-power	hp
Hundredweight	cwt
Inches	in
Inches of mercury	inHg
Independent front suspension	i.f.s.
Internal diameter	i.dia.
Kilogrammes (force)	kgf
Kilogrammes (mass)	kg
Kilogramme centimetre	kgf cm
Kilogramme metres	kgf m
Kilogrammes per square centimetre	kgf/cm²
Kilometres	km
Kilometres per hour	km/h
Kilovolts	kV
King pin inclination	k.p.i.
Left-hand	L.H.
Left-hand steering	L.H. Stg.
Left-hand thread	L.H. Thd.
Low compression	l.c.
Low tension	l.t.
Maximum	max.
Metres	m
Miniature Edison Screw	MES
Miles per gallon	m.p.g.
Miles per hour	m.p.h.
Millimetres	mm
Millimetres of mercury	mmHg
Minimum	min.
Minus (of tolerance)	—
Minute (of angle)	″
Negative (electrical)	—
Number	No.
Ounces (force)	ozf
Ounces (mass)	oz
Ounce inch (torque)	ozf in
Outside diameter	o.dia.
Overdrive	O/D
Paragraphs	para.
Part Number	Part No.
Percentage	%
Pints (Imperial)	pt
Pints (U.S.)	U.S. pt
Plus or minus	±
Plus (tolerance)	+
Positive (electrical)	+
Pounds (force)	lbf
Pounds (mass)	lb
Pounds feet (torque)	lbf ft
Pounds inches (torque)	lbf in
Pounds per square inch	lbf/in²
Radius	r
Ratio	:
Reference	ref.
Revolutions per minute	rev/min
Right-hand	R.H.
Right-hand steering	R.H. Stg.
Second (angle)	″
Second (numerical order)	2nd
Single carburetter	SC
Society of Automobile Engineers	S.A.E.
Specific gravity	sp. gr.
Square centimetres	cm²
Square inches	in²
Standard	std.
Standard wire gauge	s.w.g.
Synchronizer/synchromesh	synchro.
Third	3rd
Top dead centre	T.D.C.
Twin carburetters	TC
United Kingdom	UK
Volts	V
Watts	W
Screw threads	
American Standard Taper Pipe	N.P.T.F.
British Association	B.A.
British Standard Fine	B.S.F.
British Standard Pipe	B.S.P.
British Standard Whitworth	B.S.W.
Unified Coarse	U.N.C.
Unified Fine	U.N.F.

GENERAL SPECIFICATION DATA

ENGINE

	in	mm
Type	PE 94J	
Number of cylinders	4	
Bore	2.9 in	73.7 mm
Stroke	3.44 in	87.5 mm
Capacity	91.0 in³	1493 cm³
Firing order	1, 3, 4, 2	
Valve operation	Overhead by pushrod	
Compression ratio: l.c.	7.5 : 1	
h.c. (all U.K. and 1976 U.S.A)	9.1 : 1 (Non-catalytic converter)	
Oversize bores	+ 0.020 in	+ 0.51 mm

Crankshaft

	in	mm
Main journal diameter	2.3115 to 2.3120 in	58.713 to 58.725 mm
Minimum regrind diameter	2.2815 to 2.2820 in	57.935 to 57.948 mm
Crankpin journal diameter	1.8750 to 1.8755 in	47.625 to 47.638 mm
Minimum regrind diameter	1.8450 to 1.8455 in	46.865 to 46.878 mm
Maximum run out of centre journal (with front and rear supported)	0.003 in	0.076 mm
Maximum out of balance of shaft (with key and dowel fitted)	0.3 oz. in	3.36 g. cm
Crankshaft end-thrust	Taken on thrust washers at rear main bearing	
Crankshaft end-float	0.006 to 0.014 in	0.1524 to 0.3556 mm

Main bearings

	in	mm
Number and type	3 Thin wall type	
Length: Front, centre and rear	0.840 to 0.855 in	21.34 to 21.72 mm
End-thrust	Taken by thrust washers at rear main bearing	
Diametrical clearance	0.0005 to 0.002 in	0.013 to 0.050 mm
Undersizes	0.010, 0.020, 0.030 in	0.25, 0.51, 0.76 mm

Connecting rods

	in	mm
Type	Horizontal split big-end	
Length between centres	5.748 to 5.752 in	145.90 to 146.10 mm
Small-end bush diameter (reamed in position)	0.8126 to 0.8129 in	20.64 to 20.65 mm

Big-end bearings

	in	mm
Length	0.672 to 0.692 in	17.20 to 19.58 mm
Diametrical clearance	0.001 to 0.003 in	0.03 to 0.08 mm
Undersizes	0.010, 0.020, 0.030 in	0.25, 0.51, 0.76 mm

Gudgeon pin

	in	mm
Type	Fully floating	
Fit in connecting rod	Hand push fit	
Diameter (outer)	0.8123 to 0.8125 in	20.63 to 20.64 mm

Piston

	in	mm
Type	Aluminium, solid skirt	
Bore size: Grade F	2.8995 to 2.9000 in	73.647 to 72.66 mm
Grade G	2.9001 to 2.9006 in	73.663 to 73.673 mm
Bottom diameter of piston: Grade F	2.8984 to 2.8989 in	73.619 to 73.632 mm
Grade G	2.8990 to 2.8995 in	73.635 to 73.647 mm
Clearance of skirt in cylinder: Top	0.002 to 0.003 in	0.051 to 0.076 mm
Bottom	0.0002 to 0.0016 in	0.005 to 0.041 mm
Number of rings	3 : 2 compression 1 oil control	
Width of grooves: Top and second	0.064 to 0.065 in	1.625 to 1.650 mm
Oil control	0.1578 to 0.1588 in	3.99 to 4.01 mm
Gudgeon pin bore	0.8124 to 0.8126 in	20.63 to 20.64 mm

Piston rings

	in	mm
Compression: Type: Top	Plain, chrome plated	
Second	Tapered periphery	
Width: Top, second	0.0615 to 0.0625 in	1.575 to 1.5787 mm
Fitted gap: Top and second	0.012 to 0.022 in	0.305 to 0.559 mm
Ring to groove clearance: Top, second	0.0015 to 0.0035 in	0.038 to 0.089 mm

continued

GENERAL SPECIFICATION DATA
ENGINE — (contd.)

	in	mm
Oil control:		
Type	Two chrome faced rings with expander	
Fitted gap – chrome faced rings	0.015 to 0.055 in	0.38 to 1.40 mm
Camshaft		
Journal diameters:		
Front and Rear	1.9659 to 1.9664 in	49.93 to 49.95 mm
Centre	1.9649 to 1.9654 in	49.90 to 49.92 mm
Bore in block	1.9680 to 1.9695 in	49.980 to 50.025 mm
Diametrical clearance: Front and rear	0.0016 to 0.0036 in	0.04 to 0.09 mm
Centre	0.0026 to 0.0046 in	0.07 to 0.12 mm
End-thrust	Taken on locating plate (front end)	
End-float	0.0045 to 0.0085 in	0.120 to 0.216 mm
Drive	Single chain and sprocket from crankshaft	
Timing chain	0.375 in pitch × 62 pitches	9.52 mm pitch × 62 pitches
Tappets		
Outside diameter	0.7996 to 0.8000 in	20.30 to 20.32 mm
Length	1.75 in	44.45 mm
Rocker gear		
Rocker shaft diameter	0.5607 to 0.5612 in	14.27 to 14.35 mm
Rocker arm bore	0.563 to 0.564 in	14.30 to 14.33 mm
Valves		
Valve face angle: Inlet and Exhaust	45°	
Valve insert seat angle: Inlet and Exhaust	45½°	
Head diameter: Inlet	1.377 to 1.383 in	34.97 to 35.01 mm
Exhaust	1.168 to 1.172 in	29.66 to 29.76 mm
Stem diameter: Inlet	0.3107 to 0.3113 in	7.89 to 7.91 mm
Exhaust	0.3100 to 0.3105 in	7.874 to 7.887 mm
Stem to guide clearance: Inlet	0.0007 to 0.0023 in	0.02 to 0.06 mm
Exhaust	0.0015 to 0.0030 in	0.04 to 0.07 mm
Valve guides		
Length: Inlet and Exhaust	2.06 in	52.224 mm
Fitted height above head	0.75 in	19.050 mm
Diameter: Inlet and Exhaust:		
Outside	0.5015 to 0.502 in	12.73 to 12.75 mm
Inside	0.312 to 0.313 in	7.92 to 7.95 mm

Valve springs

	Inner (U.K. models only)	Outer
Free length	1.14 in 30 mm	1.52 in 38.6 mm
Fitted length	1.010 in 25.7 mm	1.342 in 34.2 mm
Load at top of lift	40^{+3}_{-0} lbf $18^{+1.36}_{-0}$ kgf	123^{+10}_{-0} lbf $55.8^{+4.54}_{-0}$ kgf
Number of working coils	4	4

Valve timing

Timing marks	Pointers on timing case and notch on crankshaft pulley	
Rocker clearance: Running (cold)	0.010 in	0.25 mm
Timing (No. 7 and 8 valves)	0.050 in	1.27 mm
Inlet valve: Opens	18° B.T.D.C.	
Closes	58° A.B.D.C.	
Exhaust valve: Opens	58° B.B.D.C.	
Closes	18° A.T.D.C.	

Lubrication

System	Wet sump pressure fed	
System pressure: Running	40 to 60 lbf/in²	2.81 to 4.2 kgf/cm²
Oil pump	Hobourn-Eaton eccentric lobe type	
Oil filter	Full flow; disposable cartridge type	
By-pass valve opens	8 to 12 lbf/in²	
Oil pressure relief valve opens	53 lbf/in²	3.71 kgf/cm²
Relief valve spring:		
Free length (approx)	1.53 in	38.86 mm
Fitted length	1.25 in	31.75 mm
Load at fitted length	12.5 to 15.5 lbf	5.67 to 7.04 kgf

TRANSMISSION

Gearbox		
Synchromesh	All forward gears	
Ratios: Top	1 : 1	
Third	1.433 : 1	
Second	2.1119 : 1	
First	3.4118 : 1	
Reverse	3.7529 : 1	
Overall ratios: Top	3.909 : 1	
Third	5.602 : 1	
Second	8.255 : 1	
First	13.337 : 1	
Reverse	14.670 : 1	
Road speed per 1,000 rev/min in top gear	16.4 mph	26.24 km.p.h.

continued

GENERAL SPECIFICATION DATA

TRANSMISSION — (contd.)

Rear axle

Type	Three-quarter — floating	
Ratio	3.909 : 1	

Propeller shafts

Type	Tubular	
Diameter	1¾ in	44.45 mm
Universal joints	Hardy Spicer, Needle-roller	

FUEL SYSTEM

Carburetter see 'ENGINE TUNING DATA'

Fuel pump

Make/type	AC Delco type R A 1

Air cleaner

Type	Paper element

SUSPENSION

Front

Type	Independent, coil springs	
Free length of coil spring	9.85 in	25 cm
Fitted length at load of 750 ± 15 lb (337 ± 6.8 kg)	7.08 in	18 cm
No. of effective coils	7	
Spring rate	271 lbf in	3.127 kgf m
Dampers	Lever arm type	

Rear

Type	Semi-elliptic	
Number of spring leaves	6	
Width of leaves	1.49 to 1.52 in	37.85 to 38.50 mm
Gauge of leaves	0.167 to 0.177 in	4.24 to 4.50 mm
Free camber	5.58 in	141.7 mm
Dampers	Lever arm type	

STEERING

Type	Rack and pinion	
Steering wheel turns — lock to lock	2.8	
Front wheel alignment toe-in	Parallel to ⅛ in	0 to 3.2 mm
Steering wheel diameter	15½ in	39.4 cm
Camber angle	¾°	
Castor angle	3°	
King pin inclination: Laden	6° 30' $\Big\}$ ± 1° 15'	
Unladen	6° 45'	
Steering lock angle of inner wheel with outer wheel at 20°	19° 30' ± 1° 30'	
Pinion end-float	0.010 in	0.25 mm

BRAKES

Front

Disc diameter	8.25 in	209.5 mm
Standard width	0.300 to 0.305 in	7.62 to 7.75 mm
Minimum permissible width	0.29 in	7.37 mm
Pad area (total)	18 in²	116.1 cm²
Swept area (total)	135.28 in²	871 cm²
Minimum pad thickness	1/16 in	1.59 mm

Rear

Drum diameter	7 in	177.8 mm
Lining dimensions	6.94 x 1.25 x 0.187 in	177.5 x 37.5 x 4.75 mm
Swept area (total)	27.5 in²	177 cm²
Wheel cylinder diameter	0.687 in	17.46 mm

Master cylinder:

Diameter of bore	0.75 in	19.05 mm

WHEELS

Size: Pressed spoke	4½ JSL x 13
Wire	4J x 13

TYRES

Type/size	145 SR—13
Pressures	See 'MAINTENANCE'

COOLING SYSTEM

Type	Pressurised system with expansion tank	
Thermostat: Standard (UK)	82°C	180°F
Cold climate (USA and Canada)	88°C	190°F
Pressure cap	15 lb/in²	1.5 kg/cm²
Fan belt tension (deflection on longest run)	0.5 in	13 mm
Type of pump	Centrifugal	

continued

GENERAL SPECIFICATION DATA

CLUTCH

Make	Borg and Beck	
Type	Single dry plate, diaphragm spring type	
Drive plate diameter	7¼ in	184 mm
Number of damper springs	4	
Damper spring colour	Maroon/light green (short slots), Buff/light green (long slots)	
Master cylinder bore	0.70 in	17.78 mm
Slave cylinder bore	22.23 mm	0.875 in

ELECTRICAL

System	12 volt, negative earth	
Battery type	Lucas A9/AZ9 – A11/AZ11	
Capacity at 20-hr rate	A9/AZ9: 40 amp hr A11/AZ11: 50 amp hr	

Alternator

Type	Lucas 16ACR	
Brush length – new	0.5 in	12.6 mm
Brush length – minimum protrusion from bush box moulding	0.2 in	5 mm
Brush spring pressure – when brush is pushed in flush with brush box face	9 to 13 oz	255 to 369 gm
Field winding:		
Resistance at 20° C (68° F)	3.3 ohms ± 5%	
Current flow at 12 volts	3 amperes	
Insulation test equipment	110-volt a.c. supply and 15-watt test lamp	
Stator windings:		
Continuity test equipment	12-volt d.c. supply and 36-watt test lamp	
Insulation test equipment	110-volt a.c. supply and 15-watt test lamp	
Diode current test equipment	12-volt d.c. supply and 1.5-watt test lamp	
Alternator output at 14 volts	34 amperes at 6,000 alternator rev/min	

Starter motor

Type	Lucas M35 J inertia type	
Armature:		
Commutator copper minimum thickness	0.08 in	2.03 mm
Insulation test equipment	110-volt a.c. supply and 15-watt test lamp	
Minimum brush length	3/8 in	10 mm
Brush spring pressure – when brush protrudes 1/16 in (1.5 mm) from brush box moulding	28 ozf	0.8 kgf
Brush spring and terminal post insulation test equipment	110-volt a.c. supply and 15-watt test lamp	
Field windings:		
Continuity test equipment	12-volt d.c. supply and 12-watt test lamp	
Insulation test equipment	110-watt a.c. supply and 15-watt test lamp	
Starter motor performance (obtained with a 12-volt 43 Ah (20 hour rate) battery in a 70 per cent charged condition at 20° C (68° F):		
Lock torque – with 350 to 375 amp.	7 lbf ft	0.97 kgf m
Torque at 1,000 rev/min – with 260 to 275 amp	4.4 lbf ft	0.61 kgf m
Light running current	65 amp at 8,000 to 10,000 rev/min	

Wiper motor

Type	Lucas 14W	
Running current (rack disconnected)	1.5 amp	
Wiper speed (after 60 seconds)	46 to 52 rev/min (low speed) 60 to 70 rev/min (high speed)	
Armature end-float	0.004 to 0.008 in	0.102 to 0.2 mm
Brush spring tension	5 to 7 ozf	140 to 200 gf
Minimum brush length	3/16 in	4.7 mm
Maximum pull to move rack in tubes	6 lbf	2.7 kgf

GENERAL DIMENSIONS

Track:		
Pressed spoke wheel: Front	3 ft 10 9/16 in	118.27 mm
Pressed spoke wheel: Rear	3 ft 9 in	114.30 cm
Wire wheel: Front	3 ft 10 5/16 in	117.63 cm
Wire wheel: Rear	3 ft 9¼ in	114.93 cm
Turning circle: Left lock	32 ft 1½ in	9.79 m
Turning circle: Right lock	31 ft 2½ in	9.51 m
Wheelbase	6 ft 8 in	2.03 m
Overall length	11 ft 9 in	3.6 m
Overall width: Pressed spoke wheel	4 ft 5 5/8 in	1.36 m
Overall width: Wire wheel	4 ft 8½ in	1.44 m
Overall height	4 ft 1¼ in	1.25 m
Ground clearance	3¼ in	82.55 mm

continued

GENERAL SPECIFICATION DATA

WEIGHTS — U.S.A. SPECIFICATION

	Loading conditions	Total weight	Distribution	
			Front	Rear
Kerbside	Including full fuel tank, all optional extras	1849 lb (839 kg)	941 lb (427 kg)	908 lb (412 kg)
Normal	Kerbside weight including driver, passenger	2149 lb (975 kg)	1034 lb (469 kg)	1115 lb (506 kg)
Gross	Normal weight condition refer to note below	2229 lb (1011 kg)	1003 lb (455 kg)	1226 lb (556 kg)
Maximum permissible towing weight		1344 lb (610 kg)		
Recommended towbar hitch load		75 lb (34 kg)		

WEIGHTS — U.K. SPECIFICATION

	Loading conditions	Total weight	Distribution	
			Front	Rear
Kerbside	Including full fuel tank, all optional extras	1774 lb (804 kg)	918 lb (416 kg)	856 lb (388 kg)
Normal	Kerbside weight including driver, passenger	2074 lb (941 kg)	1016 lb (461 kg)	1058 lb (480 kg)
Gross	Normal weight condition refer to note below	2154 lb (977 kg)	987 lb (448 kg)	1167 lb (529 kg)
Maximum permissible towing weight		1344 lb (610 kg)		
Recommended towbar hitch load		75 lb (34 kg)		

NOTE: Due consideration must be given to the overall weight when fully loading the car. Any loads carried on a luggage rack or downward load from a towing hitch must also be included in the maximum loading.

ENGINE TUNING DATA

Model: MG MIDGET Mk III   **Year: 1975 on (U.K. specification only)**

ENGINE

Type	PE 94J
Capacity	1493 cm³ 91.0 in³
Compression ratio	9.0 : 1
Firing order	1, 3, 4, 2
Cranking pressure	
Idle speed	650 to 680 rev/min
Fast idle speed (hot)	1,100 to 1,300 rev/min
Ignition timing † ‡	10° B.T.D.C.
Stroboscopic at 680 rev/min	
Timing marks	Pointers on timing case notch on crankshaft pulley

Valve clearance:

Inlet and Exhaust (cold)	0.010 in 0.25 mm

DISTRIBUTOR

Make/type	Lucas 45 D4
Rotation of rotor	Anti-clockwise
Dwell angle	51° ± 5°
Condenser capacity	0.18 to 0.25 microfarad
Lucas serial No.	41449
Contact breaker gap	0.014 to 0.016 in 0.35 to 0.40 mm
Centrifugal advance † ‡	2° to 6° at 1,100 rev/min
	6° to 10° at 1,400 rev/min
	8° to 12° at 2,000 rev/min
	12° to 16° at 3,200 rev/min

Vacuum advance ‡

Starts	3 in Hg
Finishes	18 in Hg
Total crankshaft degrees	12° ± 2

SPARK PLUGS

Make	Champion
Type	N–9Y; 1978: N–12Y
Gap	0.025 0.64 mm

IGNITION COIL

Make/type	Lucas 15C6
Primary resistance at 68° F	1.30 to 1.45 ohms
Ballast resistor	1.3 to 1.5 ohms

CARBURETTER

Make/type	SU Twin type HS4
Specification No.	AUD 665
Jet size	0.90 in 2.2 mm
Needle	ABT
Piston spring	Red
Choke diameter	1½ in 38.10 mm

EXHAUST EMISSION

Exhaust gas analyser reading at engine idle speed	3 to 4.5% (2% nominal)
Air pump test speed	850 rev/min

† Vacuum disconnected   ‡ Crankshaft degrees and rev/min

ENGINE TUNING DATA

Model: MG MIDGET Mk III   Year: 1975

ENGINE

Type	PE 94J
Capacity	91.0 in³ 1493 cm³
Compression ratio	7.5 : 1
Firing order	1, 3, 4, 2
Cranking pressure	
Idle speed	700 to 900 rev/min
Fast idle speed (hot)	1800 rev/min
Ignition timing:	
Stroboscopic at 800 rev/min	2° A.T.D.C.
Timing marks	Pointers on timing case notch on crankshaft pulley
Valve clearance:	
Inlet and Exhaust (cold)	0.010 in 0.25 mm

DISTRIBUTOR

Make/type	Lucas 45/DE4 (Electronic)
Rotation of rotor	Anti-clockwise
Drive resistor	9.5 ohms ± 5%
Lucas serial No.	41593
Pick-up air gap	0.014 to 0.016 in 0.35 to 0.40 mm
Centrifugal advance † ‡	0° to 7° at 1200 rev/min
	8° to 12° at 1600 rev/min
	11° to 15° at 2600 rev/min
	12° to 16° at 3200 rev/min

Vacuum retard † ‡

1. Apply vacuum 15 in hg ....   10° to 14°
2. Increase to 20 in hg ....   10° to 14°
3. Decrease to 1 in hg ....   0°

SPARK PLUGS

Make	Champion
Type	N–12Y
Gap	0.025 0.64 mm

IGNITION COIL

Make/type	Lucas 15C6
Primary resistance at 68° F	1.30 to 1.45 ohms
Ballast resistor	1.3 to 1.5 ohms

CARBURETTER

Make/type	Zenith-Stromberg Single 150 CD4
Specification No.	3754
Jet size	0.100 in 2.54
Needle	44A
Piston spring	Blue
Choke diameter	1½ in 38.10 mm

EXHAUST EMISSION

Exhaust gas analyser reading at engine idle speed	½ to 2% (2% nominal)
Air pump test speed	850 rev/min

† Vacuum disconnected   ‡ Crankshaft degrees and rev/min

ENGINE TUNING DATA

Model: MG MIDGET Mk III — Non-catalytic converter cars   Year: 1976

ENGINE
Type	PE 94J
Capacity	91.0 in³ 1493 cm³
Compression ratio	9.1 : 1
Firing order	1, 3, 4, 2
Idle speed	700 to 900 rev/min
Fast idle speed (hot)	1800 rev/min
Ignition timing:	
Stroboscopic at 800 rev/min† ‡	2° A.T.D.C.
Timing marks	Pointers on timing case notch on crank-shaft pulley
Valve clearance:	
Inlet and Exhaust (cold)	0.010 in 0.25 mm

DISTRIBUTOR
Make/type	Lucas 45/DE4 (Electronic)
Rotation of rotor	Anti-clockwise
Drive resistor	9.5 ohms ± 5%
Lucas serial No.	41646
Pick-up air gap	0.014 to 0.016 in 0.35 to 0.40 mm
Centrifugal advance † ‡	4° to 8° at 1450 rev/min
	6° to 10° at 1800 rev/min
	11° to 15° at 3200 rev/min
	12° to 16° at 5000 rev/min

Vacuum retard † ‡
1. Apply vacuum 11 in hg	10° to 14°
2. Increase to 15 in hg	10° to 14°
3. Decrease to 3 in hg	0°

SPARK PLUGS
Make	Champion
Type	N–12Y
Gap	0.025 0.64 mm

IGNITION COIL
Make/type	Lucas 15C6
Primary resistance at 68° F	1.30 to 1.45 ohms
Ballast resistor	1.3 to 1.5 ohms

CARBURETTER
Make/type	Zenith-Stromberg Single 150 CD4
Specification No.	3754
Jet size	0.100 in 2.54
Needle	44A
Piston spring	Blue
Choke diameter	1½ in 38.10 mm

EXHAUST EMISSION
Exhaust gas analyser reading at engine idle speed	½ to 2% (2% nominal)
Air pump test speed	850 rev/min

† Vacuum disconnected   ‡ Crankshaft degrees and rev/min

ENGINE TUNING DATA

Model: MG MIDGET Mk III — Catalytic converter cars   Year: 1976

ENGINE

Type	PE 94J	
Capacity	91.0 in^3	1493 cm^3
Compression ratio	7.5 : 1	
Firing order	1, 3, 4, 2	
Cranking pressure		
Idle speed	700 to 900 rev/min	
Ignition timing:		
Stroboscopic at 800 rev/min† ‡	2° A.T.D.C.	
Timing marks	Pointers on timing case notch on crank-shaft pulley	
Valve clearance:		
Inlet and Exhaust (cold)	0.010 in	0.25 mm

DISTRIBUTOR

Make/type	Lucas 45/DE4 (Electronic)	
Rotation of rotor	Anti-clockwise	
Drive resistor	9.5 ohms ± 5%	
Lucas serial No.	41593	
Pick-up air gap	0.014 to 0.016 in	0.35 to 0.40 mm
Centrifugal advance † ‡	0° to 7° at 1200 rev/min	
	8° to 12° at 1600 rev/min	
	11° to 15° at 2600 rev/min	
	12° to 16° at 3200 rev/min	

Vacuum retard † ‡
1. Apply vacuum 15 in hg	10° to 14°	
2. Increase to 20 in hg	10° to 14°	
3. Decrease to 1 in hg	0°	

SPARK PLUGS

Make	Champion	
Type	N–12Y	
Gap	0.025	0.64 mm

IGNITION COIL

Make/type	Lucas 15C6
Primary resistance at 68° F	1.30 to 1.45 ohms
Ballast resistor	1.3 to 1.5 ohms

CARBURETTER

Make/type	Zenith-Stromberg Single 150 CD4T	
Specification No.	3755	
Jet size	0.100 in	2.54
Needle	44A	
Piston spring	Blue	
Choke: Needle	D9	
Fast idle cam No.	CT 8	
Fast idle setting	0.035 in	0.9 mm
Diameter	1½ in	38.10 mm

EXHAUST EMISSION

Exhaust gas analyser reading at engine idle speed	½ to 2% (2% nominal)
Air pump test speed	850 rev/min

† Vacuum disconnected   ‡ Crankshaft degrees and rev/min

19

ENGINE TUNING DATA

Model: MG MIDGET Mk III – Californian specification   Years: **1977 and later**

ENGINE
Type	PE 94J	
Capacity	91.0 in³	1493 cm³
Compression ratio	7.5 : 1	
Firing order	1, 3, 4, 2	
Cranking pressure		
Idle speed	700 to 900 rev/min (800 rev/min nominal)	
Ignition timing: Stroboscopic at 800 rev/min† ‡	2° A.T.D.C.	
Timing marks	Pointers on timing case notch on crankshaft pulley	

Valve clearance:
Inlet and Exhaust (cold)	0.010 in	0.25 mm

DISTRIBUTOR
Make/type	Lucas 45/DE4 (Electronic)	
Rotation of rotor	Anti-clockwise	
Drive resistor	9.5 ohms ± 5%	
Lucas serial No.	41698	
Pick-up air gap	0.014 to 0.016 in	0.35 to 0.40 mm
Centrifugal advance † ‡	1° to 7° at 1200 rev/min	
	7° to 13° at 1500 rev/min	
	13° to 17° at 2600 rev/min	
	15° to 19° at 3300 rev/min	

Vacuum retard † ‡
1. Apply vacuum 11 in hg	10° to 14°	
2. Increase to 15 in hg	10° to 14°	
3. Decrease to 3 in hg	0°	

SPARK PLUGS
Make	Champion	
Type	N-12Y	
Gap	0.025	0.64 mm

IGNITION COIL
Make/type	Lucas 15C6	
Primary resistance at 68° F	1.30 to 1.45 ohms	
Ballast resistor	1.3 to 1.5 ohms	

CARBURETTER
Make/type	Zenith-Stromberg Single 150 CD4T	
Specification No.	3863	
Throat diameter	1½ in	38.10 mm
Jet size	0.100 in	2.54 mm
Needle	45K;1979:45R	
Piston spring	Blue	
Choke: Needle	D9	
Fast idle cam No.	CT8	
Fast idle setting	0.035 in	0.9 mm

EXHAUST EMISSION
Exhaust gas analyser reading at engine idle speed	½ to 6% (3% nominal)	
Air pump test speed	850 rev/min	

† Vacuum disconnected   ‡ Crankshaft degrees and rev/min

ENGINE TUNING DATA

Model: MG MIDGET Mk III — USA Federal States and Canadian specification

Years: 1977 and later

ENGINE

Type	PE 94J	
Capacity	91.0 in³	1493 cm³
Compression ratio	7.5 : 1	
Firing order	1, 3, 4, 2	
Cranking pressure		
Idle speed	700 to 900 rev/min (800 rev/min nominal)	
Ignition timing:		
Stroboscopic at 800 rev/min† ‡	10° B.T.D.C.	
Timing marks	Pointers on timing case notch on crank-shaft pulley	
Valve clearance:		
Inlet and Exhaust (cold)	0.010 in	0.25 mm

DISTRIBUTOR

Make/type	Lucas 45/DE4 (Electronic)	
Rotation of rotor	Anti-clockwise	
Drive resistor	9.5 ohms ± 5%	
Lucas serial No.	41697	
Pick-up air gap	0.014 to 0.016 in	0.35 to 0.40 mm
Centrifugal advance † ‡	1° to 7° at 1200 rev/min	
	7° to 13° at 1500 rev/min	
	13° to 17° at 2600 rev/min	
	15° to 19° at 3300 rev/min	

Vacuum advance † ‡	(5, 10.11)	
Maximum	22° at 10 inHg	
Starts	5 inHg	

SPARK PLUGS

Make	Champion	
Type	N–12Y	
Gap	0.025	0.64 mm

IGNITION COIL

Make/type	Lucas 15C6
Primary resistance at 68° F	1.30 to 1.45 ohms
Ballast resistor	1.3 to 1.5 ohms

CARBURETTER

Make/type	Zenith-Stromberg Single 150 CD4T	
Specification No.	3838	
Throat diameter	1½ in	38.10 mm
Jet size	0.100 in	2.54
Needle	44A; 1978 and later: 45Q	
Piston spring	Blue	
Choke: Needle	D9	
Fast idle cam No.	CT 8	
Fast idle setting	0.035 in	0.9 mm

EXHAUST EMISSION

Exhaust gas analyser reading at engine idle speed	½ – 6½% (3% nominal); 1978: 3 – 7% (5% nominal)
Air pump test speed	850 rev/min

† Vacuum disconnected   ‡ Crankshaft degrees and rev/min

ENGINE TUNING DATA
Model: MG MIDGET Mk III — UK specification   Year: 1978

ENGINE

Type	PE 94J
Capacity	91.0 in³ 1493 cm³
Compression ratio	9.0 : 1
Firing order	1, 3, 4, 2
Cranking pressure	
Idle speed	650 to 680 rev/min
Fast idle speed (hot) † ‡	1,100 to 1,300 rev/min
Ignition timing † ‡	
Stroboscopic at 680 rev/min	10° B.T.D.C.
Advance check at 2,000 rev/min	21° to 25° B.T.D.C.
Timing marks	Pointers on timing case notch on crank-shaft pulley

Valve clearance:

Inlet and Exhaust (cold)	0.010 in 0.25 mm

DISTRIBUTOR

Make/type	Lucas 45 D4
Rotation of rotor	Anti-clockwise
Dwell angle	51° ± 5°
Condenser capacity	0.18 to 0.25 microfarad
Lucas serial No.	41449
Contact breaker gap	0.014 to 0.016 in 0.35 to 0.40 mm
Centrifugal advance † ‡	2° to 6° at 1,100 rev/min
	6° to 10° at 1,400 rev/min
	8° to 12° at 2,000 rev/min
	12° to 16° at 3,200 rev/min

Vacuum advance ‡

Starts	3 in Hg
Finishes	18 in Hg
Total crankshaft degrees	12° ± 2°

SPARK PLUGS

Make	Champion
Type	N-12Y
Gap	0.025 0.64 mm

IGNITION COIL

Make/type	Lucas 15C6
Primary resistance at 68° F	1.30 to 1.45 ohms
Ballast resistor	1.3 to 1.5 ohms

CARBURETTER

Make/type	SU Twin type HS4
Specification No.	AUD 665
Jet size	0.90 in 2.2 mm
Needle	ABT
Piston spring	Red
Choke diameter	1½ in 38.10 mm

EXHAUST EMISSION

Exhaust gas analyser reading at engine idle speed	3 to 4.5% (2% nominal)
Air pump test speed	850 rev/min

† Vacuum disconnected   ‡ Crankshaft degrees and rev/min

TORQUE WRENCH SETTINGS

Engine

	lbf ft	kgf m
Alternator to mounting bracket and front engine plate	22	3.0
Alternator to adjusting link	20	2.8
Clutch attachment to flywheel	22	3.0
1975-1976 connecting rod bolt — Color dyed	50	6.9
Phosphated	46	6.4
1977 and later cylinder head to block (U.S.A. only)	40 to 45	5.5 to 6.2
Chainwheel to camshaft	24	3.3
Crankshaft pulley nut	150	20.7
Cylinder block drain plug	35	4.8
1975-1976 cylinder head to block	50	6.9
1977 and later connecting rod bolt (U.S.A. only)	46	6.4
Distributor to pedestal	20	2.8
Fan attachment	9	1.2
Flywheel to crankshaft:		
Cadmium plated	40	5.5
Parkerised	45	6.2
Fuel pump to cylinder block	14	1.9
Gearbox and rear engine plate to block	14	1.9
Manifold – inlet to exhaust	14	1.9
Manifold to head	25	3.5
Main bearing cap bolts	65	9.0
Oil sump drain plug	25	3.5
Oil sump to block	20	2.8
Oil pressure switch plug to cylinder head	14	1.9
Oil seal block attachment	14	1.9
Rocker cover to head	2	0.3
Rocker pedestal to cylinder head	32	4.4
Crankshaft rear seal housing	20	2.8
Rear engine mounting platform on frame	20	2.8
Sealing block to engine plate	20	2.8
Spark plug to head	20	2.8
Starter motor attachment	34	4.7
Timing cover to front engine plate:		
Small	10	1.4
Large	20	2.8
Water elbow to water pump	20	2.8
Water pump bearing housing to pump	14	1.9
Water pump to cylinder head	20	2.8
Fuel pump top cover bolt	10 to 14*	0.115 to 0.161*

Gearbox

	lbf ft	kgf m
Flywheel housing retaining bolts	28 to 30	3.9 to 4.1
Rear extension to gearbox bolts	18 to 20	2.4 to 2.7
Drive flange nut	90 to 100	12.4 to 13.8

Steering

	lbf ft	kgf m
Rack clamp bolts	20 to 22	2.77 to 3.04
Rack mounting bracket retaining bolts	17 to 18	2.35 to 2.4
Tie-rod end assembly locknut	30 to 35	4.15 to 4.84
Tie-rod end assembly ball joint nut	28 to 32	3.87 to 4.48
Tie-rod inner ball joint assembly locknut	80	11.06
Steering-wheel nut	37	5.11
Steering lock shear bolts	70*	0.8*
Column upper fixing bolts	12 to 17	1.66 to 2.35
Column pinch bolt	9 to 12	1.24 to 1.66
Steering arm bolt	39	5.4

Front suspension

	lbf ft	kgf m
Shock absorber	25 to 30	3.4 to 4.1
Hub nut	46	6.9
Swivel pin nut	40	5.5

Rear suspension

	lbf ft	kgf m
Shock absorber bolts	25 to 30	3.4 to 4.1

Brakes

	lbf ft	kgf m
Bleed screw	4 to 6	0.5 to 0.8
Master cylinder port adaptors **	15 to 19	1.7 to 2.1
Plastic reservoir fixing bolts **	5	0.69
Pressure failure switch (nylon) ***	15 *	0.173 *
Pressure failure switch assembly end plug (1975-1976)**	200 *	2.3 *
Pressure failure switch assembly end plug (1977 and later)**	400 *	4.6 *
Brake disc to hub	40 to 45	5.5 to 6.2
Calliper to stub axle	48	6.7

Rear axle and final drive

	lbf ft	kgf m
Pinion bearing pre-load	8 to 10 *	0.09 to 0.12 *
Drive flange nut	140	19.4
Crown wheel to gear carrier bolts	60	8.30
Bearing cap to gear carrier bolts	65	8.99

Electrical

	lbf ft	kgf m
Wiper motor yoke fixing bolts	20*	0.23*
Alternator pulley nut	25	3.46

Wheels

	lbf ft	kgf m
Wheel nuts	44 to 46	6.0 to 6.3

* lbf. in/ kgf. cm
** U.S.A. specification only

COMMENTS	UNIFIED	METRIC
The illustrations show metric and the equivalent Unified (U.N.F.) parts for comparison.		
Metric pipe nuts, hose ends, unions and bleed screws are coloured **GOLD** or **BLACK** and most are also identified with the letter 'M'. The correct Metric or Unified pipe flares must be used.		
End of a Metric hose is also coloured **GOLD** or **BLACK**.		
Metric parts are not counterbored; some U.N.F. threaded parts also had no counterbore; always check. If the thread of a component is in doubt, screw the hydraulic connections and bleed screw fully in with the fingers. If they cannot be screwed right in or if they are unduly slack, the threads may not be compatible.		
Metric hose seals against the bottom of the port, gap between hose hexagon and face of cylinder or calliper.		

GENERAL FITTING INSTRUCTIONS

Precautions against damage

Always fit wing and seat covers before commencing work.

Avoid spilling brake fluid or battery acid on paint work. Wash off with water immediately if this occurs.

Disconnect the battery earth lead before starting work.

Always use the recommended Service Tool or a satisfactory equivalent where specified.

Protect exposed screw threads from damage.

Safety precautions

Wear protective overalls, and use protective barrier creams when necessary.

Ensure the car is on level ground when being lifted or jacked up. Apply the handbrake and chock the wheels.

Never rely on a jack as the sole means of support when working beneath the car. Place additional safety supports beneath the car.

Ensure that any lifting apparatus has adequate load capacity for the work in hand.

Do not leave tools, lifting equipment, spilt oil etc., around or on the work area.

Cleaning components

Always use the recommended cleaning agent or equivalent.

Wherever possible clean components and the surrounding area externally before removal.

Always observe scrupulous cleanliness when cleaning dismantled components.

Do not use degreasing equipment for components containing items which could be damaged by the use of this process.

Brakes

Wash all dust from the brake assemblies, use brake cleaning fluid or denatured alcohol.

WARNING: Do not use an air-line to blow out brake dust: asbestos dust from the brake linings can be a serious health risk if inhaled.

Brake and clutch hydraulics

Two types of brake fittings are in use. Refer to the chart for identification and comments.

Warning. It is imperative that the correct brake fittings are used. The threads of components must be compatible.

Containers for hydraulic fluid must be kept absolutely clean.

Do not store hydraulic fluid in an unsealed container. It will absorb water and fluid in this condition would be dangerous to use.

Do not allow hydraulic fluid to be contaminated with mineral oil, or use a container which has previously contained mineral oil.

Do not re-use fluid bled from the system.

Always use clean brake fluid or a recommended alternative to clean hydraulic components.

Fit a blanking cap to a hydraulic union and a plug to its socket after removal to prevent the ingress of dirt.

Absolute cleanliness must be observed with hydraulic components at all times.

Joints and joint faces

Always use the recommended gaskets and/or jointing compound.

Remove all traces of old jointing material prior to re-assembly. Do not use a tool which will damage the joint faces.

Fit joints dry unless otherwise specified in the Manual.

Smooth out any scratches or burrs on the joint faces with an oil stone.

Do not allow dirt or jointing material to enter any tapped holes.

Blow out any pipes, channels or crevices with compressed air.

Where a joint is sealed with a silicone sealant peel the old sealant from the joint faces, using a razor blade if necessary. **DO NOT** use a solvent.

Service tools

Service tools are designed to enable dismantling and assembly to take place without unnnecessary damage to components and loss of time.

GENERAL FITTING INSTRUCTIONS

Always use the correct Service Tool if available. Some operations cannot be carried out without the aid of the relevant service tool.

Where a service tool is advisable and not available from the tool manufacturers, information is given to enable a tool to be manufactured locally.

Oil seals

Always renew oil seals which have been removed from their working location, either as an individual component or as part of an assembly.

Check the surface on which the seal is to run for burrs and scratches. Renew the component if the original sealing surface cannot be restored.

Lubricate the sealing lips with a recommended lubricant before use to prevent damage on initial use.

On dual lip seals, smear the area between the two lips with grease.

Protect the seal from any surface which could cause damage over which it has to pass when being fitted.

Use a protective sleeve or tape to cover the relevant surface.

Ensure that oil seals are fitted square in their housings with the sealing lip facing the lubricant to be retained.

Use a press and the recommended service tool to fit an oil seal.

If it is not possible to use a press, a hammer may be used instead.

If the correct service tool is not available, use a suitable drift approximately 0.015 in. (0.4 mm) smaller than the outside diameter of the seal.

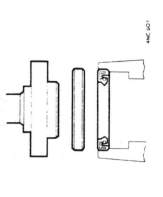

4NC 607

4NC 608

Press or drift the seal in to the depth of its housing if the housing is shouldered, or flush with the face of the housing where no shoulder is provided.

Locking devices

Always fit new locking washers, do not re-use an old one.

Always fit new split pins. Ensure that the split pin is the correct size for the hole in the bolt or stud. Fit as illustrated.

Self-locking nuts can be re-used, providing resistance can be felt when the locking portion passes over the thread of the bolt or stud. DO NOT re-use self-locking nuts in critical locations, e.g. engine bearings.

Always use the correct replacement self-locking nut.

Screw threads

Both UNF and Metric threads to ISO standards are used.

Damaged threads must always be discarded. Cleaning up threads with a die or tap impairs the strength and closeness of fit of the threads and is not recommended.

Castellated nuts must not be slackened back to accept a split pin, except in those recommended cases when this forms part of an adjustment.

Do not allow oil or grease to enter blind threaded holes. The hydraulic action on screwing in the bolt or stud could split the housing.

Always tighten a nut or bolt to the recommended torque figure. Damaged or corroded threads can affect the torque reading.

To check or retighten a bolt or screw to a specified torque figure, first slacken a quarter of a turn, then retighten to the correct figure.

Always oil threads lightly before tightening to ensure a free running thread, except in the case of self-locking nuts.

Five Thread Forms Replaced by — ISO Metric

BA	BSW	BSF	UNC	UNF	Metric Size
2			10	10	M5
1			12	12	M6
0	3/16	3/8			
	1/4	1/4	1/4	1/4	M8
	5/16	5/16	5/16	5/16	M10
	3/8	3/8	3/8	3/8	
	7/16	7/16	7/16	7/16	M12
	1/2	1/2	1/2	1/2	

4NC 362

4NC 361

4NC 360

Strength Grade 6

Strength Grade 8

Strength Grade 12

Strength Grade 14

Bolt Identification

An ISO Metric bolt or screw, made of steel and larger than 6mm in diameter can be identified by either of the symbols ISO M or M embossed or indented on top of the head.

In addition to marks to identify the manufacturer, the head is also marked with symbols to indicate the strength grade e.g. 8.8; 10.9; 12.9 or 14.9. As an alternative some bolts and screws have the M and strength grade symbol on the flats of the hexagon.

Nut Identification

A nut with an ISO metric thread is marked on one face or on one of the flats of the hexagon with the strength grade symbol 8, 12 or 14. Some nuts with a strength 4, 5 or 6 are also marked and some have the metric symbol M on the flat opposite the strength grade marking.

A clock face system is used as an alternative method of indicating the strength grade. The external chamfers or a face of the nut is marked in a position relative to the appropriate hour mark on a clock face to indicate the strength grade.

A dot is used to locate the 12 o'clock position and a dash to indicate the strength grade. If the grade is above 12, two dots identify the 12 o'clock position.

SERVICE LUBRICANTS, FUEL AND FLUIDS – CAPACITIES

Lubrication

The lubrication systems of your new car are filled with high quality oils. You should always use a high quality oil of the correct viscosity range in the engine, manual gearbox and rear axle during subsequent maintenance operations or when topping-up. The use of oils not to the correct specification can lead to high oil and fuel consumption and ultimately to damage to components.

Oil to the correct specification contains additives which disperse the corrosive acids formed by combustion and also prevent the formation of sludge which can block oilways. Additional oil additives should not be used. Servicing intervals must be adhered to.

Engine

Use a well-known brand of oil to B.L.S. OL.02 or MIL-L-2104B or A.P.1, SE quality, with viscosity band spanning the temperature range of your locality.

4NA051A

Fuel

U.S.A. non catalytic converter cars: Regular fuel
U.S.A. catalytic converter cars: Unleaded fuel
U.K. recommended octane rating: 97 RON minimum

Brake and Clutch Fluid

Use **Lockheed Universal Brake Fluid (Series 329S)** or **Castrol Girling Brake Fluid**; alternatively, use a brake fluid conforming to **F.M.V.S.S. D.O.T.3** specification with a **minimum boiling point of 260°C (500°F)**. DO NOT use any other type of fluid in the braking system.

Anti-Freeze Solutions

Use an ethylene glycol based anti-freeze conforming to specification B.S. 3151/2 or SAE J1034

The recommended quantities of anti-freeze for a car fitted with a heater for different degrees of frost protection are:

Anti-freeze Solutions: 1976 and later U.S.A. Models

Solution %	Amount of anti-freeze			Commences freezing		Frozen solid	
	U.S. pt	Pt	Litres	°C	°F	°C	°F
25	3	2½	1.42	−13	9	−26	−15
33⅓	4	3¾	1.84	−19	−2	−36	−33
50	5¾	4¾	2.7	−36	−33	−48	−53

Anti-freeze Solutions: All U.K. and 1975 U.S.A. Models

Solution %	Amount of anti-freeze			Commences freezing		Frozen solid	
	Pt	U.S. pt	Litres	°C	°F	°C	°F
25	2	2¼	1.06	−13	9	−26	−15
33⅓	2½	3	1.42	−19	−2	−36	−33
50	3¾	4½	2.13	−36	−33	−48	−53

CAPACITIES (approx)

Engine sump including filter	9.6 U.S. pt	8 pt	4.5 litres
Gearbox	1.75 U.S. pt	1½ pt	0.85 litres
Rear axle	2.1 U.S. pt	1¾ pt	1.0 litre
1975 U.S.A. and all U.K. cooling systems (with heater)	9 U.S. pt	7½ pt	4.25 litres
1976-1978 U.S.A. cooling system (with heater)	11.4 U.S. pt	9½ pt	5.42 litres
Windscreen washer bottle	4.8 U.S. pt	4 pt	2.27 litres
Fuel tank:			
U.S.A. and Canada cars	7.5 U.S. gal	6½ gal	29 litres
U.K. cars	8.6 U.S. gal	7 gal	32 litres

Synchromesh gearbox and rear axle
Top up with H.D. 90 (MIL-L-2105B) above −10°C (10°F).
Top up with H.D. 80 (MIL-L-2105B) below −5°C (20°F).
Top up with H.D. 75W (MIL-L-2105B) below −30°C (−20°F).
Complete fill with E.P. 80 (MIL-L-2105B) all temperatures.

Steering rack and grease points
Use Multipurpose Lithium Grease N.L.G.1, consistency No. 2.

MAINTENANCE – U.K. SPECIFICATION
SERVICE OPERATIONS– Summary

After Sales Service = 1,000 miles (1 500 km)
A Every 6,000 miles (10 000 km) or 6 months
B Every 12,000 miles (20 000 km) or 12 months
Items included in the 3,000 miles (5000 km) or 3 months interval Optional Inspection Check are indicated in column C

Leycare Service

After Sales	A	B	C	● ACTION / X OPERATION
●	●	●	●	Fit seat cover
X	X	X	X	Check condition and security of seats and seat belts
●	●	●	●	Drive on lift; stop engine
X	X	X	X	Check operation of lamps
X	X	X	X	Check operation of horns
X	X	X	X	Check operation of warning indicators
X	X	X	X	Check/adjust operation of windscreen washers
X	X	X	X	Check operation of windscreen wipers
X	X	X	X	Check operation of hand brake; release fully after checking
X	X	X	X	Check rear view mirrors for cracks and crazing
X	X	X	X	Check operation of window controls
●	●	●	●	Open bonnet, fit wing covers. Raise lift to convenient working height with wheels free to rotate
●	●	●	●	Remove hub cap
X	X	X	X	Mark stud to wheel relationship, remove road wheel
X	X	X	X	Check tyre complies with manufacturer's specification
X	X	X	X	Check tyre for tread depth
X	X	X	X	Check tyre visually for external cuts in fabric
X	X	X	X	Check tyre visually for external exposure of ply or cord
X	X	X	X	Check tyre visually for external lumps and bulges
X	X	X	X	Check/adjust tyre pressures
X	X	X	X	Inspect brake pads for wear and discs for condition
X	X	X	X	Check for oil leaks from steering and fluid leaks from shock absorbers
X	X	X	X	Check condition and security of steering unit, joints and gaiters
	X	X		Remove brake-drum, wipe out dust, inspect shoes for wear and drum for condition, refit drum
X	X	X	X	Adjust brakes
X	X	X		Lubricate all grease points (excluding hubs)
●	●	●	●	Refit road wheel in original position
X	X	X	X	Check tightness of road wheel nuts
●	●	●	●	Refit hub cap

* Starting at the right-hand front, complete these operations at each wheel

After Sales	A	B	C	● ACTION / X OPERATION
●	●	●	●	Raise lift to full height
X	X	X		Drain engine oil
X	X	X		Drain gearbox oil
X	X	X		Check/top up rear axle oil
X	X	X		Lubricate hand brake mechanical linkage and cables
X	X	X	X	Check visually brake pipes and unions for chafing, leaks and corrosion
X	X	X	X	Check visually fuel and clutch pipes for chafing, leaks and corrosion
X	X	X	X	Check exhaust system for leakage and security
X	X	X	X	Check security of accessible engine mountings
X	X	X		Check security of suspension fixings
●	●	●	●	Renew engine oil filter element
●	●	●		Refit engine drain plug
●				Refit gearbox drain plug
●				Clean/paint timing marks
●				Lower lift
X	X	X		Fit exhaust extractor pipe
X	X	X		Check/top up gearbox oil
X	X	X		Fill gearbox with oil
X	X	X		Check/adjust torque of cylinder head nuts
X	X	X		Check/adjust torque of rocker shaft nuts
X	X	X		Check/adjust torque of manifold nuts
X	X	X		Check/adjust valve clearances
X	X	X		Fill engine with oil
X	X	X		Check/top up engine oil
X	X	X	X	Top up carburetter piston dampers
X	X	X		Lubricate accelerator control, linkage and pedal pivot
X	X	X		Renew air cleaner elements
X	X	X	X	Check security of accessible engine mountings
X	X	X		Check driving belts, adjust or renew
X	X			Clean/adjust spark plugs
X		X		Renew spark plugs
X	X	X		Clean fuel pump filter gauze
X	X	X	X	Check/top up battery electrolyte
X	X	X	X	Clean and grease battery connections
X	X	X	X	Check/top up clutch fluid reservoir
X	X	X		Check/top up brake fluid reservoir
X	X	X		Check/top up windscreen washer reservoir
●	●	●	●	Check/top up cooling system
●	●	●		Run engine and check sealing of oil filter, stop engine
X	X	X		Recheck/top up engine oil
X	X	X		Connect electronic instruments
X	X	X		Check visually distributor points, renew if necessary
X	X	X		Check for volt drop between coil CB and earth
		X		Lubricate distributor

27

10–1

SERVICE LUBRICANTS - UK ONLY

Component	Engine and Carburetter			Syncoromesh Gearbox and Rear Axle*		Grease Points	Upper Cylinder Lubrication
Climatic Conditions	All temperatures above - 10°C (15°F)	Temperatures 10°C to - 20°C (50 to -5°F)	All temperatures below - 10°C (15°F)	All temperatures above - 10°C (15°F)	All temperatures below - 10°C (15°F)	All conditions	All conditions
Minimum performance level	British Leyland Service Fill Lubrication Oil Specifications for Passenger car and Light Commercial engines BLS 0L02			MIL-L-2105B	MIL-L-2105B	Multipurpose Lithium Grease N.L.G.L. Consistency No.2	Upper Cylinder Lubricant
Esso	Esso Uniflo 10W/50	Esso Uniflo 10W/50	Esso Extra Motor Oil 5W/20	Gearl Oil GX90/140	Esso gear Oil GX 80	Esso Multipurpose Grease II	Esso Upper Cylinder Lubricant
Mobil	Mobiloil Special 20W/50	Mobiloil Super 10W/50	Mobiloil 5W/20	Mobillube HD90	Mobillube HD80	Mobilgrease MP or MS	Mobil Upperlube
BP	BP Super Visco-Static 20/50 or 10W/40	BP Super Visco-Static 10W/30 or 10W/40	BP Super Visco-Static BP Super Visco-static 5W/20	BP Hypogear 90 EP	BP Hypogear 80 EP	BP Energrease L2	BP Cylinder Lubricant
Shell	Shell Super 20W/50	Shell Super 10W/50	Shell Super 5W/30	Shell Spirax Heavy Duty 90	Shell Spirax Heavy Duty 80	Shell Retinax A	Shell Upper Cylinder Lubricant
Duckhams	Duckhams Q. Motor Oil	Duckhams Q. 5500	Duckhams Q. 5530	Duckhams Hypoid 90S	Duckhams Hypoid 80S	Duckhams HB10 Grease	Duckhams Adcoid Liquid
Texaco	Havoline 20W/50 or 10W/40	Havoline 10W/50	Havoline 5W/50	Multigear Lubricant EP90	Multigear Lubricant EP80	Marfak All purpose	Special Upper Cylinder Lubricant
Petrofina	Fina Supergrade 20W/50 or 10W/50 or 10W/40	Fina Supergrade 10W/50 or 10W/40	Fina Supergrade 5W/50	Fina Pentonic XP 90/140	Fina Pentonic MP80	Fina HL 12	Fina Cyltonic
Castrol	Castrol GTX	Castroline	Castrol CRL 5W/20	Castrol Hypoy B 90	Castrol Hypoy B 80	Castrol LM Grease	Castrollo

* Synchromech gearbox, complete fill, E.P. 80 (MIL - L - 2105, all temperatures.
  Rear axle, complete fill, H.D. 90 (MIL - L - 2105B), all temperatures.

MAINTENANCE — U.K. SPECIFICATION

After Sales	A	B	C	● ACTION X OPERATION
●	●	●		Run engine
X	X	X		Disconnect vacuum pipe, check dwell angle, adjust points as necessary
X	X	X		Check stroboscopic ignition timing
X	X	X		Check distributor automatic advance
X	X	X		Check advance increase as vacuum pipe is reconnected
X	X	X		Check throttle operation, set to fast idle until engine reaches normal running temperature
X	X	X		Lubricate all locks and hinges (not steering lock)
	X	X	X	Check and if necessary renew windscreen wiper blades
X	X	X		Check/adjust engine idle speed and carburetter mixture setting
●	●	●		Stop engine, disconnect instruments
●	●	●	●	Remove wing covers
	●	●	●	Fill in details and fix appropriate Unipart underbonnet stickers
●	●	●	●	Close bonnet
●	●	●		Remove exhaust extractor pipe
X	X	X	X	Check fuel filler pipe tank connections
●	●	●	●	Remove spare wheel
	X	X	X	Check spare tyre complies with manufacturer's specification
	X	X	X	Check depth of tread
X	X	X	X	Check visually for external cuts in tyre fabric
X	X	X	X	Check visually for external exposure of ply or cord
X	X	X	X	Check visually for external lumps or bulges
X	X	X	X	Check/adjust tyre pressures
●	●	●	●	Refit spare wheel. Drive car off lift
X	X	X	X	Check/adjust headlamp alignment
X	X	X		Check/adjust front wheel alignment
X	X	X		Carry out road or roller test and check function of all instrumentation
X	X	X	X	Report any additional work required
X	X	X	X	Ensure cleanliness of controls, door handles, steering-wheel, etc.
●	●	●	●	Remove seat cover

Lubrication

NOTE: Ensure that the vehicle is standing on a level surface when checking the oil levels.

Weekly
(1) ENGINE. Check oil level and top up if necessary.

Every 6,000 miles or 6 months
(2) ENGINE. Drain and refill with new oil.

(3) ENGINE OIL FILTER. Remove disposable cartridge, fit new.

(4) CARBURETTERS. Top up carburetter piston dampers.

(5) ACCELERATOR. Lubricate accelerator control linkage, cable and pedal fulcrum.

(6) DISTRIBUTOR. Lubricate all parts as necessary.

(7) REAR AXLE. Check oil level, and top up if necessary.

(8) GEARBOX. Check oil level and top up if necessary.

(9) FRONT SUSPENSION (6 nipples)

(10) HAND BRAKE CABLE AND COMPENSATING LEVER (2 nipples), 1975-1976 only } Give three or four strokes with a grease gun.

(11) PROPELLER SHAFT (1 nipple), 1977 and later

LOCKS AND HINGES. Lubricate the bonnet release and safety catch and all locks and hinges. Do not oil the steering lock.

Every 30,000 miles or 36 months
(12) STEERING RACK. Lubricate steering rack — It is advisable to entrust this work to your Distributor or Dealer.

Optional lubrication at 3,000 miles or 3 months
(1) ENGINE. Check oil level and top up if necessary.

Service oils and **greases** are given in 09

MAINTENANCE — U.K. SPECIFICATION

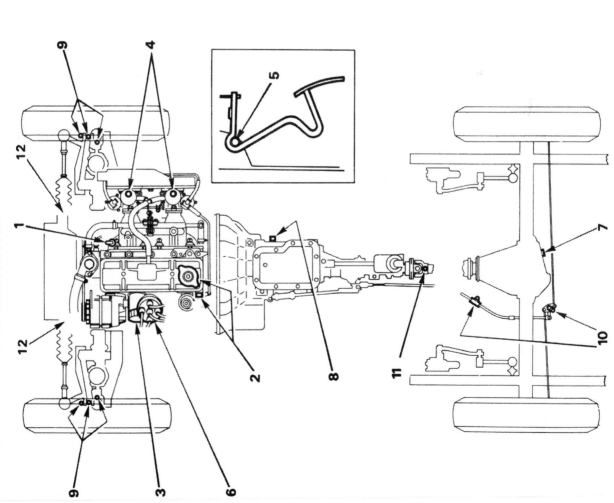

MAINTENANCE – U.K. SPECIFICATION

ENGINE

Checking engine oil level

1 Maintain the level between the 'MIN' (1a) and 'MAX' (1b) marks on the dipstick.

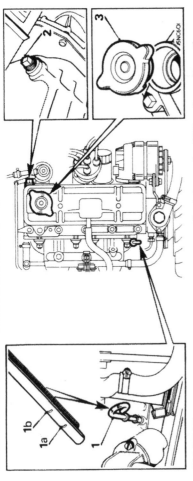

Draining and refilling the engine oil

2 Drain the oil while the engine is warm; clean the drain plug and refit.
3 Refill with the correct quantity and grade of oil. Run the engine for a short while, then allow it to stand for a few minutes before checking the level.

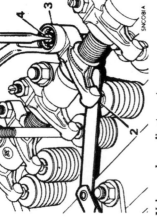

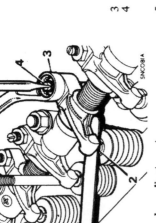

SNC001

Valve rocker adjustment

1 Remove the rocker cover.
2 Check the clearance between the valve rocker arms and the valve stems with a feeler gauge.
Clearance (cold) 0.010 in (0.25 mm).
The gauge should be a sliding fit when the engine is cold.
Check the clearance of each valve in the following order.

SNC081A

Check:

No. 1 valve	with No. 8	fully open.
" 3 "	" " 6	"
" 5 "	" " 4	"
" 2 "	" " 7	"
" 8 "	" " 1	"
" 6 "	" " 3	"
" 4 "	" " 5	"
" 7 "	" " 2	"

3 Slacken the locknut.
4 Rotate the screw, clockwise to decrease or anti-clockwise to increase the clearance.
5 Re-tighten the locknut when the clearance is correct, holding the screw against rotation.
6 Recheck the clearances.
7 Check, and if necessary renew the rocker cover gasket.
8 Refit the rocker cover and tighten the nuts to 2 lbf ft (0.3 kgf m). DO NOT OVERTIGHTEN or distortion of the cover may occur, resulting in oil leaks.

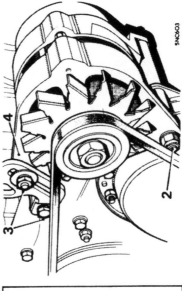

SNC003

2 Slacken the alternator securing nut and bolt.
3 Slacken the adjusting link bolts.
4 Move the alternator to the required position. Apply any leverage necessary to the alternator end bracket only, using a wooden or soft metal lever.
5 Tighten the securing nuts and bolts and recheck the tension.

Drive Belt Tension—Fan

When correctly tensioned, a total deflection of ¾ in (19 mm) under moderate hand pressure, should be possible at the midway point of the longest run between the pulleys.

Adjusting

1 Check the belt tension.

Disposable cartridge filter renewal

1 Unscrew the cartridge from the cylinder block.
2 If the adaptor remains attached to the cartridge unscrew it from the cartridge and screw it back into the cylinder block. Discard the cartridge and old seal.
3 Smear the new seal with oil and fit it into the groove in the new cartridge.
4 Wipe the engine joint face clean and smear with oil.
5 Screw the new cartridge to the adaptor, using hand force only.
6 Start the engine and check the cartridge for leaks. Check the oil level after waiting for a few minutes.

SNC585

MAINTENANCE — U.K. SPECIFICATION

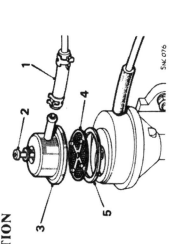

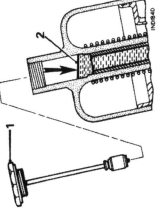

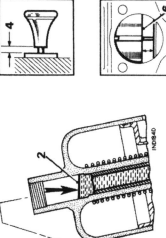

FUEL SYSTEM

Air cleaner element renewal

1. Release the fuel pipe from its clip on the container.
2. Remove the four bolts securing the air cleaner assembly to the carburetter flanges and lift the assembly from the engine.
3. Remove the bolt to release the closing plate from the container.
4. Remove and discard the elements.
5. Thoroughly clean the closing plate and container.
6. Check that the carburetter flange gasket and the closing plate gasket are in good condition.
7. Fit the four bolts to the container and assemble the elements on the four bolts.
8. Fit the closing plate, ensuring:
   a. The gasket face of the element butts against the closing plate.
   b. The holes in the carburetter flange gaskets and the element gaskets correspond with the holes in the closing plate.
9. Fit the air cleaner assembly to the carburetter flanges and secure the fuel pipe on its clip.

Fuel pump filter gauze—cleaning

1. Squeeze the ends of the clip and remove the inlet hose from the fuel pump top cover.
2. Unscrew the central bolt.
3. Remove the top cover.
4. Remove the filter gauze. Wash in clean fluid.
5. Check that the gasket is in position and in a good condition; renew if necessary.
6. Fit the gauze and top cover and secure with centre bolt.
7. Tighten the central bolt to 10-14 lbf in (0.115 to 0.161 kgf m).
8. Fit the inlet hose.
9. Start the engine and inspect the fuel pump for air and fuel leaks.
10. Check the inlet and outlet hoses for leaks and serviceability.

CARBURETTERS

Air pollution control

The carburetters incorporate features which assist in reducing exhaust emissions. Maladjustment or the fitting of parts not to the required specification may render these features ineffective.

Carburetter settings

Check and adjust

It is essential that the ignition timing, tappet clearance, distributor contact breaker and plug gaps are checked and adjusted before tuning the carburetter.

Carburetter tuning must be confined to setting the idle and fast idle speeds and mixture at idle speed. A reliable tachometer should be used.

NOTE: Where a vehicle must conform to exhaust emission control regulations, adjustments should only be carried out using a reliable tachometer and an exhaust gas analyser (CO meter).

1. Remove the air cleaner.
2. Check each piston damper, and top up if necessary with a recommended engine oil until the level is ½ in (13 mm) above the top of the hollow piston rod.
3. Check that the throttle functions correctly.
4. Ensure that the mixture control (choke) will return fully, and that the cable has ₁/₁₆ in (1.5 mm) free play before it starts to pull on the lever.
5. Check that a small clearance exists between the fast idling screws and their cams.
6. Remove the air cleaner, then raise and lower each piston with a finger, checking that it can move smoothly without any tendency to stick or bind. If it fails to move freely, refer to 19.15.28.

Piston dampers

1. Unscrew the damper cap from the top of each carburetter suction chamber and withdraw the cap and damper.
2. Top up if necessary with a recommended engine oil (preferably S.A.E. 20) until the level is ½ in (13 mm) above the top of the hollow piston rod.
3. Push the damper assembly back into position and screw the cap firmly into the suction chamber.

Accelerator mechanism

1. Lubricate the accelerator pedal pivot.
2. Lubricate the carburetter accelerator and choke linkages and cables.
3. Check carburetter throttle response to initial movement of the accelerator pedal.
4. Check carburetter throttle position when the accelerator pedal is fully depressed, and adjust, if necessary, to ensure that full throttle is obtained.

MAINTENANCE — U.K. SPECIFICATION

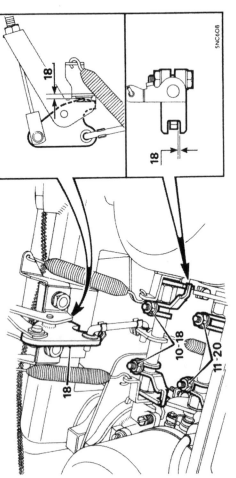

SNC608

7 Connect up a tachometer. Start the engine, run it at a fast idling speed until it attains normal running temperature and continue to run it for a further five minutes.

8 Before making any adjustments increase the engine speed to 2,500 rev/min and maintain this speed for 30 seconds to clear the intake manifold of excess fuel. Repeat this procedure at three-minute intervals if these adjustments cannot be completed within this period of time.

9 Check the idling speed with the tachometer against the figure given in DATA.
a If the reading is not correct, continue with instructions 10 to 12.
b If the idle speed is correct but is not consistent with smooth running, continue with instructions 10 to 23.

10 Slacken both throttle spindle interconnection clamp bolts.

11 Slacken both cold start interconnection clamp bolts.

12 With the engine running, check the carburetter balance with a meter or listen to the 'hiss' in each carburetter intake and turn the throttle adjusting screw in each carburetter until the intensity of the hiss is equal in both intakes and the correct idling speed is obtained (tachometer).
a If with the carburetters correctly balanced the idling is still erratic, continue with instructions 13 to 23.
b If the idling speed is correct and consistent with smooth running, follow instructions 17 to 23.

13 Screw each jet adjusting nut fully up until the jets are flush with the bridge of the carburetter or as high as possible without exceeding the bridge height, ensure both jets are in the same relative position. Turn each jet adjusting nut down two complete turns (12 flats).

14 Run the engine at idle speed. Turn the jet adjusting nuts on both carburetters one flat at a time—up to weaken or down to enrich—until the fastest

15 engine speed (tachometer) consistent with smooth running is achieved. Turn each nut up to the point where the engine speed just begins to fall to obtain the correct idle speed setting. Re-check the idling speed and adjust by turning each throttle adjusting screw an equal amount, see instruction 12.

16 EMISSION CONTROL. Using the exhaust gas analyser, check that the reading is within the limits given in 'DATA'. If the reading falls outside the limits given, reset the jet adjusting screw by the minimum amount necessary to bring the reading just within the limits. If more than half a turn is required to achieve this, the carburetter must be removed and serviced.

17 Set the throttle interconnection clamping levers until the lever pins rest on the lower arm of the forks.

18 Insert a 0.050 in (1.27 mm) feeler gauge between the throttle shaft stop and the throttle control bracket. Tighten the throttle interconnection clamping lever bolts, ensuring that there is approximately $\frac{1}{32}$ in (0.79 mm) end-float on the interconnection rod. Remove the feeler gauge. An equal clearance of 0.012 in (9.31 mm), should now exist between each lever pin and the bottom of the fork on both carburetters.

19 Run the engine at 1,500 rev/min and check the throttle linkage for correct connection by re-checking the carburetter balance.

20 With the fast idle cams of both carburetters against their stops, set the cold start inter-connections so that both cams begin to move simultaneously and check that a $\frac{1}{16}$ in (1.5 mm) free movement of the mixture control (choke) cable exists before the cable moves the cams.

21 Pull out the mixture control (choke) approximately 13 mm (½ in) until the linkage is just about to move the jet.

22 Using the balancing meter (or listening tube) to ensure equal adjustment, turn the fast idle adjusting screws to give the correct fast idle speed, see DATA.

23 Stop the engine and disconnect the instruments. Refit the air cleaner assembly.

DATA

Idling speed	650 to 680 rev/min
Fast idle speed	1100 to 1300 rev/min
Engine gas analyser reading at engine idle speed	3 to 4.5%

MAINTENANCE — U.K. SPECIFICATION

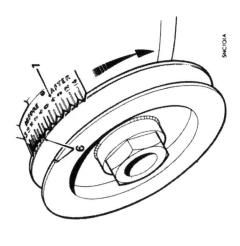

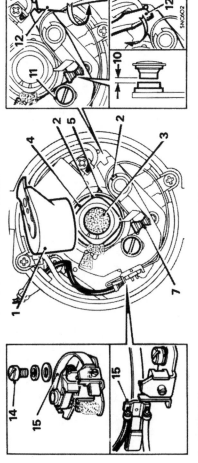

SNC602

IGNITION

Distributor—lubrication

1. Remove the distributor cover and the rotor arm.
2. Very lightly smear the cam and pivot post with grease.
3. Add a few drops of oil to the felt pad in the top of the cam spindle.
4. Add a few drops of oil through the gap between the cam spindle and the contact plate to lubricate the centrifugal weights. **Do not oil the cam wiping pad.**
5. Add a drop of oil through each of the two holes in the base plate to lubricate the contact breaker assembly central bearing every 24,000 miles (40,000 km).
6. Carefully wipe away all surplus lubricant and ensure that the contact breaker points are clean and dry.

Contact breaker—cleaning

7. Inspect the contact breaker points and if burned, clean with fine emery cloth or a fine carborundum stone. Renew pitted or worn points that cannot be rectified.
8. Wipe the contacts with a fuel-moistened cloth.

Contact breaker gap—checking

9. Turn the crankshaft until the points are fully open.

10. Check the contact gap with a feeler gauge, it should be 0.015 in (0.4 mm).

Contact breaker gap—adjusting

11. Slacken the contact set securing screw.
12. Adjust the gap by inserting a screwdriver between the slot in the end of the plate and the pipe; turn anti-clockwise to increase and clockwise to decrease the gap.
13. Tighten the securing screw.

Contact breaker set—renewing

14. Remove the securing screw, spring and plain washers.
15. Lift the contact set, press the spring and release the terminal plate from the end of the spring.
16. Wipe the points of the new contact set clean, using a fuel moistened cloth and very lightly grease the pivot post.
17. Connect the terminal plate to the end of the contact breaker spring.
18. Position the contact set on the distributor base plate and fit the securing screw.
19. Ensure that the contact breaker spring is firmly in its register on the insulator and set the contact gap.

NOTE: Whenever a new contact set has been fitted, re-check the gap after the first 500 miles (800 km). During this period the heel of the contact will have bedded-in and reduced the gap.

SNC101A

Spark plugs—clean and adjust

1. Remove the plugs and clean them, using air-blast equipment.
2. Set the gaps to 0.025 in (0.64 mm), moving the side electrode on the plug only.
3. Refit the spark plugs to the engine. **Do not overtighten.**

Ignition timing

1. Clean the timing pointers and the timing notch on the crankshaft pulley, and mark the notch on the pulley with chalk.
2. Run the engine until it attains normal running temperature, then switch off.
3. Connect a stroboscopic timing light in accordance with the manufacturer's instructions.
   WARNING: Ensure that personnel and equipment are kept clear of the cooling fan while using the timing light.
4. Run the engine at idle speed 650 to 680 rev/min.
5. Position the timing light to illuminate the crankshaft pulley and scale.
6. If the timing is correct the timing notch on the pulley will be aligned half way between the $8°$ and $12°$ BTDC pointers to give an ignition timing of $10°$ BTDC. If correct, the procedure in 7 and 8 may be ignored.
7. With the engine still running, use a second operator to slacken the clamp bolt and carefully rotate the distributor body as required until the equipment shows the correct timing.
8. Tighten the clamp bolt.

MAINTENANCE – U.K. SPECIFICATION

ELECTRICAL

Testing

Check that the lamps, horns, warning indicators, windscreen wipers and instruments are functioning correctly.

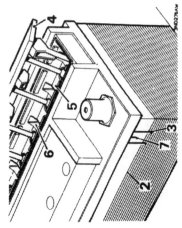

Battery

Checking

1 Ensure that the vehicle is standing on a level surface.
2 Check the level of the electrolyte which is visible through the end of the casing and should be 0.25 in (7 mm) below the red top.
3 The low indicator mark is on rear end of the case and is visible only when the battery is removed.
CAUTION: Top up only when the electrolyte level is below the top of the separators. **Do not use a naked light when checking the cells.**

Topping up

4 Raise the vent cover and tilt to one side.
5 Pour distilled water into the trough until all the rectangular filling tubes (6) are full and the bottom of the trough is just covered.
6 Press the cover firmly into position which automatically distributes the correct amount of distilled water to each battery cell.

7 The electrolyte should just cover the separator plates or, if the battery is removed, up to the high mark on the rear end of the case.
To mix the electrolyte in extremely cold conditions run the engine immediately after topping up.
CAUTION: The vent cover must be kept closed at all times, except when topping up. The electrolyte will flood if the cover is raised while charging the battery. The battery could also flood if it is topped up within half an hour of having it charged other than by the car's charging system.
8 Wipe the battery top clean and dry and smear the terminal posts with petroleum jelly as a precaution against corrosion. Ensure that the terminal screws are tight.
Clean off any corrosion from the battery and its mountings, using diluted ammonia, and then paint affected parts with anti-sulphuric paint – additional work.
NOTE: Specific gravity check and battery charging off the vehicle is additional work.

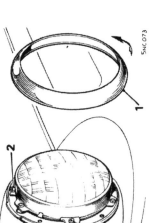

Headlamp beam alignment – adjusting

Two adjusting screws are provided on each headlamp for beam setting. The beams must be set in accordance with regulations governing the setting of headlamps.

1 Ease the bottom of the outer ring forwards and lift it off the retaining lug at the top of the lamp.
2 Turn the screw at the top of the lamp to make an adjustment in the vertical plane.
3 Turn the screw at the side of the lamp to make an adjustment in the horizontal plane.

NOTE: Beam setting is affected by the load on the car; therefore always set the beams with the normal load on the car.

Checking the charging system output

1 Connect a 0–20V moving coil voltmeter across the battery terminals.
2 Connect a 0–60A test ammeter in series with the main output cable and the '+' terminal of the alternator.
3 Start the engine, increase the engine speed and observe the ammeter.
4 If the reading exceeds 10A, continue running the engine until the reading falls below 10A.
5 The voltmeter reading should be 13.6 to 14.4V indicating that the charging system is working normally.
A voltmeter reading exceeding 14.4V indicates a defective regulator, a reading below 13.6V indicates a defective alternator or a high resistance fault in the external charging system.

WINDSCREEN WIPER BLADES AND WASHERS

Windscreen wiper blades

1 Examine the rubber blades for condition, and if these are perished or defective renew the blade assembly.
2 Pull the wiper away from the windscreen.
3 Hold the fastener and spring retainer away from the wiper arm retaining spring clip and withdraw the blade assembly from the arm.
4 Insert the end of the arm into the spring fastener of the new blade and push the new blade into engagement with the arm.
5 Lower the wiper onto the windscreen.

Checking operation

6 Press the control knob and check the operation of the washers.
7 If the delivery is incorrect turn the jet using a small screwdriver to adjust the height of the spray.

Topping up reservoir

8 Remove the filler cap and top up as necessary with a mixture of water and a recommended solvent; **do not use radiator anti-freeze.**

MAINTENANCE — U.K. SPECIFICATION

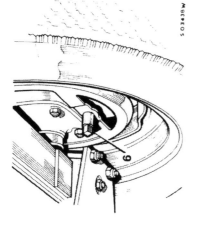

COOLING SYSTEM

WARNING: The cooling system is under pressure while the engine is hot. Allow the engine to cool before removing the expansion tank cap or the filler plug.

Examining for leaks
1 Inspect the cooling and heater systems for leaking connections and hoses, including the expansion tank to radiator hose.

Topping up/filling
2 Examine the coolant in the translucent expansion tank, the level is correct when the tank is half full.
3 If necessary remove the expansion tank cap and top up, refit the cap. If the level has fallen appreciably, suspect a leak in the cooling system

The filler plug does not normally require removing except when filling the system. However, if a leak has occurred the system may require topping up through the filling orifice.

4 Unwind the clip and remove the hose from the expansion tank.
5 Support the hose so that the free end is higher than the radiator.
6 Remove the filler plug and add coolant through the filling orifice.
7 Refit the filler plug.
8 Re-connect the hose to the expansion tank.

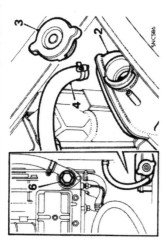

9 Top up the expansion tank if necessary.
NOTE: When the system contains anti-freeze ensure that the specific gravity of the coolant is maintained.

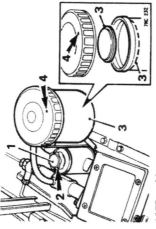

1977 and later

BRAKES

Brake hoses and pipes
Examine all hoses, pipes and unions for chafing, leaks and corrosion. It is most important that hoses are not subjected to stress and are not positioned near to other components so that chafing can occur. Rectify any leaks and replace hoses and pipes showing signs of damage or deterioration.

Topping up master cylinder reservoirs
Top up the brake master cylinder if necessary to the level mark with the recommended grade of fluid, as given in division 09. Frequent topping up is indicative of a leak in the hydraulic system which must be found and rectified immediately.
3 Examine the level of fluid and keep the reservoir filled up with fluid to the bottom of the filler neck.
4 Before replacing the filler cap, check that the breather hole is clear of obstruction by removing the centre disc of the brake reservoir cap. [To do this on a 1977 or later car, snap out the dome inside the cap, then snap it back in.]

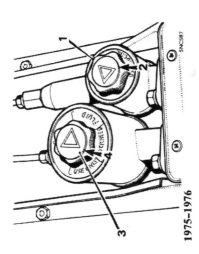

1975-1976

CLUTCH

Topping up clutch master cylinder
1 Remove the plastic filler cap and see that the fluid level is maintained at the bottom of the filler neck. Refer to division 09 for the recommended grade of fluid.
2 Before replacing the filler cap check that the breather hole is clear of obstruction.

7 Apply pressure to the brake pedal, it should feel solid. If there is any evidence of sponginess the brakes should be bled, this is additional work, refer to 70.25.02.

Checking hand brake operation
Ensure that the rear brakes have been correctly adjusted before checking the operation of the hand brake. If free play is still excessive, the hand brake cable requires adjusting, this is additional work, refer to 70.35.10.

Inspecting rear brake drum and linings
8 Chock the front wheels, release the hand brake, jack up each rear wheel in turn and place suitable supports beneath the vehicle.
9 Remove the road wheel and slacken off the brake-shoe adjuster fully.
10 Remove the two countersunk screws (pressed wheels) or the four nuts (wire wheels) and withdraw the brake drum.
11 Wash out accumulated dust from the backplate assembly and the drum with Girling Cleaning Fluid or methylated spirits (denatured alcohol) and allow to dry. Examine the drum for cracking and scoring.
WARNING: Do not blow dust from the brake assemblies — asbestos dust can be dangerous if inhaled.

Brake pedal travel and rear brake adjustment
Check brake pedal travel: if excessive, adjust the rear brakes.
5 Jack up each wheel in turn.
6 Turn the adjuster in a clockwise direction (viewed from the centre of the car) until the wheel is locked, then turn the adjuster back until the wheel can rotate without the linings rubbing. Lower the wheels.

continued

MAINTENANCE — U.K. SPECIFICATION

12 Inspect the linings for wear; if the lining material has worn down to the minimum permissible thickness of $\frac{1}{16}$ in (1.6 mm) on bonded-type shoes or close to the rivets, or will have done so before the next check is called for, the brake shoes must be renewed.

13 Refit the drum and road wheel and adjust the brake shoes. Remove the supports and lower the vehicle.

Inspecting front brake discs and pads

14 Check the thickness of the pads and renew them before the lining material has worn down to the minimum permissible thickness of $\frac{1}{16}$ in (1.6 mm). Ensure that sufficient pad material remains to allow the car to run until the next check. Examine the disc for cracking and scoring.

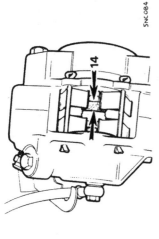

Hand brake lubrication

15 Use one of the recommended greases to charge the nipples on the hand brake balance lever and hand brake cable.

Preventive maintenance

In addition to the recommended periodical inspection of brake components it is advisable as the vehicle ages, and as a precaution against the effects of wear and deterioration, to make a more searching inspection and renew parts as necessary.

It is recommended that:

1 Brake linings, hoses and pipes should be examined at intervals no greater than those laid down in the 'MAINTENANCE SUMMARY'.

2 Brake fluid should be changed completely every 18 months or 18,000 miles (30000 km) whichever is the sooner.

3 All fluid seals and all flexible hoses in the hydraulic system should be renewed every 3 years or 36,000 miles (60000 km) whichever is the sooner. At the same time the working surface of the pistons and of the bores of the master cylinder, wheel cylinders, and other slave cylinders should be examined and new parts fitted where necessary.

Care must be taken always to observe the following points:

1 At all times use the recommended brake fluid.

2 Never leave fluid in unsealed containers. It absorbs moisture quickly and can be dangerous if used in the braking system in this condition.

3 Fluid drained from the system or used for bleeding is best discarded.

4 The necessity for absolute cleanliness throughout cannot be over-emphasised.

EXHAUST, FUEL, BRAKE AND CLUTCH PIPES

1 Check visually brake and clutch pipes and unions for chafing, leaks and corrosion.

2 Check visually fuel pipes and unions for chafing, leaks and corrosion.

3 Check exhaust system for leakage and security.

STEERING AND SUSPENSION

Checking

1 Examine the steering system and hydraulic dampers for signs of leakage and general condition of the steering rack gaiters.

2 Check the steering ball joints and the suspension for excessive free movement.

Checking front wheel alignment

When checking the front wheel alignment the following points must always be observed. See DATA.

3 The car must be at kerbside unladen trim with tyres inflated to the correct pressures and the steering-wheel in the straight-ahead position. Any free movement in the steering and suspension ball joints and suspension arms must be rectified.

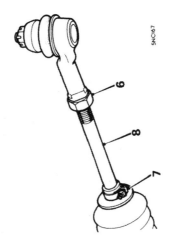

4 When a basebar-type gauge is used, take a measurement in front and behind the wheel centre at the rim edge, move the car forward half a road wheel revolution, and take another measurement at the same points on the wheel rim.

5 When an optical gauge is used, three readings must be taken, each reading at 120 degrees of wheel rim movement. The average figure must then be calculated from the readings.

Adjusting front wheel alignment

6 Slacken the locknut on both tie-rods.

7 Slacken the clip securing the rubber gaiter to the tie-rod.

8 Rotate each tie-rod (both are right-hand thread) in the required direction by an equal amount to correct the misalignment.

CAUTION: It is important that the tie-rods are adjusted to exactly equal length.

9 Tighten the tie-rod locknuts to 30 to 35 lbf ft (4.15 to 4.8 kgf m).

10 Tighten the gaiter clips.

11 Re-check the wheel alignment.

DATA

Front wheel alignment . . . . Parallel to $\frac{1}{8}$ in (0 to 3.2 mm) toe-in

MAINTENANCE – U.K. SPECIFICATION

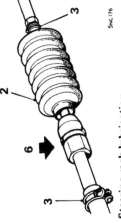

Steering rack lubrication

It is recommended that after every 30,000 miles or 3 years the steering rack is inspected and lubricated—this is additional work.

1 Clean the rack seals and the ends of the rack housing.
2 Inspect the seals for cracks, splits, signs of deterioration, or leakage of lubricant. If a seal is damaged or there are signs of lubricant leakage, the seal must be renewed, see 57.25.03.
3 Release the clips or wire securing both ends of the seals.
4 Roll the seals back to expose the rack and inner ball joints.
5 Examine the existing grease around the inner ball joint and the rack for ingress of water or dirt; if this is evident the steering rack must be removed for dismantling and inspection of the components, see 57.25.07.

CAUTION: If the vehicle is hoisted with its front wheels clear of the ground, care should be taken to avoid forceful movement of the wheels from lock to lock as damage may occur within the steering mechanism.

6 If the inner ball joint and the rack are in satisfactory condition, apply approximately 2 oz (57 gm) of a service grease around each inner ball joint and the rack including the teeth.
7 Unroll the seals, fit the protective shields and secure the seals to the rack housing with the clips.

Suspension fixings

The following fastenings should be checked for security.

8 Suspension fastenings.
9 Tie-rod ball and socket assemblies.
10 Steering-rack.
11 Steering column fixing bolts.

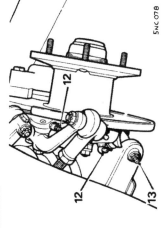

8 Smear the splines of the hub and wire wheel with grease.
9 Refit the wire wheel.
10 Lower the car.

Swivel pin lubrication

To ensure full penetration of the lubricant it is best if the front of the car is partly jacked up.

12 Use one of the approved greases to charge the two nipples on each swivel pin.

Outer fulcrum pin lubrication

13 Use one of the approved greases to charge the nipple on each fulcrum pin.

WHEELS AND TYRES

1 Check that tyres are in accordance with the manufacturer's specification: 145SR-13 radial ply.
2 Check and adjust the tyre pressures, including the spare.
Front
22 lbf/in² 1.55 kgf/cm² 1.52 bars
Rear
24 lbf/in² 1.69 kgf/cm² 1.66 bars
3 Check depth of tread.
4 Check visually for cuts in the tyre fabric, exposure of ply or cord, lumps or bulges.
5 Check tightness of the road wheel nuts: 62 Nm (45 lbf ft, 6.2 kgf m) max.

Wire wheels

6 Raise the front of the car and fit suitable safety supports under the chassis front members.

CAUTION: When the front wheels are clear of the ground, care should be taken to avoid forceful movement of the wheels from lock to lock as damage may occur within the steering mechanism.

7 Remove the road wheel.

2 Top up, allowing sufficient time for any surplus oil to run out before replacing the plug. Ensure that the correct grade of hypoid oil is used for topping up – see 'SERVICE LUBRICANTS'.

CAUTION: Do not drain the rear axle when the 'After Sales' service is carried out.

BODY

1 Lubricate the bonnet safety catch and release mechanism.
2 Lubricate all hinges and door locks.
Do not oil the steering lock.
3 Check the condition and security of the seats and seat belts and seat belt interlock.
4 Check operation of all door locks and window controls.

GENERAL

Road or roller test the vehicle and check that all the instruments function correctly.
NOTE: When checking the tightness of nuts and bolts great care must be taken not to overtighten them. A torque wrench should be used where possible – see 'TORQUE WRENCH SETTINGS'.

PROPELLER SHAFT

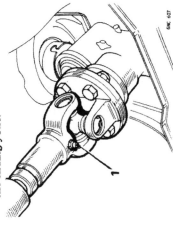

1 A nipple is provided at the front end of the propeller shaft for lubricating the sliding yoke.

GEARBOX

Checking oil level

With the vehicle standing level check that the oil is level with the bottom of the aperture.

1 Remove the filler level plug.
2 Top up, allowing sufficient time for any surplus oil to run out before replacing the plug. Ensure that the correct grade of oil is used for topping up – see 'SERVICE LUBRICANTS'.

CAUTION: Do not drain the gearbox when the 'After Sales' service is carried out.

REAR AXLE

Checking oil level

With the vehicle standing level, check that the oil is level with the bottom of the plug aperture.

1 Remove the filler level plug.
2 To lubricate, give three or four strokes of a gun filled with a recommended grease – see 'SERVICE LUBRICANTS'.

MAINTENANCE — 1975-1976 U.S.A. SPECIFICATION

FAULT FINDING CHART — NON CATALYTIC CONVERTER CARS

This chart indicates possible areas of fault causes. Progressively work through the 'possible causes', cross-referring to the 'key' opposite.

FAULT	POSSIBLE CAUSE IN ORDER OF CHECKING
Will not start	1, 2, 17, 18, 35, 36, 9, 10, 11, 12, 21, 25
Poor or erratic idle	17, 18, 36, 29, 31, 11, 13, 16, 12, 15, 14, 34, 4, 37, 22, 23, 24, 30, 3, 6, 20, 26, 38, 41, 42, 43, 44, 46, 47, 52, 53, 21, 25, 28
Hesitation or flat spot	17, 18, 27, 36, 35, 37, 32, 5, 22, 23, 25, 11, 13, 16, 12, 15, 14, 34, 4, 3, 6, 20, 26, 38, 41, 42, 43, 44, 46, 47, 52, 53, 21, 25, 28
Excessive fuel consumption	19, 30, 23, 36, 5, 37, 24, 21, 34, 4, 3, 11, 13, 16, 12, 15, 14, 52, 53, 46, 47, 6, 20, 26, 38, 41, 42, 43, 44, 25, 28
Lack of engine braking or high idle speed	36, 32, 29, 15, 31, 12, 37, 5, 21, 23, 24
Lack of engine power	17, 18, 36, 33, 5, 34, 11, 13, 16, 12, 14, 37, 23, 24, 21, 4, 3, 52, 53, 46, 47, 6, 20, 15, 26, 38, 41, 42, 43, 44, 25, 28
Engine overheating	7, 8, 12, 15, 14, 53, 47, 37, 24
Engine cuts out or stalls	17, 18, 29, 35, 36, 34, 4, 11, 13, 16, 12, 14, 37, 23, 24, 25, 6, 20, 15, 26, 38, 41, 42, 43, 44, 46, 47, 3, 21, 22, 28, 52, 53
Engine misfires	17, 18, 36, 11, 13, 16, 12, 14, 34, 4, 37, 23, 24, 3, 6, 20, 15, 26, 38, 41, 42, 43, 44
Fuel smells	19, 36, 30, 23, 42, 39, 41, 43, 44, 37, 24, 34
Engine 'runs on'	17, 36, 29, 32, 31, 41, 40, 7, 8, 12, 15, 14, 53, 47, 37, 24
Engine knock or 'pinking'	17, 12, 14, 15, 7, 8, 47, 37, 24
Arcing at plugs	13, 16
Lean running (low CO)	37, 17, 18, 23, 24, 6, 20, 15, 26, 38, 41, 42, 43, 44, 46
Rich running (excess CO)	36, 37, 43, 23, 24, 52, 53, 48, 51, 49, 50
E G R valve service interval counter/ warning light inoperative or faulty	45
Backfiring in exhaust	17, 18, 34, 4, 6, 12, 15, 20, 38, 46, 49, 26, 31
Noisy air injection pump	48, 51, 49, 50

KEY TO POSSIBLE CAUSES

Engine
1 Low battery condition or poor connections.
2 Starter system deficient.
3 Poor compressions.
4 Exhaust system leaking or blocked.
5 Fault on areas of vehicle other than engine.
6 Air leaks at inlet manifold.
7 Cooling system blocked or leaking.
8 Cylinder head gasket leaking.

Ignition
9 H.T. circuit faults.
10 L.T. power faults.
11 L.T. switching faults.
12 Ignition timing incorrect.
13 Ignition system deterioration.
14 Centrifugal advance mechanism faults.
15 Retard systems faults.
16 Spark plugs faults.

Fuel
17 Insufficient, incorrect or contaminated fuel.
18 Fuel starvation.
19 Leaking fuel.

Carburetter
20 Air leak at carburetter/manifold joint.
21 Air valve sticking in piston guide rod.
22 Obstructed float chamber or diaphragm ventilation holes.
23 Fuel level in float chamber incorrect.
24 Metering needle faults.
25 Diaphragm incorrectly located or damaged.
26 Leakage at throttle spindle, after considerable service.
27 Piston damper inoperative.
28 Air valve spring missing or incorrect.
29 Idle speed incorrectly set.
30 Leakage from fuel connection, joints or seals.
31 Incorrectly set or faulty deceleration by-pass valve.
32 Sticking throttle.
33 Throttle linkage inhibited or incorrectly set.
34 Dirty or blocked air cleaner.
35 Choke inoperative (cold engine).
36 Choke sticking on (warm engine).
37 Mixture incorrectly set.

Emission
38 Engine oil filler cap loose or leaking.
39 Fuel filler cap defective.
40 Anti run-on valve inoperative.
41 Restrictors missing or blocked.
42 Hoses blocked or leaking.
43 Adsorption canister restricted or blocked.
44 Vapour separator blocked.
45 E.G.R. valve service interval counter fault.
46 Leaks at E.G.R. valve vacuum control lines.
47 E.G.R. valve malfunction.
48 Incorrectly tensioned air pump driving belt.
49 Diverter valve malfunction.
50 Check-valve sticking.
51 Insufficient pump pressures.
52 Hot air inlet hose loose, adrift or blocked.
53 Air temperature control valve plate jammed.

MAINTENANCE — 1975–1976 U.S.A. SPECIFICATION
FAULT FINDING CHART — CATALYTIC CONVERTER CARS

This chart indicates possible areas of fault causes. Progressively work through the 'possible causes' cross referring to the 'key' opposite.

FAULT	POSSIBLE CAUSE IN ORDER OF CHECKING
Will not start	1, 2, 17, 18, 35, 9, 10, 11, 12, 21, 25
Poor or erratic idle	17, 18, 35, 29, 31, 11, 13, 16, 12, 15, 14, 34, 4, 37, 22, 23, 24, 30, 3, 6, 20, 26, 37, 40, 41, 42, 43, 46, 47, 52, 53, 21, 25, 28
Hesitation or flat spot	17, 18, 27, 35, 3, 32, 5, 22, 23, 2, 11, 13, 16, 12, 15, 14, 34, 4, 3, 6, 20, 26, 37, 40, 41, 42, 43, 45, 46, 51, 52, 21, 25, 28
Excessive fuel consumption	19, 30, 23, 35, 5, 36, 24, 21, 34, 4, 3, 11, 13, 16, 12, 15, 14, 51, 52, 45, 43, 6, 20, 26, 37, 40, 41, 42, 43, 25, 28
Lack of engine braking or high idle speed	35, 32, 29, 15, 31, 12, 36, 5, 21, 23, 24
Lack of engine power	17, 18, 35, 33, 5, 34, 11, 13, 16, 12, 14, 36, 23, 24, 21, 4, 3, 51, 52, 45, 46, 6, 20, 15, 26, 37, 40, 41, 42, 43, 25, 28
Engine overheating	7, 8, 12, 15, 14, 52, 46, 36, 24
Engine cuts out or stalls	17, 18, 29, 35, 34, 4, 11, 13, 16, 12, 14, 37, 23, 24, 25, 6, 20, 15, 26, 37, 40, 41, 42, 43, 45, 46, 3, 21, 22, 28, 52, 53
Engine misfires	17, 18, 36, 11, 13, 16, 12, 14, 34, 4, 36, 23, 24, 3, 6, 20, 15, 26, 37, 40, 41, 41, 42, 43
Fuel smells	19, 35, 30, 23, 41, 38, 40, 42, 43, 36, 24, 34
Engine 'runs on'	17, 35, 29, 32, 31, 40, 39, 7, 8, 12, 15, 14, 52, 46, 36, 24
Engine knock or 'pinking'	17, 12, 14, 15, 7, 8, 12, 15, 14, 56, 46, 36, 24
Arcing at plugs	13, 16
Lean running (low CO)	36, 17, 18, 23, 24, 6, 20, 15, 26, 37, 40, 41, 42, 43, 45
Rich running (excess CO)	35, 36, 42, 23, 24, 51, 52, 47, 50, 48, 49
E G R valve service interval counter/ warning light inoperative or faulty	44
Catalytic converter service interval counter warning light inoperative or faulty	45
Backfiring in exhaust	17, 18, 34, 4, 6, 12, 15, 20, 37, 45, 48, 26, 31
Noisy air injection pump	47, 50, 48, 49

KEY TO POSSIBLE CAUSES

Engine
1 Low battery condition or poor connections.
2 Starter system deficient.
3 Poor compressions.
4 Exhaust system leaking or blocked.
5 Faults on areas of vehicle other than engine.
6 Air leaks at inlet manifold.
7 Cooling system blocked or leaking.
8 Cylinder head gasket leaking.

Ignition
9 H.T. circuit faults.
10 L.T. power faults.
11 L.T. switching faults.
12 Ignition timing incorrect.
13 Ignition system deterioration.
14 Centrifugal advance mechanism faults.
15 Retard system faults.
16 Spark plug faults.

Fuel
17 Insufficient, incorrect or contaminated fuel.
18 Fuel starvation.
19 Leaking fuel.

Carburetter
20 Air leak at carburetter/manifold joint.
21 Air valve sticking in piston guide rod.
22 Obstructed float chamber or diaphragm ventilation holes.
23 Fuel level in float chamber incorrect.
24 Metering needle faults.
25 Diaphragm incorrectly located or damaged.
26 Leakage at throttle spindle, after considerable service.
27 Piston damper inoperative.
28 Air valve spring missing or incorrect.
29 Idle speed incorrectly set.
30 Leakage from fuel connections, joints or seals.
31 Incorrectly set or faulty deceleration by-pass valve.
32 Sticking throttle.
33 Throttle linkage inhibited or incorrectly set.
34 Dirty or blocked air cleaner.
35 Choke inoperative (cold engine).
36 Mixture incorrectly set.

Emission
37 Engine oil filler cap loose or leaking.
38 Fuel filler cap defective.
39 Anti run-on valve inoperative.
40 Restrictors missing or blocked.
41 Hoses blocked or leaking.
42 Adsorption canister restricted or blocked.
43 Vapour separator blocked.
44 E.G.R. valve service interval counter fault.
45 Catalytic converter service interval counter fault.
46 Leaks at E.G.R. valve vacuum control lines.
47 E.G.R. valve malfunction.
48 Incorrectly tensioned air pump driving belt.
49 Diverter valve malfunction.
50 Check-valve sticking.
51 Insufficient pump pressure.
52 Hot air inlet hose loose, adrift or blocked.
53 Air temperature control valve plate jammed.

MAINTENANCE — 1975-1976 U.S.A. SPECIFICATION

MAINTENANCE SUMMARY

Basic engine tuning data will be found on the Vehicle Emission Control Information label located in the engine compartment.

The following items should be checked weekly by the driver

Engine oil level
Brake fluid level
Radiator coolant level
Battery electrolyte level
Windscreen washer reservoir fluid level
All tyre pressures
All lights for operation
Horn operation
Windscreen wipers operation

MAINTENANCE INTERVALS

* These items are emission related

Service	Mileage x 1000	Monthly intervals
A	1	After Sales Service
B	3, 9, 16, 22, 28, 34, 41, 47	3
C	6, 19, 31, 44	6
D	12.5, 37.5	12
E	25, 50	24

NOTE: The service intervals are based on an annual mileage of approximately 12,500 miles. Should the vehicle complete substantially less miles than this per annum, it is recommended that a 'C' service is completed at six month intervals, and a 'D' service at 12 month intervals.

'A' SERVICE

Lubrication

Lubricate all grease points (except hubs and steering rack)
Renew engine oil.
Check/top up brake fluid reservoir
Check/top up clutch fluid reservoir
Check/top up battery electrolyte
Check/top up cooling system
Check/top up gearbox and rear axle
Check/top up screen washer reservoir
* Lubricate accelerator control linkage and pedal pivot; check operation
Lubricate all locks and hinges (not steering lock)

Engine

* Check driving belts; adjust or renew
Check cooling system hoses/pipes for security and condition
Check cooling and heater systems for leaks
* Check crankcase breathing and evaporative loss systems. Check hoses/pipes for security.
* Check security of engine bolts and mountings
* Check/adjust torque of cylinder head nuts
* Check/adjust valve clearances
* Check security of E G R valve operating lines
* Check exhaust system for leaks and security

Ignition

* Check ignition wiring for fraying, chafing and deterioration
* Check/adjust ignition timing using electronic equipment
* Check security of distributor vacuum unit line and operation of vacuum unit.

Fuel system

* Check fuel system for leaks
* Top up carburetter piston damper
* Check/adjust deceleration by-pass valve
* Check/adjust carburetter idle settings

Safety

Check tyres for tread depth, visually for cuts in tyre fabric, exposure of ply and cord structure, lumps and bulges
Check/adjust tyre pressures including spare
Check tightness of road wheel fastenings
Check condition and security of steering unit, joints and gaiters
Check security of suspension fixings
Check steering and suspension for oil/fluid leaks
Check/adjust foot and hand brake
Check visually hydraulic pipes and unions for chafing and corrosion
Check/adjust front wheel alignment
Check output of charging system
Check function of original equipment, i.e. interior and exterior lamps, horns, warning indicators, windscreen wipers and washers
Check/adjust headlamp alignment
Check operation of all door locks and window controls

Road test

Road/roller test and check operation of all instrumentation
Report additional work required

continued

MAINTENANCE — 1975-1976 U.S.A. SPECIFICATION

'B' SERVICE

Lubrication

Lubricate all grease points (except hubs and steering rack)
Check/top up engine oil
Check/top up brake fluid reservoir
Check/top up clutch fluid reservoir
Check/top up battery electrolyte
Check/top up cooling system
Check/top up gearbox and rear axle oils
Check/top up screen washer reservoir
* Lubricate accelerator control linkage and pedal pivot; check operation

Engine

Check cooling and heater systems for leaks
* Check exhaust system for leaks and security

Fuel system

* Check fuel system for leaks

Safety

Check tyres for tread depth, visually for cuts in tyre fabric, exposure of ply or cord structure, lumps or bulges
Check that tyres comply with manufacturer's specification
Check/adjust tyre pressures including spare
Check tightness of road wheel fastenings
Check condition and security of steering unit, joints and gaiters
Check steering and suspension for oil/fluid leaks
Check/adjust foot and hand brake
Check visually hydraulic pipes and unions for chafing and corrosion
Check function of original equipment, i.e. interior and exterior lamps, horns, warning indicators, windscreen wipers and washers
Check, if necessary renew, wiper blades
Check/adjust headlamp alignment

'C' SERVICE

Lubrication

Lubricate all grease points (except hubs and steering rack)
Renew engine oil and filter
Check/top up brake fluid reservoir
Check/top up clutch fluid reservoir
Check/top up battery electrolyte
Check/top up cooling system
Check/top up gearbox and rear axle oils
Check/top up screen washer reservoir
* Lubricate accelerator control linkage and pedal pivot, check operation
Lubricate all locks and hinges (not steering lock)

Engine

Check cooling and heater systems for leaks
Check cooling system hoses/pipes for security and condition
* Check exhaust system for leaks and security

Fuel system

* Check fuel system for leaks

Safety

Check tyres for tread depth, visually for cuts in tyre fabric exposure of ply or cord structure, lumps and bulges
Check that tyres comply with manufacturers specification
Check/adjust tyre pressures including spare
Check tightness of road wheel fastenings
Check condition and security of steering unit, joints and gaiters
Check security of suspension fixings
Check steering and suspension for oil/fluid leaks
Inspect brake pads for wear, discs for condition
Check/adjust foot and hand brake
Check visually hydraulic pipes and unions for chafing and corrosion
Check/adjust front wheel alignment
Check output of charging system
Check function of original equipment, i.e. interior and exterior lamps, horns, warning indicators, windscreen wipers and washers
Check, if necessary renew wiper blades
Check/adjust headlamp alignment
Check condition and security of seats, seat belts and seat belt warning system

Road test

Road/roller test and check operation of all instrumentation
Report additional work required

Brakes

It is further recommended that at 19,000 miles the brake fluid is renewed – additional work

'D' SERVICE

Lubrication

Lubricate all grease points (except hubs)
Renew engine oil and filter
Check/top up brake fluid reservoir
Check/top up clutch fluid reservoir
Check/top up battery electrolyte
Check/top up cooling system
Check/top up gearbox and rear axle oils
Check/top up screen washer reservoir
* Lubricate accelerator control linkage and pedal pivot, check operation
Lubricate all locks and hinges (not steering lock)

continued

MAINTENANCE – 1975-1976 U.S.A. SPECIFICATION

Engine
* Check driving belts; adjust or renew
* Check cooling and heater systems for leaks
  Check cooling system hoses/pipes for security and condition
* Renew carburetter air cleaner element
* Check crankcase breathing and evaporative loss systems. Check hoses/pipes and restrictors for blockage, security and condition
* Check/adjust valve clearances
* Check E G R system
* Check exhaust system for leaks and security

Ignition
* Check ignition wiring for fraying, chafing and deterioration
* Renew spark plugs
* Check security of distributor vacuum unit line and operation of vacuum unit
* Lubricate distributor
* Clean distributor cap, check for cracks and tracking
* Check coil performance on oscilloscope
* Check/adjust ignition timing using electronic equipment

Fuel system
* Clean fuel pump filter
* Check fuel system for leaks
* Top up carburetter piston damper
* Check/adjust deceleration by-pass valve
* Check/adjust carburetter idle settings
* Check condition of fuel filler cap seal

Safety
Check tyres for tread depth, visually for cuts in tyre fabric, exposure of ply or cord structure, lumps and bulges
Check that tyres comply with manufacturers specification
Check/adjust tyre pressures including spare
Check tightness of road wheel fastenings
Check condition and security of steering unit, joints and gaiters
Check security of suspension fixings
Check steering and suspension for oil/fluid leaks
Inspect brake linings/pads for wear, drums/discs for condition
Check/adjust toot and hand brake
Check visually hydraulic pipes and unions for chafing and corrosion
Check/adjust front wheel alignment
Check output of charging system
Check function of original equipment, i.e. interior and exterior lamps, horns, warning indicators, windscreen wipers and washers
Check, if necessary renew wiper blades
Check/adjust headlamp alignment
Check operation of all door locks and window controls
Check condition and security of seats, seat belts, and seat belt warning system

Road test
Road/roller test and check operation of all instrumentation
Report additional work required

Brakes
It is further recommended that every 37,500 miles the brake fluid, hydraulic seals and hoses in the brake hydraulic system are renewed – additional work

Steering
At every 37,500 miles the steering rack should be lubricated – additional work

'E' SERVICE

Lubrication
Lubricate all grease points (except hubs and steering rack)
Renew engine oil and filter
Check/top up brake fluid reservoir
Check/top up clutch fluid reservoir
Check/top up battery electrolyte
Check/top up cooling system
Check/top up gearbox and rear axle oils
Check/top up screen washer reservoir
* Lubricate accelerator control linkage and pedal pivot, check operation
* Lubricate all locks and hinges (not steering lock)

Engine
* Check driving belts; adjust or renew
  Check cooling and heater systems for leaks
  Check cooling system hoses/pipes for security and condition
* Renew carburetter air cleaner element
* Check crankcase breathing and evaporative loss systems. Check hoses/pipes and restrictors for blockage, security and condition
* Check/adjust valve clearances
* Check E G R system
* Renew catalytic converter (if fitted)
* Renew adsorption canister (every 50,000 miles)
* Check exhaust system for leaks and security

Ignition
* Check ignition wiring for fraying, chafing and deterioration
* Renew spark plugs
* Check security of distributor vacuum unit and operation of vacuum unit
* Lubricate distributor
* Clean distributor cap, check for cracks and tracking
* Check coil performance on oscilloscope
* Check/adjust ignition timing using electronic equipment

continued

MAINTENANCE — 1975-1976 U.S.A. SPECIFICATION

Fuel system

* Clean fuel pump filter
* Check fuel system for leaks
* Top up carburetter piston damper
* Check/adjust deceleration by-pass valve
* Check/adjust carburetter idle settings
* Check condition of fuel filler cap seal

Safety

Check tyres for tread depth, visually for cuts in tyre fabric, exposure of ply or cord structure, lumps and bulges

Check that tyres comply with manufacturers specification

Check/adjust tyre pressures including spare

Check tightness of road wheel fastenings

Check condition and security of steering unit, joints and gaiters

Check security of suspension fixings

Check steering and suspension for oil/fluid leaks

Inspect brake linings/pads for wear, drums/discs for condition

Check/adjust front wheel alignment

Check/adjust foot and hand brake

Check visually hydraulic pipes and unions for chafing and corrosion

Check, if necessary renew wiper blades

Check output of charging system

Check function of original equipment, i.e. interior and exterior lamps, horns, warning indicators, windscreen wipers and washers

Check/adjust headlamp alignment

Check operation of all door locks and window controls

Check condition and security of seats, seat belts and seat belt warning system

Road test

Road/roller test and check operation of all instrumentation

Report additional work required

43

LUBRICATION

NOTE: Ensure that the vehicle is standing on a level surface when checking the oil levels.

WEEKLY
(1) ENGINE. Check oil level and top up if necessary.

'A' SERVICE
(2) ENGINE. Drain and refill with new oil.
(4) THROTTLE AND CHOKE. Lubricate throttle and choke control linkages, cables, and accelerator pedal fulcrum.
(5) CARBURETTER. Top up carburetter piston damper.
(6) REAR AXLE. Check oil level, and top up if necessary.
(7) GEARBOX. Check oil level, and top up if necessary.
(9) FRONT SUSPENSION (6 nipples)
(10) HAND BRAKE CABLE (1 nipple)
(11) HAND BRAKE COMPENSATING LEVER (1 nipple)   } Give three or four strokes with a grease gun
(12) WIRE WHEELS. Lubricate wire wheel and hub splines.
LOCKS, HINGES AND LINKAGES. Lubricate all door, bonnet, boot locks and hinges (not steering lock).
FRICTION POINTS. Spray lubricant on all friction points.

'B' SERVICE
(1) ENGINE. Check oil level and top up if necessary.
(4) THROTTLE AND CHOKE. Lubricate throttle and choke control linkages, cables and accelerator pedal fulcrum.
(6) REAR AXLE. Check oil level, and top up if necessary.
(7) GEARBOX. Check oil level, and top up if necessary.
(9) FRONT SUSPENSION (6 nipples)
(10) HAND BRAKE CABLE (1 nipple)
(11) HAND BRAKE COMPENSATING LEVER (1 nipple)   } Give three or four strokes with a grease gun
(12) WIRE WHEELS. Grease wheel and hub splines.
FRICTION POINTS. Spray lubricant on all friction points.

'C' SERVICE
(2) ENGINE. Drain and refill with new oil.
(3) ENGINE OIL FILTER. Remove disposable cartridge, fit new.
(4) THROTTLE AND CHOKE. Lubricate throttle and choke control linkages, cables and accelerator pedal fulcrum.
(6) REAR AXLE. Check oil level, and top up if necessary.
(7) GEARBOX. Check oil level, and top up if necessary.
(9) FRONT SUSPENSION (6 nipples)
(10) HAND BRAKE CABLE (1 nipple)
(11) HAND BRAKE COMPENSATING LEVER (1 nipple)   } Give three or four strokes with a grease gun
(12) WIRE WHEELS. Lubricate wire wheel and hub splines.
LOCKS, HINGES AND LINKAGES. Lubricate all door, bonnet, boot locks and hinges (not steering lock); and the hand brake mechanical linkage.
FRICTION POINTS. Spray lubricant on all friction points.

'D' AND 'E' SERVICE
Carry out a 'C' service in addition to the following items (5) and (13).
(5) CARBURETTERS. Top up carburetter piston damper.
(8) STEERING. Lubricate steering rack (every 37,500 miles).
(13) DISTRIBUTOR. Lubricate all parts as necessary.

Service oils and greases are given in O9

MAINTENANCE — 1975-1976 U.S.A. SPECIFICATION

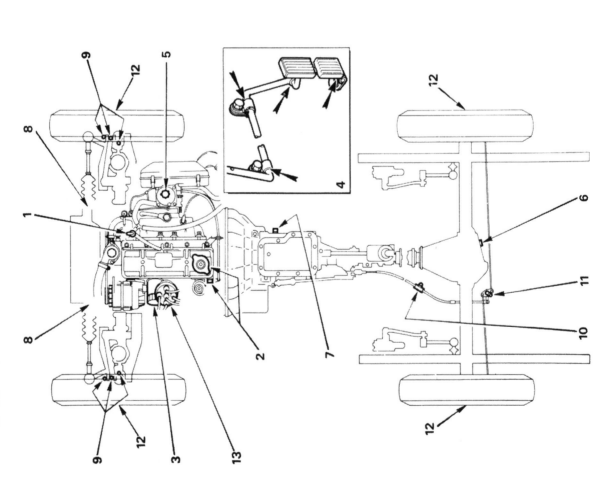

MAINTENANCE – 1975-1976 U.S.A. SPECIFICATION

ENGINE

Checking engine oil level
1 Maintain the level between the 'MIN' (1a) and 'MAX' (1b) marks on the dipstick.

Draining and refilling the engine oil
2 Drain the oil while the engine is warm; clean the drain plug and refit.
3 Refill with the correct quantity and grade of oil. Run the engine for a short while, then allow it to stand for a few minutes before checking the level.

Disposable cartridge filter renewal
1 Disconnect the hose from the air pump.
2 Unscrew the cartridge from the cylinder block.
3 If the adaptor remains attached to the cartridge unscrew it from the cartridge and screw it back into the cylinder block. Discard the cartridge and old seal.

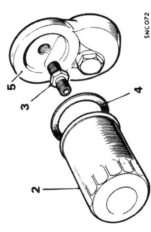
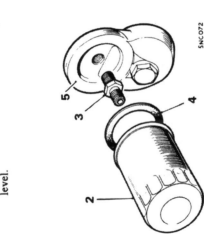

Engine mountings and bolts
Check the following fastenings for tightness:

	lbf ft	kgf m
Inlet manifold to exhaust manifold	14	1.9
Manifold to head	25	3.5
Rocker cover to head	2	0.3
Oil sump to block	20	2.8
Timing cover to front engine plate	10	1.4
Alternator to mounting bracket and front engine plate		
Alternator to adjusting link	22	3.0
E G R valve		
Engine mountings		
Air cleaner to carburetter		
Carburetter to manifold	20	2.8
Air pump		

Checking torque of cylinder head nuts
1 Remove the two nuts complete with plain and fibre washers securing the rocker cover to the cylinder head.
2 Disconnect the purge line from the rocker cover.
3 Remove the two nuts and washers securing the rocker cover to the cylinder head and slacken the air manifold support bracket screw.
4 Release the support bracket from the rocker cover rear stud.
5 Remove the rocker cover.
6 Remove the four nuts complete with washers securing the rocker shaft pedestals to the cylinder head and lift off the rocker shaft.
7 Tighten the cylinder head in a diagonal sequence to avoid distortion to a torque of 50 lbf ft (6.9 kgf m).

4 Smear the new seal with oil and fit it into the groove in the new cartridge.
5 Wipe the engine joint face clean and smear with oil.
6 Screw the new cartridge to the adaptor, using hand force only.
7 Connect the hose to the air pump.
8 Start the engine and check the cartridge for leaks. Check the oil level after waiting for a few minutes.

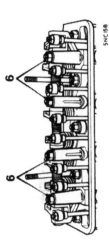

8 Refit the rocker shaft, ensuring that the adjustment screws are correctly located in the push rod cups.
9 Fit the four nuts and washers securing the rocker shaft pedestals to the cylinder head tightening the nuts evenly to a torque of 32 lbf ft (4.4 kgf m).
10 Adjust the valve clearances.

Valve rocker adjustment
1 Remove the two nuts and washers securing the rocker cover to the cylinder head.
2 Disconnect the purge line from the rocker cover.
3 Slacken the air manifold support bracket screw.
4 Release the support bracket from the rocker cover rear stud.
5 Remove the rocker cover.
6 Check the clearance between the valve rocker arms and the valve stems with a feeler gauge. Clearance (cold) 0.010 in (0.25 mm). The gauge should be a sliding fit when the engine is cold. Check the clearance of each valve in the following order.
Check:
No. 1 valve with No. 8 fully open
" 3 " " 6 " "
" 5 " " 4 " "
" 2 " " 7 " "
" 8 " " 1 " "
" 6 " " 3 " "
" 4 " " 5 " "
" 7 " " 2 " "
7 Slacken the locknut.
8 Rotate the screw, clockwise to decrease or anti-clockwise to increase the clearance.

continued

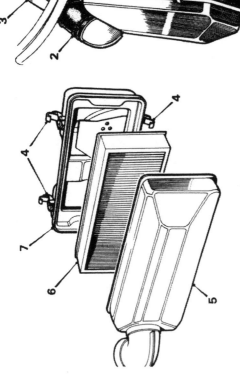

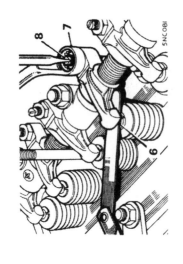

5NC081

MAINTENANCE — 1975-1976 U.S.A. SPECIFICATION

9   Re-tighten the locknut when the clearance is correct, holding the screw against rotation.

10 Recheck the clearances.

11 Check, and if necessary renew the rocker cover gasket.

12 Refit the rocker cover and position the support bracket in the rear stud, tighten the nuts to 2 lbf ft (0.3 kgf m) **DO NOT OVERTIGHTEN** or distortion of the cover may occur, resulting in oil leaks.

13 Tighten the support bracket screw.

14 Refit the purge line to the rocker cover.

15 Start the engine and check for leaks from the rocker cover gasket and filler cap.

Drive Belt Tension — Fan

When correctly tensioned, a total deflection of ¾ in (19 mm) under moderate hand pressure, should be possible at the midway point of the longest run between the pulleys.

Adjusting

1   Check the belt tension.

5NC 088A

5   Withdraw the cover.

6   Remove and discard the element.

7   Thoroughly clean the casing and cover.

8   Fit a new element and reassemble ensuring that the face of the element with the seal is fitted into the casing.

FUEL SYSTEM

Air cleaner element renewal

1   Release the hot air hose.

2   Slacken the clamp screw.

3   Remove the air temperature control assembly from the air cleaner.

4   Release the four clips.

Fuel pump filter gauze — cleaning

1   Squeeze the ends of the clip and remove the inlet hose from the fuel pump top cover.

2   Unscrew the central bolt.

3   Remove the top cover

4   Remove the filter gauze. Wash in clean fluid.

5   Check that the gasket is in position and in a good condition; renew if necessary.

6   Fit the gauze and top cover and secure with centre bolt.

7   Tighten the central bolt to 10-14 lbf in (0.115 to 0.161 kgf m).

8   Fit the inlet hose.

9   Start the engine and inspect the fuel pump for air and fuel leaks.

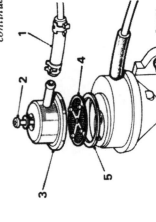

5NC 076

continued

10 Check the inlet and outlet hoses for leaks and serviceability.

5NC075

2   Slacken the alternator securing nut and bolt.

3   Slacken the adjusting link bolts.

4   Move the alternator to the required position. Apply any leverage necessary to the alternator end bracket only, using a wooden or soft metal lever.

5   Tighten the securing nuts and bolts and recheck the tension.

MAINTENANCE — 1975-1976 U.S.A. SPECIFICATION

Accelerator mechanism

1 Lubricate the accelerator pedal pivot.
2 Lubricate the carburetter accelerator and choke linkages and cables.
3 Check carburetter throttle response to initial movement of the accelerator pedal.
4 Check carburetter throttle position when the accelerator pedal is fully depressed, and adjust, if necessary, to ensure that full throttle is obtained.

Carburetter — Non catalytic converter cars

Air pollution control

The carburetter incorporates features which assist in reducing exhaust emissions. Maladjustment or the fitting of parts not to the required specifications may render these features ineffective.

Carburetter damper

1 Unscrew the damper cap.
2 Carefully raise the damper to the top of its travel.
3 Lower the damper back into the hollow piston rod. If the oil level in the hollow piston rod is correct, resistance should be felt when there is a gap of approximately ¼ in (A) between the cap and the carburetter top cover. Top up if necessary. Screw the damper cap firmly into the carburetter top cover.

Topping up

4 Remove the air cleaner.
5 Unscrew the damper cap from the carburetter top cover.
6 Raise the piston with a finger and at the same time lift the damper and carefully ease the retaining cap (6a) from the hollow piston rod to release the damper assembly from the piston.
7 With the piston raised, top up the hollow piston rod with a recommended engine oil until the oil level is ¼ in below the top of the hollow piston rod.

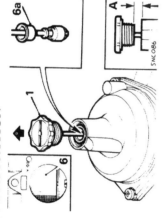

Under no circumstances should a heavy bodied lubricant be used.
8 Lower the oil level.
9 Ensure the oil level is correct.
10 Raise the piston and carefully press the retaining cup into the hollow piston rod.
11 Screw the damper cap firmly into the carburetter top cover.
12 Refit the air cleaner.

Carburetter settings

Adjustments should only be undertaken if an accurate tachometer, and exhaust gas analyser (CO meter) are available for use.

The tuning of the carburetter is confined to topping up the damper, setting idle and fast speeds, mixture strength (CO percentage), and adjusting the deceleration valve. Obtaining the correct carburetter settings depends on correct ignition timing and spark plug gaps, valve rocker clearances and on good seals at oil filler cap to the valve rocker cover, valve rocker cover to the cylinder head, engine oil dipstick to the cylinder block, carburetter to the induction manifold, exhaust manifold to the cylinder head, and all induction manifold tappings.

NOTE: Tuning must commence immediately the car reaches normal running temperature. If delay prevents the adjustment being completed within three minutes, increase the engine speed to 2000 rev/min for 30 seconds and then continue tuning. Repeat this clearing procedure at three minute intervals until tuning is completed.

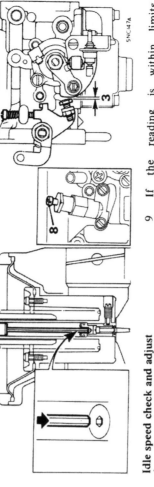

Idle speed check and adjust

1 Connect an accurate tachometer.
2 Start and warm the engine to normal running temperature.
3 Check that a small clearance exists between the fast idle screw and the cam.
4 Check the idle speed, see **DATA**, and adjust if necessary.

Mixture strength CO percentage at idle

5 Check/adjust the idle speed.
6 Disconnect the outlet hose from the air pump and plug the hose. DO NOT restrict the pump outlet otherwise damage may be caused to the air pump.
7 Recheck the idle speed.
8 Use the exhaust gas analyser in accordance with the manufacturer's instructions to check the percentage CO at idle. If the reading falls outside the prescribed limits, see **DATA**, adjust the fine idle CO screw, clockwise to enrich or anti-clockwise to weaken.

9 If the reading is within limits, continue with operations 26 onwards. If the correct CO percentage cannot be attained using the fine idle CO screw, proceed as follows:
10 Stop the engine.
11 Remove the air cleaner.
12 Raise the piston with a finger and at the same time lift the damper and carefully ease the retaining cap from the hollow piston rod to release the damper assembly from the piston.
13 Carefully insert tool S 353 into the dashpot until the outer tool engages in the air valve and the inner tool engages the hexagon in the needle adjuster plug.
   CAUTION: The outer tool must be correctly engaged and held or the carburetter diaphragm may be torn.
14 Start the engine.
15 Hold the tool firmly and turn the inner tool clockwise to enrich the mixture or anti-clockwise to weaken, as required.
16 Stop the engine.

continued

MAINTENANCE — 1975-1976 U.S.A. SPECIFICATION

17 With the piston raised, top up the hollow piston rod with a recommended engine oil until the oil level is ¼ in below the top of the hollow piston rod.
Under no circumstances should a heavy bodied lubricant be used.

18 Lower the piston.

19 Ensure the oil level is correct.

20 Raise the piston and carefully press the retaining cup into the hollow piston rod.

21 Screw the damper cap firmly into the carburetter top cover.

22 Refit the air cleaner.

23 Start the engine.

24 Recheck the idle speed.

25 Recheck the percentage CO at idle, adjusting the fine idle CO screw if necessary.

26 Stop the engine.

27 Remove the plug from the air pump hose.

28 Securely connect the hose to the air pump.

Fast idle speed — check and adjust

29 Check that the mixture control cam lever returns to its stop.

30 Pull out the mixture control knob approximately ¼ in to engage the fast idle cam in the ball locator.

31 Check that the cam is correctly engaged with the ball.

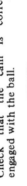

32 Check the idle speed.

33 Slacken the locknut and adjust the fast idle screw to give a fast idle speed of 1800 rev/min.

34 Tighten the adjuster lock nut, stop the engine and push the mixture control knob fully home.

Deceleration by-pass valve — check and adjust

35 Start the engine and run it at a fast idle speed until it attains normal running temperature, then run it for a further five minutes.

36 Disconnect the vacuum pipe from the distributor and place a finger over the end of the pipe.

37 The engine idle speed should rise to approximately 1300 rev/min. If the engine idle speed rises abruptly to 2000-2500 rev/min the by-pass valve is floating and adjustment is required.

38 Plug the vacuum pipe.

39 Turn the adjustment screw anti-clockwise until the engine speed falls to 1300 rev/min.

40 Momentarily increase and decrease the engine using the throttle.

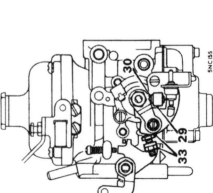

41 The engine speed should drop to approximately 1300 rev/min. Re-adjust if necessary.

42 Turn the adjustment screw ANTI-CLOCKWISE half a turn to seat the valve correctly.

43 Unplug the vacuum pipe and refit to the distributor.

DATA

Idling speed	700 to 900 rev/min
Fast idle speed (hot)	1800 rev/min
Engine gas analyser reading at engine idle speed	½ to 2% (2% nominal)

The above data is also shown on the Vehicle Emission Control Information Label located in the engine compartment.

Carburetter — Catalytic converter cars

Air pollution control

The carburetter incorporates features which assist in reducing exhaust emissions. Maladjustment or the fitting of parts not to the required specifications may render these features ineffective.

Carburetter damper

1 Unscrew the damper cap.

2 Carefully raise the damper to the top of its travel.

3 Lower the damper back into the hollow piston rod. If the oil level in the hollow piston rod is correct, resistance should be felt when there is a gap of approximately ¼ in (6 mm) (A) between the cap and the carburetter top cover. Top up if necessary. Screw the damper cap firmly into the carburetter top cover.

Topping up

4 Remove the air cleaner.

5 Unscrew the damper cap from the carburetter top cover.

6 Raise the piston with a finger and at the same time lift the damper and carefully ease the retaining cap (6a) from the hollow piston rod to release the damper assembly from the piston.

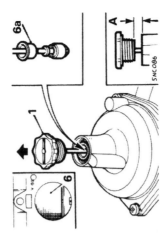

7 With the piston raised, top up the hollow piston rod with a recommended engine oil until the oil level is ¼ in (6 mm) below the top of the hollow piston rod.
Under no circumstances should a heavy bodied lubricant be used.

8 Lower the piston.

9 Ensure the oil level is correct.

10 Raise the piston and carefully press the retaining cup into the hollow piston rod.

11 Screw the damper cap firmly into the carburetter top cover.

12 Refit the air cleaner.

continued

MAINTENANCE — 1975-1976 U.S.A. SPECIFICATION

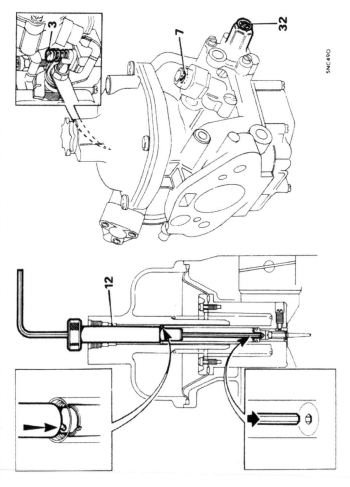

5NC49Q

Carburetter settings

Adjustments should only be undertaken if an accurate tachometer, and exhaust gas analyser (CO meter) are available for use.

The tuning of the carburetter is confined to topping up the damper, setting idle and mixture strength (CO percentage), and adjusting the deceleration valve. Obtaining the correct carburetter setting depends on correct ignition timing and spark plug gaps, valve rocker clearances and on good seals at oil filler cap to the valve rocker cover, valve rocker cover to the cylinder head, engine oil dipstick to the cylinder block, carburetter to the induction manifold, exhaust manifold to the cylinder head, and all induction manifold tappings.

NOTE: Tuning must commence immediately the car reaches normal running temperature. If delay prevents the adjustment being completed within three minutes, increase the engine speed to 2000 rev/min for 30 seconds and then continue tuning. Repeat this clearing procedure at three minute intervals until tuning is completed.

Idle speed check and adjust

1   Connect an accurate tachometer.
2   Start and warm the engine to normal running temperature.
3   Check the idle speed, see DATA, and adjust if necessary.

Mixture strength CO percentage at idle

4   Check/adjust the idle speed.
5   Disconnect the outlet hose from the air pump and plug the hose. DO NOT restrict the pump outlet otherwise damage may be caused to the air pump.
6   Recheck the idle speed.
7   Use the exhaust gas analyser in accordance with the manufacturer's instructions to check the percentage CO at idle. If the reading falls outside the prescribed limits, see DATA, adjust the fine idle CO screw, clockwise to enrich or anti-clockwise to weaken.
8   If the reading is within limits, continue with operations 25 onwards. If the correct CO percentage cannot be attained using the fine idle CO screw, proceed as follows:
9   Stop the engine.
10 Remove the air cleaner.
11 Raise the piston with a finger and at the same time lift the damper and carefully ease the retaining cap from the hollow piston rod to release the damper assembly from the piston.
12 Carefully insert tool S 353 into the dashpot until the outer tool engages in the air valve and the inner tool engages the hexagon in the needle adjuster plug. CAUTION: The outer tool must be correctly engaged and held or the carburetter diaphragm may be torn.
13 Start the engine.
14 Hold the tool firmly and turn the inner tool clockwise to enrich the mixture or anti-clockwise to weaken, as required.
15 Stop the engine.
16 With the piston raised, top up the hollow piston rod with a recommended engine oil until the oil level is ¾ in (6 mm) below the top of the hollow piston rod.
Under no circumstances should a heavy bodied lubricant be used.
17 Lower the piston.
18 Ensure the oil level is correct.
19 Raise the piston and carefully press the retaining cup into the hollow piston rod.

20 Screw the damper cap firmly into the carburetter top cover.
21 Refit the air cleaner.
22 Start the engine.
23 Recheck the idle speed.
24 Recheck the percentage CO at idle, adjusting the fine idle CO screw if necessary.
25 Stop the engine.
26 Remove the plug from the air pump hose.
27 Securely connect the hose to the air pump.

Deceleration by-pass valve — check and adjust

28 Start the engine and run it at a fast idle speed until it attains normal running temperature, then run it for a further five minutes.
29 Disconnect the vacuum pipe from the distributor and place a finger over the end of the pipe.
30 The engine idle speed should rise to approximately 1300 rev/min. If the engine idle speed rises abruptly to 2000-2500 rev/min the by-pass valve is floating and adjustment is required.
31 Plug the vacuum pipe.
32 Turn the adjustment screw anti-clockwise until the engine speed falls to 1300 rev/min.
33 Momentarily increase and decrease the engine using the throttle.
34 The engine speed should drop to approximately 1300 rev/min. Re-adjust if necessary.
35 Turn the adjustment screw ANTI-CLOCKWISE half a turn to seat the valve correctly.
36 Unplug the vacuum pipe and refit to the distributor.

DATA

Idling speed	700 to 900 rev/min
Engine gas analyser reading at engine idle speed	½ to 2% (2% nominal)

The above data is also shown on the Vehicle Emission Control Information Label located in the engine compartment.

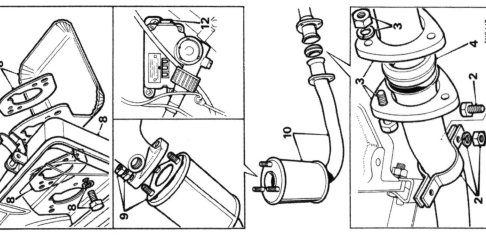

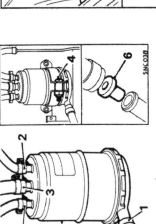

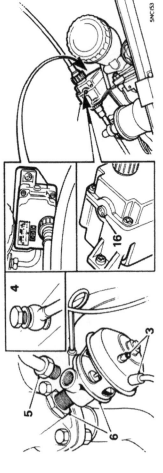

EMISSION CONTROL

Check E G R valve operating lines

1 Check for security of the push fit connections at the E G R valve, air-bleed valve, tee-piece, fuel trap and carburetter.

2 Renew any pipes which show signs of deterioration.

Check operation of E G R system

On completion of each 12,500 miles this maintenance operation will be indicated by a warning light on the console.

3 Disconnect the vacuum pipe from the E G R valve.

4 Remove the banjo bolt securing the metal pipe to the inlet manifold.

5 Unscrew the union nut securing the metal pipe to the E G R valve and remove the pipe.

6 Slacken the locknut and unscrew the E G R valve from the exhaust manifold.

7 Clean the assembly area of the E G R valve with a wire brush.

8 Use a standard spark plug machine to clean the valve and seat. Insert the valve opening into the machine and lift the diaphragm evenly. Blast the valve for approximately 30 seconds, remove and inspect. If necessary repeat until all carbon deposits are removed. Use compressed air to remove all traces of carbon grit from the valve. Use a flexiwire brush to clean inside the steel pipe — blow clear of carbon grit.

9 Renew any pipes which show signs of deterioration.

10 Refit the E G R valve.

11 Place the pipe in position to align the bottom union with the E G R valve, screw or unscrew the E G R valve as required. Place the pipe aside and tighten the E G R valve locknut.

12 Refit the steel pipe.

13 Reconnect the vacuum control pipe to the top of the E G R valve.

14 Check E G R valve operating lines for security of push fit connections at the E G R valve, air-bleed valve, tee-piece, fuel trap and carburetter.

15 Check the function of the E G R valve as follows:
Warm the engine to normal running temperature and ensure that the choke control is pushed in ('OFF'). Open and close the throttle several times and observe or feel the E G R valve, which should open and close with the changes in engine speed. The valve should close instantly when the throttle is closed.

16 Reset the E G R valve service warning indicator by inserting the key into the button and rotate to zero the counter. Remove the key.

Adsorption canister — renewal

1 Disconnect the air vent pipe.

2 Disconnect the vapour pipes.

3 Disconnect the purge pipe.

4 Remove the securing bracket nut and bolt.

5 Remove the canister.

6 Transfer the restrictor in the old canister to the new canister.

7 Fit the new canister and reconnect the air vent, vapour and purge pipes. CAUTION: Care should be taken when renewing the canister not to disturb the running-on control valve or its connections.

Renew catalytic converter and front pipe (if fitted)

1 Jack up and support the front of the car.

2 Remove the front exhaust pipe support bracket.

3 Release the exhaust front pipe from the rear pipe.

4 Remove the olive.

5 Remove the engine dipstick.

6 Remove the E G R valve, see 17.45.01.

7 Remove the air cleaner element, see 'MAINTENANCE',

8 Remove the two bolts to release the air cleaner casing, gaskets and heat shield from the carburetter.

9 Remove the six nuts securing the catalytic converter to the exhaust manifold.

10 Remove the catalytic converter and front pipe, and the exhaust flange gasket.
NOTE: Manoeuvre the engine to the L.H. side to enable the front pipe to clear the carburetter float chamber.

11 Fit a new catalytic converter and front pipe, by reversing the procedure in 1 to 10 and noting:
a Renew the exhaust flange gasket and the exhaust pipe olive.

b Renew the air cleaner gasket and heat shield if damaged or showing signs of deterioration.

12 Reset the catalytic warning indicator by inserting the key into the button, and rotating to zero the counter. Remove the key.

MAINTENANCE – 1975-1976 U.S.A. SPECIFICATION

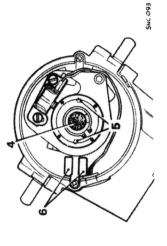

5NC093

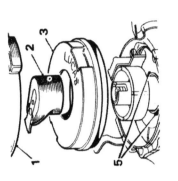

Air pump – drive belt tension

When correctly tensioned a total deflection of ½ in (13 mm) under moderate hand pressure should be possible at the midway point of the belt run.

Adjusting

1 Check the belt tension.
2 Slacken the securing bolt.
3 Slacken the two adjusting link bolts.
4 Move the air pump to the required position.
5 Tighten the bolts and re-check the belt tension.

CAUTION: Do not overtighten.

Fuel filler cap

1 Inspect the seal of the fuel filler cap for damage and wear, renew if necessary.
CAUTION: It is essential to the satisfactory operation of the evaporative loss system that the cap is always refitted correctly and tightened fully.

Purge line restrictors

1 Disconnect the purge line from the carburetter and adsorption canister.
2 Examine the orifice of the canister restrictor and carburetter restriction for obstruction.

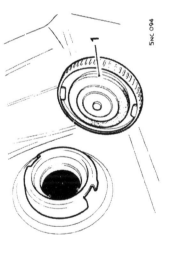

5NC074

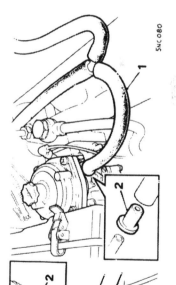

5NC094

5NC080

3 Clear any dirt or deposit using a length of wire. DO NOT use air pressure.
4 Refit the purge line assembly.

Distributor vacuum unit – checking

12 Check the security of the vacuum unit operating lines.
13 Start the engine and run it until it attains normal running temperature.
14 With the engine idling at 700 to 900 rev/min disconnect the operating line from the vacuum unit.
15 If the vacuum unit is operating correctly the engine speed will increase by approximately 500 rev/min.
16 Re-connect the operating line to the vacuum unit, ensuring a secure connection and switch off the engine.

IGNITION

Distributor – lubrication

1 Release the retaining clips and remove the cover.
2 Remove the rotor arm.
3 Remove the anti-flash shield.
4 Add a few drops of oil to the felt pad in the top of the timing rotor carrier.
5 Lubricate the pick-up plate centre bearing with a drop of oil in each ot the two holes in the base plate.
6 Apply a few drops of oil through the apertures to lubricate the centrifugal timing control.

Distributor – cleaning

7 Wipe the inside of the distributor cover, the rotor arm, and the anti-flash shield with a clean nap-free cloth. Check the carbon brush is free to move in its housing. Inspect the cap and rotor for cracks and any trace of tracking. Renew if necessary.
8 Refit the anti-flash shield ensuring that the cut-outs are aligned with the distributor cover retaining clips.
9 Refit the rotor arm and cover.

Distributor vacuum unit operating lines – checking

Check the following vacuum unit operating lines for security.
10 Carburetter to flame trap operating line.
11 Flame trap to distributor vacuum unit operating line.

Ignition coil

Check the ignition coil performance, using proprietary electronic testing equipment in accordance with the manufacturer's instructions.

Sparking plug renewal

1 Detach the high tension lead from each plug.
2 Partly unscrew each plug from the cylinder head.
3 Clean the area of the cylinder head surrounding each plug seating using compressed air or a brush.
4 Unscrew the plugs from the cylinder head and discard the plugs.
5 Set the gap between the electrodes of each new plug to the dimension given in DATA, bending the side electrode only.
6 Fit the new plugs to the engine.

continued

MAINTENANCE — 1975-1976 U.S.A. SPECIFICATION

7 Tighten each plug to 20 lbf ft (2.8 kgf m).

8 Refit the high tension lead to each plug.

DATA

Ignition coil
Make and type	Lucas 15C6
Lucas Serial No.	45243
Primary resistance at 68° F	1.30 to 1.45 ohms

Ballast resistor wire:
Resistance	1.3 to 1.5 ohms
Wire length.	63 in 160 cm

Sparking plugs
Make and type	Champion N-12Y
Gap	0.025 in 0.64 mm

Ignition wiring

Low tension circuit

1 Check the wiring connections between the drive resistor, distributor, coil and ignition switch for condition and security.

2 Check the wiring between the coil and distributor for fraying, chafing and deterioration.

3 Remove the distributor cap.

4 Check the distributor internal wiring for fraying, chafing and deterioration.

5 Check the internal distributor connections for condition and security.

6 Replace the distributor cap.

7 Report the wiring condition.

High tension circuit

8 Check the lead between coil and distributor for fraying, chafing and deterioration.

9 Check each spark plug lead for fraying, chafing and deterioration.

10 Check the high tension lead connections for condition and security.

11 Report the wiring condition.

ELECTRICAL

Testing

Check that the lamps, horns, warning indicators, windscreen wipers and instruments are functioning correctly.

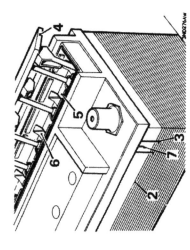

Ignition timing

1 Clean the timing pointers and the timing notch on the crankshaft pulley, and mark the notch on the pulley with chalk.

2 Run the engine until it attains normal running temperature, then switch off.

3 Connect a stroboscopic timing light in accordance with the manufacturer's instructions.
WARNING: Ensure that personnel and equipment are kept clear of the cooling fan while using the timing light.

4 Run the engine at idle speed 700 to 900 rev/min

5 Position the timing light to illuminate the crankshaft pulley and scale.

6 If the timing is correct the timing notch on the pulley will be aligned half way between the zero and 4° ATDC pointers to give an ignition timing of 2° ATDC.
If correct, the procedure in 7 and 8 may be ignored.

7 With the engine still running, use a second operator to slacken the clamp bolt and carefully rotate the distributor body as required until the equipment shows the correct timing.

8 Tighten the clamp bolt.

Battery

Checking

1 Ensure that the vehicle is standing on a level surface.

2 Check the level of the electrolyte which is visible through the end of the casing and should be 0.25 in (7 mm) below the red top.

3 The low indicator mark is on rear end of the case and is visible only when the battery is removed.
CAUTION: Top up only when the electrolyte level is below the top of the separators. **Do not use a naked light when checking the cells.**

Topping up

4 Raise the vent cover and tilt to one side.

5 Pour distilled water into the trough until all the rectangular filling tubes (6) are full and the bottom of the trough is just covered.

6 Press the cover firmly into position which automatically distributes the correct amount of distilled water to each battery cell.

continued

MAINTENANCE – 1975-1976 U.S.A. SPECIFICATION

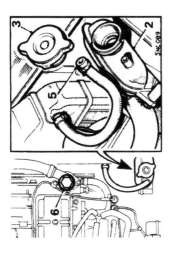

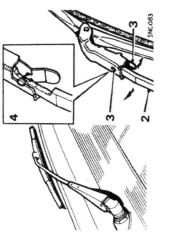

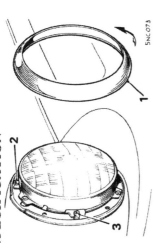

7 The electrolyte should just cover the separator plates or, if the battery is removed, up to the high mark on the rear end of the case.

To mix the electrolyte in extremely cold conditions run the engine immediately after topping up.

CAUTION: The vent cover must be kept closed at all times, except when topping up. The electrolyte will flood if the cover is raised while charging the battery. The battery could also flood if it is topped up within half an hour of having it charged other than by the car's charging system.

8 Wipe the battery top clean and dry and smear the terminal posts with petroleum jelly as a precaution against corrosion. Ensure that the terminal screws are tight.

Clean off any corrosion from the battery and its mountings, using diluted ammonia, and then paint affected parts with anti-sulphuric paint – additional work.

NOTE: Specific gravity check and battery charging off the vehicle is additional work.

Checking the charging system output

1 Connect a 0–20V moving coil voltmeter across the battery terminals.

2 Connect a 0–60A test ammeter in series with the main output cable and the '+' terminal of the alternator.

3 Start the engine, increase the engine speed and observe the ammeter.

4 If the reading exceeds 10A, continue running the engine until the reading falls below 10A.

5 The voltmeter reading should be 13.6 to 14.4V indicating that the charging system is working normally.
A voltmeter reading exceeding 14.4V indicates a defective regulator, a reading below 13.6V indicates a defective alternator or a high resistance fault in the external charging system.

Headlamp beam alignment – adjusting

Two adjusting screws are provided on each headlamp for beam setting. The beams must be set in accordance with regulations governing the setting of headlamps.

1 Ease the bottom of the outer ring forwards and lift it off the retaining lug at the top of the lamp.

2 Turn the screw at the top of the lamp to make an adjustment in the vertical plane.

3 Turn the screw at the side of the lamp to make an adjustment in the horizontal plane.

NOTE: Beam setting is affected by the load on the car; therefore always set the beams with the normal load on the car.

WINDSCREEN WIPER BLADES AND WASHERS

Windscreen wiper blades

1 Examine the rubber blades for condition, and if these are perished or defective renew the blade assembly.

2 Pull the wiper away from the windscreen.

3 Hold the fastener and spring retainer away from the wiper arm retaining spring clip and withdraw the blade assembly from the arm.

4 Insert the end of the arm into the spring fastener of the new blade and push the new blade into engagement with the arm.

5 Lower the wiper onto the windscreen.

Checking operation

6 Switch on the ignition and press the end of the switch lever and check the operation of the washers.

7 If the delivery is incorrect turn the jet using a small screwdriver to adjust the height of the spray.

Topping up reservoir

8 Remove the filler cap and top up as necessary with a mixture of water and a recommended solvent; do not use radiator anti-freeze.

COOLING SYSTEM

WARNING: The cooling system is under pressure while the engine is hot. Allow the engine to cool before removing the expansion tank cap or the filler plug.

Examining for leaks

1 Inspect the cooling and heater systems for leaking connections and hoses, including the expansion tank to radiator hose.

Topping up/filling

2 Examine the coolant in the expansion tank, the level is correct when the tank is half full.

3 If necessary remove the expansion tank cap and top up, refit the cap. If the level has fallen appreciably, suspect a leak in the cooling system.

The filler plug does not normally require removing except when filling the system. However, if a leak has occurred the system may require topping up through the filling orifice.

4 Unwind the clip and remove the hose from the expansion tank.

5 Support the hose so that the free end is higher than the radiator.

6 Remove the filler plug and add coolant through the filling orifice.

7 Refit the filler plug.

8 Re-connect the hose to the expansion tank.

9 Top up the expansion tank if necessary.

NOTE: When the system contains anti-freeze ensure that the specific gravity of the coolant is maintained.

CLUTCH

Topping up clutch master cylinder

1 Remove the plastic filler cap and see that the fluid level is maintained at the bottom of the filler neck. Refer to division 09 for the recommended grade of fluid.

2 Before replacing the filler cap check that the breather hole is clear of obstruction.

continued

MAINTENANCE — 1975-1976 U.S.A. SPECIFICATION

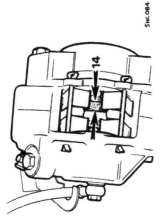

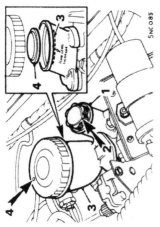

BRAKES

Brake hoses and pipes

Examine all hoses, pipes and unions for chafing, leaks and corrosion. It is most important that hoses are not subjected to stress and are not positioned near to other components so that chafing can occur. Rectify any leaks and replace hoses and pipes showing signs of damage or deterioration.

Topping up master cylinder reservoirs

Top up the brake master cylinder if necessary to the level mark with the recommended grade of fluid, as given in division 09. Frequent topping up is indicative of a leak in the hydraulic system which must be found and rectified immediately.

3 Examine the level of fluid and keep the reservoir filled up with fluid to the bottom of the filler neck.

4 Before replacing the filler cap, check that the breather hole is clear of obstruction by removing the centre disc of the brake reservoir cap.

Brake pedal travel and rear brake adjustment

Check brake pedal travel: if excessive, adjust the rear brakes.

5 Jack up each wheel in turn.

6 Turn the adjuster in a clockwise direction (viewed from the centre of the car) until the wheel is locked, then turn the adjuster back until the wheel can rotate without the linings rubbing. Lower the wheels.

7 Apply pressure to the brake pedal, it should feel solid. If there is any evidence of sponginess the brakes should be bled, this is additional work, refer to 70.25.02.

Checking hand brake operation

Ensure that the rear brakes have been correctly adjusted before checking the operation of the hand brake. If free play is still excessive, the hand brake cable requires adjusting, this is additional work, refer to 70.35.10.

Inspecting rear brake drum and linings

8 Chock the front wheels, release the hand brake, jack up each rear wheel in turn and place suitable supports beneath the vehicle.

9 Remove the road wheel and slacken off the brake-shoe adjuster fully.

10 Remove the two countersunk screws (pressed wheels) or the four nuts (wire wheels) and withdraw the brake drum.

11 Wash out accumulated dust from the backplate assembly and the drum with Girling Cleaning Fluid or methylated spirits (denatured alcohol) and allow to dry. Examine the drum for cracking and scoring.
WARNING: Do not blow dust from the brake assemblies — asbestos dust can be dangerous if inhaled.

12 Inspect the linings for wear; if the lining material has worn down to the minimum permissible thickness of $\frac{1}{16}$ in (1.6 mm) on bonded-type shoes or close to the rivets, or will have done so before the next check is called for, the brake shoes must be renewed.

13 Refit the drum and road wheel and adjust the brake shoes. Remove the supports and lower the vehicle.

Inspecting front brake discs and pads

14 Check the thickness of the pads and renew them before the lining material has worn down to the minimum permissible thickness of $\frac{1}{16}$ in (1.6 mm). Ensure that sufficient pad material remains to allow the car to run until the next check. Examine the disc for cracking and scoring.

Hand brake lubrication

15 Use one of the recommended greases to charge the nipples on the hand brake balance lever and hand brake cable.

Preventive maintenance

In addition to the recommended periodical inspection of brake components it is advisable as the vehicle ages, and as a precaution against the effects of wear and deterioration, to make a more searching inspection and renew parts as necessary.

It is recommended that:

1 Brake linings, hoses and pipes should be examined at intervals no greater than those laid down in the 'MAINTENANCE SUMMARY'.

2 Brake fluid should be changed completely every 18 months or 19,000 miles (30000 km) whichever is the sooner.

3 All fluid seals and all flexible hoses in the hydraulic system should be renewed every 3 years or 37,500 miles (60000 km) whichever is the sooner. At the same time the working surface of the pistons and of the bores of the master cylinder, wheel cylinders, and other slave cylinders should be examined and new parts fitted where necessary.

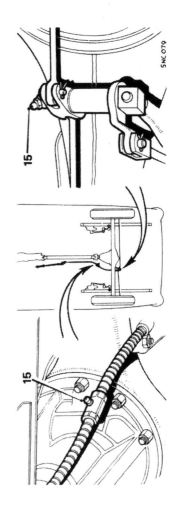

continued

MAINTENANCE – 1975-1976 U.S.A. SPECIFICATION

Care must be taken always to observe the following points:

1 At all times use the recommended brake fluid.
2 Never leave fluid in unsealed containers. It absorbs moisture quickly and can be dangerous if used in the braking system in this condition.
3 Fluid drained from the system or used for bleeding is best discarded.
4 The necessity for absolute cleanliness throughout cannot be over-emphasised.

EXHAUST, FUEL, BRAKE AND CLUTCH PIPES

1 Check visually brake and clutch pipes and unions for chafing, leaks and corrosion.
2 Check visually fuel pipes and unions for chafing, leaks and corrosion.
3 Check exhaust system for leakage and security.

STEERING AND SUSPENSION

Checking

1 Examine the steering system and hydraulic dampers for signs of leakage and general condition of the steering rack gaiters.
2 Check the steering ball joints and the suspension for excessive free movement.

Checking front wheel alignment

When checking the front wheel alignment the following points must always be observed. See DATA.

3 The car must be at kerbside unladen trim with tyres inflated to the correct pressures and the steering-wheel in the straight-ahead position. Any free movement in the steering and suspension ball joints and suspension arms must be rectified.

DATA

Front wheel alignment . . . .

Parallel to ⅛ in
(0 to 3.2 mm) toe-in

---

4 When a basebar-type gauge is used, take a measurement in front and behind the wheel centre at the rim edge, move the car forward half a road wheel revolution, and take another measurement at the same points on the wheel rim.
5 When an optical gauge is used, three readings must be taken, each reading at 120 degrees of wheel rim movement. The average figure must then be calculated from the readings.

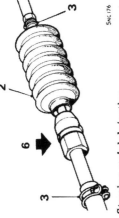

SNC167

Adjusting front wheel alignment

6 Slacken the locknut on both tie-rods.
7 Slacken the clip securing the rubber gaiter to the tie-rod.
8 Rotate each tie-rod (both are right-hand thread) in the required direction by an equal amount to correct the misalignment.
CAUTION: It is important that the tie-rods are adjusted to exactly equal length.
9 Tighten the tie-rod locknuts to 30 to 35 lbf ft (4.15 to 4.8 kgf m).
10 Tighten the gaiter clips.
11 Re-check the wheel alignment.

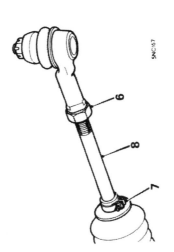

SNC176

Steering rack lubrication

It is recommended that after every 37,500 miles or 3 years the steering rack is inspected and lubricated—this is additional work.

1 Clean the rack seals and the ends of the rack housing.
2 Inspect the seals for cracks, splits, signs of deterioration, or leakage of lubricant. If a seal is damaged or there are signs of lubricant leakage, the seal must be renewed, see 57.25.03.
3 Release the clips or wire securing both ends of the seals.
4 Roll the seals back to expose the rack and inner ball joints.
5 Examine the existing grease around the inner ball joint and the rack for ingress of water or dirt; if this is evident the steering rack must be removed for dismantling and inspection of the components, see 57.25.07.
6 If the inner ball joint and the rack are in satisfactory condition, apply approximately 2 oz (57 gm) of a service grease around each inner ball joint and the rack including the teeth.
7 Unroll the seals, fit the protective shields and secure the seals to the rack housing with the clips.
CAUTION: If the vehicle is hoisted with its front wheels clear of the ground, care should be taken to avoid forceful movement of the wheels from lock to lock as damage may occur within the steering mechanism.

Suspension fixings

The following fastenings should be checked for security.

14 Suspension fastenings.
15 Tie-rod ball and socket assemblies.
16 Steering-rack.
17 Steering column fixing bolts.

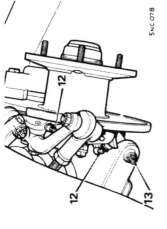

SNC078

Swivel pin lubrication

To ensure full penetration of the lubricant it is best if the front of the car is partly jacked up.

12 Use one of the approved greases to charge the two nipples on each swivel pin.

Outer fulcrum pin lubrication

13 Use one of the approved greases to charge the nipple on each fulcrum pin.

WHEELS AND TYRES

i Check that tyres are in accordance with the manufacturer's specification: 145SR-13 radial ply.
2 Check and adjust the tyre pressures, including the spare.
Front:
22 lbf/in² 1.55 kgf/cm² 1.52 bars
Rear:
24 lbf/in² 1.69 kgf/cm² 1.66 bars
3 Check depth of tread.
4 Check visually for cuts in the tyre fabric, exposure of ply or cord, lumps or bulges.
5 Check tightness of the road wheel nuts: 62 Nm (45 lbf ft, 6.2 kgf m) max.

continued

MAINTENANCE – 1975-1976 U.S.A. SPECIFICATION

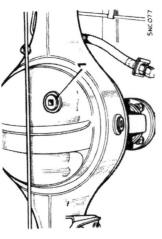

Wire wheels

6 Raise the front of the car and fit suitable safety supports under the chassis front members.

CAUTION: When the front wheels are clear of the ground, care should be taken to avoid forceful movement of the wheels from lock to lock as damage may occur within the steering mechanism.

7 Remove the road wheel.
8 Smear the splines of the hub and wire wheel with grease.
9 Refit the wire wheel.
10 Lower the car.

GEARBOX

Checking oil level

With the vehicle standing level check that the oil is level with the bottom of the aperture.

1 Remove the filler level plug.
2 Top up, allowing sufficient time for any surplus oil to run out before replacing the plug.
Ensure that the correct grade of oil is used for topping up – see **'SERVICE LUBRICANTS'.**

CAUTION: Do not drain the gearbox when the **'After Sales'** service is carried out.

REAR AXLE

Checking oil level

With the vehicle standing level, check that the oil is level with the bottom of the plug aperture.

1 Remove the filler level plug.
2 Top up, allowing sufficient time for any surplus oil to run out before replacing the plug. Ensure that the correct grade of hypoid oil is used for topping up – see **'SERVICE LUBRICANTS'.**

CAUTION: Do not drain the rear axle when the **'After Sales'** service is carried out.

BODY

1 Lubricate the bonnet safety catch and release mechanism.
2 Lubricate all hinges and door locks.
   Do not oil the steering lock.
3 Check the condition and security of the seats and seat belts and seat belt interlock.
4 Check operation of all door locks and window controls.

GENERAL

Road or roller test the vehicle and check that all the instruments function correctly. **NOTE:** When checking the tightness of nuts and bolts great care must be taken not to overtighten them. A torque wrench should be used where possible – see **'TORQUE WRENCH SETTINGS'.**

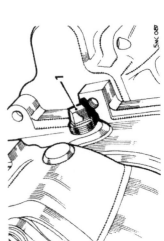

MAINTENANCE — 1977 AND LATER U.S.A. SPECIFICATION
FAULT FINDING CHART

This chart indicates possible areas of fault causes. Progressively work through the 'possible causes' cross referring to the 'key' opposite.

FAULT	POSSIBLE CAUSE IN ORDER OF CHECKING
Will not start	1, 2, 17, 18, 35, 9, 10, 11, 12, 21
Poor or erratic idle	17, 29, 25, 36, 16, 10, 11, 12, 15, 13, 37, 40, 41, 42, 43, 6, 4, 20, 18, 30, 19, 22, 32, 33, 34, 23, 21, 28, 24, 22, 26, 44, 45, 31, 48, 14, 49, 50, 8, 3
Hesitation or flat spot	17, 18, 27, 36, 32, 5, 22, 23, 24, 11, 13, 16, 12, 15, 34, 4, 6, 20, 26, 37, 40, 41, 42, 43, 44, 49, 50, 21, 28, 3, 14, 45
Excessive fuel consumption	19, 30, 23, 5, 36, 24, 21, 34, 4, 11, 13, 16, 12, 15, 49, 50, 44, 6, 20, 26, 37, 40, 41, 42, 43, 28, 3, 14, 45
Lack of engine braking or high idle speed	32, 29, 15, 31, 12, 36, 5, 21, 23, 24
Lack of engine power	17, 18, 33, 5, 34, 11, 13, 16, 12, 36, 23, 24, 21, 4, 49, 50, 44, 6, 20, 15, 26, 37, 40, 41, 42, 43, 28, 14, 3, 45
Engine overheating	7, 12, 15, 50, 36, 24, 8, 14, 45
Engine cuts out or stalls	17, 18, 29, 35, 34, 4, 11, 13, 16, 12, 36, 23, 24, 6, 20, 15, 26, 37, 40, 41, 42, 43, 44, 46, 3, 21, 22, 28, 49, 50, 14, 45, 3
Engine misfires	17, 18, 11, 13, 16, 12, 14, 4, 36, 23, 24, 6, 20, 15, 26, 37, 40, 41, 42, 43, 14, 3
Fuel smells	19, 30, 23, 41, 38, 40, 42, 43, 36, 24, 34
Engine 'runs on'	17, 29, 32, 31, 40, 39, 7, 12, 15, 50, 36, 24, 8, 14, 45
Engine knock or 'pinking'	17, 12, 15, 7, 12, 50, 36, 24, 14, 8, 45
Arcing at plugs	13, 16
Lean running (low CO)	36, 17, 18, 23, 24, 6, 20, 15, 26, 37, 40, 41, 42, 43, 45
Rich running (excess CO)	36, 42, 23, 24, 49, 50, 46, 47
Backfiring in exhaust	17, 18, 34, 4, 6, 12, 15, 20, 37, 44, 26, 31
Noisy air injection pump	46, 47, 48

KEY TO POSSIBLE CAUSES

Engine
1 Low battery condition or poor connections.
2 Starter system deficient.
3 Poor compressions.
4 Exhaust system leaking or blocked.
5 Faults on areas of vehicle other than engine.
6 Air leaks at inlet manifold.
7 Cooling system blocked or leaking.
8 Cylinder head gasket leaking.

Ignition
9 H.T. circuit faults.
10 L.T. power faults.
11 L.T. switching faults.
12 Ignition timing incorrect.
13 Ignition system deterioration.
14 Centrifugal advance mechanism faults.
15 Retard system faults.
16 Spark plug faults.

Fuel
17 Insufficient, incorrect or contaminated fuel.
18 Fuel starvation.
19 Leaking fuel.

Carburetter
20 Air leak at carburetter/manifold joint.
21 Air valve sticking in piston guide rod.
22 Obstructed float chamber or diaphragm ventilation holes.
23 Fuel level in float chamber incorrect.
24 Metering needle faults.
25 Diaphragm incorrectly located or damaged.
26 Leakage at throttle spindle, after considerable service.
27 Piston damper inoperative.
28 Air valve spring missing or incorrect.
29 Idle speed incorrectly set.
30 Leakage from fuel connections, joints or seals.
31 Incorrectly set or faulty deceleration by-pass valve.
32 Sticking throttle.
33 Throttle linkage inhibited or incorrectly set.
34 Dirty or blocked air cleaner.
35 Choke inoperative (cold engine).
36 Mixture incorrectly set.

Emission
37 Engine oil filler cap loose or leaking.
38 Fuel filler cap defective.
39 Anti run-on valve inoperative.
40 Restrictors missing or blocked.
41 Hoses blocked or leaking.
42 Adsorption canister restricted or blocked.
43 Vapour separator blocked.
44 Leaks at E.G.R. valve vacuum control lines.
45 E.G.R. valve malfunction.
46 Incorrectly tensioned air pump driving belt.
47 Check-valve sticking.
48 Insufficient pump pressure.
49 Hot air inlet hose loose, adrift or blocked.
50 Air temperature control valve plate jammed.

MAINTENANCE — 1977 AND LATER U.S.A. SPECIFICATION
MAINTENANCE SUMMARY

Basic engine tuning data will be found on the Vehicle Emission Control Information label located in the engine compartment.

The following items should be checked weekly by the driver

Engine oil level
Brake fluid level
Radiator coolant level
Battery electrolyte level
Windscreen washer reservoir fluid level
All tyre pressures
All lights for operation
Horn operation
Windscreen wipers operation

MAINTENANCE INTERVALS

* These items are emission related

Service	Mileage x 1000	Monthly intervals
A	1	After Sales Service
B	3, 9, 16, 22, 28, 34, 41, 47	3
C	6, 19, 31, 44	6
D	12.5, 37.5	12
E	25, 50	24

NOTE: The service intervals are based on an annual mileage of approximately 12,500 miles. Should the vehicle complete substantially less miles than this per annum, it is recommended that a 'C' service is completed at six month intervals, and a 'D' service at 12 month intervals.

'A' SERVICE

Lubrication
Lubricate all grease points (except hubs and steering rack)
Renew engine oil.
Check/top up brake fluid reservoir
Check/top up clutch fluid reservoir
Check/top up battery electrolyte
Check/top up cooling system
Check/top up gearbox and rear axle
Check transmission for oil leaks
* Lubricate accelerator control linkage (and pedal pivot); check operation
Lubricate all locks and hinges (not steering lock)

Engine
Check for oil leaks
* Check driving belts; adjust or renew
* Check cooling and heater systems for leaks, and hoses for security and condition
* Check crankcase breathing and evaporative loss system hoses for security
Check security of engine mountings
* Check/adjust torque of cylinder head nuts
* Check/adjust valve clearances
* Check security of E G R valve operating lines
* Check exhaust system for leaks and security

Ignition
* Check ignition wiring for fraying, chafing and deterioration
* Check/adjust ignition timing using electronic equipment
* Check security of distributor vacuum unit line
* Check operation of distributor vacuum unit (California only)

Fuel system
* Check fuel system for leaks, pipes and unions for chafing and corrosion
* Top up carburetter piston damper
* Check/adjust deceleration by-pass valve
* Check/adjust carburetter idle settings

Safety
Check/adjust operation of all washers, and top up reservoir
Check tyres for external cuts in tyre fabric, exposure of ply or cord structure, lumps or bulges
Check/adjust tyre pressures including spare
Check tightness of road wheel fastenings
Check condition and security of steering unit, joints and gaiters
Check security of suspension fixings
Check steering rack and suspension for oil/fluid leaks
Check/adjust foot and hand brake
Check visually hydraulic hoses, pipes and unions for chafing, cracks, leaks and corrosion
Check/adjust front wheel alignment
Check output of charging system
Check function of original equipment, i.e. interior and exterior lamps, horns, wipers and warning indicators
Check/adjust headlamp alignment
Check operation of all door, bonnet, and luggage compartment locks
Check operation of window controls
Check condition and security of seats and seat belts

Road test
Road/roller test and check function of all instrumentation

continued

MAINTENANCE — 1977 AND LATER U.S.A. SPECIFICATION

'B' SERVICE

Lubrication
Lubricate all grease points (except hubs and steering rack)
Check/top up engine oil
Check/top up brake fluid reservoir
Check/top up clutch fluid reservoir
Check/top up battery electrolyte
Check/top up cooling system
Check/top up gearbox and rear axle oils
Check transmission for oil leaks
* Lubricate accelerator control linkage (and pedal pivot); check operation

Engine
Check for oil leaks
* Check cooling and heater systems for leaks and hoses for security and condition
* Check exhaust system for leaks and security

Fuel system
* Check fuel system for leaks, pipes and unions for chafing and corrosion

Safety
Check/adjust operation of all washers, and top up reservoir
Check tyres for tread depth, and visually for external cuts in fabric, exposure of ply or cord structure, lumps or bulges
Check that tyres comply with manufacturer's specification
Check/adjust tyre pressures including spare
Check tightness of road wheel fastenings
Check condition and security of steering unit, joints and gaiters
Check steering rack and suspension for oil/fluid leaks
Check/adjust foot and hand brake
Check visually hydraulic hoses, pipes and unions for chafing, cracks, leaks and corrosion
Check output of charging system
Check function of original equipment, i.e. interior and exterior lamps, horns, wipers and warning indicators
Check, if necessary renew, wiper blades
Check/adjust headlamp alignment
Check condition and security of seats and seat belts
Check operation of seat belt warning system
Check rear view mirror for cracks and crazing

Road test
Report additional work required

59

'C' SERVICE

Lubrication
Lubricate all grease points (except hubs and steering rack)
Renew engine oil and filter
Check/top up brake fluid reservoir
Check/top up clutch fluid reservoir
Check/top up battery electrolyte
Check/top up cooling system
Check/top up gearbox and rear axle oils
Check transmission for oil leaks
Lubricate hand brake mechanical linkage
* Lubricate accelerator control linkage (and pedal pivot); check operation
Lubricate all locks and hinges (not steering lock)

Engine
Check for oil leaks
* Check cooling and heater system for leaks, and hoses for security and condition
* Check exhaust system for leaks and security

Fuel system
* Check fuel system for leaks, pipes and unions for chafing and corrosion

Safety
Check/adjust operation of all washers, and top up reservoir
Check tyres for tread depth and visually for external cuts in fabric exposure of ply or cord structure, lumps and bulges
Check that tyres comply with manufacturers specification
Check/adjust tyre pressures including spare
Check tightness of road wheel fastenings
Check condition and security of steering unit, joints and gaiters
Check security of suspension fixings
Check steering rack and suspension for oil/fluid leaks
Inspect brake pads for wear, discs for condition
Check/adjust foot and hand brake
Check visually hydraulic hoses, pipes and unions for chafing, cracks, leaks and corrosion
Check/adjust front wheel alignment
Clean and grease battery connections
Check output of charging system
Check function of original equipment, i.e. interior and exterior lamps, horns, wipers and warning indicators.
Check, if necessary renew wiper blades
Check/adjust headlamp alignment
Check operation of all door, bonnet and luggage compartment locks
Check condition and security of seat and seat belts
Check operation of seat belt warning system
Check rear view mirror for cracks and crazing

Road test
Road/roller test and check function of all instrumentation
Report additional work required

Brakes
It is further recommended that at 19,000 miles the brake fluid is renewed — additional work

10-33

MAINTENANCE — 1977 AND LATER U.S.A. SPECIFICATION

'D' SERVICE

Lubrication
Lubricate all grease points (except hubs)
Lubricate steering rack (every 37,500 miles only)
Renew engine oil and filter
Check/top up brake fluid reservoir
Check/top up clutch fluid reservoir
Check/top up battery electrolyte
Check/top up cooling system
Check/top up gearbox and rear axle oils
Check transmission for oil leaks
Lubricate hand brake mechanical linkage
* Lubricate distributor
* Lubricate accelerator control linkage (and pedal pivot); check operation
Lubricate all locks and hinges (not steering lock)

Engine
Check for oil leaks
* Check driving belts; adjust or renew
* Check cooling and heater systems for leaks and hoses for security and condition
* Renew carburetter air cleaner element
* Check air injection system hoses/pipes for condition and security
* Check air intake temperature control system
* Check crankcase breathing and evaporative loss systems. Check hoses/pipes and restrictors for blockage, security and condition
* Check/adjust valve clearances
* Check exhaust system for leaks and security

Ignition
* Check ignition wiring for fraying, chafing and deterioration
* Renew spark plugs
* Check security of distributor vacuum unit line
* Check operation of distributor vacuum unit (California only)
* Clean distributor cap, check for cracks and tracking
* Check coil performance on oscilloscope,
* Check/adjust ignition timing using electronic equipment

Fuel system
* Clean fuel pump filter
* Check fuel system for leaks, pipes and unions for chafing and corrosion
* Top up carburetter piston damper
* Check/adjust deceleration by-pass valve
* Check/adjust carburetter idle settings
* Check condition of fuel filler cap seal

Safety
Check/adjust operation of all washers, and top up reservoir
Check tyres for tread depth, and visually for external cuts in fabric, exposure of ply or cord structure, lumps and bulges
Check that tyres comply with manufacturers specification
Check/adjust tyre pressures including spare
Check tightness of road wheel fastenings
Check condition and security of steering unit, joints and gaiters
Check security of suspension fixings
Check steering rack and suspension for oil/fluid leaks
Inspect brake linings/pads for wear, drums/discs for condition
Check/adjust foot and hand brake
Check visually hydraulic hoses, pipes and unions for chafing, cracks, leaks and corrosion
Check front wheel alignment
Clean and grease battery connections
Check output of charging system
Check function of original equipment, i.e. interior and exterior lamps, horns, wipers and warning indicators
Check, if necessary renew wiper blades
Check/adjust headlamp alignment
Check operation of all door, bonnet and luggage compartment locks
Check operation of window controls
Check condition and security of seats and seat belts
Check operation of seat belt warning system
Check rear view mirror for cracks or crazing

Road test
Road/roller test and check operation of all instrumentation
Report additional work required.

Brakes
It is further recommended that every 37,500 miles the brake fluid, hydraulic seals and hoses in the brake hydraulic system are renewed. Examine working surfaces of pistons and bores in master, slave and wheel cylinders — additional work

Steering
At every 37,500 miles the steering rack should be lubricated — additional work

MAINTENANCE — 1977 AND LATER U.S.A. SPECIFICATION
'E' SERVICE

Lubrication

Lubricate all grease points (except hubs and steering rack)
Renew engine oil and filter
Check/top up brake fluid reservoir
Check/top up clutch fluid reservoir
Check/top up battery electrolyte
Check/top up cooling system
Check/top up gearbox and rear axle oils
Check transmission for oil leaks
Lubricate hand brake mechanical linkage
* Lubricate distributor
* Lubricate accelerator control linkage and pedal pivot, check operation
Lubricate all locks and hinges (not steering lock)

Engine

* Check for oil leaks
* Check driving belts; adjust or renew
* Check cooling and heater systems for leaks and hoses for security and condition
* Renew carburetter air cleaner element
* Check air injection system hoses/pipes for condition and security
* Check air intake temperature control system
* Check crankcase breathing and evaporative loss systems. Check hoses/pipes and restrictors for blockage, security and condition
* Check/adjust valve clearances
* Check E G R system } (every 50,000 miles)
* Check adsorption canister
* Renew catalytic converter (every 25,000 miles, California only)
* Check exhaust system for leaks and security

Ignition

* Check ignition wiring for fraying, chafing and deterioration
* Renew spark plugs
* Check security of distributor vacuum unit line
* Check operation of distributor vacuum unit (California only)
* Clean distributor cap, check for cracks and tracking
* Check coil performance on oscilloscope
* Check/adjust ignition timing using electronic equipment

Fuel system

* Clean fuel pump filter
* Check fuel system for leaks, pipes and unions for chafing and corrosion
* Top up carburetter piston damper
* Check/adjust deceleration by-pass valve
* Check/adjust carburetter idle settings
* Check condition of fuel filler cap seal

Safety

Check/adjust operation of all washers, and top up reservoir
Check tyres for tread depth, and visually for external cuts in fabric, exposure of ply or cord structure, lumps and bulges
Check that tyres comply with manufacturers specification
Check/adjust tyre pressures including spare
Check tightness of road wheel fastenings
Check condition and security of steering unit, joints and gaiters
Check security of suspension fixings
Check steering rack and suspension for oil/fluid leaks
Inspect brake linings/pads for wear, drums/discs for condition
Check/adjust foot and hand brake
Check visually hydraulic hoses, pipes and unions for chafing, cracks, leaks and corrosion
Check front wheel alignment
Clean and grease battery connections
Check output of charging system
Check, if necessary renew wiper blades
Check function of original equipment, i.e. interior and exterior lamps, horns, wipers and warning indicators
Check/adjust headlamp alignment
Check operation of all door, bonnet, and luggage compartment locks
Check operation of window controls
Check condition and security of seats and seat belts
Check operation of seat belt warning system
Check rear view mirror for cracks and crazing

Road test

Road/roller test and check operation of all instrumentation
Report additional work required

61

LUBRICATION

NOTE: Ensure that the vehicle is standing on a level surface when checking the oil levels.

WEEKLY

(1) ENGINE. Check oil level and top up if necessary.

'A' SERVICE

(2) ENGINE. Drain and refill with new oil.
(4) THROTTLE. Lubricate throttle control linkage, cable and accelerator pedal fulcrum
(5) CARBURETTER. Top up carburetter piston damper.
(6) REAR AXLE. Check oil level, and top up if necessary.
(7) GEARBOX. Check oil level, and top up if necessary.
(9) FRONT SUSPENSION. (6 nipples) ⎫ Give three or four strokes
(10) PROPELLER SHAFT. (1 nipple) ⎬ with a grease gun
(11) WIRE WHEELS ONLY. Lubricate wire wheel and hub splines.
LOCKS, HINGES AND LINKAGES. Lubricate all door, bonnet, luggage compartment locks and hinges **(not steering lock).**
FRICTION POINTS. Spray lubricant on all friction points.

'B' SERVICE

(1) ENGINE. Check oil level and top up if necessary.
(4) THROTTLE. Lubricate throttle control linkage, cable and accelerator pedal fulcrum.
(6) REAR AXLE. Check oil level, and top up if necessary.
(7) GEARBOX. Check oil level, and top up if necessary.
(9) FRONT SUSPENSION. (6 nipples) ⎫ Give three or four strokes
(10) PROPELLER SHAFT. (1 nipple) ⎬ with a grease gun
(11) WIRE WHEELS ONLY. Grease wheel and hub splines.
FRICTION POINTS. Spray lubricant on all friction points.

'C' SERVICE

(2) ENGINE. Drain and refill with new oil.
(3) ENGINE OIL FILTER. Remove disposable cartridge, fit new.
(4) THROTTLE. Lubricate throttle control linkage, cable and accelerator pedal fulcrum.
(6) REAR AXLE. Check oil level, and top up if necessary.
(7) GEARBOX. Check oil level, and top up if necessary.
(9) FRONT SUSPENSION. (6 nipples) ⎫ Give three or four strokes
(10) PROPELLER SHAFT. (1 nipple) ⎬ with a grease gun
(11) WIRE WHEELS ONLY. Lubricate wire wheel and hub splines.
LOCKS, HINGES AND LINKAGES. Lubricate all door, bonnet, luggage compartment locks and hinges **(not steering lock);** and the hand brake mechanical linkage.
FRICTION POINTS. Spray lubricant on all friction points.

D' AND 'E' SERVICE

Carry out a 'C' service in addition to the following items (5) and (12).
(5) CARBURETTERS. Top up carburetter piston damper.
(8) STEERING. Lubricate steering rack (every 37,500 miles).
(12) DISTRIBUTOR. Lubricate all parts as necessary.

Service oils and greases are given in O9

MAINTENANCE — 1977 AND LATER U.S.A. SPECIFICATION

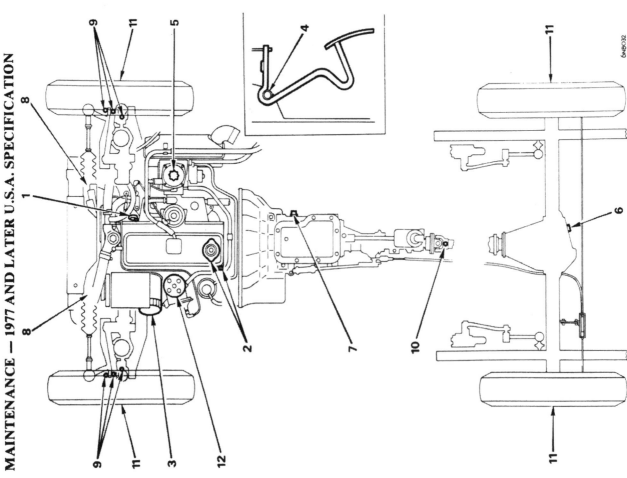

6NBO32

MAINTENANCE – 1977 AND LATER U.S.A. SPECIFICATION

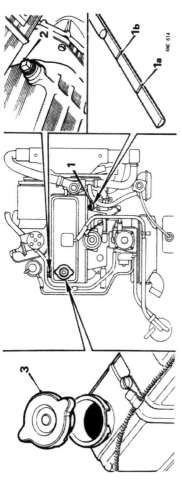

ENGINE

Checking engine oil level

1 Maintain the level between the 'MIN' (1a) and 'MAX' (1b) marks on the dipstick.

Draining and refilling the engine oil

2 Drain the oil while the engine is warm; clean the drain plug and refit.

3 Refill with the correct quantity and grade of oil. Run the engine for a short while, then allow it to stand for a few minutes before checking the level.

Disposable cartridge filter renewal

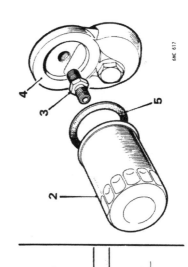

1 Disconnect the hose from the air pump.

2 Unscrew the cartridge from the cylinder block.

3 If the adaptor remains attached to the cartridge unscrew it from the cartridge and screw it back into the cylinder block. Discard the cartridge and old seal.

4 Wipe the engine joint face clean and smear with oil.

5 Smear the new seal with oil and fit it into the groove in the new cartridge.

6 Screw the new cartridge to the adaptor, using hand force only.

7 Connect the hose to the air pump.

8 Start the engine and check the cartridge for leaks. Check the oil level after waiting for a few minutes.

Engine mountings and bolts

Check the following fastenings for tightness:

	lbf ft	kgf m
Inlet manifold to exhaust manifold	14	1.9
Manifold to head	25	3.5
Rocker cover to head	2	0.3
Oil sump to block	20	2.8
Timing cover to front engine plate	10	1.4
Alternator to mounting bracket and front engine plate	22	3.0
Alternator to adjusting link		
E G R valve		
Engine mountings		
Air cleaner to carburetter		
Carburetter to manifold	20	2.8
Air pump		

Checking torque of cylinder head nuts

1 Disconnect the purge pipe from the rocker cover.

2 Unscrew the rocker cover retaining screws and lift the capillary tube brackets aside (when fitted).

3 Release the collar and seal from the rocker cover.

4 Remove the rocker cover and gasket.

5 Remove the four nuts complete with washers securing the rocker shaft pedestals to the cylinder head and lift off the rocker shaft.

6 Tighten the cylinder head in a diagonal sequence to avoid distortion to a torque of 46 lbf ft (6.4 kgf m).

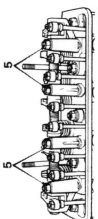

7 Refit the rocker shaft, ensuring that the adjustment screws are correctly located in the push rod cups.

8 Fit the four nuts and washers securing the rocker shaft pedestals to the cylinder head tightening the nuts evenly to a torque of 32 lbf ft (4.4 kgf m).

9 Adjust the valve clearances.

Valve rocker adjustment

1 Disconnect the purge pipe from the rocker cover.

2 Unscrew the rocker cover retaining screws and lift the capillary tube brackets aside.

3 Release the collar and seal from the rocker cover.

4 Remove the rocker cover and gasket.

5 Check the clearance between the valve rocker arms and the valve stems with a feeler gauge.

Clearance (cold) 0.010 in (0.25 mm). The gauge should be a sliding fit when the engine is cold.

Check the clearance of each valve in the following order.

Check:

No. 1 valve with No. 8 fully open
" 3 " " 6 "
" 5 " " 4 "
" 2 " " 7 "
" 8 " " 1 "
" 6 " " 3 "
" 4 " " 5 "
" 7 " " 2 "

6 Slacken the locknut.

7 Rotate the screw, clockwise to decrease or anti-clockwise to increase the clearance.

continued

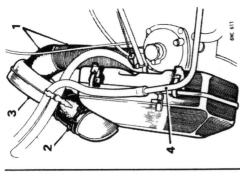

6MC 611

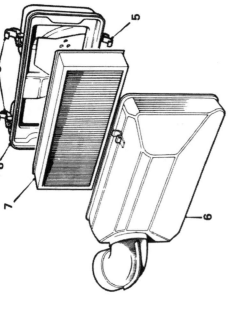

MAINTENANCE — 1977 AND LATER U.S.A. SPECIFICATION

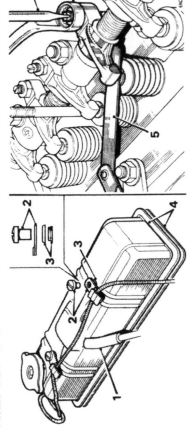

6MC 613

8 Re-tighten the locknut when the clearance is correct, holding the screw against rotation.
9 Recheck the clearances.
10 Check, and if necessary renew the rocker cover gasket.
11 Refit the rocker cover and position the capillary tube support brackets, tighten the screws to 2 lbf ft (0.3 kgf m). DO NOT OVERTIGHTEN or distortion of the cover may occur, resulting in oil leaks.
12 Refit the purge line to the rocker cover.
13 Start the engine and check for leaks from the rocker cover gasket and filler cap.

Drive Belt Tension — Fan

When correctly tensioned, a total deflection of ¾ in (19 mm) under moderate hand pressure, should be possible at the midway point of the longest run between the pulleys.

Adjusting

1 Check the belt tension.

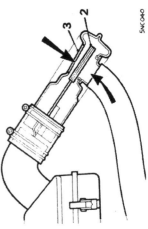

6MC 616

2 Slacken the alternator securing nut and bolt.
3 Slacken the adjusting link bolts.
4 Move the alternator to the required position. Apply any leverage necessary to the alternator end bracket only, using a wooden or soft metal lever.
5 Tighten the securing nuts and bolts and recheck the tension.

FUEL SYSTEM

Air cleaner element renewal

1 Release the hot air hose.
2 Slacken the securing slip screw.
3 Remove the air temperature control assembly from the air cleaner.
4 Release the purge pipe from the air cleaner casing.
5 Release the four clips.

6 Withdraw the cover.
7 Remove and discard the element.
8 Thoroughly clean the casing and cover.
9 Fit a new element and reassemble ensuring that the face of the element with the seal is fitted into the casing.

Air temperature control valve — check

1 Ensure that the engine and air cleaner are cold.
2 Check the position of the valve plate.
3 The valve plate should be against the cold air intake (hot air position).
4 Start the engine and run it to normal operating temperature.
5 Observe the action of the valve plate which should move towards the hot air hose (cold air position).

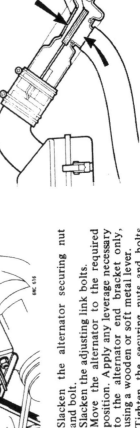

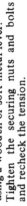

5NC040

MAINTENANCE — 1977 AND LATER U.S.A. SPECIFICATION

SNC490

6NC 608

6a

SNC086

Fuel pump filter gauze — cleaning

1 Squeeze the ends of the clip and remove the inlet hose from the fuel pump top cover.
2 Unscrew the centre bolt.
3 Remove the top cover.
4 Remove the filter gauze. Wash in clean fuel.
5 Check that the gasket is in position and in a good condition; renew if necessary.
6 Fit the filter gauze and top cover and secure with the centre bolt.
7 Tighten the centre bolt to 10-14 lbf in (0.115 to 0.161 kgf m).
8 Fit the inlet hose.
9 Start the engine and inspect the fuel pump for air and fuel leaks.
10 Check the inlet and outlet hoses for leaks and serviceability.

Carburetter

Air pollution control

The carburetter incorporates features which assist in reducing exhaust emissions. Maladjustment or the fitting of parts not to the required specifications may render these features ineffective.

Carburetter damper

1 Unscrew the damper cap.
2 Carefully raise the damper to the top of its travel.
3 Lower the damper back into the hollow piston rod. If the oil level in the hollow piston rod is correct, resistance should be felt when there is a gap of approximately ¼ in (6 mm) (A) between the cap and the carburetter top cover. Top up if necessary. Screw the damper cap firmly into the carburetter top cover.

Topping up

4 Remove the air cleaner.
5 Unscrew the damper cap from the carburetter top cover.
6 Raise the piston with a finger and at the same time lift the damper and carefully ease the retaining cap (6a) from the hollow piston rod to release the damper assembly from the piston.
7 With the piston raised, top up the hollow piston rod with a recommended engine oil until the oil level is ¼ in (6 mm) below the top of the hollow piston rod.
Under no circumstances should a heavy bodied lubricant be used.
8 Lower the piston.
9 Ensure the oil level is correct.
10 Raise the piston and carefully press the retaining cup into the hollow piston rod.
11 Screw the damper cap firmly into the carburetter top cover.
12 Refit the air cleaner.

Carburetter settings

Adjustments should only be undertaken if an accurate tachometer, and exhaust gas analyser (CO meter) are available for use.

The tuning of the carburetter is confined to topping up the damper, setting idle and mixture strength (CO percentage), and adjusting the deceleration valve. Obtaining the correct carburetter setting depends on correct ignition timing and spark plug gaps, valve rocker clearances and on good seals at oil filler cap to the valve rocker cover, valve rocker cover to the cylinder head, engine oil dipstick to the cylinder block, carburetter to the induction manifold, exhaust manifold to the cylinder head, and all induction manifold tappings.

NOTE: Tuning must commence immediately the car reaches normal running temperature. If delay prevents the adjustment being completed within three minutes, increase the engine speed to 2000 rev/min for 30 seconds and then continue tuning. **Repeat this clearing procedure at three minute intervals until tuning is completed.**

Idle speed check and adjust

1 Connect an accurate tachometer.
2 Start and warm the engine to normal running temperature.
3 Check the idle speed, see DATA, and adjust if necessary.

Mixture strength CO percentage at idle

4 Check/adjust the idle speed.
5 Disconnect the outlet hose from the air pump and plug the hose. DO NOT restrict the pump outlet otherwise damage may be caused to the air pump.
6 Recheck the idle speed.
7 Use the exhaust gas analyser in

EMISSION CONTROL

Check E G R valve operating lines

1 Check for security of the push fit connections at the E G R valve, fuel trap and carburetter.
2 Renew any pipes which show signs of deterioration.

Check operation of E G R system

3 Disconnect the vacuum pipe from the E G R valve.
4 Remove the pipe connecting the E G R valve to the induction manifold.
5 Slacken the locknut and unscrew the E G R valve from the exhaust manifold.
6 Clean the assembly area of the E G R valve with a wire brush.
7 Use a standard spark plug machine to clean the valve and seat. Insert the valve opening into the machine and lift the diaphragm evenly. Blast the valve for approximately 30 seconds, remove and inspect. If necessary repeat until all carbon deposits are removed. Use compressed air to remove all traces of carbon grit from the valve. Use a flexiwire brush to clean inside the 'U' shaped pipe – blow clear of carbon grit.
8 Renew any pipes which show signs of deterioration.
9 Screw the E G R valve locknut to the top of the threads.
10 Screw the valve into the manifold.
11 Place the 'U' shaped pipe in position to align the unions with the E G R valve and induction manifold adaptor, screw or unscrew the E G R valve as required. Place the pipe aside.
12 Tighten the locknut.
13 Refit the connecting pipe.
14 Reconnect the vacuum control pipe to the top of the E G R valve.
15 Check E G R valve operating lines for security of push fit connections at the E G R valve, fuel trap and carburetter.

continued

68C 600A

Accelerator mechanism

1 Lubricate the accelerator pedal pivot.
2 Lubricate the carburetter accelerator linkages and cables.
3 Check carburetter throttle response to initial movement of the accelerator pedal.
4 Check carburetter throttle position when the accelerator pedal is fully depressed, and adjust, if necessary, to ensure that full throttle is obtained.

MAINTENANCE — 1977 AND LATER U.S.A. SPECIFICATION

accordance with the manufacturer's instructions to check the percentage CO at idle. If the reading falls outside the prescribed limits, see DATA, adjust the fine idle CO screw, clockwise to enrich or anti-clockwise to weaken.
8 If the reading is within limits, continue with operations 25 onwards. If the correct CO percentage cannot be attained using the fine idle CO screw, proceed as follows:
9 Stop the engine.
10 Remove the air cleaner.
11 Raise the piston with a finger and at the same time lift the damper and carefully ease the retaining cap from the hollow piston rod to release the damper assembly from the piston.
12 Carefully insert tool S 353 into the dashpot until the outer tool engages in the air valve and the inner tool engages the hexagon in the needle adjuster plug. CAUTION: The outer tool must be correctly engaged and held or the carburetter diaphragm may be torn.
13 Start the engine.
14 Hold the tool firmly and turn the inner tool clockwise to enrich the mixture or anti-clockwise to weaken, as required.
15 Stop the engine.
16 With the piston raised, top up the hollow piston rod with a recommended engine oil until the oil level is ¼ in (6 mm) below the top of the hollow piston rod. Under no circumstances should a heavy bodied lubricant be used.
17 Lower the piston.
18 Ensure the oil level is correct.
19 Raise the piston and carefully press the retaining cup into the hollow piston rod.
20 Screw the damper cap firmly into the carburetter top cover.
21 Refit the air cleaner.
22 Start the engine.
23 Recheck the idle speed.
24 Recheck the percentage CO at idle, adjusting the fine idle CO screw if necessary.
25 Stop the engine.
26 Remove the plug from the air pump hose.
27 Securely connect the hose to the air pump.

Deceleration by-pass valve – check and adjust

28 Start the engine and run it at a fast idle speed until it attains normal running temperature, then run it for a further five minutes.
29 Disconnect the vacuum pipe from the distributor and place a finger over the end of the pipe.
30 The engine idle speed should rise to approximately 1300 rev/min. If the engine idle speed rises abruptly to 2000-2500 rev/min the by-pass valve is floating and adjustment is required.
31 Plug the vacuum pipe.
32 Turn the adjustment screw anti-clockwise until the engine speed falls to 1300 rev/min.
33 Momentarily increase and decrease the engine speed using the throttle.
34 The engine speed should drop to approximately 1300 rev/min. Re-adjust if necessary.
35 Turn the adjustment screw ANTI-CLOCKWISE half a turn to seat the valve correctly.
36 Unplug the vacuum pipe and refit to the distributor.

DATA

Idling speed .... 700 to 900 rev/min (800 rev/min nominal)

Exhaust gas content (carbon monoxide) at idle speed (1975–1977) ½ to 6% (3% nominal). California only
½ to 6½% (3% nominal). All remaining Federal States and Canada

Exhaust gas content (carbon monoxide) at idle speed (1978) ½ to 6% (3% nominal). California only
1 to 5% (3% nominal). Canada and USA except California

The above data is also shown on the Vehicle Emission Control Information Label located in the engine compartment.

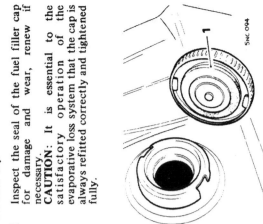

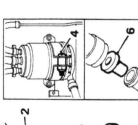

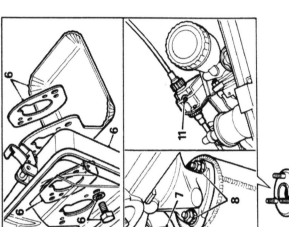

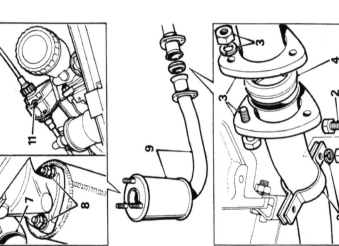

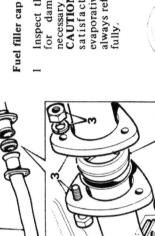

MAINTENANCE — 1977 AND LATER U.S.A. SPECIFICATION

16 Check the function of the E G R valve as follows:
Warm the engine to normal running temperature. Open and close the throttle several times and observe or feel the E G R valve, which should open and close with the changes in engine speed.
The valve should close instantly when the throttle is closed.

Adsorption canister — renewal (1977 only)

[**NOTE:** The evaporative loss system is radically different on the 1978 models. Please refer to **page 330** for detailed special maintenance instructions.]

Adsorption canister — renewal

1 Disconnect the air vent pipe.
2 Disconnect the vapour pipes.
3 Disconnect the purge pipe.
4 Remove the securing bracket nut and bolt.
5 Remove the canister.
6 Transfer the restrictor in the old canister to the new canister.
7 Fit the new canister and reconnect the air vent, vapour and purge pipes. **CAUTION**: Care should be taken when renewing the canister not to disturb the running-on control valve (if fitted) or its connections.

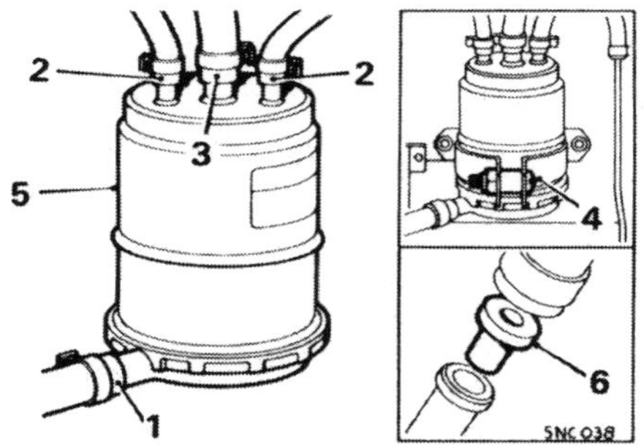

Renew catalytic converter and front pipe

1 Jack up and support the front of the car.
2 Remove the catalytic converter support bracket.
3 Release the catalytic converter from the rear pipe.
4 Remove the olive.
5 Remove the carburetter and place to one side, see 2 to 9, 30.15.15.
6 Remove the two screws to release the air cleaner casing and heat shield from the carburetter.
7 Press in the retaining clips and remove the pre-heater duct.
8 Remove the six nuts securing the catalytic converter to the exhaust manifold.
9 Remove the catalytic converter and front pipe, and the exhaust manifold flange gasket.
10 Fit a new catalytic converter and front pipe, by reversing the procedure in 1 to 9 and noting:
  a Renew the exhaust manifold flange gasket and the exhaust pipe olive.
  b Renew the air cleaner gasket and heat shield if damaged or showing signs of deterioration.
11 Reset the catalytic warning indicator by inserting the key into the button, and rotating to zero the counter. Remove the key.

Air pump — drive belt tension
When correctly tensioned a total deflection of ½ in (13 mm) under moderate hand pressure should be possible at the midway point of the belt run.

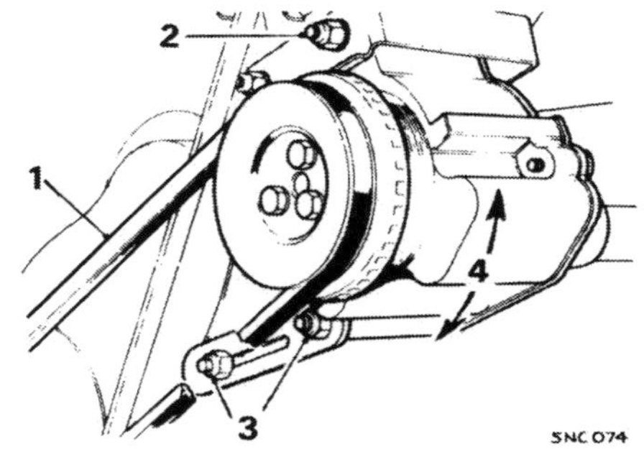

Adjusting

1 Check the belt tension.
2 Slacken the securing bolt.
3 Slacken the two adjusting link bolts.
4 Move the air pump to the required position.
5 Tighten the bolts and re-check the belt tension.
CAUTION: Do not overtighten.

Fuel filler cap

1 Inspect the seal of the fuel filler cap for damage and wear, renew if necessary.
CAUTION: It is essential to the satisfactory operation of the evaporative loss system that the cap is always refitted correctly and tightened fully.

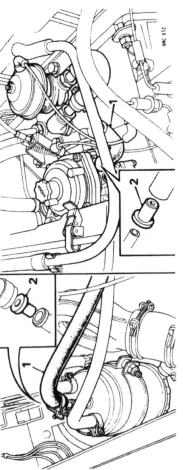

6MC 612

Purge line restrictors

1 Disconnect the purge line from the carburetter and adsorption canister.
2 Examine the orifice of the canister restrictor and carburetter restriction for obstruction.
3 Clear any dirt or deposit using a length of wire. DO NOT use air pressure.
4 Refit the purge line assembly.

IGNITION

Distributor — lubrication

1 Release the retaining clips and remove the cover.
2 Remove the rotor arm.
3 Remove the anti-flash shield.
4 Add a few drops of oil to the felt pad in the top of the timing rotor carrier.
5 Lubricate the pick-up plate centre bearing with a drop of oil in each ot the two holes in the base plate.
6 Apply a few drops of oil through the apertures to lubricate the centrifugal timing control.

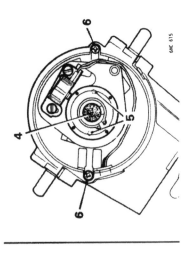

6MC 615

Distributor — cleaning

7 Wipe the inside of the distributor cover, the rotor arm, and the anti-flash shield with a clean nap-free cloth. Check the carbon brush is free to move in its housing. Inspect the cap and rotor for cracks and any trace of tracking. Renew if necessary.
8 Refit the anti-flash shield ensuring that the cut-outs are aligned with the distributor cover retaining clips.
9 Refit the rotor arm and cover.

Distributor vacuum unit operating lines — checking

Check the following vacuum unit operating lines for security.
10 Carburetter to flame trap operating line.
11 Flame trap to distributor vacuum unit operating line.

Distributor vacuum unit — checking — California only

12 Check the security of the vacuum unit operating lines.
13 Start the engine and run it until it attains normal running temperature.
14 With the engine idling at 700 to 900 rev/min disconnect the operating line from the vacuum unit.
15 If the vacuum unit is operating correctly the engine speed will increase by approximately 500 rev/min.
16 Re-connect the operating line to the vacuum unit, ensuring a secure connection and switch off the engine.

Ignition coil

Check the ignition coil performance, using proprietary electronic testing equipment in accordance with the manufacturer's instructions.

Sparking plug renewal

1 Detach the high tension lead from each plug.
2 Partly unscrew each plug from the cylinder head.
3 Clean the area of the cylinder head surrounding each plug seating using compressed air or a brush.
4 Unscrew the plugs from the cylinder head and discard the plugs.
5 Set the gap between the electrodes of each new plug to the dimension given in DATA, bending the side electrode only.
6 Fit the new plugs to the engine.
7 Tighten each plug to 20 lbf ft (2.8 kgf m).
8 Refit the high tension lead to each plug.

DATA

Ignition coil

Make and type	Lucas 15C6	
Lucas Serial No.	45243	
Primary resistance at 68° F	1.30 to 1.45 ohms	
Ballast resistor wire:		
Resistance	1.3 to 1.5 ohms	
Wire length	63 in	160 cm

Sparking plugs

Make and type	Champion N-12Y	
Gap	0.025 in	0.64 mm

MAINTENANCE — 1977 AND LATER U.S.A. SPECIFICATION

Ignition wiring

Low tension circuit

1 Check the wiring connections between the ballast resistor, drive resistor, distributor, coil and ignition switch for condition and security.

2 Check the wiring between coil and distributor for fraying, chafing and deterioration.

3 Remove the distributor cap.

4 Check the distributor internal wiring for fraying, chafing and deterioration.

5 Check the internal distributor connections for condition and security.

6 Replace the distributor cap.

7 Report the wiring condition.

High tension circuit

8 Check the lead between coil and distributor for fraying, chafing and deterioration.

9 Check each spark plug lead for fraying, chafing and deterioration.

10 Check the high tension lead connections for condition and security.

11 Report the wiring condition.

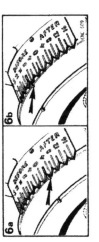

ELECTRICAL

Testing

Check that the lamps, horns, warning indicators, windscreen wipers and instruments are functioning correctly.

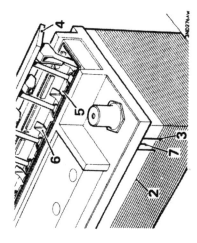

Ignition timing

1 Clean the timing pointers and the timing notch on the crankshaft pulley, and mark the notch on the pulley with chalk.

2 Run the engine until it attains normal running temperature, then switch off.

3 Connect a stroboscopic timing light in accordance with the manufacturer's instructions.

WARNING: Ensure that personnel and equipment are kept clear of the cooling fan while using the timing light.

4 Run the engine at 800 rev/min max.

5 Position the timing light to illuminate the crankshaft pulley and scale.

6 a CALIFORNIA ONLY: If the timing is correct the timing notch on the pulley will be aligned half way between the zero and 4° A.T.D.C. pointers to give an ignition timing of 2° A.T.D.C. If correct, the procedure in 7 and 8 may be ignored.

b ALL REMAINING FEDERAL STATES AND CANADA: If the timing is correct the timing notch on the pulley will be aligned half way between the 8° and 12° B.T.D.C. pointers to give an ignition timing of 10° B.T.D.C. If correct, the procedure in 7 and 8 may be ignored.

7 With the engine still running, use a second operator to slacken the clamp bolt and carefully rotate the distributor body as required until the equipment shows the correct timing.

8 Tighten the clamp bolt.

Battery

Checking

1 Ensure that the vehicle is standing on a level surface.

2 Check the level of the electrolyte which is visible through the end of the casing and should be 0.25 in (7 mm) below the red top.

3 The low indicator mark is on the rear end of the case and is visible only when the battery is removed.

CAUTION: Top up only when the electrolyte level is below the top of the separators. Do not use a naked light when checking the cells.

Topping up

4 Raise the vent cover and tilt to one side.

5 Pour distilled water into the trough until all the rectangular filling tubes (6) are full and the bottom of the trough is just covered.

6 Press the cover firmly into position which automatically distributes the correct amount of distilled water to each battery cell.

MAINTENANCE – 1977 AND LATER U.S.A. SPECIFICATION

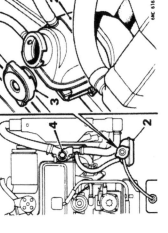

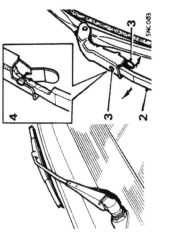

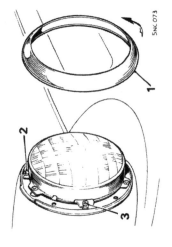

7 The electrolyte should just cover the separator plates or, if the battery is removed, up to the high mark on the rear end of the case.

To mix the electrolyte in extremely cold conditions run the engine immediately after topping up.

CAUTION: The vent cover must be kept closed at all times, except when topping up. The electrolyte will flood if the cover is raised while charging the battery. The battery could also flood if it is topped up within half an hour of having it charged other than by the car's charging system.

8 Wipe the battery top clean and dry and smear the terminal posts with petroleum jelly as a precaution against corrosion. Ensure that the terminal screws are tight.

Clean off any corrosion from the battery and its mountings, using diluted ammonia, and then paint affected parts with anti-sulphuric paint – additional work.

NOTE: Specific gravity check and battery charging off the vehicle is additional work.

Checking the charging system output

1 Connect a 0–20V moving coil voltmeter across the battery terminals.
2 Connect a 0–60A test ammeter in series with the main output cable and the '+' terminal of the alternator.
3 Start the engine, increase the engine speed and observe the ammeter.
4 If the reading exceeds 10A, continue running the engine until the reading falls below 10A.
5 The voltmeter reading should be 13.6 to 14.4V indicating that the charging system is working normally.
A voltmeter reading exceeding 14.4V indicates a defective regulator, a reading below 13.6V indicates a defective alternator or a high resistance fault in the external charging system.

Checking operation

6 Switch on the ignition and press the end of the switch lever and check the operation of the washers.
7 If the delivery is incorrect turn the jet using a small screwdriver to adjust the height of the spray.

Topping up reservoir

8 Remove the filler cap and top up as necessary with a mixture of water and a recommended solvent; do not use radiator anti-freeze.

Headlamp beam alignment – adjusting

Two adjusting screws are provided on each headlamp for beam setting. The beams must be set in accordance with regulations governing the setting of headlamps.

1 Ease the bottom of the outer ring forwards and lift it off the retaining lug at the top of the lamp.
2 Turn the screw at the top of the lamp to make an adjustment in the vertical plane.
3 Turn the screw at the side of the lamp to make an adjustment in the horizontal plane.

NOTE: Beam setting is affected by the load on the car; therefore always set the beams with the normal load on the car.

WINDSCREEN WIPER BLADES AND WASHERS

Windscreen wiper blades

1 Examine the rubber blades for condition, and if these are perished or defective renew the blade assembly.
2 Pull the wiper away from the windscreen.
3 Hold the fastener and spring retainer away from the wiper arm retaining spring clip and withdraw the blade assembly from the arm.
4 Insert the end of the arm into the spring fastener of the new blade and push the new blade into engagement with the arm.
5 Lower the wiper onto the windscreen.

The filler plug does not normally require removing except when filling the system. However, if a leak has occurred the system may require topping up through the filling orifice.

4 Remove the filler plug and add coolant through the filling orifice until the level is up to the bottom of the threads.

Refit the filler plug.

5 Top up the expansion tank with coolant to the half-full point and refit the cap.
6 Run the engine until normal operating temperature is reached. Stop the engine and allow the system to cool.
7 Remove the filler plug and top up to the bottom of the threads and refit the filler plug.
8 Top up the expansion tank to the half-full point and refit the cap.

NOTE: When the system contains anti-freeze ensure that the specific gravity of the coolant is maintained.

COOLING SYSTEM

WARNING: The cooling system is under pressure while the engine is hot. Allow the engine to cool before removing the expansion tank cap or the filler plug.

Examining for leaks

1 Inspect the cooling and heater systems for leaking connections and hoses, including the expansion tank to water outlet elbow.

Topping up/filling

2 Examine the coolant in the expansion tank, the level is correct when the tank is half full.
3 If necessary remove the expansion tank cap and top up, refit the cap. If the level has fallen appreciably, suspect a leak in the cooling system.

CLUTCH

Topping up clutch master cylinder

1 Remove the plastic filler cap and see that the fluid level is maintained at the bottom of the filler neck. Refer to division 09 for the recommended grade of fluid.
2 Before replacing the filler cap check that the breather hole is clear of obstruction.

continued

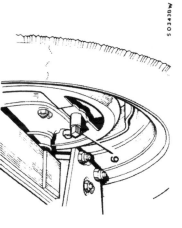

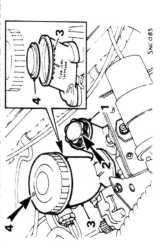

SNC085

BRAKES

Brake hoses and pipes

Examine all hoses, pipes and unions for chafing, leaks and corrosion. It is most important that hoses are not subjected to stress and are not positioned near to other components so that chafing can occur. Rectify any leaks and replace hoses and pipes showing signs of damage or deterioration.

Topping up master cylinder reservoirs

Top up the brake master cylinder if necessary to the level mark with the recommended grade of fluid, as given in division 09. Frequent topping up is indicative of a leak in the hydraulic system which must be found and rectified immediately.

3 Examine the level of fluid and keep the reservoir filled up with fluid to the bottom of the filler neck.

4 Before replacing the filler cap, check that the breather hole is clear of obstruction by removing the centre disc of the brake reservoir cap.

Brake pedal travel and rear brake adjustment

Check brake pedal travel: if excessive, adjust the rear brakes.

5 Jack up each wheel in turn.

6 Fully release the hand brake, turn the adjuster in a clockwise direction (viewed from the centre of the car) until the wheel is locked, then turn the adjuster back until the wheel can rotate without the linings rubbing. Lower the wheels.

S0349BW

---

12 Inspect the linings for wear; if the lining material has worn down to the minimum permissible thickness of $\frac{1}{16}$ in (1.6 mm) on bonded-type shoes or close to the rivets, or will have done so before the next check is called for, the brake shoes must be renewed.

13 Refit the drum and road wheel and adjust the brake shoes. Remove the supports and lower the vehicle.

Inspecting front brake discs and pads

14 Check the thickness of the pads and renew them before the lining material has worn down to the minimum permissible thickness of $\frac{1}{16}$ in (1.6 mm). Ensure that sufficient pad material remains to allow the car to run until the next check. Examine the disc for cracking and scoring.

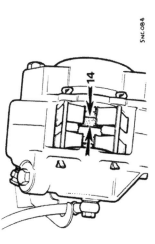

SNC084

7 Apply pressure to the brake pedal, it should feel solid. If there is any evidence of sponginess the brakes should be bled, this is additional work, refer to 70.25.02.

Checking hand brake operation

Ensure that the rear brakes have been correctly adjusted before checking the operation of the hand brake. If free play is still excessive, the hand brake cable requires adjusting, this is additional work, refer to 70.35.10.

Inspecting rear brake drum and linings

8 Chock the front wheels, release the hand brake, jack up each rear wheel in turn and place suitable supports beneath the vehicle.

9 Remove the road wheel and slacken off the brake-shoe adjuster fully.

10 Remove the two countersunk screws (pressed wheels) or the four nuts (wire wheels) and withdraw the brake drum. Wash out accumulated dust from the backplate assembly and the drum with Girling Cleaning Fluid or methylated spirits (denatured alcohol) and allow to dry. Examine the drum for cracking and scoring.

11 **WARNING: Do not blow dust from the brake assemblies – asbestos dust can be dangerous if inhaled.**

Hand brake lubrication

15 Grease the hand brake clevis pins.

Preventive maintenance

In addition to the recommended periodical inspection of brake components it is advisable as the vehicle ages, and as a precaution against the effects of wear and deterioration, to make a more searching inspection and renew parts as necessary.

It is recommended that:

1 Brake linings, hoses and pipes should be examined at intervals no greater than those laid down in the 'MAINTENANCE SUMMARY'.

2 Brake fluid should be changed completely every 18 months or 19,000 miles (30000 km) whichever is the sooner.

3 All fluid seals and all flexible hoses in the hydraulic system should be renewed every 3 years or 37,500 miles (60000 km) whichever is the sooner. At the same time the working surface of the pistons and of the bores of the master cylinder, wheel cylinders, and other slave cylinders should be examined and new parts fitted where necessary.

Care must be taken always to observe the following points:

1 At all times use the recommended brake fluid.

2 Never leave fluid in unsealed containers. It absorbs moisture quickly and can be dangerous if used in the braking system in this condition.

3 Fluid drained from the system or used for bleeding is best discarded.

4 The necessity for absolute cleanliness throughout cannot be over-emphasised.

MAINTENANCE – 1977 AND LATER U.S.A. SPECIFICATION

EXHAUST, FUEL, BRAKE AND CLUTCH PIPES

1 Check visually brake and clutch pipes and unions for chafing, leaks and corrosion.

2 Check visually fuel pipes and unions for chafing, leaks and corrosion.

3 Check exhaust system for leakage and security.

STEERING AND SUSPENSION

Checking

1 Examine the steering system and hydraulic dampers for signs of leakage and general condition of the steering rack gaiters.

2 Check the steering ball joints and the suspension for excessive free movement.

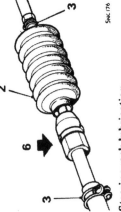

Checking front wheel alignment

When checking the front wheel alignment the following points must always be observed. See **DATA**.

3 The car must be at kerbside unladen trim with tyres inflated to the correct pressures and the steering-wheel in the straight-ahead position. Any free movement in the steering and suspension ball joints and suspension arms must be rectified.

DATA

Front wheel alignment . . . .

4 Using an optical gauge, take two readings, each reading at 180 degrees of wheel movement. The average figure must then be calculated from the readings.

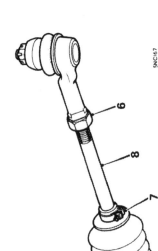

Adjusting front wheel alignment

6 Slacken the locknut on both tie-rods.

7 Slacken the clip securing the rubber gaiter to the tie-rod.

8 Rotate each tie-rod (both are right-hand thread) in the required direction by an equal amount to correct the misalignment. **CAUTION: It is important that the tie-rods are adjusted to exactly equal length.**

9 Tighten the tie-rod locknuts to 30 to 35 lbf ft (4.15 to 4.8 kgf m).

10 Tighten the gaiter clips.

11 Re-check the wheel alignment.

Parallel to $\frac{1}{8}$in
(0 to 3.2 mm) toe-in

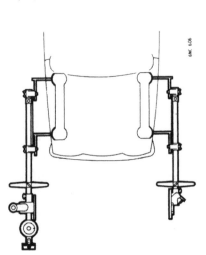

Swivel pin lubrication

To ensure full penetration of the lubricant it is best if the front of the car is partly jacked up.

12 Use one of the approved greases to charge the two nipples on each swivel pin.

Outer fulcrum pin lubrication

13 Use one of the approved greases to charge the nipple on each fulcrum pin.

Steering rack lubrication

It is recommended that after every 37,500 miles or 3 years the steering rack is inspected and lubricated – this is additional work.

1 Clean the rack seals and the ends of the rack housing.

2 Inspect the seals for cracks, splits, signs of deterioration, or leakage of lubricant. If a seal is damaged or there are signs of lubricant leakage, the seal must be renewed, see 57.25.03.

3 Release the clips or wire securing both ends of the seals.

4 Roll the seals back to expose the rack and inner ball joints.

5 Examine the existing grease around the inner ball joint and the rack for ingress of water or dirt; if this is evident the steering rack must be removed for dismantling and inspection of the components, see 57.25.07.

6 If the inner ball joint and the rack are in satisfactory condition, apply approximately 2 oz (57 gm) of a service grease around each inner ball joint and the rack including the teeth.

7 Unroll the seals, fit the protective shields and secure the seals to the rack housing with the clips. **CAUTION:** If the vehicle is hoisted with its front wheels clear of the ground, care should be taken to avoid forceful movement of the wheels from lock to lock as damage may occur within the steering mechanism.

Suspension fixings

The following fastenings should be checked for security.

14 Suspension fastenings.

15 Tie-rod ball and socket assemblies.

16 Steering-rack.

17 Steering column fixing bolts.

WHEELS AND TYRES

1 Check that tyres are in accordance with the manufacturer's specification: 145SR-13 radial ply.

2 Check and adjust the tyre pressures, including the spare.
Front:
22 lbf/in^2 1.55 kgf/cm^2 1.52 bars
Rear:
24 lbf/in^2 1.69 kgf/cm^2 1.66 bars

3 Check depth of tread.

4 Check visually for cuts in the tyre fabric, exposure of ply or cord, lumps or bulges.

5 Check tightness of the road wheel nuts: 62 Nm (45 lbf ft, 6.2 kgf m) max.

continued

MAINTENANCE — 1977 AND LATER U.S.A. SPECIFICATION

Wire wheels

6 Raise the front of the car and fit suitable safety supports under the chassis front members.
CAUTION: When the front wheels are clear of the ground, care should be taken to avoid forceful movement of the wheels from lock to lock as damage may occur within the steering mechanism.

7 Remove the road wheel.

8 Smear the splines of the hub and wire wheel with grease.

9 Refit the wire wheel.

10 Lower the car.

GEARBOX

Checking oil level

With the vehicle standing level check that the oil is level with the bottom of the aperture.

1 Remove the filler level plug.

2 Top up, allowing sufficient time for any surplus oil to run out before replacing the plug.
Ensure that the correct grade of oil is used for topping up — see 'SERVICE LUBRICANTS'.
CAUTION: Do not drain the gearbox when the 'After Sales' service is carried out.

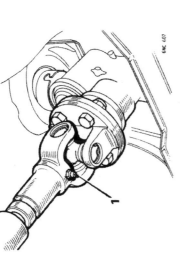

2 Top up, allowing sufficient time for any surplus oil to run out before replacing the plug. Ensure that the correct grade of hypoid oil is used for topping up — see 'SERVICE LUBRICANTS'.
CAUTION: Do not drain the rear axle when the 'After Sales' service is carried out.

BODY

1 Lubricate the bonnet safety catch and release mechanism.

2 Lubricate all hinges and door locks.
Do not oil the steering lock.

3 Check the condition and security of the seats and seat belts and seat belt interlock.

4 Check operation of all door locks and window controls.

GENERAL

Road or roller test the vehicle and check that all the instruments function correctly.
NOTE: When checking the tightness of nuts and bolts great care must be taken not to overtighten them. A torque wrench should be used where possible — see 'TORQUE WRENCH SETTINGS'.

PROPELLER SHAFT

1 A nipple is provided at the front end of the propeller shaft for lubricating the sliding yoke.

2 To lubricate, give three or four strokes of a gun filled with a recommended grease — see 'SERVICE LUBRICANTS'.

REAR AXLE

Checking oil level

With the vehicle standing level, check that the oil is level with the bottom of the plug aperture.

1 Remove the filler level plug.

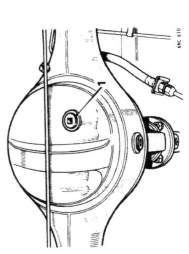

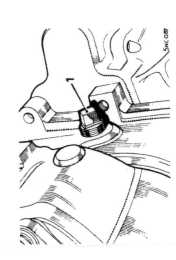

ENGINE – U.K. SPECIFICATION

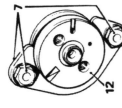
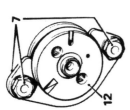

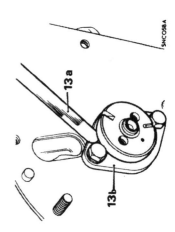

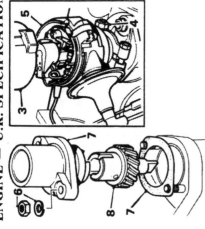

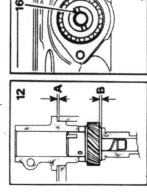

11 Remove the two nuts and washers to release the fuel pump from the cylinder block, and place aside.
12 Withdraw the camshaft.

Refitting

13 Reverse the procedure in 1 to 12 noting:
   a Check that the camshaft end-float is within 0.0045 to 0.0085 in (0.120 to 0.216 mm).
   b Renew the locating plate if the end-float is excessive.
   c Check the valve timing, see 12.65.08.
   d Ensure that the fan drive belt is correctly tensioned, see 'MAINTENANCE'.

---

13 Remove the pedestal, shaft assembly and washer.
14 Turn the crankshaft to bring No. 1 piston to T.D.C. on compression stroke.
15 Lower the drive gear into the bush, allowing it to turn as it meshes with the camshaft gear and ensuring that it engages with the oil pump drive dog.
16 The gear is correctly positioned when the offset slot is in the position shown in the illustration.
17 Reverse the procedure in 1 to 7.
18 Check the ignition timing, see 'MAINTENANCE'.
[NOTE: To prevent undue wear when the engine is first started, lightly lubricate the gear with motor oil during installation.]

CAMSHAFT 12.13.02
Remove and refit

Removing
1 Remove the radiator, see 26.40.01.
2 Remove the fan belt.
3 Remove the water pump housing complete with water pump and fan, see 26.50.03.
4 Remove the crankshaft pulley, see 12.21.01.
5 Remove the timing gear cover, see 12.65.01.
6 Remove the timing chain and gears, see 12.65.12.
7 Remove the bolts securing the cam locating plate and withdraw the plate.
8 Remove the cylinder head gasket, see 12.29.02.
9 Remove the cam followers and identify for reassembly.
[NOTE: Used cam followers should never be interchanged. The best way to identify them for reassembly is to wipe dry each follower as you remove it. Then use waterproof ink or a waterproof felt-tipped marker to write an identification number on the follower. During reassembly, lightly lubricate the cam followers with assembly lubricant (available from automotive supply stores) or with a thin coat of multipurpose grease. Doing this will prevent undue cam lobe and cam follower wear when the engine is first started.]
10 Remove the distributor drive shaft, see 12.10.22.

Refitting
NOTE: An end-float of 0.005 in ±0.002 in (0.13 mm ±0.05 mm) must exist between the end of the distributor pedestal and the drive gear. The end-float is controlled by the selective use of gaskets between the pedestal and cylinder block. Measure the end-float using the following procedure.

9 Measure, note the thickness of, and fit a plain washer 0.5 in (12.7 mm) dia. over the drive shaft below the gear.
10 Fit the shaft assembly and washer into the bush, ensuring that the oil pump drive is mated with the shaft.
NOTE: Use a screwdriver to turn the oil pump drive: try the drive gear in a different position in order to be sure that it is mated correctly.
11 Fit the distributor pedestal into position without the gasket.
12 Measure the gap between the pedestal and cylinder block (A) and subtract from the thickness of the washer (B). The result is gear end-float (or load) which must be adjusted, by gaskets, to give the correct end-float.

Example 1

	in	mm
Thickness of washer (B)	0.100	2.54
Pedestal/cylinder block gap (A)	0.098	2.49
= gear end-float	+0.002	+0.05
add gasket of	0.003	0.08
for correct end-float of	0.005	0.13

Example 2

	in	mm
Thickness of washer (B)	0.100	2.45
Pedestal/cylinder block gap (A)	0.110	2.79
= gear load of	0.010	0.25
add gasket ot	0.015	0.38
for correct end-float of	0.005	0.13

[NOTE: To prevent abrasive dirt from entering the engine, thoroughly clean the pedestal and the surrounding part of the cylinder block before you remove the pedestal.]

DISTRIBUTOR DRIVE SHAFT 12.10.22
Remove and refit

Removing
1 Disconnect the battery.
2 Remove the heater air intake hose.
3 Remove the distributor cap and leads.
4 Remove the nut, bolt and washer securing the distributor and clamp assembly to the pedestal.
5 Detach the distributor from the pedestal and place aside.
6 Remove the two nuts and washers securing the distributor pedestal to the cylinder block.
7 Remove the pedestal and gasket.
8 Remove the distributor drive shaft.

ENGINE – U.K. SPECIFICATION

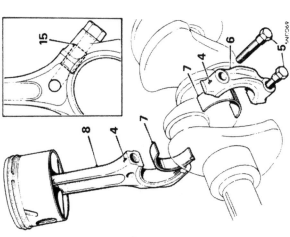

CONNECTING RODS AND PISTONS   12.17.01

Remove and refit

Service tool: 18G 55 A

Removing
1. Disconnect the battery.
2. Remove the cylinder head gasket, see 12.29.02.
3. Remove the sump.
4. Check the identification marks on the connecting rods and bearing caps.
5. Remove the connecting rod bolts.
6. Remove the bearing caps, complete with the bolt bushes.
7. Remove the bearing shells.
8. Remove the pistons and connecting rods upwards from the cylinder block.
9. Retain the bearing shells in their respective connecting rods and bearing caps.

Refitting
10. Lubricate the pistons, cylinder bores and crankpins with clean engine oil.

[NOTE: Lubricate the pistons, the piston rings, and the cylinders with engine oil only. Other lubricants may interfere with the proper seating of new piston rings. If the engine is to be stored for some time following repairs — or if you are installing new bearing shells — it is advisable to use assembly lubricant (available from automotive supply stores) or a light coating of multipurpose grease on the crankpins rather than ordinary motor oil.]

11. Fit the pistons and connecting rods to their original bores, noting:
    a. The mark ▲ is pointing to the front of the engine.
    b. The open face of the big-end bearing is towards the non-thrust side of the cylinder bore.
12. Stagger the piston ring gaps, avoid having a gap on the thrust side of the piston.
13. Use 18G 55A to compress the piston rings.
14. Push the pistons into the cylinder bore.
15. Check that the connecting rod bolt bushes are correctly positioned.
16. Fit the bearing shells to the connecting rods and the bearing caps.
17. Pull the connecting rods onto the crankpins and fit the bearing caps. Use new bolts and tighten to 50 lbf ft (colour dyed bolts) or 46 lbf ft (phosphated bolts).
18. Reverse the procedure in 1 o 3.
19. Refill the sump with the correct quantity of oil.
20. Refill the cooling system.

CONNECTING RODS AND PISTONS

Overhaul   12.17.10

Gudgeon pin bush – remove and refit 1 to 3, 15 to 18, and
22 to 23   12.17.13

NOTE: Do not mix components during this operation.

Dismantling
1. Remove the connecting rods and pistons, see 12.17.01.
2. Remove the circlips from the pistons.
3. Remove the gudgeon pin.

4. Remove the piston from the connecting rod.
5. Remove the piston rings from the piston.
6. Clean the pistons, removing all carbon deposits, particularly from the piston ring grooves.
7. Remove the big-end bearing shells.

Inspection
[CAUTION: Every check and fitting operation described here is essential. If you lack the skills or the proper equipment, please turn this work over to your Authorized Dealer or to a qualified automotive repair shop.]

8. Examine the gudgeon pin and check for wear – see DATA.
9. Check the piston dimensions to grade and bore – see DATA.
10. Check the dimensions of piston ring grooves – see DATA.
11. Check the piston ring gaps in the bores – see DATA.
12. Check the piston ring to groove clearance – see DATA.
13. Check the small end bushes for wear,

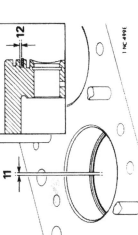

and if necessary, press out the old bush.
14. Check the connecting rods for bend and twist.

Reassembly
[NOTE: If wear has left ridges of metal around the tops of the cylinders (known as top cylinder ridges), you should not replace the piston rings unless these ridges are first removed with a special ridge reaming tool. If unremoved, the ridges may break the new top rings.]

15. Press the new bush into the connecting rod aligning the oil holes.
16. Ream the new bush – see DATA.
17. Fit the piston over the connecting rod and press in the gudgeon pin – hand push fit at 16°C (68°F).

NOTE: Ensure the piston is fitted the correct way on the connecting rod. The crown of the piston is marked ▲ (front) and the cylinder No. stamped on the connecting rod and cap side facing the camshaft.

18. Refit the circlips.
19. Fit the oil control ring expander to the bottom groove followed by the bottom rail and the top rail, ensuring that the ends of the expander are butting but not overlapped.
20. Fit the stepped ring to the second groove in the piston with the face marked 'TOP' towards the top of the piston.

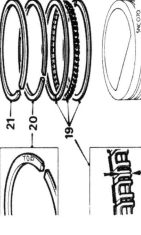

21. Fit the plain compression ring to the top groove.
22. Separate the ring gaps equally on the non-thrust side of the piston.
23. Refit the connecting rods and pistons, see 12.17.01.

continued

ENGINE — U.K. SPECIFICATION

DATA

Pistons

Bore size:	Grade F	2.8995 to 2.9000 in (73.647 to 72.66 mm)
	Grade G	2.9001 to 2.9006 in (73.663 to 73.673 mm)
Bottom diameter of piston:	Grade F	2.8984 to 2.8989 in (73.619 to 73.632 mm)
	Grade G	2.8990 to 2.8995 in (73.635 to 73.647 mm)

Pistons available: Oil control	+0.20 in (+0.53 mm)
Groove width: Top and second	0.1578 to 0.1588 in (3.99 to 4.01 mm)
Ring width: Top and second	0.064 to 0.065 in (1.625 to 1.650 mm)
	0.0615 to 0.0625 in (1.575 to 1.5787 mm)

Connecting rods

Small end bush (fitted) dia.	0.8126 to 0.8129 in (20.64 to 20.65 mm)
Gudgeon pin diameter	0.8123 to 0.8125 in (20.63 to 20.64 mm)

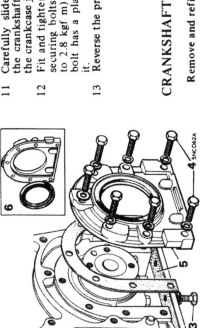

CRANKSHAFT PULLEY   12.21.01

Remove and refit

Removing

1 Remove the radiator, see 26.40.01.
2 Remove the fan.
3 Slacken the alternator adjusting link bolts and mounting bolt and remove the drive belt.
4 Remove the steering-column pinch bolt and nut.
5 Remove the steering-rack mounting brackets, see 57.33.04.
6 Detach the steering-rack from the column and carefully manoeuvre it forwards and downwards to give access to the crankshaft pulley retaining nut.
7 Remove the starter motor, see 86.60.01.
8 Fit a flywheel locking tool to the starter motor aperture.
9 Remove the crankshaft pulley retaining nut.
10 Remove the crankshaft pulley.

Refitting

11 Reverse the procedure in 1 to 10 noting:
  a Tighten the crankshaft retaining nut to 150 lbf ft (20.7 kgf m).
  b Check the fan belt tension, see 'MAINTENANCE'.

---

11 Carefully slide the seal housing over the crankshaft and into contact with the crankcase joint face.
12 Fit and tighten evenly the seal housing securing bolts to 16 to 20 lbf ft (2.2 to 2.8 kgf m) and ensure that the top bolt has a plain copper washer under it.
13 Reverse the procedure in 1 to 3.

CRANKSHAFT REAR OIL SEAL   12.21.20

Remove and refit

Removing

1 Remove the flywheel, see 12.53.07.
2 Remove the seven bolts to release the gearbox adaptor plate from its dowels on the cylinder block.
3 Remove the two bolts securing the sump to the rear oil seal housing.
4 Remove the seven set screws and washers securing the oil seal housing to the crankcase.
5 Remove the oil seal housing assembly taking care not to damage the sump gasket.
6 Press out the oil seal from the housing.

Refitting

7 Smear the outside diameter of the new oil seal with grease and press into the housing, lip face to crankshaft.
8 Clean the crankcase joint face, removing all traces of old gasket and jointing compound.
9 Coat the crankcase face with sealing compound and smear the crankshaft with oil.
10 Place a new gasket in position on the crankcase joint face.

CRANKSHAFT

Remove and refit	12.21.33
Crankshaft end-float — check and adjust 12 to 13, and 28 to 32	12.21.26

Removing

1 Remove the engine assembly, see 12.41.01.
2 Remove the clutch assembly, see 33.10.01.
3 Remove the four bolts securing the flywheel to the crankshaft.
4 Remove the flywheel, see 12.53.07.
5 Remove the seven set screws and washers securing the engine rear adaptor plate to the cylinder block.
6 Remove the engine rear adaptor plate.
7 Remove the water pump housing, see 26.50.03.
8 Remove the timing chain and gears, see 12.65.12.
9 Remove the bolts securing the camshaft locating plate.
10 Remove the camshaft locating plate.
11 Remove the front mounting plate, see 12.25.10.
12 Remove the dipstick.
13 Remove the sump and gasket.
14 Remove the crankshaft drive key.
15 Remove the shims if fitted.
16 Remove the two screws securing the front sealing block.
17 Remove the front sealing block and gaskets.
18 Remove the crankshaft rear oil seal housing, see 12.21.20.

continued

ENGINE — U.K. SPECIFICATION

19 Check the identification marks on the connecting rod bearing caps and main bearing caps.
20 Remove the connecting rod bearings, caps and bottom half bearings.
21 Remove the main bearing caps and bottom half bearings.
22 Remove the thrust washers from the rear main bearing.
23 Lift out the crankshaft.
24 Remove the main bearing top half shells and ensure that the bearing shells are identified with their respective locations for correct reassembly.
25 Remove the crankshaft spigot bush.

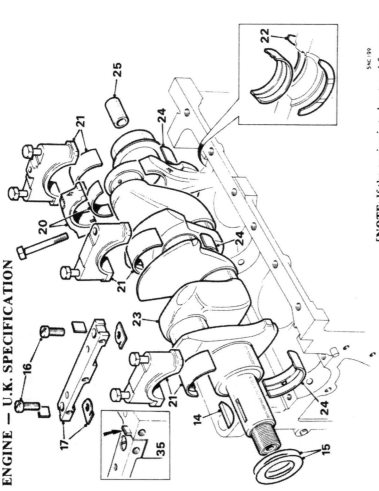

SNC 199

[NOTE: If the engine is to be stored for some time following repairs, it is advisable to use assembly lubricant (available from automotive supply stores) or a light coating of multipurpose grease on the crankpins rather than an ordinary engine oil. Many experienced mechanics choose to use assembly lubricant whenever new bearing shells are installed.]

Refitting

26 Smear the crankshaft spigot bush with zinc oxide grease and refit.
27 Fit the main bearings top half shells to the crankcase.
28 Fit the crankshaft to the crankcase.
29 Fit the thrust washers to the rear main bearing.
30 Fit the bearing shells to the lower main bearing caps.
31 Fit the main bearing caps and tighten the bolts to 50 to 65 lbf ft (2.2 to 2.8 kgf m).

32 Check the crankshaft end-float; adjust with selective thrust washers.
33 Refit the connecting rods to the crankshaft. Use new bolts and tighten to 50 lbf ft (6.9 kgf m) —colour dyed bolts or 46 lbf ft (6.4 kgf m) — phosphated bolts.
34 Fit the front sealing block to the crankcase, using jointing compound on the gaskets. Do not tighten the screws.
35 Drive new wedges into the slots.
36 Align the face of the sealing block with the crankcase and tighten the screws.
37 Trim the protruding ends of the wedges.
38 Fit the crankshaft rear oil seal, see 12.21.20.
39 Fit the sump, renewing the gasket. Tighten the retaining set screws to 16 to 20 lbf ft.
40 Fit the engine rear adaptor plate.

41 Fit the flywheel, see 12.53.07, ensuring that the crankshaft spigot bush is in position.
42 Fit the clutch assembly, see 33.10.01.
43 Fit the front mounting plate and gasket noting:
    a Remove all traces of old gasket and jointing compound from the cylinder block face.
    b Smear the cylinder block face of the new gasket with jointing compound.
44 Fit the camshaft locating plate.
45 Fit the timing chain and sprockets, see 12.65.12.
46 Check the valve timing, see 12.65 08.
47 Fit the oil thrower ensuring that the dished periphery faces the timing cover.
48 Fit the timing chain cover, see 12.65.01.
49 Fit the crankshaft pulley, tightening the retaining nut to 150 lbf ft (20.7 kgf m).
50 Fit the thermostat and water pump housing assembly. Ensure that a new gasket is fitted, see 26.45.10.
51 Fit the engine assembly to the car, see 12.41.01.

DATA

Crankshaft

Main bearing journal diameter	2.3115 to 2.3120 in (58.713 to 58.725 mm)
Crankpin diameter	1.8750 to 1.8755 in (47.625 to 47.638 mm)
Crankshaft end-float tolerance	0.006 to 0.014 in (0.152 to 0.356 mm)
Maximum out of balance of shaft (with key and dowel fitted)	0.3 oz in (3.36 g cm)
Maximum run out of centre journal (with front and rear supported)	0.003 in (0.076 mm)
Thrust washer oversizes	0.005 in (0.13 mm)
Available bearing undersizes	0.010, 0.020, 0.030 in (0.25, 0.51, 0.76 mm)

12.21.01

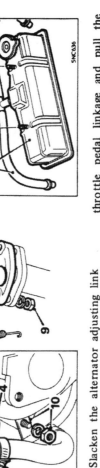

ENGINE – U.K. SPECIFICATION

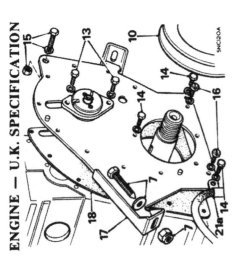

CYLINDER BLOCK FRONT MOUNTING PLATE GASKET   12.25.10

Remove and refit

Removing

1 Disconnect the battery, see 26.40.01.
2 Remove the radiator, see 26.40.01.
3 Remove the fan belt.
4 Remove the water housing complete with water pump and fan, see 26.50.03.
5 Remove the three nuts, bolts and washers securing the exhaust pipe to the exhaust manifold.
6 Support the engine.
7 Remove the nuts, bolts and washers securing the L.H. and R.H. engine mountings to the front mounting plate.
8 Raise the engine assembly to allow removal of the crankshaft pulley.
9 Remove the crankshaft pulley nut.
10 Withdraw the crankshaft pulley.
11 Remove the timing gear cover, see 12.65.01.
12 Remove the timing chain and gears, see 12.65.12.
13 Remove the bolts securing the camshaft locating plate and withdraw the plate.

14 Remove the three set screws and washers securing the mounting plate to the cylinder block.
15 Remove the nut, bolt and washer securing the alternator bracket to the mounting plate.
16 Remove the two set screws and washers securing the mounting plate to the sealing block.
17 Remove the front mounting plate.
18 Remove the front mounting plate gasket.

Refitting

19 Remove all traces of old jointing compound from the cylinder block face.
20 Coat the cylinder block face of the new gasket with Wellseal jointing compound.
21 Reverse the procedure in 1 to 18 noting:
  a Fit the engine earth lead to the mounting plate.
  b Fit a new thermostat and water pump housing gasket.

CYLINDER HEAD GASKET   12.29.02

Remove and refit

Removing

1 Disconnect the battery.
2 Disconnect the bottom radiator hose to drain the cooling system.
3 Remove the carburetters and air cleaner assembly, see 19.15.11.
4 Remove the temperature transmitter from the thermostat housing, unclip the capillary tube from the induction manifold water pipe and move the capillary tube aside.
5 Remove the fan guard from the radiator.

6 Slacken the alternator adjusting link bolt.
7 Remove the three bolts securing the thermostat and water pump housing to the cylinder head.
8 Disconnect the thermostat housing hose, the heater by-pass hose, and the heater control valve hose from the induction manifold.
9 Remove the three nuts, bolts and washers securing the exhaust pipe to the exhaust manifold.
10 Remove the exhaust manifold nut securing the water return pipe support bracket and detach the bracket from the manifold stud.
11 Disconnect the throttle cable from the manifold stud.

throttle pedal linkage and pull the cable into the engine compartment.
12 Disconnect the spark plug leads, detach the distributor cap from the distributor and move the cap and leads aside.
13 Remove the rocker cover complete with breather hose.
14 Remove the four nuts and washers securing the rocker shaft to the cylinder head and lift off the rocker shaft.
15 Remove the push rods, keeping them in their installed order.
16 Remove the ten nuts and washers securing the cylinder head to the block.

10 Check the valve guides, renew if worn.

11 Check the valves and renew valves with bent or worn stems (see **DATA**) or where the thickness of the valve head is reduced to 0.0312 in (0.8 mm) or below.

12 Check the valve springs – see **DATA**. Renew as necessary.

Valve guides

13 Using service tool 60A, with adaptor S 60A-2A assemble the replacement valve guide in the tool with the chamfered end uppermost (leading). Position the tool on the combustion chamber face of the cylinder head and pull the replacement guide in and the old guide out. Ensure that the guide protrusion above the cylinder head top face is correct, see **DATA**.

Valve seat inserts

14 Machine the cylinder head to the dimensions given.
NOTE: When fitting a pair of valve seat inserts it will be necessary to machine the cylinder head and fit the first insert before machining the cylinder head for the second insert.

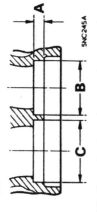

14

5NC245A

15 Press in the valve seat insert and peen over the cylinder head casting material to secure.

16 Cut seats in the inserts to the dimensions given in **DATA**.

EXHAUST

A   0.250 to 0.255 in (6.35 to 6.48 mm)
B   1.249 to 1.250 in (31.72 to 31.75 mm)

INLET

A   0.250 to 0.255 in (6.35 to 6.48 mm)
C   1.484 to 1.485 in (37.69 to 37.72 mm)

Reassembling

17 Lap in all the valves using carborundum paste.

18 Reverse the procedure in 2 to 8.

19 Refit the cylinder head, fitting a new gasket.

DATA

Valves

		Inlet	Exhaust
Valve insert seat angle: Inlet and exhaust		$45\frac{1}{2}°$	
Head diameter:	Inlet	1.377 to 1.383 in (34.97 to 35.01 mm)	
	Exhaust	1.168 to 1.172 in (29.66 to 29.76 mm)	
Stem diameter:	Inlet	0.3107 to 0.3113 in (7.89 to 7.91 mm)	
	Exhaust	0.3100 to 0.3105 in (7.874 to 7.887 mm)	
Stem to guide clearance:	Inlet	0.0007 to 0.0023 in (0.02 to 0.06 mm)	
	Exhaust	0.0015 to 0.0030 in (0.04 to 0.07 mm)	

Valve guides

Length: Inlet and exhaust . . . . 2.06 in (52.224 mm)
Fitted height above head . . . . 0.75 in (19.050 mm)
Diameter: Inlet and exhaust:
            Outside . . . . 0.5015 to 0.502 in (12.73 to 12.75 mm)
            Inside . . . . 0.312 to 0.313 in (7.92 to 7.95 mm)

Valve springs

	Inner	Outer
Free length	1.14 in (30 mm)	1.52 in (38.6 mm)
Fitted length	1.01 in (25.7 mm)	1.342 in (1.29 mm)
Load at top of lift	$40^{+3}_{\,0}$ lbf ($18 \pm 1\cdot36$ kgf)	$123^{+10}_{\ \ 0}$ lbf ($55.8^{+4.54}_{\ \ 0}$ kgf)
Number of working coils	4	4

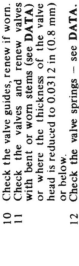

5NCH2

17 Remove the engine lifting bracket and the fuel pipe bracket.

18 Lift off the cylinder head assembly.

19 Remove the cylinder head gasket and discard.

Refitting

20 Reverse the procedure in 1 to 19 noting:

a Use a new gasket, with the side of the gasket marked 'TOP' upwards.

b Tighten the cylinder head nuts gradually in the sequence shown to a torque of 50 lbf ft (6.9 kgf m).

c Tighten the rocker shaft pedestal nuts to a torque of 26 to 32 lbf ft (3.6 to 4.4 kgf m).

d Fill the cooling system, see 'MAINTENANCE'.

e Check the fan belt tension, see 'MAINTENANCE'.

21 Adjust the valve clearances, see 'MAINTENANCE'.

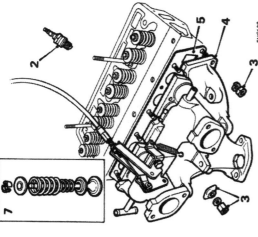

5NC628

CYLINDER HEAD

Overhaul   12.29.19

Service tool: 18G; 45, 60A. S 60A-2A

Dismantling

1 Remove the cylinder head, see 12.29.02.

2 Remove the spark plugs.

3 Remove the nuts, washers and clamps securing the manifold assembly to the cylinder head.

4 Remove the induction and exhaust manifold assembly.

5 Remove the manifold gasket.

6 Compress the valve springs using 18G 45.

7 Remove the valve cotter halves and the valve springs complete with the spring cups and seats.

8 Remove the inlet and exhaust valves and retain in their assembly order.

Inspection

9 Check each valve seat face; if necessary recondition the seat, removing the minimum amount of metal necessary to correct the seat. Fit valve seat inserts if the seats cannot be restored by refacing.

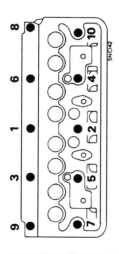

12.25.10

ENGINE — U.K. SPECIFICATION
ROCKER SHAFT

Remove and refit   12.29.54

Removing

1 Disconnect the breather pipe from the rocker cover.
2 Remove the rocker cover.
3 Remove the four nuts and washers securing the rocker shaft pedestals to the cylinder head.
4 Lift off the rocker shaft.

Refitting

5 Reverse the procedure in 1 to 4 noting:
    a.   Tighten the pedestal nuts to 26 to 32 lbf ft (3.6 to 4.4 kgf m).
6 Adjust the valve clearances, see 'MAINTENANCE'.

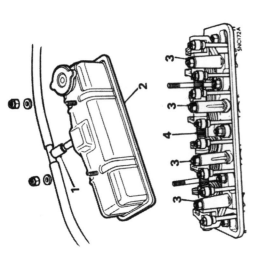

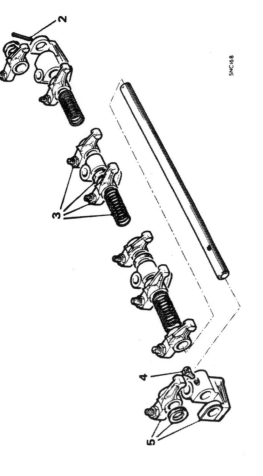

ROCKER SHAFT ASSEMBLY

Overhaul   12.29.55

Dismantling

1 Remove the rocker shaft, see 12.29.54.
2 Withdraw the split pin from the front end of the rocker shaft.
3 Slide off the rockers, pedestals, springs and spacers from the front end of the shaft, noting the order for reassembly.
4 Remove the screw locating the rear pedestal to the shaft.
5 Remove the rear pedestal complete with washer and rocker.

Reassembling

6 Reverse the procedure in 1 to 5 noting:
    a   Renew all worn components.
    b   Ensure that the oil-ways in the rockers and shaft are clear.
    c   Apply Loctite 221 to the rear pedestal locating screw.
    d   Ensure that the rear pedestal locating screw engages correctly in the rocker shaft.
7 Adjust the valve clearances, see 'MAINTENANCE'.

80

ENGINE AND GEARBOX ASSEMBLY

Remove and refit   12.37.01

Removing

1 Remove the bonnet.
2 Disconnect the battery.
3 Remove the car heater air intake hose.
4 Remove the radiator, see 26.40.01.
5 Remove the cooling fan.
6 Drain the engine oil.
7 Remove the carburetters and air cleaner assembly, see 19.15.11.
8 Detach the accelerator cable from the accelerator pedal arm and pull the cable into the engine compartment.
9 Remove the three nuts, bolts and washers securing the exhaust pipe to the exhaust manifold and remove the gasket.
10 Disconnect the heater hose from the water return pipe.
11 Disconnect the heater control valve hose from the inlet manifold.
12 Disconnect the water temperature transmitter from the thermostat housing, unclip the capillary tube from the induction manifold water pipe and place aside.
13 Disconnect the alternator lead plug at the alternator.
14 Disconnect the high tension ignition leads and remove the distributor cap.
15 Disconnect the low tension distributor leads.
16 Disconnect the oil pressure gauge pipe from the engine.
17 Remove the bolt securing the engine earth strap to the engine and move the earth strap aside.
18 Disconnect the lead from the starter motor.
19 Remove the three nuts and bolts securing the exhaust front pipe to the rear pipe and collect the olive.
20 Disconnect the petrol hose from the petrol pipe at the union in the gearbox tunnel.
21 Disconnect the reverse light switch leads at the connector in the gearbox tunnel, detach the lead from the clip and pull the lead clear of the brake pipe.

22 Remove the bolt securing the speedometer drive clamp to the gearbox.
23 Remove the clamp and withdraw the speedometer drive. Refit the clamp and bolt.
24 Remove the nut and bolt on the clamp securing the clutch slave cylinder to the gearbox.
25 Pull the clutch slave cylinder rearwards and place aside.
26 Remove the four nuts, bolts and washers securing the propeller shaft to the gearbox.
27 Remove the two bolts and washers securing the rear mounting bracket to the floor panel.
28 Remove the gearbox tunnel carpet.
29 Remove the four screws securing the gear lever gaiter assembly.
30 Lift the gaiter assembly, press and turn the gear lever retaining cover and lift the assembly complete with the anti-rattle cup and spring from the gearbox.
31 Remove the two bolts and washers securing the rear mounting bracket to the gearbox tunnel.
32 Fit the engine lifting slings to the two engine lifting brackets using a shorter sling on the front bracket to ensure that the engine and gearbox assembly tilts at an angle of approximately 70 during removal.
33 Take the weight of the engine and gearbox assembly on the lifting slings and remove the two nuts, bolts and washers from the R.H. and L.H. front engine mountings.
34 Lift the engine and gearbox from the car using a second operator to lift the gearbox rear coupling over the crossmember in the gearbox tunnel.

Refitting

35 Reverse the procedure in 1 to 34.

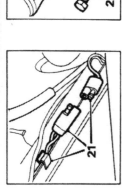
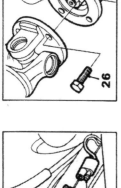
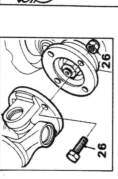
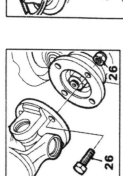

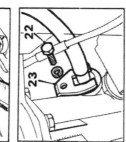

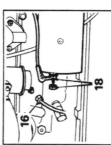
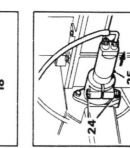

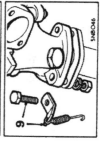
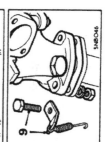

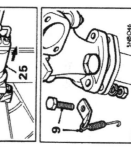
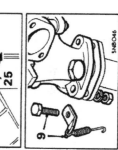

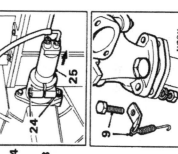
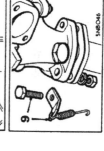
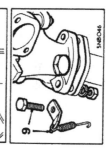

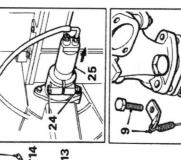
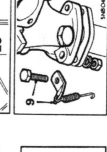

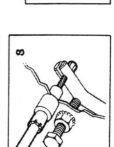
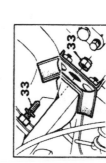
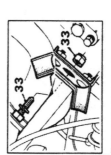
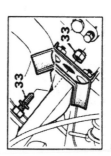

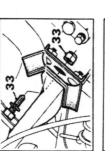

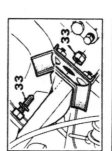
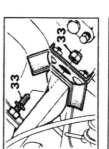
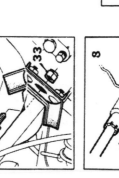

ENGINE – U.K. SPECIFICATION

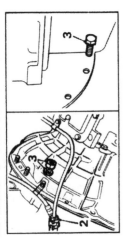  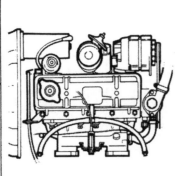 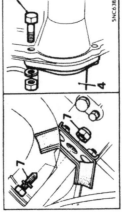

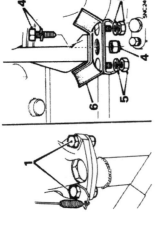

ENGINE ASSEMBLY

Remove and refit   12.41.01

Removing

1 Disconnect or remove as necessary the ancillary equipment from the engine, see 12.37.01.
2 Disconnect the fuel inlet hose from the pump.
3 Remove the nuts, bolts and washers securing the gearbox housing and starter motor to the engine.
4 Detach the starter motor and place aside on the longitudinal member.
5 Support the gearbox.
6 Fit engine lifting slings to the engine lifting brackets.
7 Take the weight of the engine assembly on the lifting slings and remove the nuts, two bolts and washers from the R.H. and L.H. front engine mountings.
8 Lift the engine assembly from the car.

Refitting

9 Reverse the procedure in 1 to 8.

ENGINE MOUNTING FRONT R.H   12.45.03

Remove and refit

Removing

1 Slacken the three nuts and bolts securing the exhaust manifold to the exhaust pipe.
2 Remove the fan guard from the radiator.
3 Support the engine.
4 Remove the nut, bolt and washer securing the engine mounting to the engine mounting foot.
5 Remove the two nuts and washers securing the engine mounting to the body bracket.
6 Raise the engine and remove the engine mounting.

Refitting

7 Reverse the procedure in 1 to 6.

ENGINE MOUNTING FRONT L.H.   12.45.01

Remove and refit

Removing

1 Remove the fan guard from the radiator.
2 Support the engine.
3 Remove the two nuts and washers securing the engine mounting to the body bracket.
4 Remove the nut, bolt and washer securing the engine mounting to the engine mounting foot.
5 Raise the engine and remove the engine mounting.

Refitting

6 Reverse the procedure in 1 to 5.

FLYWHEEL   12.53.07

Remove and refit

Removing

1 Remove the clutch assembly, see 33.10.01.
2 Remove the four bolts securing the flywheel to the crankshaft.
3 Remove the flywheel.

Refitting

4 Clean the flywheel mating face. Check the locating dowel for damage, and ensure that the crankshaft spigot bush is correctly positioned.
5 Fit the flywheel to the crankshaft, locating it over the dowel in the crankshaft.
6 Tighten the flywheel retaining bolts evenly to 40 to 45 lbf ft (5.5 to 6.2 kgf m).
7 Using a dial indicator gauge, check the flywheel for run-out, not to exceed 0.002 in (0.051 mm) at 3.0 in (76.2 mm) radius from the spigot centre. Check concentricity, not to exceed 0.004 in (0.100 mm).
8 Refit the clutch assembly, see 33.10.01.

STARTER RING GEAR

Remove and refit   12.53.19

Removing
1 Disconnect the battery.
2 Remove the flywheel, see 12.53.07.
3 Drill a hole ¼ in (6.35 mm) diameter between any two teeth of the ring gear.
4 Hold the flywheel assembly in a soft jaw vice.
5 Place a cloth of heavy material over the ring gear for protection against flying fragments.
WARNING: Ensure adequate protection, particularly for the eyes, to prevent possible injury from flying fragments, particularly when the ring gear is split.
6 Place a cold chisel immediately above the centre line of the drilled hole and strike sharply to split the ring gear.

Refitting
7 Heat the replacement starter ring gear uniformly to a maximum of 200°C.
8 Place the flywheel on a flat surface, clutch face side uppermost, and clean the ring gear locating register.
9 Locate the ring gear and hold in position until it contracts sufficiently to grip the flywheel.
10 Allow the ring gear to cool gradually to avoid distortion.
11 Refit the flywheel, see 12.53.07, and check that ring gear eccentricity does not exceed 0.010 in (0.254 mm).

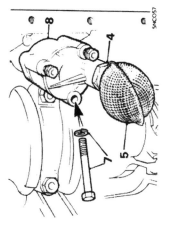

OIL PUMP

Remove and refit 1 to 3 and 7 to 9   12.60.26

Oil pick-up strainer 1 to 6, and 9   12.60.20

Removing
1 Drain the sump.
2 Remove the bolts securing the sump to the crankcase.
3 Remove the sump and gasket.
4 Release the oil strainer locknut.
5 Unscrew the oil strainer from the oil pump cover plate.
6 Wash the oil strainer in petrol and allow to dry before refitting.
7 Remove the three bolts and washers securing the oil pump to the crankcase.
8 Remove the oil pump assembly.

Refitting
9 Reverse the procedure in 1 to 8 as necessary, ensuring that the oil pump drive shaft engages correctly into the drive gear shaft.

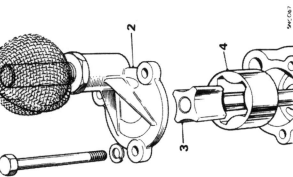
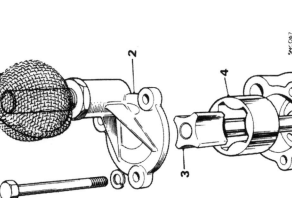

the outer rotor is at the driving end of the pump body.
7 With a straight edge across the pump body face, check the clearance between the rotors and the straight edge.
8 Check the clearance between the inner and outer rotors.
9 Check the clearance between the outer rotor and the pump body.
10 Renew the pump assembly if the clearances or end-floats measured in 7 to 9 exceed the figures given in DATA.
11 Check the cover plate for scoring, and test on a surface plate for distortion. Renew if necessary.
12 Check the pump spindle bearing surface in the pump body for excessive wear.

Reassembling
13 Reverse the procedure in 1 to 4 noting:
a. Ensure that the outer rotor is installed in the pump body with its chamfered end at the driving end of the pump body.
b. Ensure that absolute cleanliness is observed.

OIL PUMP

Overhaul   12.60.32

Dismantling
1 Remove the oil pump, see 12.60.26.
2 Remove the cover plate complete with strainer.
3 Remove the inner rotor and shaft assembly.
4 Remove the outer rotor.

Inspecting
5 Clean all components.
6 Install the rotors in the pump body ensuring that the chamfered edge of

DATA
Oil pump

Inner rotor end-float	0.0004 in (0.1 mm)
Outer rotor end-float	0.0004 in (0.1 mm)
Rotor lobe clearance	0.010 in (0.25 mm)
Outer rotor to pump body diametrical clearance	0.008 in (0.2 mm)

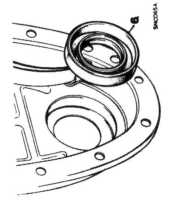

5NCO55A

3 Remove the timing gear cover and gasket.
4 Remove the oil seal from the timing cover.

Refitting
5 Dip the new oil seal in engine oil before refitting.
6 Fit the new oil seal to the timing gear cover, using 18G 134 and 18G 134 BM.
7 Reverse the procedure in 1 to 3 noting:
a. Fit a new gasket ensuring that it locates on the dowels.
b. To facilitate refitment of the cover, compress the chain tensioner with a suitably bent length of rod, taking care not to damage the gasket when withdrawing the rod.

TIMING GEAR COVER OIL SEAL

Remove and refit   12.65.05
Timing gear cover 1 to 4 and 8   12.65.01

Service tool: 18G 134, 18G 134 BM

Removing
1 Remove the crankshaft pulley, see 12.21.01.
2 Remove the eleven set screws, and one nut complete with washers securing the timing gear cover to the cylinder block.

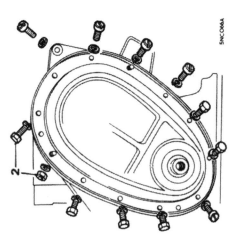

5NCO46A

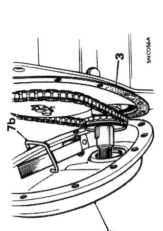

5NCO56A

ENGINE — U.K. SPECIFICATION

OIL PRESSURE RELIEF VALVE

Remove and refit   12.60.56

Removing
1 Unscrew the relief valve body from the cylinder block.
2 Remove the washer and discard.
3 Withdraw the plunger.
4 Remove the spring.

Refitting
5 Reverse the procedure in 1 to 4 noting:
a Renew the washer.
b Renew the spring if the free length is not in accordance with the figure given in DATA.

DATA
Oil pressure relief valve spring free length   1.53 in (38.8 mm)

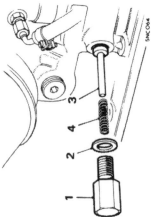

5NCO64

84

ENGINE – U.K. SPECIFICATION

VALVE TIMING

Check 12.65.08

1 Remove the rocker cover.
2 Adjust the rocker clearances of Nos. 7 and 8 valves to 0.050 in (1.27 mm), to give a working clearance.
3 Turn the crankshaft until No. 1 piston is at T.D.C. on compression stroke, indicated by the mark on the crankshaft pulley coinciding with the pointer on the timing cover.
4 Check that Nos. 1 and 2 valves are fully closed by inserting a feeler gauge between the valve tip and rocker pad to ascertain clearance.
5 Using two feeler gauges of the same thickness, check that the rocker clearances on Nos. 7 and 8 valves are equal. Oscillate the crankshaft to achieve this condition, but ensure that when the rocker clearances are the same the conditions in instructions 3 and 4 are maintained within a few degrees.
6 Should the valve timing prove to be incorrect, retiming will be necessary.
7 Re-adjust Nos. 7 and 8 valves to 0.010 in (0.25 mm).
8 Refit the rocker cover.

DATA
Valve timing

Inlet valve: Opens	18° B.T.D.C.
Closes	58° A.B.D.C.
Exhaust valve: Opens	58° B.B.D.C.
Closes	18° A.T.D.C.

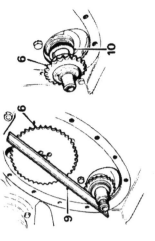

SNC.159

Refitting

7 Remove the crankshaft drive key.
8 Temporarily fit both gear wheels.
9 Check the alignment of the gear wheels by placing a straight edge across the teeth of both gears.
10 Correct any misalignment by fitting selective shims behind the crankshaft gear wheel.
11 Remove the gear wheels.
12 Refit the drive key.
13 Assemble the timing chain and gear wheels and locate the engine ensuring that the marks on the gear wheels and the camshaft are aligned.
14 Refit the camshaft gear wheel securing bolts.
15 Check the timing chain wear by placing a straight edge along the slack run of chain. If movement at the mid-point exceeds 0.4 in (10 mm) renew the chain.
16 Remove the camshaft gear wheel securing bolts, fit a new lock plate and refit the bolts.
17 Refit the oil thrower with the dished periphery towards the timing gear cover.
18 Refit the timing gear cover, see 12.65.01.
NOTE: If new gear wheels are fitted make a punch mark on the crankshaft and camshaft gear wheels on a line scribed between the centres of the two gear wheels. Make also a punch mark on the camshaft and a corresponding mark on the camshaft gear wheel.

TIMING CHAIN AND GEARS

Remove and refit 12.65.12

Removing

1 Remove the timing gear cover, see 12.65.01.
2 Remove the oil thrower.
3 Turn the crankshaft until the timing marks on each gear are opposite each other.
4 When the marks on the timing gears are aligned the centre punch marks in the centre of the camshaft gear and on the camshaft should be aligned. Note that the camshaft centre punch mark is visible through the hole in the camshaft gear.
5 Bend back the lock plate tabs and remove the two bolts securing the gear wheel to the camshaft.
6 Taking care not to turn the crankshaft or camshaft, remove both gears together with the timing chain.

ENGINE – U.S.A. SPECIFICATION

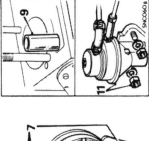

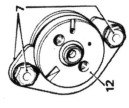

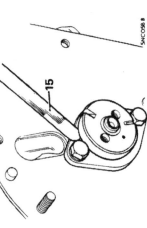

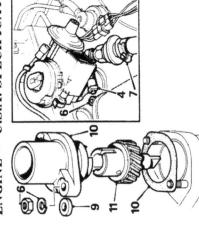

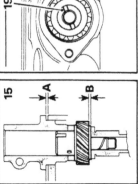

[NOTE: To prevent abrasive dirt from entering the engine, thoroughly clean the pedestal and the surrounding part of the cylinder block before you remove the pedestal.]

DISTRIBUTOR DRIVE SHAFT

Remove and refit   12.10.22

Removing

1 Disconnect the battery.
2 Remove the heater air intake hose.
3 Remove the distributor cap and leads.
4 Remove the nut, bolt and washer securing the distributor and clamp assembly to the pedestal.
5 Detach the distributor from the pedestal and place aside.
6 Remove the two nuts and washers securing the diverter valve bracket and the distributor pedestal to the cylinder block.

7 Disconnect the air hose from the check valve.
8 Detach the diverter valve bracket from the cylinder block stud.
9 Remove the two spacers from the cylinder block studs.
10 Remove the pedestal and gasket.
11 Remove the distributor drive shaft.

Refitting

NOTE: An end-float of 0.005 in ±0.002 in (0.13 mm ±0.05 mm) must exist between the end of the distributor pedestal and the drive gear. The end-float is controlled by the selective use of gaskets on the pedestal/cylinder block interface. Measure the end-float using the following procedure.

12 Measure, note the thickness of, and fit a plain washer 0.5 in (12.7 mm) dia. over the drive shaft below the gear.
13 Fit the shaft assembly and washer into the bush, ensuring that the oil pump drive is mated with the shaft.
NOTE: Use a screwdriver to turn the oil pump drive: try the drive gear in a different position in order to be sure that it is mated correctly.
14 Fit the distributor pedestal into position without the gasket.
15 Measure the gap between the pedestal and cylinder block (A) and subtract from the thickness of the washer (B). The result is gear end-float (or load) which must be adjusted, by gaskets, to give the correct end-float.

Example 1

	in	mm
Thickness of washer (B)	0.100	2.54
Pedestal/cylinder block gap (A)	0.098	2.49
= gear end-float	+0.002 / 0.003	+0.05 / 0.08
add gasket of	0.005	0.13
for correct end-float of	0.005	0.13

Example 2

	in	mm
Thickness of washer (B)	0.100	2.45
Pedestal/cylinder block gap (A)	0.110	2.79
= gear load of	−0.010 / 0.015	−0.25 / 0.38
add gasket of	0.015	0.38
for correct end-float of	0.005	0.13

16 Remove the pedestal, shaft assembly and washer.
17 Turn the crankshaft to bring No. 1 piston to T.D.C. on compression stroke.
18 Lower the drive gear into the bush, allowing it to turn as it meshes with the camshaft gear and ensuring that it engages with the oil pump drive dog.
19 The gear is correctly positioned when the offset slot is in the position shown in the illustration.
20 Reverse the procedure in 1 to 10.
21 Check the ignition timing, see 'MAINTENANCE'.

[NOTE: To prevent undue wear when the engine is first started, lightly lubricate the gear with motor oil during installation.]

CAMSHAFT

Remove and refit   12.13.02

Removing

1 Remove the radiator, see 26.40.01.
2 Remove the air pump drive belt.
3 Remove the fan belt.
4 Remove the crankshaft pulley, see 12.21.01.
5 Remove the timing gear cover, see 12.65.01.
6 Remove the timing chain and gears, see 12.65.12.
7 Remove the bolts securing the cam locating plate and withdraw the plate.
8 Remove the cylinder head gasket, see 12.29.02, noting it is NOT necessary to remove the water pump housing from the head.
9 Remove the cam followers and identify for reassembly.

[NOTE: Used cam followers should never be interchanged. The best way to identify them for reassembly is to wipe dry each follower as you remove it. Then use waterproof ink or a waterproof felt-tipped marker to write an identification number on the follower. During reassembly, lightly lubricate the cam followers with assembly lubricant (available from automotive supply stores) or with a thin coat of multipurpose grease. Doing this will prevent undue cam lobe and cam follower wear when the engine is first started.]

10 Remove the distributor drive shaft, see 12.10.22.

11 Remove the two nuts and washers to release the fuel pump from the cylinder block, and place aside.
12 Withdraw the camshaft.

Refitting

13 Mark the new camshaft with a punch mark in the position corresponding to that of the camshaft being replaced.
14 Fit the camshaft and the locating plate.
15 Check that the camshaft end-float is within 0.0045 to 0.0085 in (0.120 to 0.216 mm); renew the locating plate if end-float is excessive.
16 Refit the timing chain and gears, see 12.65.12.
17 Refit the fuel pump.
18 Refit the distributor drive shaft, see 12.10.22.
19 Refit the cam followers.
20 Refit the cylinder head gasket, see 12.29.02.
21 Reverse the procedure in 1 to 5, ensuring that the fan and air pump drive belts are correctly tensioned, see 'MAINTENANCE'.

ENGINE – U.S.A. SPECIFICATION

CONNECTING RODS AND PISTONS

Remove and refit   12.17.01

Service tool: 18G 55 A

Removing
1 Disconnect the battery.
2 Remove the cylinder head gasket, see 12.29.02.
3 Remove the sump.
4 Check the identification marks on the connecting rods and bearing caps.
5 Remove the connecting rod bolts.
6 Remove the bearing caps, complete with the bolt bushes.
7 Remove the bearing shells.
8 Remove the pistons and connecting rods upwards from the cylinder block.
9 Retain the bearing shells in their respective connecting rods and bearing caps.

Refitting
10 Lubricate the pistons, cylinder bores and crankpins with clean engine oil.

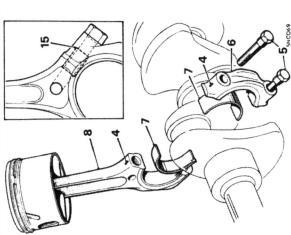

[NOTE: Lubricate the pistons, the piston rings, and the cylinders with engine oil only. Other lubricants may interfere with the proper seating of new piston rings. If the engine is to be stored for some time following repairs — or if you are installing new bearing shells — it is advisable to use assembly lubricant (available from automotive supply stores) or a light coating of multipurpose grease on the crankpins rather than ordinary motor oil.]

11 Fit the pistons and connecting rods to their original bores, noting:
  a The mark ▲ is pointing to the front of the engine.
  b The open face of the big-end bearing is towards the non-thrust side of the cylinder bore.
12 Stagger the piston ring gaps, avoid having a gap on the thrust side of the piston.
13 Use 18G 55A to compress the piston rings.
14 Push the pistons into the cylinder bore.
15 Check that the connecting rod bolt bushes are correctly positioned.
16 Fit the bearing shells to the connecting rods and the bearing caps.
17 Pull the connecting rods onto the crankpins and fit the bearing caps. Use new bolts and tighten to 50 lbf ft (colour dyed bolts) or 46 lbf ft (phosphated bolts).
[NOTE: On 1977 models, torque the bolts to 40 to 45 lbf ft.]
18 Reverse the procedure in 1 o 3.
19 Refill the sump with the correct quantity of oil.
20 Refill the cooling system.

CONNECTING RODS AND PISTONS

Overhaul   12.17.10

Gudgeon pin bush – remove and refit 1 to 3, 15 to 18, and   12.17.13
22 to 23

NOTE: Do not mix components during this operation.

Dismantling
1 Remove the connecting rods and pistons, see 12.17.01.

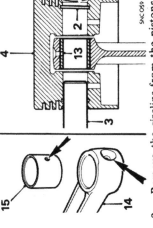

2 Remove the circlips from the pistons.
3 Remove the gudgeon pin.
4 Remove the piston from the connecting rod.
5 Remove the piston rings from the piston.
6 Clean the pistons, removing all carbon deposits, particularly from the piston ring grooves.
7 Remove the big-end bearing shells.

Inspection
[CAUTION: Every check and fitting operation described here is essential. If you lack the skills or the proper equipment, please turn this work over to your Authorized Dealer or to a qualified automotive repair shop.]

8 Examine the gudgeon pin and check for wear – see Data.
9 Check the piston dimensions to grade and bore – see Data.
10 Check the dimensions of piston ring grooves – see Data.
11 Check the piston ring gaps in the bores – see Data.
12 Check the piston ring to groove clearance – see Data.

13 Check the small end bushes for wear, and if necessary, press out the old bush.
14 Check the connecting rods for bend and twist.

Reassembly
[NOTE: If wear has left ridges of metal around the tops of the cylinders (known as top cylinder ridges), you should not replace the piston rings unless these ridges are first removed with a special ridge reaming tool. If unremoved, the ridges may break the new top rings.]

15 Press the new bush into the connecting rod aligning the oil holes.
16 Ream the new bush – see Data.
17 Fit the piston over the connecting rod and press in the gudgeon pin – hand push fit at 16°C (68°F).
NOTE: Ensure the piston is fitted the correct way on the connecting rod. The crown of the piston is marked ▲ (front) and the cylinder No. stamped on the connecting rod and cap side facing the camshaft.
18 Refit the circlips.
19 Fit the oil control ring expander to the bottom groove followed by the bottom rail and the top rail, ensuring that the ends of the expander are butting but not overlapped.
20 Fit the stepped ring to the second groove in the piston with the face marked 'TOP' towards the top of the piston.

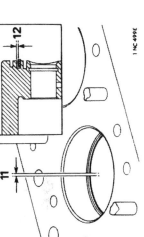

21 Fit the plain compression ring to the top groove.
22 Separate the ring gaps equally on the non-thrust side of the piston.
23 Refit the connecting rods and pistons, see 12.17.01.
continued

11 Carefully slide the seal housing over the crankshaft and into contact with the crankcase joint face.
12 Fit and tighten evenly the seal housing securing bolts to 16 to 20 lbf ft (2.2 to 2.8 kgf m) and ensure that the top bolt has a plain copper washer under it.
13 Reverse the procedure in 1 to 3.

CRANKSHAFT 12.21.33

Remove and refit

Crankshaft end-float — check and adjust 12 to 13, and 28 to 32 12.21.26

Removing
1 Remove the engine assembly, see 12.41.01.
2 Remove the clutch assembly, see 33.10.01.
3 Remove the four bolts securing the flywheel to the crankshaft.
4 Remove the flywheel, see 12.53.07.
5 Remove the seven set screws and washers securing the engine rear adaptor plate to the cylinder block.
6 Remove the engine rear adaptor plate.
7 Remove the water pump and thermostat housing, see 26.45.10.
8 Remove the timing chain and gears, see 12.65.12.
9 Remove the bolts securing the camshaft locating plate.
10 Remove the camshaft locating plate.
11 Remove the front mounting plate, see 12.25.10.
12 Remove the dipstick.
13 Remove the sump and gasket.
14 Remove the crankshaft drive key.
15 Remove the shims if fitted.
16 Remove the two screws securing the front sealing block.
17 Remove the front sealing block and gaskets.
18 Remove the crankshaft rear oil seal housing, see 12.21.20.
continued

CRANKSHAFT REAR OIL SEAL 12.21.20

Remove and refit

Removing
1 Remove the flywheel, see 12.53.07.
2 Remove the seven bolts to release the adaptor plate from the dowels on the cylinder block.
3 Remove the two bolts securing the sump to the rear oil seal housing.
4 Remove the seven set screws and washers securing the oil seal housing to the crankcase.
5 Remove the oil seal housing assembly taking care not to damage the sump gasket.
6 Press out the oil seal from the housing.

Refitting
7 Smear the outside diameter of the new oil seal with grease and press into the housing, lip face to crankshaft.
8 Clean the crankcase joint face, removing all traces of old gasket and jointing compound.
9 Coat the crankcase face with sealing compound and smear the crankshaft with oil.
10 Place a new gasket in position on the crankcase joint face.

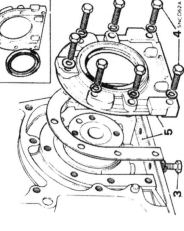
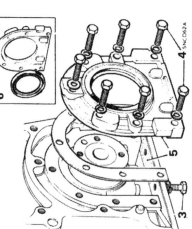

ENGINE — U.S.A. SPECIFICATION

DATA

Pistons
Bore size: Grade F .... 2.8995 to 2.9000 in (73.647 to 72.66 mm)
Grade G .... 2.9001 to 2.9006 in (73.663 to 73.673 mm)
Bottom diameter of piston: Grade F ... 2.8984 to 2.8989 in (73.619 to 73.632 mm)
Grade G ... 2.8990 to 2.8995 in (73.635 to 73.647 mm)
Pistons available .... +0.20 in (+0.53 mm)
Groove width: Oil control .... 0.1578 to 0.1588 in (3.99 to 4.01 mm)
Ring width: Top and second .... 0.064 to 0.065 in (1.625 to 1.650 mm)
Top and second .... 0.0615 to 0.0625 in (1.575 to 1.5787 mm)

Connecting rods
Small end bush (fitted) dia. .... 0.8126 to 0.8129 in (20.64 to 20.65 mm)
Gudgeon pin diameter .... 0.8123 to 0.8125 in (20.63 to 20.64 mm)

CRANKSHAFT PULLEY 12.21.01

Remove and refit

Removing
1 Remove the radiator, see 26.40.01.
2 Remove the fan.
3 Remove the air pump and drive belt, see 17.25.07.
4 Remove the fan belt.
5 Remove the carburetter, see 1 to 9, 30.15.15.
6 Press in the retaining clips and remove the pre-heater duct.
7 Remove the six nuts securing the catalytic converter to the exhaust manifold.
8 Support the engine.
9 Remove the nuts, bolts and washers securing the L.H. and R.H. engine mountings to the front mounting plate.
10 Raise the engine assembly to allow removal of the crankshaft pulley.
11 Remove the crankshaft pulley nut.
12 Withdraw the crankshaft pulley.

Refitting
13 Reverse the procedure in 1 to 12, noting:
a Fit a new exhaust manifold flange gasket.
b Ensure that the fan and air pump drive belts are correctly tensioned, see 'MAINTENANCE'.

ENGINE — U.S.A. SPECIFICATION

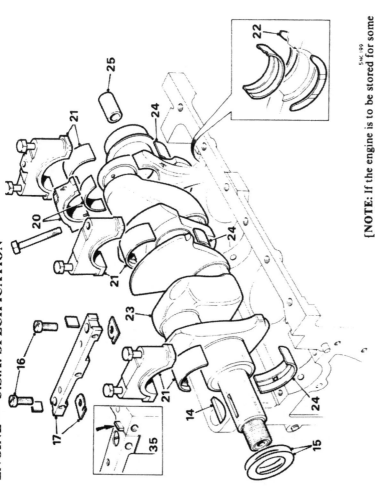

19 Check the identification marks on the connecting rod bearing caps and main bearing caps.
20 Remove the connecting rod bearings caps and bottom half bearings.
21 Remove the main bearing caps and bottom half bearings.
22 Remove the thrust washers from the rear main bearing.
23 Lift out the crankshaft.
24 Remove the main bearing top half shells and ensure that the bearing shells are identified with their respective locations for correct reassembly.
25 Remove the crankshaft spigot bush.

[NOTE: If the engine is to be stored for some time following repairs, it is advisable to use assembly lubricant (available from automotive supply stores) or a light coating of multipurpose grease on the crankpins rather than an ordinary engine oil. Many experienced mechanics choose to use assembly lubricant whenever new bearing shells are installed.]

Refitting

26 Smear the crankshaft spigot bush with zinc oxide grease and refit.
27 Fit the main bearings top half shells to the crankcase.
28 Fit the crankshaft to the crankcase.
29 Fit the thrust washers to the rear main bearing.
30 Fit the bearing shells to the lower main bearing caps.
31 Fit the main bearing caps and tighten the bolts to 50 to 65 lbf ft (2.2 to 2.8 kgf m).

32 Check the crankshaft end-float; adjust with selective thrust washers.
33 Refit the connecting rods to the crankshaft. Use new bolts and tighten to 50 lbf ft (6.9 kgf m) — colour dyed bolts or 46 lbf ft (6.4 kgf m) phosphated bolts.
34 Fit the front sealing block to the crankcase, using jointing compound on the gaskets. Do not tighten the screws.
35 Drive new wedges into the slots.
36 Align the face of the sealing block with the crankcase and tighten the screws.
37 Trim the protruding ends of the wedges.
38 Fit the crankshaft rear oil seal, see 12.21.20.
39 Fit the sump, renewing the gasket. Tighten the retaining set screws to 16 to 20 lbf ft.
40 Fit the engine rear adaptor plate.

41 Fit the flywheel, see 12.53.07, ensuring that the crankshaft spigot bush is in position.
42 Fit the clutch assembly, see 33.10.01.
43 Fit the front mounting plate and gasket noting:
   a Remove all traces of old gasket and jointing compound from the cylinder block face.
   b Smear the cylinder block face of the new gasket with jointing compound.
44 Fit the camshaft locating plate.
45 Fit the timing chain and sprockets, see 12.65.12.
46 Check the valve timing, see 12.65 08.
47 Fit the oil thrower ensuring that the dished periphery faces the timing cover.
48 Fit the timing chain cover, see 12.65.01.
49 Fit the crankshaft pulley, tightening the retaining nut to 150 lbf ft (20.7 kgf m).
50 Fit the thermostat and water pump housing assembly. Ensure that a new gasket is fitted, see 26.45.10.
51 Fit the engine assembly to the car, see 12.41.01.

DATA
Crankshaft

Main bearing journal diameter	2.3115 to 2.3120 in (58.713 to 58.725 mm)
Crankpin diameter	1.8750 to 1.8755 in (47.625 to 47.638 mm)
Crankshaft end-float tolerance	0.006 to 0.014 in (0.152 to 0.356 mm)
Maximum out of balance of shaft (with key and dowel fitted)	0.3 oz in (3.36 g cm)
Maximum run out of centre journal (with front and rear supported)	0.003 in (0.076 mm)
Thrust washer oversizes	0.005 in (0.13 mm)
Available bearing undersizes	0.010, 0.020, 0.030 in (0.25, 0.51, 0.76 mm)

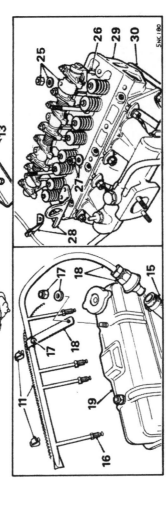

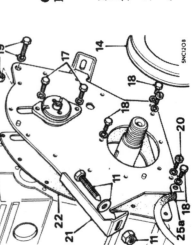

ENGINE — U.S.A. SPECIFICATION

CYLINDER BLOCK FRONT MOUNTING PLATE GASKET

Remove and refit   12.25.10

Removing
1. Disconnect the battery.
2. Remove the radiator, see 26.40.01.
3. Remove the air pump and drive belt, see 17.25.07.
4. Remove the fan belt.
5. Remove the water pump housing complete with water pump and fan, see 26.50.03.
6. Remove the air cleaner, see 'MAINTENANCE'.
7. Remove the two bolts to release the air cleaner casing and heat shield from the carburetter.
8. Press in the retaining clips and remove the pre-heater duct.
9. Remove the six nuts securing the catalytic converter to the exhaust manifold.
10. Support the engine.
11. Remove the nuts, bolts and washers securing the L.H. and R.H. engine mountings to the front mounting plate.
12. Raise the engine to allow removal of the crankshaft pulley.
13. Remove the crankshaft pulley nut.
14. Withdraw the crankshaft pulley.
15. Remove the timing gear cover, see 12.65.01.
16. Remove the timing chain and gears, see 12.65.12.
17. Remove the bolts securing the camshaft locating plate and withdraw the plate.
18. Remove the three set screws and washers securing the mounting plate to the cylinder block.
19. Remove the nut, bolt and washer securing the alternator bracket to the mounting plate.
20. Remove the two set screws and washers securing the mounting plate to the sealing block.
21. Remove the front mounting plate.
22. Remove the front mounting plate gasket.

Refitting
23. Remove all traces of old jointing compound from the cylinder block face.
24. Coat the cylinder block face of the new gasket with Wellseal or equivalent jointing compound.
25. Reverse the procedure in 1 to 22, noting:
   a Fit the engine earth lead to the mounting plate.
   b Fit a new thermostat and water pump housing gasket.
   c Fit a new exhaust manifold flange gasket.

CYLINDER HEAD GASKET — 1975-1976

Remove and refit   12.29.02

Removing
1. Disconnect the battery.
2. Disconnect the bottom radiator hose to drain the cooling system.
3. Remove the air temperature control valve hot air hose.
4. Disconnect the distributor vacuum pipe from the carburetter.
5. Disconnect the E.G.R. valve vacuum pipes from the carburetter.
6. Disconnect the breather pipe from the rocker cover.
7. Disconnect the fuel line from the carburetter.
8. Remove the two nuts and washers securing the carburetter assembly to the induction manifold.
9. Detach the carburetter assembly from the induction manifold and place to one side.
10. Unclip the distributor vacuum pipe flame-trap and move aside.
11. Remove the temperature transmitter from the thermostat housing, unclip the capillary tube from the air manifold and move aside.
12. Disconnect the thermostat housing hose from the induction manifold.
13. Remove the fan guard from the radiator.

continued

ENGINE – U.S.A. SPECIFICATION

14 Unscrew the three water pump housing bolts from the cylinder head.

15 Disconnect the diverter valve hose from the check valve.

16 Unscrew the four air manifold unions from the cylinder head.

17 Remove the rocker cover nuts and washers and slacken the air manifold support bracket screw.

18 Release the support bracket from the rear rocker cover stud and remove the air manifold and check valve assembly.

19 Remove the rocker cover.

20 Disconnect the spark plug leads.

21 Disconnect the exhaust manifold from the exhaust pipe.

22 Disconnect the running-on control valve vacuum pipe from the induction manifold.

23 Disconnect the heater control valve hose and the heater by-pass hose from the induction manifold.

24 Remove the exhaust manifold nut holding the heater return pipe bracket.

25 Remove the four nuts and washers securing the rocker shaft to the cylinder head and lift off the rocker shaft.

26 Remove the push rods, keeping them in their installed order.

27 Remove the ten nuts and washers securing the cylinder head to the block.

28 Remove the engine lifting bracket and the fuel pipe clips.

29 Lift off the cylinder head assembly.

30 Remove the cylinder head gasket and discard.

Refitting

31 Reverse the procedure in 1 to 30 noting:

a Use a new gasket, with the side of the gasket marked 'TOP' upwards.

b Slacken the alternator adjusting link nut and bolt to allow refitment of the three thermostat and water pump housing bolts to the cylinder head.

c Tighten the cylinder head nuts gradually in the sequence shown to a torque of 50 lbf ft (6.9 kgf m).

d Tighten the rocker shaft pedestal nuts to a torque of 26 to 32 lbf ft (3.6 to 4.4 kgf m).

e Fill the cooling system, see 'MAINTENANCE'.

32 Adjust the valve clearances, see 'MAINTENANCE'.

CYLINDER HEAD GASKET
– 1977 and later

Remove and refit   12.29.02

Removing

1 Disconnect the battery.

2 Drain the cooling system, see 26.10.01.

3 Remove the carburetter and place to one side, see 1 to 9, 30.15.15.

4 Disconnect the temperature transmitter from the thermostat housing.

5 Disconnect the thermostat housing from the induction manifold.

6 Remove the fan guard from the radiator.

7 Unscrew the three water pump housing bolts from the cylinder head.

8 Remove the bolt securing the flame trap bracket to the manifold and place the bracket to one side.

9 Disconnect the heater control valve hose from the induction manifold.

continued

continued

pull the replacement guide in and the old guide out. Ensure that the guide protrusion above the cylinder head top face is correct, see **DATA**.

Valve seat inserts

17 Machine the cylinder head to the dimensions given.
NOTE: When fitting a pair of valve seat inserts it will be necessary to machine the cylinder head and fit the first insert before machining the cylinder head for the second insert.

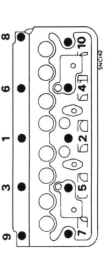

17

18 Press in the valve seat insert and peen over the cylinder head casting material to secure.
19 Cut seats in the inserts to the dimensions given in **DATA**.

EXHAUST

All 1975 engines and 1976 h.c. engines
A 0.250 to 0.255 in (6.35 to 6.48 mm)
B 1.249 to 1.250 in (31.72 to 31.75 mm)

1976 l.c. engines
A 0.260 to 0.265 in (32 to 32.13 mm)
B 1.254 to 1.255 in (31.85 to 31.87 mm)

INLET

All 1975 engines and 1976 h.c. engines
A 0.250 to 0.255 in (6.35 to 6.48 mm)
C 1.484 to 1.485 in (37.69 to 37.72 mm)

1976 l.c. engines
A 0.260 to 0.265 in (32 to 32.13 mm)
C 1.489 to 1.490 in (37.74 to 37.84 mm)

Reassembling

20 Lap in all the valves using carborundum paste.
21 Reverse the procedure in 2 to 11.
22 Refit the cylinder head, fitting a new gasket.

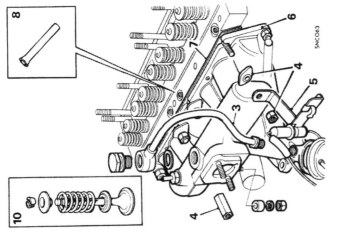

Inspection

12 Check each valve seat face; if necessary recondition the seat, removing the minimum amount of metal necessary to correct the seat. Fit valve seat inserts if the seats cannot be restored by refacing.
13 Check the valve guides, renew if worn.
14 Check the valves and renew valves with bent or worn stems (see DATA) or where the thickness of the valve head is reduced to 0.0312 in (0.8 mm) or below.
15 Check the valve springs — see DATA. Renew as necessary.

Valve guides

16 Using service tool 60A, with adaptor S 60A-2A assemble the replacement valve guide in the tool with the chamfered end uppermost (leading). Position the tool on the combustion chamber face of the cylinder head and

ENGINE — U.S.A. SPECIFICATION

10 Disconnect the running-on control valve hose (if fitted) from the induction manifold.
11 Slacken the nut securing the air pipe retaining clip to the gearbox.
12 Disconnect the air pipe from the exhaust manifold.
13 Press in the retaining clips and remove the pre-heater duct.
14 Remove the six nuts securing the catalytic converter to the exhaust manifold.
15 Remove the nut and washer securing the heater return pipe to the cylinder head stud.
16 Remove the rocker cover screws.
17 Withdraw the rocker cover placing the water temperature gauge capillary tube to one side.
18 Remove the four nuts and washers securing the rocker shaft to the cylinder head and lift off the rocker shaft.
19 Remove the push-rods, keeping them in their installed order.
20 Remove the 10 nuts and washers securing the cylinder head to the block.
21 Remove the engine lifting bracket.
22 Disconnect the spark plug leads.
23 Remove the cylinder head and gasket.

Refitting

24 Reverse the procedure in 1 to 23, noting:
a Use a new gasket, with the side of the gasket marked 'TOP' upwards.
b Slacken the alternator adjusting link nut and bolt to allow refitment of the three thermostat and water pump housing bolts to the cylinder head.
c Tighten the cylinder head nuts gradually in the sequence shown to a torque of 46 lbf ft (6.4 kgf m).
d Tighten the rocker shaft pedestal nuts to a torque of 26 to 32 lbf ft (3.6 to 4.4 kgf m).
e Fit a new exhaust manifold flange gasket.
f Fill the cooling system, see 'MAINTENANCE'.
g Adjust the valve clearances, see 'MAINTENANCE'.

CYLINDER HEAD — 1975-1976   12.29.19

Overhaul

Service tool: 18G 45, 60A, S 60A-2A

Dismantling

1 Remove the cylinder head, see 12.29.02.
2 Remove the spark plugs.
3 Remove the E.G.R. valve pipe.
4 Remove the nuts, washers and clamps securing the manifold assembly to the cylinder head.
5 Remove the E.G.R. valve and distributor vacuum pipe flame trap bracket.
6 Remove the induction and exhaust manifold assembly.
7 Remove the manifold gasket.
8 Remove the four injection tubes from the cylinder head.
9 Compress the valve springs using 18G 45.
10 Remove the valve cotter halves and the valve springs complete with the spring cups and seats.
11 Remove the inlet and exhaust valves and retain their assembly order.

ENGINE — U.S.A. SPECIFICATION

DATA

Valves
Valve insert seat angle: Inlet and exhaust	45½°
Head diameter: Inlet	1.377 to 1.383 in (34.97 to 35.01 mm)
Exhaust	1.168 to 1.172 in (29.66 to 29.76 mm)
Stem diameter: Inlet	0.3107 to 0.3113 in (7.89 to 7.91 mm)
Exhaust	0.3100 to 0.3106 in (7.874 to 7.889 mm)
Stem to guide clearance: Inlet	0.0007 to 0.0023 in (0.02 to 0.06 mm)
Exhaust	0.0015 to 0.0030 in (0.04 to 0.07 mm)

Valve guides
Length: Inlet and exhaust	2.06 in (52.224 mm)
Fitted height above head	0.75 in (19.050 mm)
Diameter: Inlet and exhaust:	
Outside	0.5015 to 0.502 in (12.73 to 12.75 mm)
Inside	0.312 to 0.313 in (7.92 to 7.95 mm)

Valve springs
Free length	1.52 in (38.6 mm)
Fitted length	1.342 in (1.29 mm)
Load at top of lift	123 $\pm^{10}_{0}$ lbf (55.8 $\pm^{4.54}_{0}$ kgf)
Number of working coils	3¾

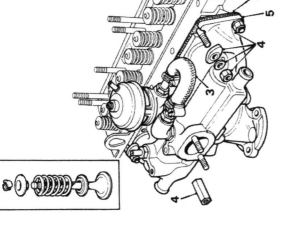

CYLINDER HEAD
— 1977 and later

Overhaul   12.29.19

Service tool: 18G 45, 60A, S 60A-2A

Dismantling
1 Remove the cylinder head, see 12.29.02.
2 Remove the spark plugs.
3 Remove the pipe connecting the E G R valve to the induction manifold.
4 Remove the nuts, washers and clamps securing the manifold assembly to the cylinder head.
5 Remove the induction and exhaust manifold assembly.
6 Remove the manifold gasket.
7 Compress the valve springs using 18G 45.
8 Remove the valve cotter halves and the valve springs complete with the spring cups and seats.
9 Remove the inlet and exhaust valves and retain their assembly order.

Inspection
10 Check each valve seat face; if necessary recondition the seat, removing the minimum amount of metal necessary to correct the seat. Fit valve seat inserts if the seats cannot be restored by refacing.
11 Check the valve guides, renew if worn.
12 Check the valves and renew valves with bent or worn stems (see DATA) or where the thickness of the valve head is reduced to 0.0312 in (0.8 mm) or below.
13 Check the valve springs – see DATA. Renew as necessary.

Valve guides
14 Using service tool 60A, with adaptor S 60A-2A assemble the replacement valve guide in the tool with the chamfered end uppermost (leading). Position the tool on the combustion chamber face of the cylinder head and pull the replacement guide in and the old guide out. Ensure that the guide protrusion above the cylinder head top face is correct, see DATA.

Valve seat inserts
15 Machine the cylinder head to the dimensions given.
NOTE: When fitting a pair of valve seat inserts it will be necessary to machine the cylinder head and fit the first insert before machining the cylinder head for the second insert.

15

SKC245B

16 Press in the valve seat insert and peen over the cylinder head casting material to secure.
17 Cut seats in the inserts to the dimensions given in DATA.

EXHAUST
A 0.260 to 0.265 in (32 to 32.13 mm)
B 1.254 to 1.255 in (31.85 to 31.87 mm)

INLET
A 0.260 to 0.265 in (32 to 32.13 mm)
C 1.489 to 1.490 in (37.74 to 37.84 mm)

Reassembling
20 Lap in all the valves using carborundum paste.
21 Reverse the procedure in 2 to 11.
22 Refit the cylinder head, fitting a new gasket.

continued

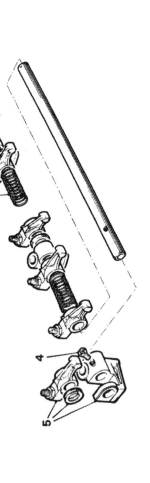

ENGINE – U.S.A. SPECIFICATION

DATA

Valves

Valve insert seat angle: Inlet and exhaust	$45\frac{1}{2}°$
Head diameter: Inlet	1.377 to 1.383 in (34.97 to 35.01 mm)
Exhaust	1.168 to 1.172 in (29.66 to 29.76 mm)
Stem diameter: Inlet	0.3107 to 0.3113 in (7.89 to 7.91 mm)
Exhaust	0.3100 to 0.3106 in (7.874 to 7.889 mm)
Stem to guide clearance: Inlet	0.0007 to 0.0023 in (0.02 to 0.06 mm)
Exhaust	0.0015 to 0.0030 in (0.04 to 0.07 mm)

Valve guides

Length: Inlet and exhaust	2.06 in (52.224 mm)
Fitted height above head	0.75 in (19.050 mm)
Diameter: Inlet and exhaust:	
Outside	0.5015 to 0.502 in (12.73 to 12.75 mm)
Inside	0.312 to 0.313 in (7.92 to 7.95 mm)

Valve springs

Free length	1.52 in (38.6 mm)
Fitted length	1.342 in (1.29 mm)
Load at top of lift	$123 {\pm 10 \atop 0}$ lbf ($55.8 {+4.54 \atop 0}$ kgf)
Number of working coils	$3\frac{3}{4}$

ROCKER SHAFT 12.29.54

Remove and refit

Removing

1 Disconnect the purge pipe from the rocker cover.
2 Remove the rocker cover screws and washers and place the coolant temperature gauge capillary tube to one side.
3 Remove the rocker cover and gasket.
4 Remove the four nuts and washers securing the rocker shaft pedestals to the cylinder head.
5 Lift off the rocker shaft.

Refitting

6 Reverse the procedure in 1 to 5, noting:
  a Fit a new rocker cover gasket if necessary.
  b Tighten the pedestal nuts to 26 to 32 lbf ft (3.6 to 4.4 kgf m).
  c Adjust the valve clearances, see 'MAINTENANCE'.
  d Ensure that the collars and seals are in place when refitting the rocker cover screws.

ROCKER SHAFT ASSEMBLY 12.29.55

Overhaul

Dismantling

1 Remove the rocker shaft, see 12.29.54.
2 Withdraw the split pin from the front end of the rocker shaft.
3 Slide off the rockers, pedestals, springs and spacers from the front end of the shaft, noting the order for reassembly.
4 Remove the screw locating the rear pedestal to the shaft.
5 Remove the rear pedestal complete with washer and rocker.

Reassembling

6 Reverse the procedure in 1 to 5 noting:
  a Renew all worn components.
  b Ensure that the oil-ways in the rockers and shaft are clear.
  c Apply Loctite 221 to the rear pedestal locating screw.
  d Ensure that the rear pedestal locating screw engages correctly in the rocker shaft.
7 Adjust the valve clearances, see 'MAINTENANCE'.

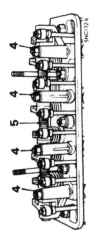

SNC172 B

ENGINE AND GEARBOX ASSEMBLY — 1975-1976　12.37.01

Remove and refit

Removing

1　Remove the bonnet.
2　Disconnect the battery.
3　Remove the car heater air intake hose.
4　Remove the radiator, see 26.40.01.
5　Remove the cooling fan.
6　Drain the engine oil.
7　Disconnect the carburetter assembly from the induction manifold and place aside, see 30.15.15.
8　Remove the three nuts and bolts securing the exhaust manifold to the exhaust pipe.
9　Disconnect the running-on control valve vacuum pipe from the inlet manifold.
10　Disconnect the heater hose from the water return pipe.
11　Disconnect the heater control valve hose from the inlet manifold.
12　Disconnect the water temperature capillary tube from the thermostat housing and the air manifold and check valve assembly.
13　Remove the rear rocker cover nut and slacken the air manifold support screw.
14　Release the support bracket from the rocker cover stud.
15　Disconnect the diverter valve hose from the check valve.
16　Unscrew the air manifold unions from the cylinder head and remove the air manifold and check valve assembly.
17　Disconnect the alternator lead plug at the alternator.
18　Disconnect the high tension ignition leads and remove the distributor cap.
19　Disconnect the low tension distributor leads.
20　Remove the air pump, see 17.25.07.
21　Disconnect the oil pressure gauge pipe from the engine.
22　Remove the bolt securing the engine earth strap to the engine and move the earth strap aside.
23　Disconnect the lead from the starter motor.
24　Remove the three nuts and bolts securing the exhaust front pipe to the rear pipe.

25　Disconnect the petrol hose from the petrol pipe at the union in the gearbox tunnel.
26　Disconnect the leads to the reverse light switch on the gearbox.
27　Remove the bolt securing the speedometer drive clamp to the gearbox.
28　Remove the clamp and withdraw the speedometer drive. Refit the clamp and bolt.
29　Remove the nut and bolt on the clamp securing the clutch slave cylinder to the gearbox.
30　Pull the clutch slave cylinder rearwards and place aside.
31　Detach the gearbox restraint cable from the gearbox.
32　Remove the four nuts, bolts and washers securing the propeller shaft to the gearbox.
33　Remove the two bolts and washers securing the rear mounting bracket to the floor panel.
34　Remove the gearbox tunnel carpet.
35　Remove the four screws securing the gear lever gaiter assembly.
36　Lift the gaiter assembly, press and turn the gear lever retaining cover and lift the assembly complete with the anti-rattle cup and spring from the gearbox.
37　Remove the two bolts and washers securing the rear mounting bracket to the gearbox tunnel.
38　Remove the two nuts securing the R.H. and L.H. front engine mountings to the engine bearer brackets.
39　Fit engine lifting brackets to the two engine lifting brackets using a shorter sling on the front bracket to ensure that the engine and gearbox assembly tilts at an angle of approximately 70° during removal.
40　Take the weight of the engine and gearbox assembly on the lifting slings and remove the two bolts and washers from the R.H. and L.H. front engine mountings.
41　Lift the engine and gearbox from the car using a second operator to lift the gearbox rear coupling over the crossmember in the gearbox tunnel.

Refitting
42　Reverse the procedure in 1 to 41.

ENGINE — U.S.A. SPECIFICATION

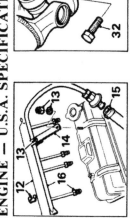
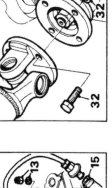

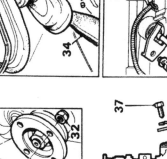
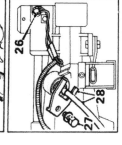
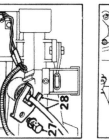
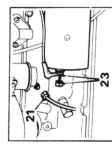
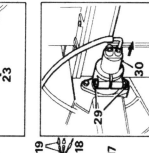
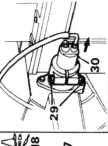

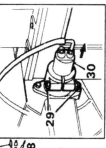

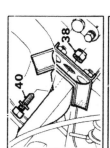
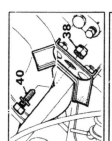

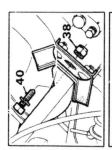
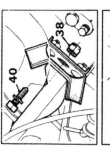

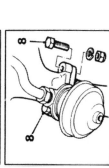

SNC 202A

ENGINE AND GEARBOX ASSEMBLY — 1977 and later   12.37.01

Remove and refit

Removing

1 Remove the bonnet.
2 Disconnect the battery.
3 Remove the car heater air intake hose.
4 Remove the radiator, see 26.40.01.
5 Remove the cooling fan.
6 Drain the engine oil.
7 Remove the catalytic converter, see 17.15.01.
8 Disconnect the running-on control valve vacuum pipe from the inlet manifold.
9 Disconnect the heater hose from the water return pipe.
10 Disconnect the heater control valve hose from the inlet manifold.
11 Disconnect the coolant temperature gauge capillary tube from the thermostat housing and the rocker cover and place aside.
12 Disconnect the hose from the check valve.
13 Disconnect the alternator lead plug at the alternator.
14 Disconnect the high tension ignition leads and remove the distributor cap.
15 Disconnect the low tension distributor leads.
16 Remove the air pump, see 17.25.07.
17 Disconnect the oil pressure gauge pipe from the engine.
18 Remove the bolt securing the engine earth strap to the engine and move the earth strap aside.
19 Disconnect the lead from the starter motor.
20 Disconnect the petrol hose from the petrol pipe at the union in the gearbox tunnel.
21 Disconnect the leads to the reverse light switch on the gearbox.
22 Remove the bolt securing the speedometer drive clamp to the gearbox.
23 Remove the clamp and withdraw the speedometer drive. Refit the clamp and bolt.
24 Remove the nut and bolt on the clamp securing the clutch slave cylinder to the gearbox.
25 Pull the clutch slave cylinder rearwards and place aside.
26 Detach the gearbox restraint cable from the gearbox.
27 Remove the four nuts, bolts and washers securing the propeller shaft to the gearbox.
28 Remove the two bolts and washers securing the rear mounting bracket to the floor panel.
29 Remove the gearbox tunnel carpet.
30 Remove the four screws securing the gear lever gaiter assembly.
31 Lift the gaiter assembly, press and turn the gear lever retaining cover and lift the assembly complete with the anti-rattle cup and spring from the gearbox.
32 Remove the two bolts and washers securing the rear mounting bracket to the gearbox tunnel.
33 Remove the two nuts securing the R.H. and L.H. front engine mountings to the engine bearer brackets.
34 Fit engine lifting slings to the two engine lifting brackets using a shorter sling on the front bracket to ensure that the engine and gearbox assembly tilts at an angle of approximately 70 during removal.
35 Take the weight of the engine and gearbox assembly on the lifting slings and remove the two bolts and washers from the R.H. and L.H. front engine mountings.
36 Lift the engine and gearbox from the car using a second operator to lift the gearbox rear coupling over the cross-member in the gearbox tunnel.

Refitting

37 Reverse the procedure in 1 to 36.

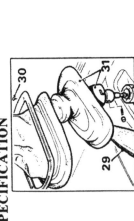
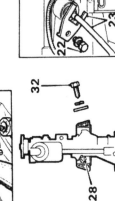
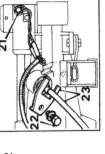
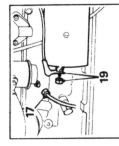
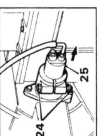

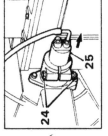

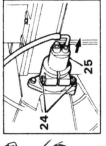
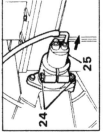
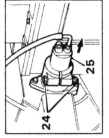

ENGINE – U.S.A. SPECIFICATION

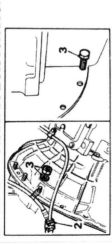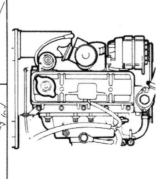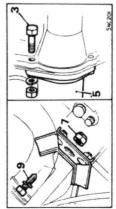

ENGINE ASSEMBLY — 1975-1976   12.41.01

Remove and refit

Removing

1 Disconnect or remove as necessary the ancillary equipment from the engine, see 12.37.01.
2 Disconnect the fuel inlet hose from the pump.
3 Remove the nuts, bolts and washers securing the gearbox housing and starter motor to the engine.
4 Move the gearbox restraint cable aside.
5 Detach the starter motor and place aside on the longitudinal member.
6 Support the gearbox.
7 Remove the two nuts securing the R.H. and L.H. front engine mountings to the engine bearer brackets.
8 Fit engine lifting slings to the engine lifting brackets.
9 Take the weight of the engine assembly on the lifting slings and remove the two bolts and washers from the R.H. and L.H. front engine mountings.
10 Lift the engine assembly from the car.

Refitting

11 Reverse the procedure in 1 to 10.

ENGINE ASSEMBLY — 1977 and later   12.41.01

Remove and refit

Removing

1 Disconnect or remove as necessary the ancillary equipment from the engine, see 12.37.01.
2 Disconnect the fuel inlet hose from the pump.
3 Remove the nuts, bolts and washers securing the gearbox housing and starter motor to the engine.
4 Move the gearbox restraint cable aside.
5 Detach the starter motor and place aside on the longitudinal member.
6 Support the gearbox.
7 Remove the two nuts securing the R.H. and L.H. front engine mountings to the engine bearer brackets.
8 Fit engine lifting slings to the engine lifting brackets.
9 Take the weight of the engine assembly on the lifting slings and remove the two bolts and washers from the R.H. and L.H. front engine mountings.
10 Lift the engine assembly from the car.

Refitting

11 Reverse the procedure in 1 to 10.

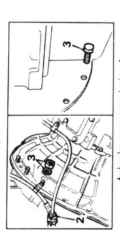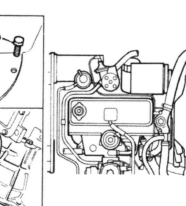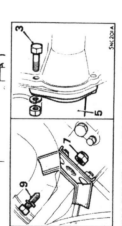

ENGINE MOUNTING FRONT L.H.   12.45.01

Remove and refit

Removing

1 Remove the air pump, see 17.25.07.
2 Remove the fan guard from the radiator.
3 Support the engine.
4 Remove the two nuts and washers securing the engine mounting to the body bracket.
5 Remove the nut, bolt and washer securing the engine mounting to the engine mounting foot.
6 Raise the engine and remove the engine mounting.

Refitting

7 Reverse the procedure in 1 to 6.

ENGINE MOUNTING FRONT R.H. — 1975-1976   12.45.03

Remove and refit

Removing

1 Slacken the three nuts and bolts securing the exhaust manifold to the exhaust pipe.

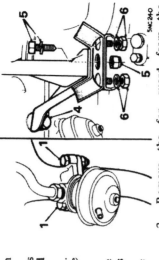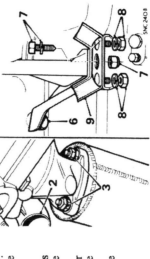

Remove the fan guard from the radiator.
2 Support the engine.
3 Slacken the bolt securing the engine restraint bracket to the cylinder block.
4 Remove the nut, bolt and. washer securing the engine mounting to the engine mounting foot.
5 Remove the two nuts and washers securing the engine mounting to the body bracket.
6 Raise the engine and remove the engine mounting.

Refitting

7 Reverse the procedure in 1 to 7.

ENGINE MOUNTING FRONT R.H. — 1977 and later   12.45.03

Remove and refit

Removing

1 Remove the carburetter and place aside, see 2 to 9, 30.15.15.
2 Press in the retaining clips and remove the pre-heater duct.   *continued*

Refitting

8 Reverse the procedure in 1 to 7.

97

12.37.01 USA

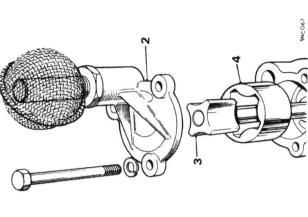
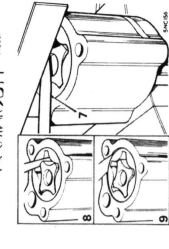

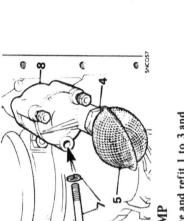

ENGINE – U.S.A. SPECIFICATION

3 Remove the six nuts securing the catalytic converter to the exhaust manifold.
4 Remove the fan guard from the radiator.
5 Support the engine.
6 Slacken the bolt securing the engine restraint bracket to the cylinder block.
7 Remove the nut, bolt and washer securing the engine mounting to the engine mounting foot.
8 Remove the two nuts and washers securing the engine mounting to the body bracket.
9 Raise the engine and remove the engine mounting.

Refitting
10 Reverse the procedure in 1 to 9.

FLYWHEEL

Remove and refit   12.53.07

Removing
1 Remove the clutch assembly, see 33.10.01.
2 Remove the four bolts securing the flywheel to the crankshaft.
3 Remove the flywheel.

Refitting
4 Clean the flywheel mating face. Check the locating dowel for damage, and ensure that the crankshaft spigot bush is correctly positioned.
5 Fit the flywheel to the crankshaft, locating it over the dowel in the crankshaft.

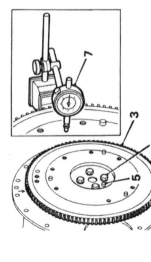

6 Tighten the flywheel retaining bolts evenly to 40 to 45 lbf ft (5.5 to 6.2 kgf m).
7 Using a dial indicator gauge, check the flywheel for run-out, not to exceed 0.002 in (0.051 mm) at 3.0 in (76.2 mm) radius from the spigot centre. Check concentricity, not to exceed 0.004 in (0.100 mm).
8 Refit the clutch assembly, see 33.10.01.

STARTER RING GEAR

Remove and refit   12.53.19

Removing
1 Disconnect the battery.
2 Remove the flywheel, see 12.53.07.
3 Drill a hole ¼ in (6.35 mm) diameter between any two teeth of the ring gear.
4 Hold the flywheel assembly in a soft jaw vice.
5 Place a cloth of heavy material over the ring gear for protection against flying fragments.
WARNING: Ensure adequate protection, particularly for the eyes, to prevent possible injury from flying fragments when the ring gear is split.
6 Place a cold chisel immediately above the centre line of the drilled hole and strike sharply to split the ring gear.

Refitting
7 Heat the replacement starter ring gear uniformly to a maximum of 200°C.
8 Place the flywheel on a flat surface, clutch face side uppermost, and clean the ring gear locating register.
9 Locate the ring gear and hold in position until it contracts sufficiently to grip the flywheel.
10 Allow the ring gear to cool gradually to avoid distortion.
11 Refit the flywheel, see 12.53.07, and check that ring gear eccentricity does not exceed 0.010 in (0.254 mm).

OIL PUMP

Remove and refit 1 to 3 and 7 to 9   12.60.26

Oil pick-up strainer 1 to 6, and 9   12.60.20

Removing
1 Drain the sump.
2 Remove the bolts securing the sump to the crankcase.
3 Remove the sump and gasket.
4 Release the oil strainer locknut.
5 Unscrew the oil strainer from the oil pump cover plate.
6 Wash the oil strainer in petrol and allow to dry before refitting.
7 Remove the three bolts and washers securing the oil pump to the crankcase.
8 Remove the oil pump assembly.

Refitting
9 Reverse the procedure in 1 to 8 as necessary, ensuring that the oil pump drive shaft engages correctly into the drive gear shaft.

OIL PUMP

Overhaul   12.60.32

Dismantling
1 Remove the oil pump, see 12.60.26.
2 Remove the cover plate complete with strainer.
3 Remove the inner rotor and shaft assembly.
4 Remove the outer rotor.

Inspecting
5 Clean all components.
6 Install the rotors in the pump body ensuring that the chamfered edge of the outer rotor is at the driving end of the pump body.
7 With a straight edge across the pump body face, check the clearance between the rotors and the straight edge.

ENGINE – U.S.A. SPECIFICATION

8 Check the clearance between the inner and outer rotors.
9 Check the clearance between the outer rotor and the pump body.
10 Renew the pump assembly if the clearances or end-floats measured in 7 to 9 exceed the figures given in DATA.
11 Check the cover plate for scoring, and test on a surface plate for distortion. Renew if necessary.
12 Check the pump spindle bearing surface in the pump body for excessive wear.

DATA
Oil pump

Inner rotor end-float	0.0004 in (0.1 mm)
Outer rotor end-float	0.0004 in (0.1 mm)
Rotor lobe clearance	0.010 in (0.25 mm)
Outer rotor to pump body diametrical clearance	0.008 in (0.2 mm)

OIL PRESSURE RELIEF VALVE

Remove and refit   **12.60.56**

Removing
1 Unscrew the relief valve body from the cylinder block.
2 Remove the washer and discard.
3 Withdraw the plunger.
4 Remove the spring.

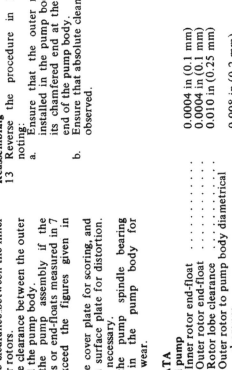

DATA

Oil pressure relief valve spring free length	1.53 in (38.8 mm)

Reassembling
13 Reverse the procedure in 1 to 4 noting:
   a. Ensure that the outer rotor is installed in the pump body with its chamfered end at the driving end of the pump body.
   b. Ensure that absolute cleanliness is observed.

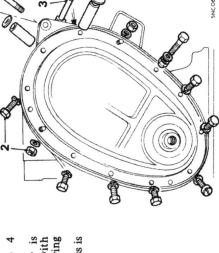

Refitting
5 Reverse the procedure in 1 to 4 noting:
   a Renew the washer.
   b Renew the spring if the free length is not in accordance with the figure given in **DATA**.

3 Withdraw the bottom air pump bolt and remove the spacer.
4 Remove the timing gear cover and gasket.
5 Remove the oil seal from the timing cover.

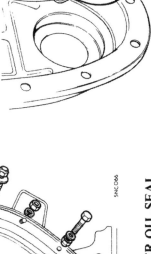

TIMING GEAR COVER OIL SEAL

Remove and refit   **12.65.05**
Timing gear cover 1 to 4 and 8   **12.65.01**

Service tool: 18G 134, 18G 134 BM

Removing
1 Remove the crankshaft pulley, see 12.21.01.
2 Remove the eight set screws, one bolt and three nuts complete with washers and spacer securing the timing gear cover to the cylinder block and air pump adjusting links.

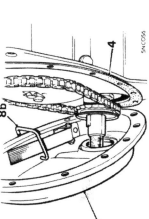

Refitting
6 Dip the new oil seal in engine oil before refitting.
7 Fit the new oil seal to the timing gear cover, using 18G 134 and 18G 134 BM.
8 Reverse the procedure in 1 to 4 noting:
   a. Fit a new gasket ensuring that it locates on the dowels.
   b. To facilitate refitment of the cover, compress the chain tensioner with a suitably bent length of rod, taking care not to damage the gasket when withdrawing the rod.

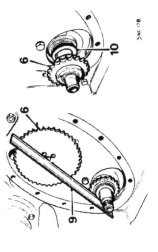

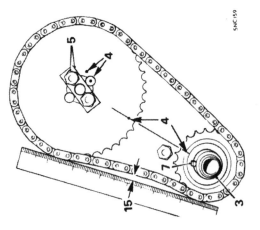

ENGINE – U.S.A. SPECIFICATION

VALVE TIMING

Check   12.65.08

1 Remove the rocker cover.
2 Adjust the rocker clearances of Nos. 7 and 8 valves to 0.050 in (1.27 mm), to give a working clearance.
3 Turn the crankshaft until No. 1 piston is at T.D.C. on compression stroke, indicated by the mark on the crankshaft pulley coinciding with the pointer on the timing cover.
4 Check that Nos. 1 and 2 valves are fully closed by inserting a feeler gauge between the valve tip and rocker pad to ascertain clearance.
5 Using two feeler gauges of the same thickness, check that the rocker clearances on Nos. 7 and 8 valves are equal. Oscillate the crankshaft to achieve this condition, but ensure that when the rocker clearances are the same the conditions in instructions 3 and 4 are maintained within a few degrees.
6 Should the valve timing prove to be incorrect, retiming will be necessary.
7 Re-adjust Nos. 7 and 8 valves to 0.010 in (0.25 mm).
8 Refit the rocker cover.

DATA

Valve timing

Inlet valve:	Opens	18° B.T.D.C.
	Closes	58° A.B.D.C.
Exhaust valve:	Opens	58° B.B.D.C.
	Closes	18° A.T.D.C.

Refitting

7 Remove the crankshaft drive key.
8 Temporarily fit both gear wheels.
9 Check the alignment of the gear wheels by placing a straight edge across the teeth of both gears.
10 Correct any misalignment by fitting selective shims behind the crankshaft gear wheel.
11 Remove the gear wheels.
12 Refit the drive key.
13 Assemble the timing chain and gear wheels and locate the engine ensuring that the marks on the gear wheels and the camshaft are aligned.
14 Refit the camshaft gear wheel securing bolts.
15 Check the timing chain wear by placing a straight edge along the slack run of chain. If movement at the mid-point exceeds 0.4 in (10 mm) renew the chain.
16 Remove the camshaft gear wheel securing bolts, fit a new lock plate and refit the bolts.
17 Refit the oil thrower with the dished periphery towards the timing gear cover.
18 Refit the timing gear cover, see 12.65.01.
NOTE: If new gear wheels are fitted make a punch mark on the crankshaft and camshaft gear wheels on a line scribed between the centres of the two gear wheels. Make also a punch mark on the camshaft and a corresponding mark on the camshaft gear wheel.

TIMING CHAIN AND GEARS

Remove and refit   12.65.12

Removing

1 Remove the timing gear cover, see 12.65.01.
2 Remove the oil thrower.
3 Turn the crankshaft until the timing marks on each gear are opposite each other.
4 When the marks on the timing gears are aligned the centre punch marks in the centre of the camshaft gear and on the camshaft should be aligned. Note that the camshaft centre punch mark is visible through the hole in the camshaft gear.
5 Bend back the lock plate tabs and remove the two bolts securing the gear wheel to the camshaft.
6 Taking care not to turn the crankshaft or camshaft, remove both gears together with the timing chain.

EMISSION CONTROL — 1975-1976

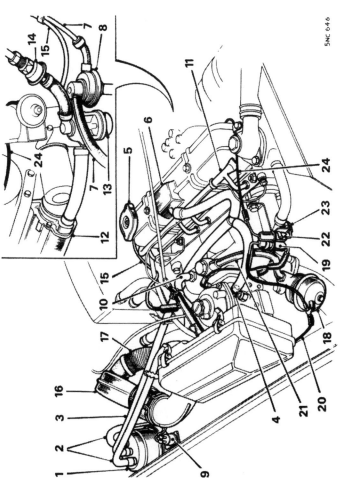

5NC 646

THE EMISSION CONTROL COMPONENTS

1 Charcoal adsorption canister
2 Vapour lines
3 Purge line
4 Restricted connection
5 Sealed oil filler cap
6 Oil separator/flame trap (arrester)
7 Fuel pipe
8 Fuel pump
9 Running-on control valve
10 Running-on control pipe
11 Air manifold
12 Air pump
13 Diverter valve
14 Check valve

15 Diverter valve pipe
16 Air temperature control valve
17 Hot air hose
18 Exhaust gas/recirculation valve
19 E G R valve flame trap
20 E G R valve line to carburetter choke cam
21 E G R valve pipe
22 Distributor flame trap
23 Distributor flame trap line to carburetter
24 Flame trap line to distributor vacuum unit

EXHAUST EMISSION CONTROL

General description

Air pressure is fed from an air pump via an injection manifold to the cylinder head exhaust port of each cylinder. A diverter valve in the air delivery line re-directs the supply of air pressure to atmosphere during conditions of deceleration and engine over-run. A check valve also in the air delivery line prevents blow-back from high pressure exhaust gases.

IMPORTANT: The efficient operation of the system is dependent on the engine being correctly tuned. The ignition and spark plug settings, valve clearances, and carburetter adjustments given for a particular engine (see 'ENGINE TUNING DATA') must be strictly adhered to at all times.

Air pump

The rotary vane type air pump is mounted on the front of the cylinder head and is belt driven from the crankshaft pulley. Provision is made for tensioning the belt.

Air is drawn into the pump through the radial intakes around the pulley.

Diverter valve

The diverter valve is fitted in the air delivery line between the air pump and the check valve. The valve re-directs excessive air pressure to atmosphere at high engine speed and also during conditions of deceleration and engine over-run.

Check valve

The check valve fitted in the pump discharge line to the injection manifold, protects the pump from the back-flow of exhaust gases.

Exhaust gas recirculation valve

The E G R valve is mounted on the exhaust manifold and controls a flow of exhaust gas from the exhaust manifold to the inlet manifold. The control signal is taken from a throttle edge tapping which gives no recirculation at idle speed. With the throttle open the degree of recirculation is dependent upon inlet manifold depression. At full throttle there is insufficient signal to open the valve. A cut-out valve breaks the signal to the E G R valve when the choke is in operation by opening an air bleed into the vacuum line.

Carburetter

The carburetter is manufactured to a special exhaust emission control specification and is tuned to give optimum engine performance with maximum emission control.

The metering needle is arranged in such a manner that it is always lightly spring loaded against the side of the jet to ensure consistency of fuel metering. A throttle by-pass valve limits the inlet manifold depression and ensures that during conditions of engine over-run the air/fuel mixture enters the engine cylinders in a combustible condition consistent with low emission levels.

Running-on control valve

The solenoid-operated valve is connected by hoses between the adsorption canister ventilation connection of the evaporative loss control system and the inlet manifold. A third hose connected to the valve is open to atmosphere for canister ventilation while the engine is running normally. The electrical circuit of the solenoid is connected through the ignition switch and an oil pressure operated switch.

The valve is fitted to prevent prolonged running-on.

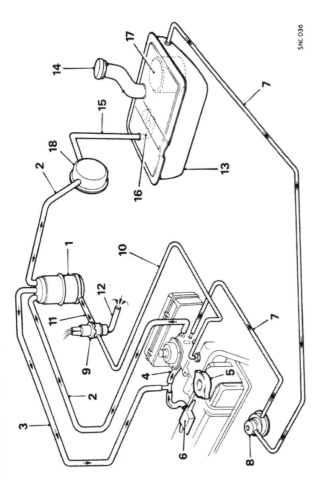

5NC 036

THE LAYOUT OF THE FUEL EVAPORATIVE LOSS CONTROL SYSTEM

1 Charcoal adsorption canister
2 Vapour lines
3 Purge line
4 Restricted connection
5 Sealed oil filter cap
6 Oil separator/flame trap (arrester)
7 Fuel pipe
8 Fuel pump
9 Running-in control valve
10 Running-on control pipe
11 Running-on control hose
12 Air vent pipe
13 Fuel tank
14 Sealed fuel filler cap
15 Vapour line
16 Vapour tube
17 Capacity limiting tank
18 Separation tank

EVAPORATIVE LOSS CONTROL

General description

The system is designed to collect vapour from the fuel in the fuel tank. The vapour is stored in an adsorption canister while the engine is stopped, and then after the engine is re-started, passed through the crankcase emission control system to the combustion chambers. While the car is being driven the vapours are drawn directly to the crankcase emission control system.

Ventilation tubes on the fuel tank ensure that vapours are vented through the control system.

To prevent spillage of fuel by displacement due to expansion, sufficient capacity is available to accommodate the amount of fuel from a full tank which would be displaced by a high temperature rise.

The position of the vent pipe connections prevents liquid fuel being carried with the vapour to the adsorption canister.

IMPORTANT: The fuel and oil filler caps seal the system, and it is essential for its efficient function that they are correctly refitted after removal.

Adsorption canister

The adsorption or vapour storage canister mounted in the engine compartment contains activated charcoal (carbon) granules. Filter pads are fitted at both sides of the charcoal to filter incoming ventilating air and to prevent the granules from leaving the canister through the purge line. Vapour tubes from the fuel tank, carburetter and the purge line to the carburetter depression chamber are connected to the ports on the top of the canister. The port on the bottom section provides a connection for the ventilating air tube.

Fuel vapour entering the canister through the vapour tubes is adsorbed and held by the charcoal. When the engine is started, air is drawn by the crankcase emission control system through the ventilation tube and into the canister. As the air passes over the charcoal granules the vapours are given up and are carried with the air through the crankcase emission control system to the combustion chambers.

Fuel expansion

To ensure that sufficient space is available to accommodate fuel displaced by expansion due to high ambient temperatures the fuel filler breather produces an air lock which prevents the tank being completely filled with fuel, thereby ensuring that sufficient space is always available for expansion.

CRANKCASE EMISSION CONTROL

General description

The engine breather outlet is connected by hoses to the controlled depression chamber (the chamber between the piston and the throttle disc valve) of the carburetter. Engine fumes and blow-by gases are drawn from the crankcase by the depression in this chamber, through an oil separator flame trap (arrestor) incorporated in the top of the valve rocker cover, and from there to the depression chamber. Air for engine breathing is drawn through the filtered adsorption canister of the evaporative loss control system and joins the engine fumes and blow-by gases drawn from the crankcase. A restrictor in the adsorption canister connection reduces the air flow to ensure crankcase depression under all conditions.

EMISSION CONTROL – 1975-1976

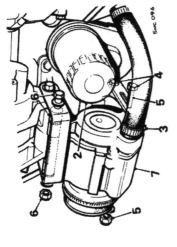

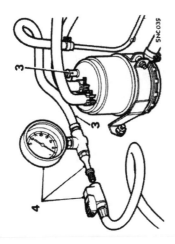

EVAPORATIVE LOSS CONTROL

Leak testing   17.15.01

NOTE: As a preliminary check for leaks on the induction and evaporative loss control systems, temporarily block the air vent pipe of the running-on control valve while the engine is idling. If no air leaks exist in the systems the engine will stop almost immediately; if the engine continues to run, an air leak is indicated.

If a fault in the operation of the system is suspected or components other than the canister have been removed and refitted, the evaporative loss control system must be pressure-tested for leaks as follows.

Testing

1 Check that there is at least one gallon of fuel in the fuel tank.
2 Run the engine for one minute to prime the fuel system.
3 Stop the engine, slacken the clip and disconnect the fuel tank ventilation pipe at the canister.
4 Connect a 0 to 10 lbf in² pressure gauge, a Schrader valve, and a low-pressure air supply (tyre pump) to the disconnected pipe.
5 Pressurize the system until 1 lbf in² is registered on the gauge. WARNING: Do not exceed this pressure at any time.
6 Check that the gauge is maintained for 10 seconds without falling more than 0.5 lbf in². If the reading is not maintained, check the system for leaks commencing with the fuel filler cap and seal.
7 Make a visual check for fuel leakage.
8 Remove the fuel tank filler cap and check that the gauge falls to zero.
9 Remove the test equipment.
10 Reconnect the fuel tank ventilation pipe to the canister.
11 Tighten the retaining clip.

AIR PUMP

Test   17.25.01

Faulty operation of the air pump is generally indicated by excessive noise from the pump.

1 Check the pump drive belt for correct tension; if incorrect, refer to 'MAINTENANCE'.
2 Connect a tachometer to the engine in accordance with the instrument maker's instructions.
3 Slacken the clip and disconnect the air supply hose at the diverter valve.
4 Connect 0 to 10 lbf in² pressure gauge to the diverter valve hose.
5 Run the engine at the air pump test speed as given in 'ENGINE TUNING DATA'. A gauge reading of not less than 1 to 1.50 lbf in² should be registered.
6 If the recommended air pump output pressure is not obtained, fit a new air pump, see 17.25.07.

AIR MANIFOLD

Remove and refit   17.25.17

Removing

1 Disconnect the hose from the check valve.
2 Holding the air manifold connection to prevent it twisting, unscrew the check valve from the air manifold.
3 Release the temperature gauge capillary tube clips from the air manifold.
4 Remove the support bracket screw and nut.
5 Remove the rocker cover rear nut and washer.
6 Release the support bracket from the rear rocker cover stud.
7 Unscrew the four air manifold unions from the cylinder head and remove the air manifold.
8 Remove the support bracket from the air manifold.

Refitting

9 Reverse the procedure in 1 to 8.

AIR PUMP

Remove and refit   17.25.07

Removing

1 Disconnect the air vent hose bracket and remove the hose.
2 Remove the oil filter cartridge.
3 Disconnect the air hose from the pump connection.
4 Slacken the mounting and adjusting link bolts and remove the drive belt from the pump pulley.
5 Unscrew the nut and remove the adjusting link bolt.
6 Support the pump, unscrew the nut and remove the top mounting bolt and spacer.
7 Remove the air pump.

Refitting

8 Reverse the procedure in 1 to 7.

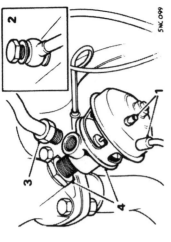

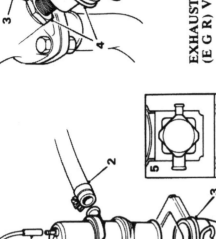

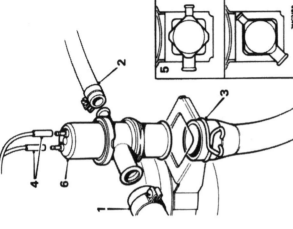

EXHAUST GAS RECIRCULATION (E G R) VALVE

Remove and refit   17.45.01

Removing

1. Disconnect the vacuum pipe from the E G R valve.
2. Remove the banjo bolt securing the metal pipe to the inlet manifold.
3. Unscrew the union nut securing the metal pipe to the E G R valve.
4. Slacken the locknut and unscrew the E G R valve from the exhaust manifold.

Refitting

5. Screw the valve into the manifold.
6. Place the pipe in position to align the bottom union with the E G R valve, screw or unscrew the E G R valve as required. Place the pipe aside.
7. Tighten the locknut.
8. Reverse the procedure in 1 to 3.
9. Reset the E G R valve service interval counter.

RUNNING-ON CONTROL VALVE

Remove and refit   17.40.01

Removing

1. Slacken the clip and disconnect the running-on control hose from the valve.
2. Disconnect the running-on control pipe from the valve.
3. Squeeze the ends of the wire clip and disconnect the vent pipe from the bottom of the valve.
4. Disconnect the electrical leads from the valve.
5. Turn the valve 45° to align the base with the body panel cut-out.
6. Remove the running-on control valve.

Refitting

7. Reverse the procedure in 1 to 6.

AIR TEMPERATURE CONTROL VALVE

Check   17.30.02

Checking

1. Ensure that the engine and air cleaner are cold.
2. Check the position of the valve plate.
3. The valve plate should be against the cold air intake (hot air position).
4. Start the engine and run it to normal operating temperature.
5. Observe the action of the valve plate which should move towards the hot air hose (cold air position).

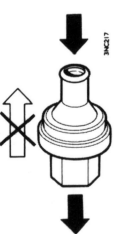

EMISSION CONTROL — 1975-1976

CHECK VALVE

Test   17.25.22

Testing

CAUTION: Do not use a pressure air supply for this test.

1. Remove the check valve, see 17.25.17.
2. Blow through the valve, orally, in turn from each connection. Air should only pass through the valve when blown from the air supply hose connection. If air passes through the valve when blown from the air manifold connection, renew the check valve.
3. Refit the check valve.

DIVERTER VALVE

Remove and refit   17.25.26

Removing

1. Release the air intake hose from the heater.
2. Disconnect the hose from the check valve.
3. Disconnect the air pump hose from the diverter valve bracket.
4. Remove the vacuum pipe from the diverter valve.
5. Remove the nuts and bolts to release the diverter valve and gasket.
6. Remove the vacuum pipe connector from the valve.
7. Remove the check valve hose from the diverter valve.

Refitting

8. Reverse the procedure in 1 to 6.

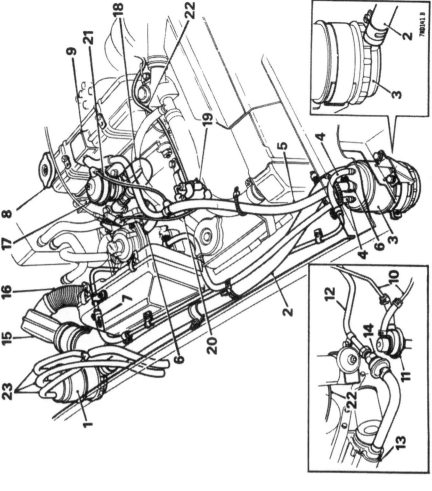

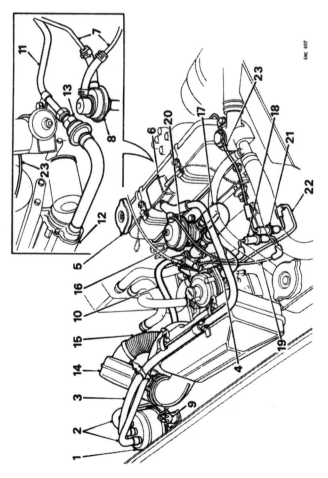

EMISSION CONTROL — 1977 AND LATER

1977 EMISSION CONTROL COMPONENTS

1   Charcoal adsorption canister
2   Vapour lines
3   Purge line
4   Restricted connection
5   Sealed oil filler cap
6   Oil separator/flame trap (arrester)
7   Fuel pipe
8   Fuel pump
9   Running-on control valve } (if fitted)
10 Running-on control pipe }
11 Air injection pipe
12 Air pump
13 Check valve
14 Air temperature control valve
15 Hot air hose
16 Exhaust gas/recirculation valve
17 E G R valve pipe
18 E G R valve flame trap
19 E G R valve flame trap line to carburetter
20 Flame trap line to E G R valve
21 Distributor flame trap
22 Distributor flame trap line to carburetter
23 Flame trap line to distributor vacuum unit

1978 and later EMISSION CONTROL COMPONENTS — Canada and U.S.A. except California

1   Secondary charcoal adsorption canister
2   Canister inter-connecting pipe
3   Primary charcoal adsorption canister
4   Vapour lines
5   Purge line
6   Restricted connection
7   Restrictor
8   Sealed oil filler cap
9   Oil separator/flame trap (arrester)
10 Fuel pipe
11 Fuel pump
12 Air injection pipe
13 Air pump
14 Check valve
15 Air temperature control valve
16 Hot air hose
17 Exhaust gas recirculation valve
18 E.G.R. valve pipe
19 Flame trap
20 Flame trap line to carburetter
21 Flame trap line to E.G.R. valve
22 Flame trap line to distributor vacuum unit
23 Vent pipes

17.00.01 [77 and later]

EMISSION CONTROL – 1977 and later

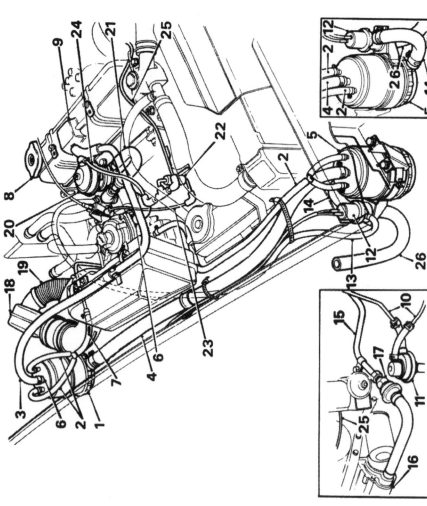

EXHAUST EMISSION CONTROL

General description

Air pressure is fed from an air pump via an injection pipe to the exhaust manifold. A check valve in the air delivery line prevents blow-back from high pressure exhaust gases.

IMPORTANT: The efficient operation of the system is dependent on the engine being correctly tuned. The ignition and spark plug settings, valve clearances, and carburetter adjustments given for a particular engine (see 'ENGINE TUNING DATA') must be strictly adhered to at all times.

Air pump

The rotary vane type air pump is mounted on the front of the cylinder head and is belt driven from the crankshaft pulley. Provision is made for tensioning the belt.

Air is drawn into the pump through the radial intakes around the pulley.

A relief valve fitted in the pump re-directs excessive air pressure to atmosphere at high engine speed and also during conditions of deceleration and engine over-run.

Check valve

The check valve fitted in the pump discharge line to the injection manifold, protects the pump from the back-flow of exhaust gases.

The valve shuts if the air pressure ceases while the engine is running; for example, if the pump drive belt should break.

Catalytic converter

The catalytic converter is fitted in the exhaust system, between the exhaust manifold flange and the exhaust pipe, in order to reduce the carbon monoxide and hydrocarbon emissions.

Exhaust gas recirculation valve

The E G R valve is mounted on the exhaust manifold and controls a flow of exhaust gas from the exhaust manifold to the inlet manifold. The control signal is taken from a throttle edge tapping which gives no recirculation at idle speed. With the throttle open the degree of recirculation is dependent upon inlet manifold depression. At full throttle there is insufficient signal to open the valve.

Carburetter

The carburetter is manufactured to a special exhaust emission control specification and is tuned to give optimum engine performance with maximum emission control.

The metering needle is arranged in such a manner that it is always lightly spring loaded against the side of the jet to ensure consistency of fuel metering. A throttle by-pass valve limits the inlet manifold depression and ensures that during conditions of engine over-run the air/fuel mixture enters the engine cylinders in a combustible condition consistent with low emission levels.

Running-on control valve (if fitted)

The solenoid-operated valve is connected by hoses between the adsorption canister ventilation connection of the evaporative loss control system and the inlet manifold. A third hose connected to the valve is open to atmosphere for canister ventilation while the engine is running normally. The electrical circuit of the solenoid is connected through the ignition switch and an oil pressure operated switch.

The valve is fitted to prevent prolonged running-on.

EVAPORATIVE LOSS CONTROL

General description

The system is designed to collect vapour from the fuel in the fuel tank. The vapour is stored in an adsorption canister while the engine is stopped, and then after the engine is re-started, passed through the crankcase emission control system to the combustion chambers. While the car is being driven the vapours are drawn directly to the crankcase emission control system.

Ventilation tubes on the fuel tank ensure that vapours are vented through the control system.

To prevent spillage of fuel by displacement due to expansion, sufficient capacity is available to accommodate the amount of fuel from a full tank which would be displaced by a high temperature rise.

1978 AND LATER EMISSION CONTROL COMPONENTS – California only

1 Primary charcoal adsorption canister
2 Vapour lines
3 Purge line
4 Canister inter-connecting pipe
5 Secondary charcoal adsorption canister
6 Restricted connection
7 Restrictor
8 Sealed oil filler cap
9 Oil separator/flame trap (arrester)
10 Fuel pipe
11 Fuel pump
12 Running-on control valve
13 Running-on control pipe
14 Running-on control hose
15 Air injection pipe
16 Air pump
17 Check valve
18 Air temperature control valve
19 Hot air hose
20 Exhaust gas recirculation valve
21 E.G.R. valve pipe
22 Flame trap
23 Flame trap line to carburetter
24 Flame trap line to E.G.R. valve
25 Flame trap line to distributor vacuum unit
26 Air vent pipe

EMISSION CONTROL — 1977 and later

LAYOUT OF THE FUEL EVAPORATIVE LOSS CONTROL SYSTEM (1977 only)

1 Charcoal adsorption canister	10 Running-on control pipe
2 Vapour lines	11 Running-on control hose } (if fitted)
3 Purge line	12 Air vent pipe
4 Restricted connection	13 Fuel tank
5 Sealed oil filter cap	14 Sealed fuel filler cap
6 Oil separator/flame trap (arrester)	15 Vapour line
7 Fuel pipe	16 Vapour tube
8 Fuel pump	17 Capacity limiting tank
9 Running-on control valve (if fitted)	18 Separation tank

For safety reasons a restrictor is fitted in the vapour hose prior to its connection to the primary adsorption canister to permit small air flows which are likely to occur with fuel vapour or replacement air, and to prevent the possibility of liquid fuel being carried with the vapour to the adsorption canisters under fuel filling conditions.

IMPORTANT: The fuel and oil filler caps seal the system, and it is essential for its efficient function that they are correctly refitted after removal.

Adsorption canister

The adsorption or vapour storage canisters mounted in the engine compartment contain activated charcoal (carbon) granules. Filter pads are fitted at both sides of the charcoal to filter incoming ventilating air and to prevent the granules from leaving the canister through the purge line.

LAYOUT OF THE FUEL EVAPORATIVE LOSS CONTROL SYSTEM Canada and U.S.A. except California (1978 and later only)

1 Secondary charcoal adsorption canister	9 Oil separator flame trap (arrester)
2 Primary charcoal adsorption canister	10 Fuel pipe
3 Canister inter-connecting pipe	11 Fuel pump
4 Vapour lines	12 Fuel tank
5 Purge line	13 Sealed fuel filler cap
6 Restricted connection	14 Vapour line
7 Restrictor	15 Vapour tube
8 Sealed oil filler cap	16 Capacity limiting tank
	17 Separation tank
	18 Vent pipes

Canada and USA except California: Vapour tubes from the fuel tank, carburetter and purge line from the engine breather system are connected to the ports on top of the primary canister. The primary and secondary canisters are inter-connected.

California only: Vapour tubes from the fuel tank, carburetter and purge line from the engine breather system are connected to the ports on the top of the primary and secondary canisters. The primary and secondary canisters are inter-connected. The port on the bottom section of the secondary canister provides a connection for the running-on control valve hose.

Fuel vapour entering the canisters through the vapour tubes and inter-connecting pipe is adsorbed and held by the charcoal. When the engine is started, air is drawn by the crankcase emission

LAYOUT OF THE FUEL EVAPORATIVE LOSS CONTROL SYSTEM — California (1978 and later only)

1 Primary charcoal adsorption canister	11 Fuel pump
2 Vapour lines	12 Running-on control valve
3 Purge line	13 Running-on control pipe
4 Canister inter-connecting pipe	14 Running-on control hose
5 Secondary charcoal adsorption canister	15 Air vent pipe
6 Restricted connection	16 Fuel tank
7 Restrictor	17 Sealed fuel filler cap
8 Sealed oil filler cap	18 Vapour line
9 Oil separator/flame trap (arrester)	19 Vapour tube
10 Fuel pipe	20 Capacity limiting tank
	21 Separation tank

control system into the canister(s). As the air passes over the charcoal granules the vapours are given up and are carried with the air through the crankcase emission control system to the combustion chambers.

Fuel expansion

To ensure that sufficient space is available to accommodate fuel displaced by expansion due to high ambient temperatures the fuel filler breather produces an air lock which prevents the tank being completely filled with fuel, thereby ensuring that sufficient space is always available for expansion.

CRANKCASE EMISSION CONTROL – USA and Canada

General description

The engine breather outlet is connected by hoses to the controlled depression chamber (the throttle disc valve) of the carburetter. Engine fumes and blow-by gases are drawn from the crankcase by the depression in this chamber, through an oil separator flame trap (arrester) incorporated in the top of the valve rocker cover, and from there to the depression chamber. Air for engine breathing is drawn through the filtered adsorption canister of the evaporative lose control system and joins the engine fumes and blow-by gases drawn from the crankcase. A restrictor in the adsorption canister connection reduces the air flow to ensure crankcase depression under all conditions.

107

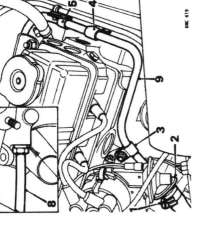

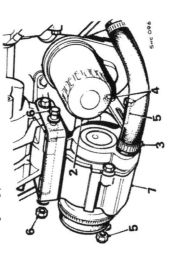

EMISSION CONTROL — 1977 and later

EVAPORATIVE LOSS CONTROL — USA and Canada

Leak testing   17.15.01

Canada and U.S.A. — 1977

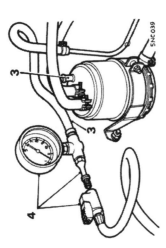

NOTE: California only. As a preliminary check for leaks on the induction and evaporative loss control systems, temporarily block the air vent pipe of the running-on control valve while the engine is idling. If no air leaks exist in the systems the engine will stop almost immediately; if the engine continues to run, an air leak is indicated.

If a fault in the operation of the system is suspected or components other than the two canisters have been removed and refitted, the evaporative loss control system must be pressure-tested for leaks as follows.

Canada and U.S.A. except California — 1978 and later

Testing

1 Check that there is at least one gallon of fuel in the fuel tank.
2 Run the engine for one minute to prime the fuel system.
3 Stop the engine, slacken the clip, and disconnect the hose as shown.
4 Connect a 0 to 10 lbf in² pressure gauge, a Schrader valve, and a low-pressure air supply (tyre pump) to the disconnected pipe.
5 Pressurize the system until 1 lbf in² is registered on the gauge. WARNING: Do not exceed this pressure at any time.
6 Check that the gauge is maintained for 10 seconds without falling more than 0.5 lbf in². If the reading is not maintained, check the system for leaks commencing with the fuel filler cap and seal.
7 Make a visual check for fuel leakage.
8 Remove the fuel tank filler cap and check that the gauge falls to zero.
9 Remove the test equipment.
10 Reconnect the fuel tank ventilation pipe to the canister.
11 Tighten the retaining clip.

California only — 1978 and later

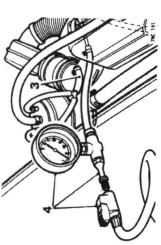

1 Check the pump drive belt for correct tension; if incorrect, refer to 'MAINTENANCE'.
2 Connect a tachometer to the engine in accordance with the instrument maker's instructions.
3 Slacken the clip and disconnect the air supply hose at the diverter valve.
4 Connect 0 to 10 lbf in² pressure gauge to the diverter valve hose.
5 Run the engine at the air pump test speed as given in 'ENGINE TUNING DATA'. A gauge reading of not less than 1 to 1.50 lbf in² should be registered.
6 If the recommended air pump output pressure is not obtained, fit a new air pump, see 17.25.07.

AIR INJECTION PIPE

Remove and refit   17.25.20

Removing

1 Disconnect the hose from the check valve.
2 Holding the air injection pipe connection to prevent it twisting, unscrew the check valve from the air injection pipe.
3 Remove the nut and washer securing the air injection pipe bracket and distributor pedestal to the cylinder block.
4 Slacken the nut to release the air injection pipe bracket from the gearbox casing.
5 Release the clip retaining the fuel pipe bracket to the air injection pipe.
6 Remove the air cleaner, see 'MAINTENANCE'.
7 Remove the two screws and washers to release the air cleaner casing and heat shield from the carburetter.
8 Disconnect the air injection pipe from the exhaust manifold.
9 Remove the air injection pipe.

Refitting

10 Reverse the procedure in 1 to 9.

AIR PUMP

Remove and refit   17.25.07

Removing

1 Disconnect the air vent hose bracket and remove the hose.
2 Remove the oil filter cartridge.
3 Disconnect the air hose from the pump connection.
4 Slacken the mounting and adjusting link bolts and remove the drive belt from the pump pulley.
5 Unscrew the nut and remove the adjusting link bolt.
6 Support the pump, unscrew the nut and remove the top mounting bolt and spacer.
7 Remove the air pump.

Refitting

8 Reverse the procedure in 1 to 7.

AIR PUMP

Test   17.25.01

Faulty operation of the air pump is generally indicated by excessive noise from the pump.

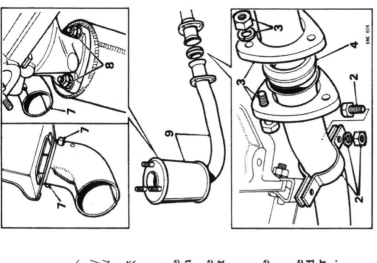

EMISSION CONTROL — 1977 and later

RUNNING-ON CONTROL VALVE   17.40.01

Remove and refit

Removing

1 Slacken the clip and disconnect the running-on control hose from the valve.
2 Disconnect the running-on control pipe from the valve.
3 Squeeze the ends of the wire clip and disconnect the vent pipe from the bottom of the valve.
4 Disconnect the electrical leads from the valve.
5 Turn the valve 45° to align the base with the body panel cut-out.
6 Remove the running-on control valve.

Refitting

7 Reverse the procedure in 1 to 6.

CHECK VALVE

Test   17.25.22

Testing

CAUTION: Do not use a pressure air supply for this test.

1 Remove the check valve, see 17.25.17.
2 Blow through the valve, orally, in turn from each connection. Air should only pass through the valve when blown from the air supply hose connection. If air passes through the valve when blown from the air manifold connection, renew the check valve.
3 Refit the check valve.

AIR TEMPERATURE CONTROL VALVE

Check   17.30.02

Checking

1 Ensure that the engine and air cleaner are cold.
2 Check the position of the valve plate.
3 The valve plate should be against the cold air intake (hot air position).
4 Start the engine and run it to normal operating temperature.
5 Observe the action of the valve plate which should move towards the hot air hose (cold air position).

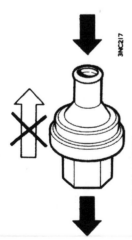

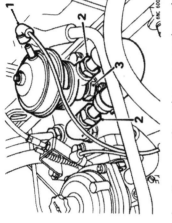

2 Remove the pipe connecting the EGR valve to the induction manifold.
3 Slacken the locknut and unscrew the EGR valve from the exhaust manifold.

Refitting

4 Screw the locknut to the top of the threads.
5 Screw the valve into the manifold.
6 Place the pipe in position to align the unions with the EGR valve and induction manifold adaptor, screw or unscrew the EGR valve as required.
7 Place the pipe aside.
   Tighten the locknut.
8 Reverse the procedure in 1 and 2.

EXHAUST GAS RECIRCULATION (EGR) VALVE   17.45.01

Remove and refit

Removing

1 Disconnect the vacuum pipe from the EGR valve.

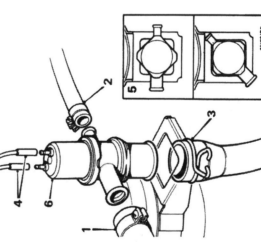

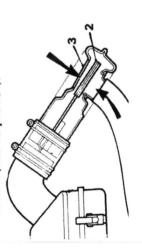

8 Remove the six nuts securing the catalytic converter to the exhaust manifold.
9 Remove the catalytic converter together with the manifold flange gasket from the car.

Refitting

10 Fit a new catalytic converter, by reversing the procedure in 1 to 9, noting:
  a Renew the exhaust manifold flange gasket and exhaust pipe olive.
  b Renew the carburetter manifold gasket.
11 CALIFORNIA ONLY. Reset the service interval counter by inserting the key into the button, and rotating the counters to zero. Remove the key.

CATALYTIC CONVERTER

Remove and refit   17.50.01

Removing

1 Jack up and support the front of the car.
2 Remove the catalytic converter support bracket.
3 Release the catalytic converter from the rear pipe.
4 Remove the olive.
5 Remove the carburetter and place to one side, see 30.15.15, instructions 2 to 9.
6 Remove the two screws retaining the air cleaner casing and heat shield to the carburetter.
7 Press in the retaining clips and remove the pre-heater duct.

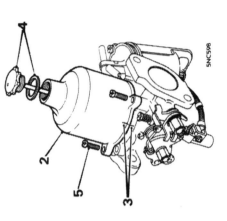

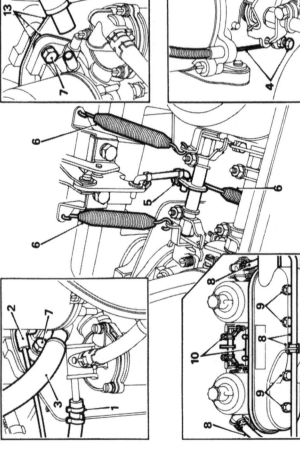

CARBURETTERS

Remove and refit   19.15.11

[Warning: **Fuel and fuel vapors will be discharged during the following procedure. Do not smoke or work near heaters or other fire hazards. Have a fire extinguisher handy.**]

Removing

1   Disconnect the fuel feed hose from the rear carburetter.

2   Disconnect the distributor vacuum pipe from the rear carburetter.

3   Disconnect the engine breather hose and adaptor from each carburetter.

4   Release the mixture control (choke) cable from the rear carburetter and remove the trunnion and screw.

5   Detach the throttle control linkage lever from the arm on the throttle interconnection rod and remove the retaining clip.

6   Detach the three throttle return springs from the carburetter linkage.

7   Remove the four bolts and washers to release the carburetters and air cleaner assembly from the induction manifold and collect the heat shield and gaskets.

8   Detach the fuel pipe from the clip on the air cleaner and disconnect the fuel hoses from the carburetter float chambers.

9   Remove the four bolts to release the air cleaner assembly and gaskets from the carburetters.

10   Separate the carburetters and collect the throttle interconnection rod and the cold start interconnection rod.

Refitting

11   Reverse the procedure in 8 to 10.

12   Fit the four bolts and washers to the carburetter flanges.

13   Fit the heat shield, with a gasket either side, to the carburetters.

14   Fit the assembly to the induction manifold, starting the two top bolts first and checking that the gaskets are in position before the bolts are tightened.

15   Reverse the procedure in 1 to 6 and check and adjust the carburetter settings, see MAINTENANCE.

CARBURETTERS

Overhaul and adjust   19.15.18

[CAUTION: **Please read the instructions thoroughly before you attempt carburetor repairs. If you lack the necessary skills or tools we suggest you leave this work to an Authorized Dealer or other qualified shop. Before taking a removed carburetor in for repair, thoroughly clean its exterior but do not undertake any disassembly.**]

Dismantling

1   Remove the carburetters, see 19.15.11.

2   Thoroughly clean the outside of the carburetters.

3   Mark the relative position of the suction chamber and the carburetter body.

4   Remove the damper and its washer.

5   Unscrew the suction chamber securing screws and lift off the chamber.

6   Remove the piston spring.

7   Carefully lift out the piston assembly and empty the oil from the piston rod.

8   Remove the guide locking screw and withdraw the needle assembly, taking care not to bend the needle. Withdraw the needle from the guide and remove the spring from the needle.

9   Push the piston lifting pin upwards, detach its securing circlip and withdraw the pin and spring downwards.

10   Release the pick-up lever return spring from its retaining lug.

11   Support the plastic moulded base of the jet and remove the screw retaining the jet pick-up link and link bracket (when fitted).

continued

FUEL SYSTEM — U.K. SPECIFICATION

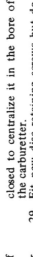

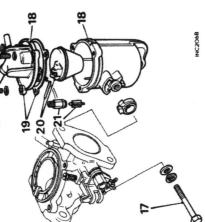

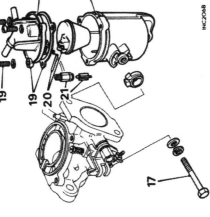

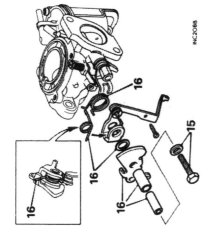

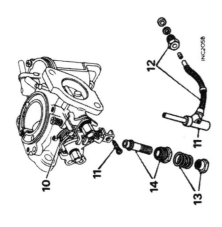

12 Unscrew the flexible jet tube sleeve nut from the float-chamber and withdraw the jet assembly. Note the gland, washer and ferrule at the end of the jet tube.

13 Remove the jet adjusting nut and spring.

14 Unscrew the jet locking nut and detach the nut and jet bearing; withdraw the bearing from the nut.

15 Unscrew and remove the lever pivot bolt and spacer.

16 Detach the lever assembly and return springs, noting the pivot bolt tubes, skid washer and the locations of the cam and pick-up lever springs.

17 Remove the float-chamber securing bolt and the chamber.

18 Mark the float-chamber lid location.

19 Remove the lid securing screws and detach the lid with its joint washer and float.

20 Hold the float hinge pin at its serrated end and withdraw the pin and float.

21 Extract the float needle from its seating and unscrew the seating from the lid.

22 Close the throttle and mark the relative position of the throttle disc and the carburetter flange. CAUTION: Do not mark the throttle disc in the vicinity of the limit valve.

23 Unscrew the disc retaining screws, open the throttle and ease the disc from its slot in the throttle spindle. Store the disc in a safe place until required for assembly.

24 Tap back the tabs of the lock washer securing the spindle nut; remove the nut and detach the lever arm, washer and throttle spindle; note the location of the lever arm in relation to the spindle and carburetter body.

Inspecting

25 Examine the components as follows:
   a Check the throttle spindle in the body for excessive play, and renew if necessary.
   b Examine the float needle for wear, i.e. small ridges or grooves in the seat of the needle, and that the spring-loaded plunger on the opposite end operates freely.

Replace the needle and seating if necessary.
   c Inspect all other components for wear and damage; renew unserviceable components.

Reassembling

26 Refit the spindle to the body, with the countersunk holes in the spindle facing outwards.

27 Assemble the spacing washer, lever, lock washer and securing nut, ensure that the idling stop on the lever is against the idling screw abutment on the body in the closed throttle position. Tighten the spindle nut and lock with the tab washer.

28 Insert the throttle disc into the spindle slot; note the markings for reassembling, i.e. the limit valve positioned at the bottom of the disc with the head of the valve towards the engine. Manoeuvre the disc in the spindle until the throttle can be closed, snap the throttle open and closed to centralize it in the bore of the carburetter.

29 Fit new disc retaining screws but do not fully tighten, check that the disc closes fully and adjust its position as necessary. Tighten the screws fully and spread their split ends just enough to prevent them turning.

30 Screw the seating into the float-chamber; do not overtighten. Insert the needle coned-end first into the seating.

31 Refit the float to the chamber lid and insert the hinge pin.

32 Refit the float-chamber lid with a new joint washer, noting the securing screw markings, tighten the securing screws evenly.

33 Refit the float-chamber to the body and tighten the retaining bolt.

34 Refit the piston lifting pin, spring and circlip.

35 Clean fuel deposits off the suction chamber and piston with fuel or methylated spirit and wipe dry. CAUTION: DO not use abrasives.

continued

111

FUEL SYSTEM – U.K. SPECIFICATION

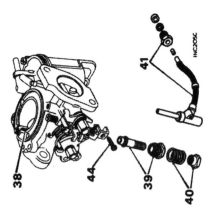

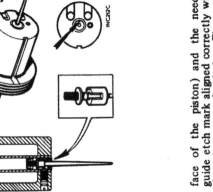
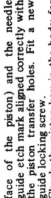

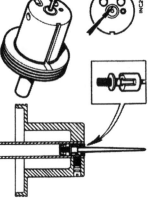

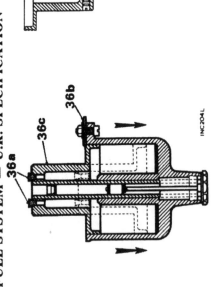

36 Check the operation of the suction chamber and piston (without the spring fitted) as follows:

a Refit the damper and washer to the suction chamber; temporarily plug the piston transfer holes with rubber plugs or Plasticine and insert the piston fully into the suction chamber.

b Secure a large flat washer to one of the fixing holes with a screw and nut so that it overlaps the bore.

c With the assembly upside-down, hold the piston and check the time taken for the suction chamber to fall the full extent of its travel. The time taken should be five to seven seconds; if this time is exceeded, check the piston and chamber for cleanliness and mechanical damage. Renew the assembly if the time taken is still not within these limits.

37 Fit the spring and guide to the needle and insert the assembly into the piston (with the guide fitted flush with the face of the piston) and the needle guide etch mark aligned correctly with the piston transfer holes. Fit a new guide locking screw.

38 Check the piston key in the body for security.

39 Refit the jet bearing; fit and tighten the jet locking nut.

40 Refit the spring and jet adjustment nut; screw the nut up as far as possible.

41 Insert the jet into the bearing, fit the brass sleeve nut, washer and gland to the end of the flexible tube (if removed). The tube must project a minimum of $\frac{3}{16}$ in (4.8 mm) beyond the gland. Tighten the brass sleeve nut until the gland is compressed; overtightening can cause leakage.

42 Refit the piston, spring and suction chamber to the body (noting the assembly marks) and tighten the securing screws evenly.

43 Reverse the instructions 16 and 15.

44 Hold up the choke lever to relieve pressure on the jet pick-up link, refit the link bracket (when fitted), support the end of the moulded jet and tighten the securing screw.

45 Screw the jet adjusting nut down two complete turns (12 flats) to provide the initial setting.

46 Refit the carburetters, see 19.15.11.

47 Tune the carburetters, see MAINTENANCE.

FLOAT CHAMBER NEEDLE AND SEAT

Remove and refit   19.15.24

Removing

1 Disconnect the engine breather hose and adaptor from the carburetter.

2 Detach the fuel pipe from the clip on the air cleaner container.

3 Disconnect the fuel hose(s) from the float chamber.

4 Mark the float chamber and float chamber lid for assembly.

5 Remove the three screws securing the float chamber lid.

6 Remove the lid and float assembly.

7 Hold the float pin at its serrated end and withdraw the pin to release the float from the lid.

8 Extract the float needle from its seating and unscrew the float chamber seat from the lid.

Inspecting

9 Examine the float needle for wear, i.e. small ridges or grooves in the seat of the needle; also check that the spring loaded plunger on the opposite end operates freely. Renew the needle and seat if the needle is worn.

Refitting

10 Clean any sediment from the float chamber and fit a new joint washer if required.

11 Reverse the procedure in 1 to 8.

FUEL SYSTEM – U.K. SPECIFICATION

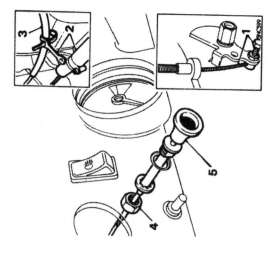

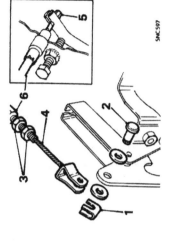

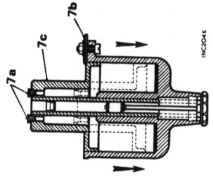

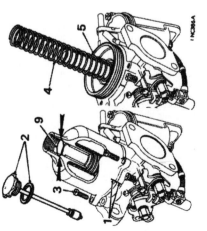

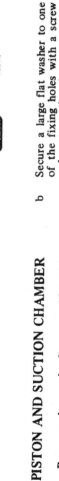

PISTON AND SUCTION CHAMBER

Remove, clean and refit   19.15.28

Removing

1 Mark the relative position of the suction chamber and the carburetter body.
2 Remove the damper and its washer.
3 Unscrew the suction chamber securing screws and lift off the chamber.
4 Remove the piston spring.
5 Carefully lift out the piston assembly and empty the oil from the piston rod.
6 Clean fuel deposits off the suction chamber and piston with fuel or methylated spirit and wipe dry.

CAUTION: Do not use abrasives.

7 Check the operation of the suction chamber and piston (without the spring fitted) as follows:

a Refit the damper and washer to the suction chamber; temporarily plug the piston transfer holes with rubber plugs or Plasticine and insert the piston fully into the suction chamber.

b Secure a large flat washer to one of the fixing holes with a screw and nut so that it overlaps the bore.

c With the assembly upside-down, hold the piston and check the time taken for the suction chamber to fall the full extent of its travel. The time taken should be five to seven seconds; if this time is exceeded, check the piston and chamber for cleanliness and mechanical damage. Renew the assembly if the time taken is still not within these limits.

Refitting

8 Refit the piston, spring and suction chamber to the carburetter (noting the assembly marks) and tighten the screws evenly.
9 Top up each piston damper with multigrade engine oil until the level is ½ in (13 mm) above the top of the hollow piston rod.
10 Refit each piston damper with its washer.

THROTTLE CABLE

Remove and refit   19.20.06

Removing

1 Remove the clip securing the throttle linkage retaining pin.
2 Remove the retaining pin.
3 Slacken the locknut and unscrew the adjusting nut from the outer cable abutment.
4 Release the cable from the support bracket.
5 Disconnect the cable from the throttle pedal linkage.
6 Remove the cable assembly from the car.

Refitting

7 Reverse the procedure in 1 to 6, adjusting the outer cable abutment nuts to take up any slack in the inner cable.

MIXTURE CONTROL (CHOKE) CABLE ASSEMBLY

Remove and refit   19.20.13

Removing

1 Slacken the trunnion screw and release the inner cable from the carburetter linkage.
2 Remove the strap to release the cable from the heater hose.
3 Remove the rubber sleeve from the cable.
4 Unscrew the cable securing nut behind the fascia.
5 Pull the cable assembly from the fascia, collecting the nut and washer.

Refitting

6 Reverse the procedure in 1 to 5, checking that the mixture control knob has ⅟₁₆ in (2 mm) free movement before the cable starts to pull on the lever.

FUEL SYSTEM – U.K. SPECIFICATION

FUEL PUMP

Remove and refit   19.45.08

[**WARNING: Fuel and fuel vapors will be discharged during the following procedure. Do not smoke or work near heaters or other fire hazards. Have a fire extinguisher handy.**]

Removing

1 Squeeze the ends of the clip and remove the inlet hose.
2 Squeeze the ends of the clip, and remove the outlet hose.
3 Remove the two securing nuts and spring washers.
4 Remove the pump and gasket.

Refitting

5 Reverse the procedure in 1 to 4 using a new gasket.

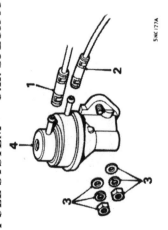

FUEL TANK

Remove and refit   19.55.01

[**Warning: Fuel and fuel vapors will be discharged during the following procedure. Do not smoke or work near heaters or other fire hazards. Have a fire extinguisher handy.**]

Service tool: 18G 1001

1 Disconnect the battery.
2 Slacken the clip and disconnect the filler hose from the fuel tank inlet pipe.
3 Detach the harness clips from the front mounting flange of the fuel tank.
4 Disconnect the fuel gauge tank unit electrical connection.
5 Support the fuel tank.
6 Disconnect the fuel pipe from the fuel tank.
   NOTE: As no facility for draining is provided, a clean container, should be placed beneath the tank before removing the feed pipe if the tank is full.
7 Remove the nuts, spring washers and plain washers securing the tank to the boot floor noting the position of the harness retaining clip.
8 Remove the fuel tank.
9 Remove the wire from the fuel gauge tank unit.
10 Remove the fuel gauge tank unit using tool 18G 1001.
11 Remove the pad from the filler neck.

Refitting
12 Reverse the procedure in 1 to 11.

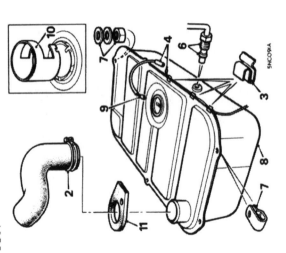

moves the E G R air bleed valve fully home.

19 Start the engine and run until normal operating temperature is reached then adjust the fast idle, see 'MAINTENANCE'.

18 Check the adjustment of the mixture control as follows:
  a Pull out the control and check that the starter lever abuts against its stop.
  b Push the control in and check that the stop on the starter lever

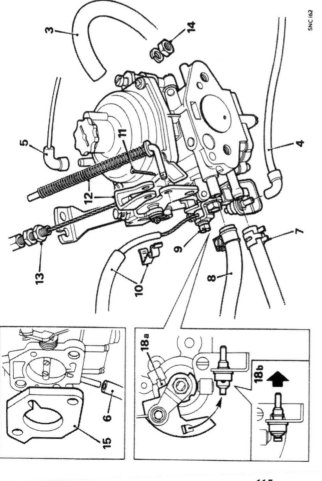

SNC448

SNC162

FUEL SYSTEM — U.S.A. SPECIFICATION

CARBURETTER — Non catalytic converter cars — 1975-1976

Remove and refit   19.15.09

[WARNING: Fuel and fuel vapors will be discharged during the following procedure. Do not smoke or work near heaters or other fire hazards. Have a fire extinguisher handy.]

Removing
1 Remove the air cleaner element, see 'MAINTENANCE'.
2 Remove the two bolts to release the air cleaner cover and gasket.
3 Remove the purge pipe.
4 Remove the pipe from the E G R air bleed valve.
5 Remove the E G R valve flame-trap pipe.
6 Remove the anti-run on valve pipe.
7 Squeeze the ends of the clip and remove the fuel delivery pipe.
8 Slacken the clip and remove the vapour pipe.

9 Slacken the screw securing the mixture control inner cable to the starter box lever.
10 Pull the mixture control cable from its clip on the carburetter.
11 Remove the split pin from the spring retaining rod.
12 Remove the spring retaining rod complete with spring to release the throttle cable yoke from the carburetter.
13 Unscrew the nut from the outer cable abutment to release the throttle cable from the support bracket.
14 Remove the two nuts securing the carburetter to the induction manifold.
15 Remove the carburetter and insulating block.

Refitting
16 Reverse the procedure in 1 to 15.
17 Adjust the throttle cable abutment nuts to take up slack in the inner cable.

CARBURETTER — Catalytic converter cars — 1975-1976

Remove and refit   19.15.09

[WARNING: Fuel and fuel vapors will be discharged during the following procedure. Do not smoke or work near heaters or other fire hazards. Have a fire extinguisher handy.]

Removing
1 Remove the air cleaner element, see 'MAINTENANCE'.
2 Remove the two bolts to release the air cleaner cover, gasket and heat shield.
3 Remove the purge pipe.
4 Remove the E G R valve flame trap pipe.
5 Disconnect the distributor vacuum pipe flame trap elbow from the vacuum pipe.
6 Remove the distributor vacuum pipe from the carburetter.

7 Squeeze the ends of the clip and remove the fuel delivery pipe.
8 Slacken the clip and remove the vapour pipe.
9 Slacken the clips and remove the two water hoses from the auto-choke.
10 Disconnect the carburetter link rod ball joint from the roller lever.
11 Remove the two nuts securing the carburetter to the induction manifold.
12 Remove the carburetter and insulating block.

Refitting
13 Reverse the procedure in 1 to 12.
14 Check and adjust the automatic fuel enrichment unit, see 19.15.47.
15 Tune the carburetter, see 'MAINTENANCE'.

FUEL SYSTEM – U.S.A. SPECIFICATION

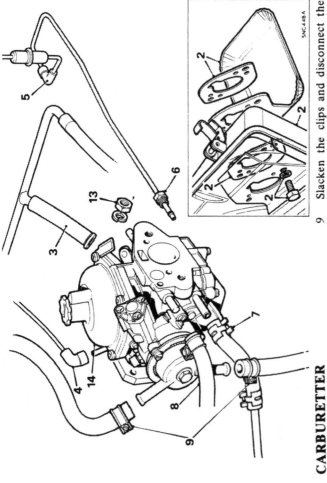

CARBURETTER
– 1977 and later

Remove and refit   19.15.09

[WARNING: Fuel and fuel vapors will be
discharged during the following procedure.
Do not smoke or work near heaters or other
fire hazards. Have a fire extinguisher handy.]

Removing

1   Remove the air cleaner element, see
    'MAINTENANCE'.

2   Remove the two bolts to release the
    air cleaner cover, gasket and heat
    shield.

3   Remove the purge pipe.

4   Remove the E G R valve flame trap
    pipe.

5   Disconnect the distributor flame trap
    elbow from the vacuum pipe.

6   Remove the distributor vacuum pipe
    from the carburetter.

7   Squeeze the ends of the clip and
    disconnect the fuel pipe.

8   Slacken the clip and remove the
    vapour hose.

9   Slacken the clips and disconnect the
    two water hoses from the auto-choke.

10 Remove the two screws and washers
    to release the throttle cable abutment
    bracket from the induction manifold.

11 Unscrew the throttle cable adjuster
    lower locknut and release the throttle
    cable and throttle return spring from
    the abutment bracket.

12 Remove the split pin and washers to
    release the throttle cable and throttle
    return spring from the carburetter
    throttle lever.

13 Remove the two nuts securing the
    carburetter to the induction manifold.

14 Remove the carburetter and insulating
    block.

Refitting

15 Check and adjust the automatic fuel
    enrichment unit (auto-choke), see
    19.15.47.

16 Reverse the procedure in 1 to 14.

17 Top up the cooling system, see
    'MAINTENANCE'.

18 Tune the carburetter, see
    'MAINTENANCE'.

FUEL SYSTEM – U.S.A. SPECIFICATION

CARBURETTER – Non catalytic converter cars

Overhaul and adjust   19.15.17

[CAUTION: Please read the instructions thoroughly before you attempt carburetor repairs. If you lack the necessary skills or tools we suggest you leave this work to an Authorized Dealer or other qualified shop. Before taking a removed carburetor in for repair, thoroughly clean its exterior but do not undertake any disassembly.]

Service tool: S353

Dismantling

1 Remove the carburetter, see 19.15.09.
2 Unscrew the damper cap.
3 Raise the piston with a finger and at the same time carefully ease the retaining cap from the air valve assembly.
4 Pull the bottom plug from the float chamber.
5 Drain the carburetter of oil and fuel.
6 Remove the 'O' ring from the plug.
7 Remove the six screws securing the float-chamber to the body.
8 Remove the float-chamber and gasket.
9 Remove the float assembly by gently prising the spindle from the clip at each end.
10 Remove the needle valve and washer.
11 Remove the four screws securing the top cover to the body.
12 Remove the top cover.
13 Remove the spring.
14 Remove the air valve assembly.
15 Remove the four screws securing the diaphragm and retaining ring to the air valve assembly.
16 Remove the diaphragm and the retaining ring.
17 Slacken the grubscrew in the side of the air valve.
18 Insert the tool S353 into the stem of the air valve, turn it anti-clockwise approximately two turns, withdraw the needle and housing by pulling it firmly and straight with the fingers.

CAUTION: The needle adjuster is a captive assembly in the stem of the air valve and no attempt should be made to remove it.

19 Remove the two screws securing the starter box to body and remove the starter box.
20 Remove the E G R air-bleed valve and bracket.
21 Remove the nut and lockwasher from the starter spindle.
22 Remove the choke cable lever and fast idle cam from the spindle.
23 Remove the starter disc assembly from the starter body.
24 Remove the 'C' clip.
25 Remove the spring from the starter disc spindle.
26 Remove the two screws securing the idle air regulator assembly to the body.

27 Remove the idle air regulator and gasket.
28 Remove the three screws securing the deceleration by-pass valve to the body.
29 Remove the deceleration by-pass valve and gasket.
30 Remove the three cross-head screws to release the base plate from the valve housing.
31 Remove the spring, valve and gaskets from the deceleration by-pass valve body.
32 Remove the star washer to release the adjustment screw from the valve housing.
33 Remove the 'O' ring seal from the adjustment screw and unscrew the locknut.
34 Remove the idle adjustment screw and spring.
35 Remove the split pin, withdraw the clevis pin and washers to disconnect the linkage from the throttle spindle lever.
36 Remove the retaining nut and remove the lever from the throttle spindle.
37 Remove the retainer and spring from the throttle spindle.

Inspection

38 Wash all components in clean fuel, allow to drain dry or use compressed air. Place all components on a clean surface.
39 Examine the condition of all components for wear, paying special attention to needle and seat, air valve and diaphragm all of which should be renewed unless in exceptionally good condition. Use clean compressed air to blow through all ports, needle valve and starter box.
40 Renew the carburetter if the components of the starter box, idle and air regulator or deceleration by-pass valve are damaged.

Reassembling

41 Fit the spring and retainer to the throttle spindle.
42 Refit the throttle lever and secure with the nut.
43 Connect the linkage to the throttle lever.

continued

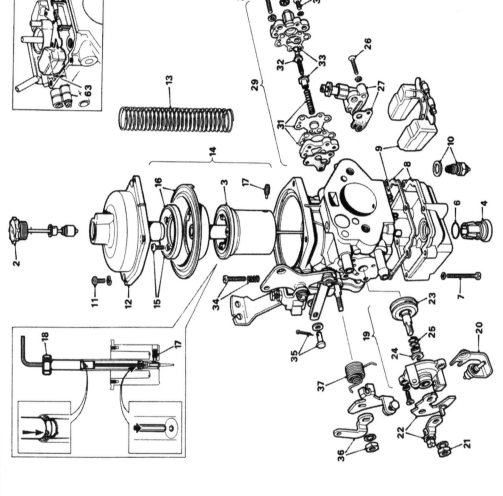

FUEL SYSTEM — U.S.A. SPECIFICATION

44 Refit the throttle adjustment screw and spring.

45 Fit the deceleration by-pass valve sandwiched between the gaskets to the base plate, ensuring the register for the spring is towards the valve body.

46 Assemble the spring and deceleration by-pass valve body to the base plate and secure with the three cross-head screws.

47 Fit the deceleration by-pass valve and gasket to the body of the carburetter and secure with the three screws.

48 Refit the spring to the spindle and secure with the 'C' clip.

49 Refit the disc assembly to the starter body ensuring the lug with the detent ball is between the slot of the disc and the largest of the series of holes.

50 Refit the cam lever and choke cable lever, ensuring the cam lever is located on the detent ball.

51 Secure the levers with the lockwasher and nut.

52 Refit the starter and E G R air bleed valve bracket to the carburetter body and secure with two screws.

53 Insert the needle housing assembly into the bottom of the air valve.

54 Fit tool S353, turning clockwise to engage the threads of the needle valve assembly with the adjusting screw; continue turning until the slot in the needle housing is aligned with the grub screw.

55 Tighten the grub screw.

NOTE: The grub screw does not tighten on the needle housing but locates into the slot. This ensures that, during adjustment, the needle will remain in its operating position, i.e. biased, by a spring in the needle housing, towards the air cleaner side of the carburetter.

56 Fit the diaphragm, locating the inner tag into the recess of the air valve.

57 Fit the diaphragm retaining ring and secure with four screws.

58 Fit the air valve assembly, locating the outer tag and rim of the diaphragm in complementary recesses in the carburetter body.

59 Fit the carburetter top cover with the bulge on the housing neck towards the air intake.

60 Fit and evenly tighten the top cover securing screws.

61 Fit the needle valve and sealing washer.

62 Fit the float assembly by levering the pivot pin gently into position.

63 Check the float height by measuring the distance between the carburetter gasket face and the highest point of the floats. The float height must be equal and set to 16 to 17 mm (0.625 to 0.672 in). Adjust by bending the tabs ensuring that the tab sits on the needle valve at right angles.

64 Fit the float-chamber gasket.

65 Fit the float-chamber and secure with the six screws.

66 Fit the 'O' ring to the bottom plug.

67 Press the bottom plug into the float chamber.

68 Fit the carburetter, see 19.15.09.

69 Fill the carburetter damper dashpot with recommended engine oil, using the damper as a dipstick, until the threaded plug is 6 mm (0.25 in) above the dashpot when resistance is felt, see 'MAINTENANCE'.

70 Raise the piston and carefully press the damper retaining cap into the air valve.

71 Screw the damper cap onto the top cover.

72 Tune the carburetter, see 'MAINTENANCE'.

CARBURETTER — Catalytic converter cars

Overhaul and adjust   19.15.17

[CAUTION: Please read the instructions thoroughly before you attempt carburetor repairs. If you lack the necessary skills or tools we suggest you leave this work to an Authorized Dealer or other qualified shop. Before taking a removed carburetor in for repair, thoroughly clean its exterior but do not undertake any disassembly.]

Service tool: S353

Dismantling

1 Remove the carburetter, see 19.15.09.

2 Unscrew the damper cap.

3 Raise the piston with a finger and at the same time carefully ease the retaining cap from the air valve assembly.

4 Pull the bottom plug from the float chamber.

5 Drain the carburetter of oil and fuel.

6 Remove the 'O' ring from the plug.

7 Remove the six screws securing the float-chamber to body.

8 Remove the float-chamber and gasket.

9 Remove the float assembly by gently prising the spindle from the clip at each end. Note that the metal plate supporting the floats is positioned towards the outside of the float.

10 Remove the needle valve and washer.

11 Remove the four screws securing the top cover to the body.

12 Remove the top cover.

13 Remove the spring.

14 Remove the air valve assembly, noting the position of the diaphragm outer tag in the carburetter body.

15 Remove the four screws securing the diaphragm and retaining ring to the air valve assembly.

16 Remove the diaphragm and the retaining ring, noting the position of the diaphragm inner tag in the air valve assembly.

17 Slacken the grubscrew in the side of the air valve.

18 Insert the tool S 353 into the stem of the air valve, turn the tool centre spindle anti-clockwise two or three complete turns; the needle housing assembly will be progressively exposed from the air valve as the tool is turned.

19 Remove the grubscrew and pull out the needle and housing assembly. Remove the tool.
CAUTION: The needle adjuster is a captive assembly in the stem of the air valve and no attempt should be made to remove it.

20 Unclip and remove the idle air regulator cover.

21 Remove the two screws securing the idle air regulator assembly to the body.

22 Remove the idle air regulator and gasket.

23 Remove the three screws securing the deceleration by-pass valve to the body.

24 Remove the deceleration by-pass valve and gasket.

25 Remove the three cross-head screws to release the base plate from the valve housing.

26 Remove the spring, valve and gaskets from the deceleration by-pass valve body.

27 Remove the star washer to release the adjustment screw from the valve housing.

28 Remove the 'O' ring seal from the adjustment screw and unscrew the locknut.

29 Remove the nut, washer, linkage rod lever retaining the auto-choke operating lever.

30 Remove the auto choke operating lever, bush and spring.

31 Remove the stop lever and spring.

32 Remove the three screws securing the auto-choke to the body.

33 Remove the auto-choke and gasket.

34 Remove the bolt and washer retaining the auto-choke water jacket.

35 Remove the water jacket and sealing ring.

36 Remove the three screws securing the heat mass.

37 Remove the heat mass and its insulator.

38 Remove the vacuum kick piston cover and gasket.

Inspection

39 Wash all components in clean fuel, allow to drain dry or use compressed air. Place all components on a clean surface.

continued

FUEL SYSTEM — U.S.A. SPECIFICATION

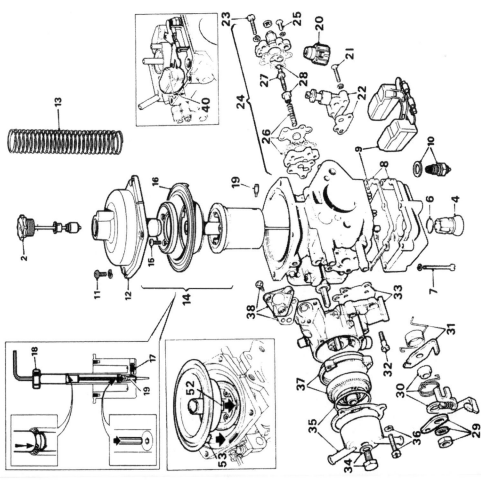

40 Examine the condition of all components for wear, paying special attention to needle and seat, air valve and diaphragm all of which should be renewed unless in exceptionally good condition. Use clean compressed air to blow through all ports, needle valve and starter box.

41 Renew the carburetter if the components of the auto-chock idle and air regulator or deceleration by-pass valve are damaged.

Reassembling

42 Fit the spring and stop lever.

43 Fit the spring bush and auto choke operating lever.

44 Fit the linkage rod lever, washer and nut.

45 Fit the deceleration by-pass valve sandwiched between the gaskets to the base plate, ensuring the register for the spring is towards the valve body.

46 Assemble the spring and deceleration by-pass valve body to the base plate and secure with the three cross-head screws.

47 Fit the deceleration by-pass valve and gasket to the body of the carburetter and secure with the three screws.

48 Refit the spring to the spindle and secure with the 'C' clip.

49 Insert the needle housing assembly into the bottom of the air valve.

50 Fit tool S353, turning clockwise to engage the threads of the needle valve assembly with the adjusting screw; continue turning until the slot in the needle housing is aligned with the grub screw.

51 Tighten the grub screw.
NOTE: The grub screw does not tighten on the needle housing but locates into the slot. This ensures that, during adjustment, the needle will remain in its operating position, i.e. biased, by a spring in the needle housing, towards the air cleaner side of the carburetter.

52 Fit the diaphragm, locating the inner tag into the recess of the air valve.

53 Fit the diaphragm retaining ring and secure with four screws.

54 Fit the air valve assembly, locating the outer tag and rim of the diaphragm in complementary recesses in the carburetter body.

55 Fit the carburetter top cover with the bulge on the housing neck towards the air intake.

56 Fit and evenly tighten the top cover securing screws.

57 Fit the needle valve and sealing washer.

58 Fit the float assembly by levering the pivot pin gently into position.

59 Check the float height by measuring the distance between the carburetter gasket face and the highest point of the floats. The float height must be equal and set to 16 to 17 mm (0.625 to 0.672 in). Adjust by bending the tabs ensuring that the tab sits on the needle valve at right angles.

60 Fit the float-chamber gasket.

61 Fit the float-chamber and secure with the six screws.

62 Fit the 'O' ring to the bottom plug.

63 Press the bottom plug into the float chamber.

64 Check and adjust the auto-choke, see 19.15.09.

65 Fit the carburetter, see 19.15.47.

66 Fill the carburetter damper dashpot with recommended engine oil using the damper as a dipstick, until the threaded plug is 6 mm (0.25 in) above the dashpot when resistance is felt, see 'MAINTENANCE'.

67 Raise the piston and carefully press the damper retaining cap into the air valve.

68 Screw the damper cap onto the top cover.

69 Tune the carburetter, see 'MAINTENANCE'.

FUEL SYSTEM — U.S.A. SPECIFICATION

AUTOMATIC FUEL ENRICHMENT (Auto-choke)

Check and adjust   19.15.47

1 Remove the carburetter, see 19.15.09.
2 Remove the throttle butterfly and wedge it open.
3 Remove the bolt and washer retaining the auto-choke water jacket.
4 Remove the water jacket and sealing ring.
5 Remove the three screws and spring washers retaining the heat mass.
6 Remove the heat mass and its insulator.
7 Rotate the operating arm and carry out the checks detailed in operations 8, 9 and 10.
8 Check the vacuum kick piston and rod for full and free movement.
9 Check that the fast idle cam and thermostat lever are free on the pivot.
10 Move the cam from the lever and ensure it returns under spring influence to the lever; ensure it remains there when the lever is rotated.
11 Remove the throttle wedge.
12 Set the gap 'A' between the choke and throttle levers to 3/32 in (2.4 mm) by turning the idle speed screw.
13 Slacken the locknut and adjust the throttle stop screw to obtain a clearance 'B' of 0.035 in (0.9 mm) measured between the end of the fast idle pin and the cam.
14 Lock the adjusting screw by tightening the locknut.
15 Reverse the procedure in 3 to 6 noting:
a Ensure that the moving end of the temperature coil registers over the operating arm.
b Renew the water jacket sealing ring if necessary.
c Do not tighten the clamp plate screws or the water jacket centre bolt.
16 Align the index mark on the heat mass with the datum mark on the auto-choke body.

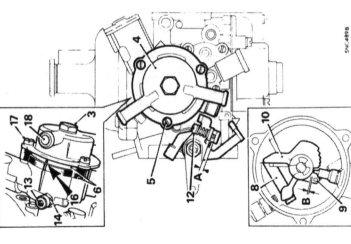

17 Tighten the clamp plate screws to 8 to 10 lbf in (0.092 to 0.115 kgf m).
18 Position the water jacket pipe connections correctly and tighten the centre bolt to 65 to 75 lbf in (0.749 to 0.865 kgf m).
19 Refit the carburetter, see 19.15.09.
20 Tune the carburetter, see 'MAINTENANCE'.

THROTTLE LINKAGE — Catalytic converter cars — 1975-1976

Check and adjust   19.20.05

1 Connect an accurate tachometer.
2 Start and warm the engine to normal operating temperature.
3 Check the idle speed and adjust if necessary to 700 to 900 rev/min, see 'MAINTENANCE'.
4 Check the mixture CO percentage at idle, see 'MAINTENANCE'.
5 Adjust the link rod to give a gap 'A' of 0.010 in (0.254 mm) to 0.190 in (4.83 mm) between the roller and progression lever.
6 Adjust the position of the outer cable at the abutment to take up any slack in the inner cable. Tighten the nuts.

THROTTLE CABLE — Non catalytic converter cars — 1975-1976

Remove and refit   19.20.06

Removing
1 Remove the split pin from the spring retaining rod.
2 Remove the spring retaining rod complete with spring to release the throttle cable yoke from the carburetter.
3 Unscrew the nut from the outer cable abutment to release the cable from the support bracket.
4 Release the cable from the accelerator pedal.
5 Remove the cable from the body.

Refitting
6 Reverse the procedure in 1 to 5, adjusting the outer cable abutment nuts to take up slack in the inner cable.

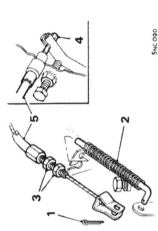

THROTTLE CABLE — Catalytic converter cars — 1975-1976

Remove and refit   19.20.06

Removing
1 Unscrew the nut from the outer cable abutment to release the cable from the support bracket.
2 Release the inner cable from the progression lever.
3 Release the cable from the accelerator pedal.
4 Remove the cable from the body.

Refitting
5 Reverse the procedure in 1 to 4.
6 Adjust the throttle linkage, see 19.20.05.

FUEL SYSTEM — U.S.A. SPECIFICATION

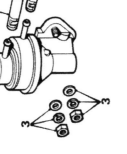

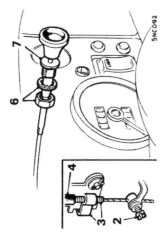

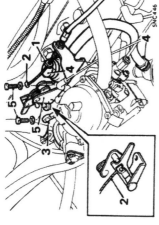

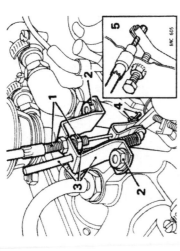

THROTTLE CABLE — 1977 and later

Remove and refit   19.20.06

Removing

1 Unscrew the throttle cable adjuster lower locknut and release the throttle cable from the abutment bracket.
2 Remove the two screws securing the abutment bracket to the induction manifold.
3 Release the abutment bracket from the throttle return spring rod, collecting the return spring.
4 Remove the split pin and washers to release the throttle cable and throttle return spring rod from the carburetter throttle lever.
5 Release the cable from the throttle pedal.
6 Remove the cable from the body.

Refitting

7 Reverse the procedure in 1 to 6.

THROTTLE LINKAGE — Catalytic converter cars — 1975-1976

Remove and refit   19.20.07

Removing

1 Unscrew the nut from the outer cable abutment to release the cable from the support bracket.
2 Release the inner cable from the progression lever.
3 Detach the link rod from the roller lever.
4 Slacken the union nut and the banjo bolt securing the metal pipe to the E G R valve and inlet manifold.
5 Remove the two bolts to release the throttle linkage from the manifold.

Refitting

6 Reverse the procedure in 1 to 4.
7 Adjust the throttle linkage, see 19.20.05.
8. Check the mixture CO percentage at idle, see 'MAINTENANCE'.

MIXTURE CONTROL (CHOKE) CABLE ASSEMBLY — 1975-1976

Remove and refit   19.20.13

Removing

1 Disconnect the battery.
2 Slacken the screw securing the inner cable to the starter box lever.
3 Pull the cable from its clip on the carburetter.
4 Remove the outer sleeve from the cable.
5 Remove the centre console eight securing screws and move the centre console aside.
6 Unscrew the cable securing nut from behind the fascia.
7 Pull the cable from the fascia, collecting the securing nut and washer.

Refitting

8 Reverse the procedure in 1 to 7.
9 Check the adjustment of the mixture control as follows:
   a   Pull out the control and check that the starter lever abuts against its stop.
   b   Push the control in and check that the stop on the starter lever moves the E G R air bleed valve fully home.
10 Start the engine and run until normal operating temperature is reached then adjust the fast idle, see 'MAINTENANCE'.

FUEL PUMP

Remove and refit   19.45.08

Removing

1 Disconnect the battery.
2 Remove the car heater air intake hose bracket screw and nut and remove the air intake hose.
3 Remove the two securing nuts and spring washerss.
4 Squeeze the ends of the clip and remove the inlet hose.

[WARNING: Fuel will be discharged as you disconnect the hoses. Do not smoke or work near heaters or other fire hazards. Have a fire extinguisher handy.]

5 Squeeze the ends of the clip and remove the outlet hose.
6 Remove the fuel pump and gasket.

Refitting

7 Reverse the procedure in 1 to 6 using a new gasket.

FUEL SYSTEM – U.S.A. SPECIFICATION

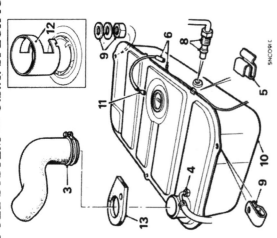

SNC09IC

FUEL TANK

Remove and refit　　19.55.01

Service tool: 18G 1001

Removing
1 Disconnect the battery.
2 Unscrew the spare wheel retaining screw and move the spare wheel away from the fuel tank filler hose.
3 Slacken the clip, and disconnect the filler hose from the fuel tank inlet pipe.

[WARNING: Fuel vapors will be present when you detach the hose. Do not smoke or work near heaters or other fire hazards. Have a fire extinguisher handy.]

4 Unscrew the separator tank flexible pipe from the fuel tank.
5 Disconnect the wiring from the harness clips on the front mounting flange of the fuel tank.
6 Disconnect the fuel gauge tank unit electrical connection.
7 Support the fuel tank.
8 Disconnect the fuel pipe from the fuel tank.

NOTE: As no facility for draining is provided, a clean container should be placed beneath the tank before removing the feed pipe if the tank is full.

9 Remove the nuts, spring and plain washers securing the tank to the boot floor, noting the wiring clip.
10 Remove the fuel tank.
11 Remove the wire from the fuel gauge tank unit.
12 Remove the fuel gauge tank unit using tool 18G 1001.
13 Remove the pad from the filler neck.

Refitting
14 Reverse the procedure in 1 to 13.

FUEL FILLER NECK

Remove and refit　　19.55.07

Removing
1 Slacken the clip securing the hose to the filler neck, and move the clip forward along the hose.

[WARNING Fuel vapors will be present when you detach the hose. Do not smoke or work near heaters or other fire hazards. Have a fire extinguisher handy.]

2 Withdraw the filler neck.
3 Remove the seal.
4 a Inspect the restrictor and check that the trap door will open, and that it will close under its own spring pressure. If the restrictor is faulty, fit a new restrictor.
  b Release the three locating tongues.
  c Withdraw the restrictor.

Refitting
5 a Fit the sleeve to the filler neck, aligning the vent hole in the sleeve with the stamp mark 'TOP' on the filler neck.
  b Secure the sleeve in position by the three locating tongues.
  c The filler neck must be fitted with the word 'TOP' uppermost.
6 Fit a new seal if necessary.
7 Reverse the procedure in 1 and 2.

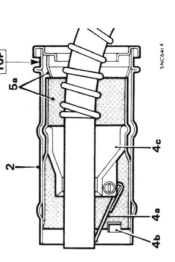

SNC041A

COOLING SYSTEM – U.K. SPECIFICATION

RADIATOR

Remove and refit   26.40.01

Removing

WARNING: If the cooling system is hot remove the expansion tank filler cap slowly to release the pressure gradually from the cooling system.

[CAUTION: Do not drain the cooling system while it is hot. Doing this could cause the cylinder head or the engine block to warp.]

1 Disconnect the bottom hose to drain the cooling system.
2 Disconnect the expansion tank hose from the radiator.
3 Disconnect the top hose from the thermostat housing.
4 Disconnect the car heater air intake hose bracket from the body and ease the air hose rearwards.
5 Remove the two screws securing the radiator cowl to the bonnet platform.
6 Remove the four radiator cowl securing bolts and nuts.

7 Lift out the radiator complete with cowl.
8 Disconnect the thermostat housing hose from the radiator.
9 Remove the four bolts to release the fan guard and radiator cowl from the radiator.

Refitting

10 Reverse the procedure in 1 to 9.
11 Refill the cooling system, see 'MAINTENANCE'.

THERMOSTAT

Remove and refit   26.45.01

Removing

1 Remove the radiator bottom hose to drain the cooling system.
2 Remove the radiator top hose.
3 Remove the two studs and spring washers securing the thermostat elbow to the thermostat and water pump housing.
4 Release the carburetter vacuum pipe retaining clip.
5 Remove the elbow and gasket.
6 Remove the thermostat.

Refitting

7 Reverse the procedure in 1 to 6, using 'MAINTENANCE'.
8 Refill the cooling system, see 'MAINTENANCE'.

THERMOSTAT

Testing   26.45.09

1 If the thermostat is stuck in the open position renew the thermostat.
2 Immerse the thermostat in water heated to the temperature stamped on the thermostat.
3 Renew the thermostat if it fails to open.
4 Allow the thermostat to cool. If it sticks in the open position, renew the thermostat.

THERMOSTAT AND WATER PUMP HOUSING

Remove and refit   26.45.10

Removing

1 Disconnect the bottom hose to drain the cooling system.
2 Disconnect the top hose from the thermostat housing.
3 Disconnect the induction manifold hose from the thermostat housing.
4 Disconnect the return water pipe union at the rear of the water pump housing.
5 Remove the temperature transmitter.
6 Remove the two bolts to release the fan guard from the radiator.
7 Slacken the alternator adjusting link bolts and mounting bolt and detach the drive belt from the alternator pulley and the crankshaft pulley.
8 Remove the three bolts securing the thermostat and water pump housing to the cylinder head. Note the length and position of each bolt.

9 Remove the thermostat and water pump housing complete with water pump and fan.
10 Remove the three nuts and washers and detach the water pump and fan assembly from the housing.
11 Remove the induction manifold hose adaptor.
12 Remove the temperature transmitter adaptor.
13 Remove the return water pipe adaptor.
14 Remove the thermostat elbow and thermostat.

Refitting

15 Reverse the procedure in 1 to 14 and check the fan belt tension, see 'MAINTENANCE'.

WATER PUMP

Remove and refit   26.50.01

Removing

1 Remove the radiator, see 26.40.01.
2 Slacken the alternator adjusting link bolts and mounting bolt and detach the drive belt from the water pump pulley.
3 Remove the four bolts and washers to release the fan from the water pump.
4 Remove the three nuts and washers securing the water pump to the thermostat and water pump housing.
5 Remove the water pump and gasket.

Refitting

6 Reverse the procedure in 1 to 5 and check the fan belt tension, see 'MAINTENANCE'.

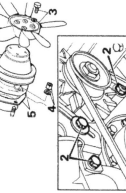

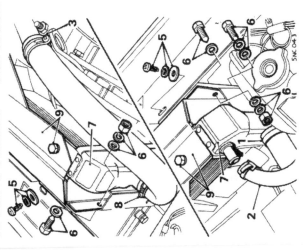

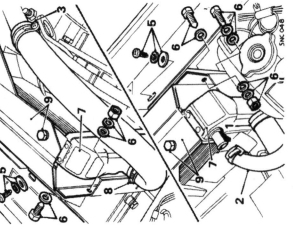

COOLING SYSTEM – U.S.A. SPECIFICATION COOLANT

Drain and refill   26.10.01

Draining

WARNING: If the cooling system is hot, remove the expansion tank filler cap slowly to release the pressure gradually from the cooling system.

[**CAUTION:** Do not drain the cooling system while it is hot. Doing this could cause the cylinder head or the engine block to warp.]

1. Stand the car on level ground.
2. Remove the expansion tank cap, and the filler plug from the thermostat elbow.
3. Position a container to collect the coolant.
4. Slacken the hose clip and disconnect the bottom hose at the radiator.
5. Remove the cylinder block drain plug.
   NOTE: There is no provision for draining the heater, expansion tank or spill tank.

Refilling

6. Refit the drain plug and bottom hose.
7. Check that all hose connections are tight.
8. Fill the system with coolant through the thermostat elbow filler until the level is up to the bottom of the threads, refit the filler plug.
9. Top up the expansion tank to the half-full point and refit the cap.
10. Run the engine until normal operating temperature is reached, then switch off the engine.
11. Allow the engine to cool, then remove the expansion tank cap.
12. Remove the filler plug and top up once more to the bottom of the threads. Refit the filler plug.
13. Top up the expansion tank to the half-full point and refit the cap.

COOLING SYSTEM

Pressure test   26.10.07

1. Check and top-up the cooling system.
   NOTE: Ensure the expansion tank cap is fitted before the filler plug is removed.
2. Run the engine until the system is warm. Switch off the engine.
3. Turn the expansion tank cap slowly to release the pressure in the system gradually, and remove the cap.
4. Fit the pressure tester to the expansion tank.
5. Pump up the system to the pressure indicated on the expansion tank cap. $15 = 15 \, \text{lbf/in}^2$ or $1.0 \, \text{kgf/cm}^2$.
6. Check that the pressure is held for 10 seconds.

7. Check for leaks.
8. If the pressure drops and no leaks are visible, an internal leak is indicated.
9. Fit the cap to the pressure tester and check that it opens at approximately the correct pressure.

4NC261

RADIATOR – 1975-1976

Remove and refit   26.40.01

Removing

WARNING: If the cooling system is hot remove the expansion tank filler cap slowly to release the pressure gradually from the cooling system.

[**CAUTION:** Do not drain the cooling system while it is hot. Doing this could cause the cylinder head or the engine block to warp.]

1. Disconnect the bottom hose to drain the cooling system.
2. Disconnect the expansion tank hose from the radiator.
3. Disconnect the top hose from the thermostat housing.
4. Disconnect the car heater air intake hose bracket from the body and ease the air hose rearwards.
5. Remove the two screws securing the radiator cowl to the bonnet platform.
6. Remove the four radiator cowl securing bolts and nuts.
7. Lift out the radiator complete with cowl.
8. Disconnect the thermostat housing hose from the radiator.

9. Remove the four bolts to release the fan guard and radiator cowl from the radiator.

Refitting

10. Reverse the procedure in 1 to 9.
11. Refill the cooling system, see 'MAINTENANCE'.

124

COOLING SYSTEM – U.S.A. SPECIFICATION

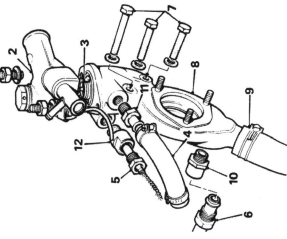

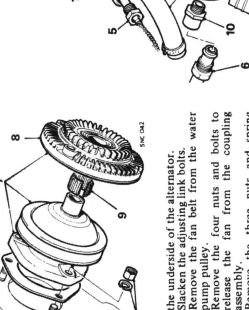

Refitting

10 Reverse the procedure in 2 to 9.
11 Refill the cooling system, see 26.10.01.

THERMOSTAT   26.45.01

Remove and refit

Removing

1 Partly drain the cooling system, see 26.10.01.
2 Disconnect the outlet hose from the water outlet elbow.
3 Remove the two studs and spring washers securing the water outlet elbow to the thermostat and water pump housing.
4 Release the carburetter vacuum pipe retaining clip.
5 Place the elbow and gasket to one side.
6 Remove the thermostat.

Refitting

7 Reverse the procedure in 2 to 6, using a new thermostat housing gasket.
8 Refill the cooling system, see 26.10.01.

THERMOSTAT   26.45.09

Testing

1 If the thermostat is stuck in the open position, renew the thermostat.
2 Immerse the thermostat in water heated to the temperature stamped on the thermostat.
3 Renew the thermostat if it fails to open.
4 Allow the thermostat to cool. If it sticks in the open position, renew the thermostat.

WATER PUMP   26.50.01

Remove and refit

Service tool: 18G 2

Removing

1 Remove the radiator, see 26.40.01.
2 Slacken the securing nut and bolt on the underside of the alternator.
3 Slacken the adjusting link bolts.
4 Remove the fan belt from the water pump pulley.
5 Remove the four nuts and bolts to release the fan from the coupling assembly.
6 Remove the three nuts and spring washers securing the water pump to the thermostat and water pump housing.
7 Remove the water pump and coupling assembly.
8 Using 18G 2, withdraw the fan coupling.
9 Remove the tolerance ring.

Refitting

10 Refit the tolerance ring to the water pump spindle.
11 Holding the tolerance ring in its locating groove on the spindle, press on the fan coupling.
12 Reverse the procedure in 1 to 7.

WATER PUMP HOUSING   26.50.03

Remove and refit

Removing

1 Remove the water pump complete with fan, see 26.50.01.
2 Remove the water outlet elbow and gasket.
3 Withdraw the thermostat.
4 Disconnect the induction manifold hose at the water outlet elbow.
5 Remove the temperature transmitter.
6 Disconnect the return water pipe union at the rear of the water pump housing.
7 Remove the three bolts securing the water pump housing to the cylinder head. Note the length and position of each bolt.
8 Withdraw the water pump housing.
9 Remove the bottom hose.
10 Remove the return water pipe union adaptor.
11 Remove the induction manifold hose adaptor.
12 Remove the temperature transmitter adaptor.

Refitting

13 Reverse the procedure in 1 to 12.

RADIATOR — 1977 and later   26.40.01

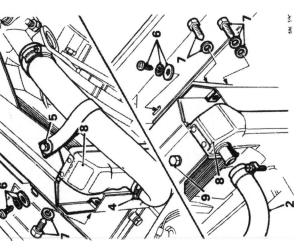

Remove and refit

Removing

1 Drain the cooling system, see 26.10.01.
2 Disconnect the top hose from the radiator.
3 Disconnect the heater air intake hose bracket from the body and ease the intake hose rearwards.
4 Disconnect the water outlet elbow hose from the radiator.
5 Remove the bolt, washer, strap and spacer retaining the water outlet hose.
6 Remove the two screws securing the radiator cowl to the bonnet lock platform.
7 Remove the four radiator cowl securing bolts.
8 Lift out the radiator complete with cowl.
9 Remove the three bolts to release the fan guard and radiator cowl from the radiator.

MANIFOLD AND EXHAUST SYSTEM – U.K. SPECIFICATION

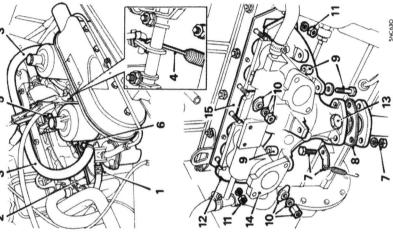

FRONT PIPE

Remove and refit   30.10.09

Removing

1 Raise and support the front of the car.
2 Release the fuel pipe from the clip on the air cleaner body.
3 Remove the four bolts securing the air cleaner to the carburetters.
4 Remove the air cleaner.
5 Disconnect the main throttle return spring from the throttle lever.
6 Remove the three nuts, bolts and washers securing the front pipe to the exhaust manifold, and collect the throttle return spring and bracket.
7 Release the front pipe from the exhaust manifold and remove the gasket.
8 Remove the three nuts, bolts and washers securing the front pipe to the rear pipe.
9 Remove the front pipe and collect the olive.

Refitting

10 Reverse the procedure in 1 to 9, noting:

a Fit a new front pipe to manifold gasket, if necessary.
b Tighten the front pipe to manifold bolts before tightening the front pipe to rear pipe bolts.
c Fit new air cleaner gaskets, if necessary.

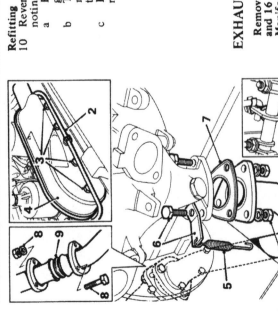

EXHAUST MANIFOLD

Remove and refit 1 to 13   30.15.10
and 16 to 26   30.15.15
Manifold gaskets 1 to 26

Removing

1 Disconnect the fuel feed line from the rear carburetter.
2 Disconnect the distributor vacuum pipe from the rear carburetter.
3 Disconnect the breather hose from each carburetter.
4 Disconnect the main throttle return spring from the throttle lever.
5 Remove the two screws securing the throttle control bracket to the induction manifold.
6 Remove the securing bolts and washers to release the carburetter and air cleaner assembly, heat shield and gaskets from the induction manifold and place aside.
7 Remove the three nuts, bolts and washers securing the exhaust system to the exhaust manifold, and collect the throttle return spring and bracket.
8 Release the exhaust system from the exhaust manifold and remove the gasket.
9 Remove the two bolts and washers securing the induction manifold to the exhaust manifold and withdraw the spacers.
10 Remove the six nuts, washers and clamps securing the manifolds to the cylinder head.
11 Remove the two nuts securing the ends of the exhaust manifold to the cylinder head and remove the water return pipe bracket from the rear stud.
12 Withdraw the exhaust manifold from the cylinder head.
13 Remove the plug from the exhaust manifold.
14 Pull the induction manifold clear of the cylinder head studs.
15 Remove the manifold gasket.

Refitting

16 Refit the plug to the exhaust manifold.
17 Fit a new manifold gasket to the cylinder head.
18 Position the exhaust manifold on the cylinder head studs.
19 Position the induction manifold on the cylinder head dowels.
20 Fit the water return pipe bracket to the rear stud.
21 Refit the clamps and washers and do up the eight retaining nuts finger tight.
22 Refit the spacers between the induction manifold and exhaust manifold and do up the bolts finger tight.
23 Finally tighten the exhaust manifold outer nuts.
24 Finally tighten the six remaining nuts securing the manifold clamps.
25 Finally tighten the two bolts retaining the induction manifold to the exhaust manifold.
26 Reverse the procedure in 1 to 8, fitting a new exhaust manifold flange gasket.

MANIFOLD AND EXHAUST SYSTEM – U.K. SPECIFICATION

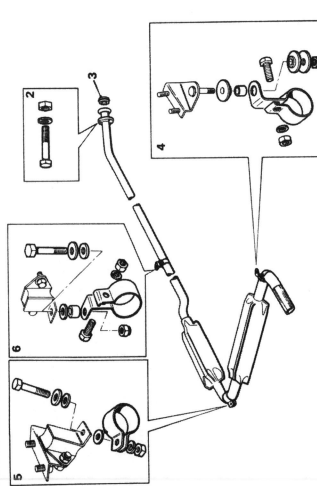

TAILPIPE AND SILENCERS

Remove and refit   30.10.22

Removing

1 Raise the rear of the car and support on stands beneath the rear axle.
2 Remove the three nuts, bolts and washers to release the rear pipe from the front pipe.
3 Remove the olive.
4 Remove the nut, plain washer, rubber bushes and spacer securing the rear clip.
5 Remove the nut, bolt and washers securing the intermediate clip.
6 Remove the nut, bolt, washers and spacer securing the front clip and remove the rear exhaust pipe assembly.
7 Remove the bolts where necessary and detach the mounting clips from the rear exhaust pipe.

Refitting

8 Reverse the procedure in 1 to 7, noting:
  a Renew the rubber bushes and insulating washers where necessary.
  b Ensure that the rubber bushes, insulating washers and spacers are correctly positioned.
  c Leave all the clips slack until after the complete exhaust system has been refitted; then tighten the clips.

INDUCTION MANIFOLD   30.15.02

Remove and refit

Removing

1 Drain the cooling system.
2 Disconnect the fuel feed line from the rear carburetter.
3 Disconnect the distributor vacuum pipe from the rear carburetter.
4 Disconnect the breather hose from each carburetter.
5 Disconnect the main throttle return spring from the throttle lever.
6 Remove the two screws securing the throttle control bracket to the induction manifold.
7 Remove the securing bolts and washers to release the carburetter and air cleaner assembly, heat shield and gaskets from the induction manifold and place aside.
8 Remove the clip retaining the capillary tube to the induction manifold water pipe.
9 Disconnect the three hoses from the induction manifold water pipes.
10 Remove the two bolts and washers securing the induction manifold to the exhaust manifold and withdraw the spacers.
11 Remove the six nuts, washers and clamps securing the manifolds to the cylinder head.
12 Withdraw the induction manifold from the cylinder head.
13 Remove the plug from the induction manifold.

Refitting

14 Refit the plug to the induction manifold.
15 Position the induction manifold on the cylinder head dowels.
16 Refit the six clamps and washers and do up the nuts finger tight.
17 Refit the spacers between the induction manifold and exhaust manifold and do up the bolts finger tight.
18 Finally tighten the six nuts retaining the manifold clamps.
19 Finally tighten the two bolts retaining the induction manifold to the exhaust manifold.
20 Reverse the procedure in 1 to 9.

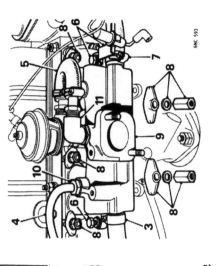

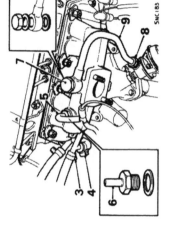

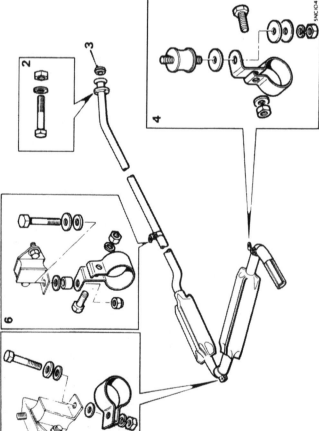

TAIL PIPE AND SILENCERS

Remove and refit   30.10.22

Removing

1 Raise the rear of the car and support on stands beneath the rear axle.

2 Release the rear pipe from the front pipe.

3 Remove the olive.

4 Remove the nut, bolt, washers and spacers securing the tail pipe bracket.

5 Remove the bolt, washers and spacers securing the intermediate pipe.

6 Remove the bolt, washers and spacers securing the front bracket and remove the rear exhaust pipe.

7 Remove the bolts where necessary and detach the mounting brackets from the rear exhaust pipe.

Refitting

8 Reverse the procedure in 1 to 7, noting:

a Renew rubber mountings where necessary.

b Ensure the rubber mountings and spacers are correctly positioned.

c Leave all clamps slack until after the complete exhaust system has been refitted; then tighten the clamps.

INDUCTION MANIFOLD — 1975-1976

Remove and refit   30.15.02

Removing

1 Drain the cooling system.

2 Release the carburetter assembly from the induction manifold, see 30.15.15.

3 Disconnect the heater hose from the induction manifold.

4 Disconnect the heater by-pass hose from the induction manifold.

5 Remove the running-on control valve vacuum pipe from the induction manifold.

6 Remove the running-on control valve vacuum pipe adaptor from the induction manifold.

7 Remove the banjo bolt securing the metal pipe to the induction manifold.

8 Unscrew the union nut securing the metal pipe to the E.G.R. valve.

9 Remove the metal pipe connecting the E.G.R. valve to the induction manifold.

10 Remove the induction manifold, see 30.15.15.

Refitting

11 Fit the manifold assembly to the cylinder head, see 30.15.15.

12 Reverse the procedure in 1 to 9.

INDUCTION MANIFOLD — 1977 and later

Remove and refit   30.15.02

Removing

1 Drain the cooling system, see 26.10.01.

2 Release the carburetter assembly from the induction manifold, see 30.15.15.

3 Disconnect the heater hose from the induction manifold.

4 Remove the running-on control valve vacuum pipe (if fitted) from the induction manifold.

5 Remove the hose connecting the E G R valve to the induction manifold.

6 Remove the two bolts retaining the induction manifold to the exhaust manifold and place the flame trap bracket to one side.

7 Disconnect the thermostat housing hose from the induction manifold.

8 Remove the six nuts, washers and clamps retaining the induction manifold to the cylinder head.

9 Withdraw the induction manifold from the cylinder head studs.

10 Remove the running-on control valve vacuum pipe adaptor (if fitted).

11 Remove the E G R valve hose adaptor.

Refitting

12 Reverse the procedure in 1 to 11, noting:

Fit the two larger clamps and two washers to the two inner lower cylinder head studs; start the two longer nuts on the studs before fitting the manifold to the cylinder head.

MANIFOLD AND EXHAUST SYSTEM — U.S.A. SPECIFICATION

EXHAUST MANIFOLD — 1975-1976   30.15.10

Remove and refit

Removing

1. Remove the manifold gaskets, see 21.30.15.15.
2. Remove the exhaust manifold.
3. Slacken the locknut and unscrew the E.G.R. valve from the exhaust manifold.

Refitting

4. Fit the manifold assembly to the cylinder head, see 30.15.15.
5. Fit the water return pipe bracket to the cylinder head and manifold assembly.
6. Fit the flame trap bracket to the cylinder head and manifold assembly.
7. Fit the remaining nuts, washers and clamps securing the manifold assembly to the cylinder head.
8. Connect the water return pipe to the thermostat housing.
9. Connect the thermostat housing hose to the induction manifold.
10. Fit the nut and washer securing the exhaust manifold to the induction manifold.
11. Screw the E.G.R. valve into the exhaust manifold.
12. Place the metal pipe in position to align the bottom with the E.G.R. valve, screw or unscrew the E.G.R. valve as required. Place the pipe aside.
13. Tighten the locknut.
14. Fit the metal pipe to the E.G.R. valve.

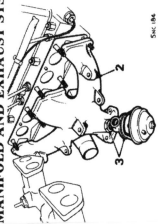

15. Fit the banjo bolt to secure the metal pipe to the induction manifold.
16. Fit the carburetter assembly, see 30.15.15.

MANIFOLD GASKETS — 1975-1976   30.15.15

Remove and refit

Removing

1. Drain the cooling system.
2. Remove the air temperature control valve hot air hose.
3. Disconnect the distributor vacuum pipe from the carburetter.
4. Disconnect the E.G.R. valve vacuum pipes from the carburetter.
5. Disconnect the breather pipe from the rocker cover.
6. Disconnect the fuel line from the carburetter.

[WARNING: Fuel will be discharged when you disconnect the fuel pipe. Do not smoke or work near heaters or other fire hazards. Have a fire extinguisher handy.]

7. Remove the securing nuts and washers to release the carburetter assembly and insulating block from the induction manifold and place aside.
8. Remove the banjo bolt securing the metal pipe to the induction manifold.
9. Unscrew the union nut securing the metal pipe to the E.G.R. valve.
10. Remove the metal pipe connecting the E.G.R. valve to the induction manifold.

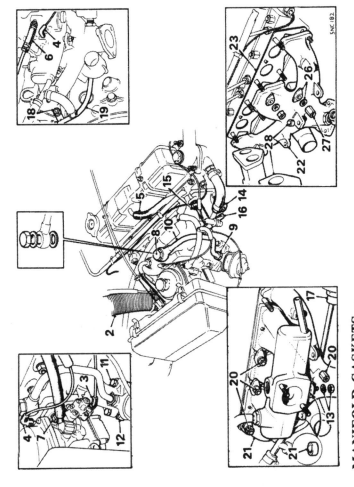

11. Remove the three nuts, bolts and washers securing the exhaust system to the exhaust manifold.
12. Release the exhaust system from the exhaust manifold and remove the gasket.
13. Remove the nut and washer securing the exhaust manifold to the inlet manifold.
14. Disconnect the thermostat housing hose from the induction manifold.
15. Remove the nut securing the flame trap bracket to the cylinder head and manifold assembly.
16. Release the flame trap bracket and place aside.
17. Disconnect the water return pipe at the thermostat housing.
18. Remove the nut securing the water return pipe bracket to the cylinder head and manifold assembly.
19. Release the water return pipe bracket and place aside.
20. Remove the remaining six nuts, washers and clamps securing the manifold assembly to the cylinder head.
21. Pull the manifold assembly away from the cylinder head sufficiently to allow the induction manifold to be lifted aside and the spacer removed.
22. Remove the exhaust manifold clear of the cylinder head studs.
23. Remove the manifold gasket.

Refitting

24. Fit a new manifold gasket to the cylinder head.
25. Position the exhaust manifold on the cylinder head studs.
26. Fit the two larger clamps and two washers to the two inner lower cylinder head studs.
27. Start the two longer nuts on the two inner lower cylinder head studs.
28. Fit the induction manifold complete with spacer to the exhaust manifold and locate the induction manifold on the cylinder head dowels ensuring that the two clamps are correctly positioned.
29. Push on the manifold assembly.
30. Reverse the procedure in 1 to 20, fitting a new exhaust manifold flange gasket.

MANIFOLD AND EXHAUST SYSTEM — U.S.A. SPECIFICATION

MANIFOLD GASKETS — 1977 and later

Remove and refit 1 to 17, 19, 21 to 27	30.15.15
Exhaust manifold — remove and refit 1 to 27	30.15.10

Removing

1 Drain the cooling system, see 26.10.01.
2 Remove the air temperature control valve hot air hose.
3 Disconnect the distributor vacuum pipe from the carburetter.
4 Disconnect the EGR valve vacuum pipe from the carburetter.
5 Disconnect the purge pipe from the rocker cover.
6 Disconnect the fuel pipe from the carburetter.

[WARNING: Fuel will be discharged when you disconnect the fuel pipe. Do not smoke or work near heaters or other fire hazards. Have a fire extinguisher handy.]

7 Remove the throttle cable abutment bracket complete with throttle cable from the induction manifold.
8 Disconnect the EGR valve flame trap pipe.
9 Remove the securing nuts and washers to release the carburetter assembly and insulating block from the induction manifold and place aside.
10 Raise and support the front of the car.
11 Remove the catalytic converter support bracket.
12 Release the catalytic converter from the rear exhaust pipe.
13 Press in the retaining clips and remove the pre-heater duct.
14 Remove the six nuts securing the catalytic converter to the exhaust manifold.
15 Release the catalytic converter from the exhaust manifold and remove the manifold flange gasket.
16 Remove the two bolts securing the induction manifold to the exhaust manifold and place the flame trap bracket to one side.
17 Disconnect the thermostat housing hose from the induction manifold.
18 Slacken the EGR valve locknut.

19 Remove the pipe connecting the EGR valve to the induction manifold.
20 Remove the EGR valve from the exhaust manifold.
21 Remove the six nuts, washers and clamps securing the induction manifold to the cylinder head.
22 Withdraw the induction manifold and place to one side.
23 Slacken the nut securing the air pipe retaining clip to the gearbox casing.
24 Disconnect the air pipe from the exhaust manifold.
25 Disconnect the water return pipe from the water pump housing.
26 Remove the two nuts and washers retaining the exhaust manifold to the cylinder head.
27 Remove the exhaust manifold and gasket.

Refitting

28 Fit a new manifold gasket to the cylinder head.
29 Position the exhaust manifold on the cylinder head studs.
30 Fit the two larger clamps and two washers to the inner lower cylinder head studs.
31 Start the two longer nuts on the two inner lower cylinder head studs.
32 Fit the induction manifold to the exhaust manifold and locate the induction manifold on the cylinder head dowels ensuring that the two clamps are correctly positioned.
33 Reverse the procedure in 1 to 26, noting:
a Fit a new exhaust manifold flange gasket and exhaust pipe olive.
b Before fitting the EGR valve, screw the locknut to the top of the threads, screw the EGR valve into the manifold aligning the 'U' shaped pipe and the valve as necessary before tightening the locknut.

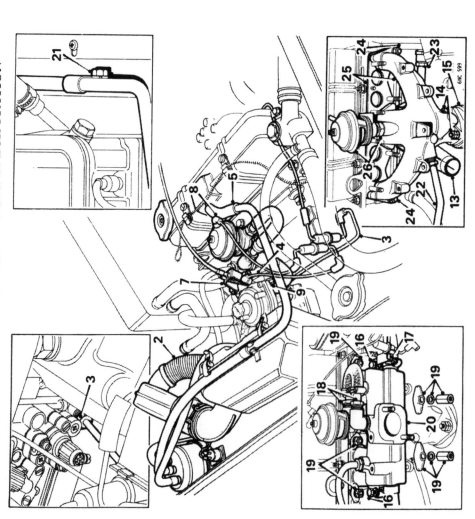

30.10.22 [USA]

130

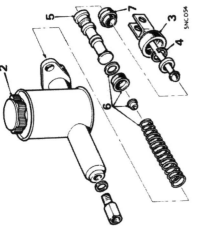

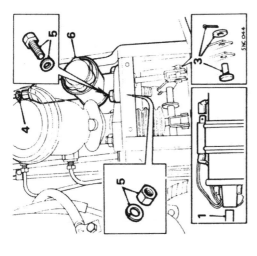

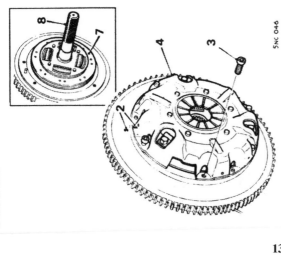

c Place the plate onto tool 18G 1196, hold the tool in a vice, spin the plate and check for excessive run-out of the plate.

d Check for loose springs and elongated apertures in the spring housings.

e Examine the splines for wear and check that the centre hub is not loose.

Refitting

7 Refit the clutch driven plate to the flywheel with the side marked 'FLYWHEEL SIDE' facing towards the flywheel.

8 Centralize the clutch driven plate using tool 18G 1196.

9 Refit the clutch cover, aligning the assembly marks on the flywheel and clutch unit, and progressively tighten the securing screws.

10 Remove tool 18G 1196.

11 Refit the gearbox, see 37.20.01.

CLUTCH ASSEMBLY

Remove and refit   33.10.01

Service tool: 18G 1196

Removing

1 Remove the gearbox, see 37.20.01.

2 Check the reassembly marks on the clutch and flywheel.

3 Remove the clutch cover securing screws.

4 Remove the clutch cover and driven plate.

Inspecting

5 Clean the clutch unit and inspect as follows:

  a Check the pressure plate for scoring or damage.

  b Examine the diaphragm spring components for wear and fractures.

6 Inspect the driven plate as follows:

  a Check the linings for oil contamination and/or burning.

  b Examine the linings for uneven wear on each clutch face.

HYDRAULIC SYSTEM   33.15.01

Bleeding

1 Top up the master cylinder, using a recommended brake fluid, see 09. NOTE: Brake fluid can have a detrimental effect on paintwork; ensure that fluid is not allowed to contact painted surfaces.

2 Attach a rubber tube to the bleed nipple on the slave cylinder and immerse the other end of the tube into a translucent container containing brake fluid.

3 Open the bleed nipple approximately three-quarters of a turn; pump the pedal and hold it down at the end of its stroke and close the bleed screw before allowing the pedal to return to its normal position. Continue this series of operations until clear fluid free from air bubbles is delivered into the container. Ensure that the master cylinder fluid level does not fall so low that air can enter the system during bleeding.

4 Top up master cylinder to the bottom of the filler neck.

MASTER CYLINDER

Overhaul   33.20.07

Dismantling

1 Remove the master cylinder, see 33.20.01.

2 Remove the filler cap and drain the fluid.

3 Detach the rubber boot from the body and slide the boot along the push rod.

4 Release the circlip retaining the push rod, and withdraw the push rod complete with circlip, dished washer and rubber boot.

5 Remove the piston with its secondary cup seal.

6 Remove the piston washer, main cup seal spring retainer and spring.

7 Remove the secondary cup seal from the piston by carefully stretching it over the end of the piston.

Inspecting

8 Wash the master cylinder body in industrial methylated spirit and dry thoroughly. Clean all internal parts in brake fluid.

9 Check the cylinder bore; if it is not scored or ridged new seals can be fitted.
Renew the unit if the bore is scored or ridged.

MASTER CYLINDER

Remove and refit   33.20.01

Removing

1 Remove the H.T. lead from the ignition coil and the white and blue lead from the ballast resistor.

2 Remove the four screws to release the cover plate complete with ignition coil.

3 Withdraw the split pin and washer and remove the clevis pin.

4 Unscrew the pipe union from the master cylinder.

5 Remove the bolts and nuts, flat and spring washers securing the master cylinder to the pedal box.

6 Remove the master cylinder.

Refitting

7 Reverse the procedure in 1 to 6.

8 Bleed the clutch hydraulic system, see 33.15.01.

continued

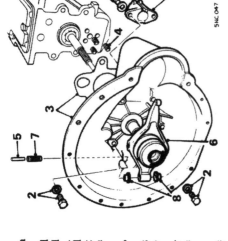

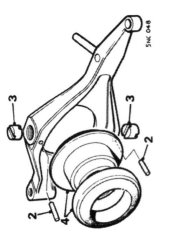

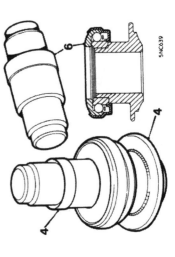

CLUTCH

Reassembling

10 Immerse all internal components in brake fluid and assemble when wet.

11 Stretch the new secondary cup seal over the piston with the lip of the seal facing towards the head of the piston.

12 Fit the spring retainer into the small diameter end of the spring and insert the spring into the body, large diameter first.

13 Fit the main cup seal, cup seal washer, piston and push rod.

CAUTION: When fitting the cup seals carefully enter the lip edge of the cup seals into the barrel first.

14 Smear the sealing areas of the rubber boot with Lockheed disc brake lubricant or Girling rubber grease.

15 Fit the circlip and rubber boot.

16 Refit the master cylinder, see 33.20.01.

CLUTCH HOUSING COVER   33.25.10

Remove and refit

Removing

1 Remove the gearbox, see 37.20.01.

2 Remove the five bolts retaining the clutch housing to the gearbox, noting that the bottom bolt is fitted with a copper washer.

3 Remove the clutch housing and gasket.

4 Remove the three laygear pre-load springs.

5 Drive the pin retaining the clutch withdrawal lever from the clutch housing.

6 Remove the operating lever from the housing.

7 Remove the splined sleeve from the operating lever.

8 Remove the retaining pin bushes from the housing.

9 Remove the slave cylinder housing.

Refitting

10 Reverse the procedure in 1 to 9 noting:

a The splined sleeve must be fitted to the operating lever before the lever is fitted to the clutch housing.

b When fitting the operating lever ensure that the push rod is positioned through the slave cylinder housing.

CLUTCH RELEASE BEARING   33.25.12

Remove and refit

Service tool: 18G 1270

Removing

1 Remove the operating lever, see 33.25.10.

2 Press out each Mills pin from the operating lever.

3 Remove each bearing sleeve plug, and release the bearing from the operating lever.

4 Mount the assembly on a suitable press and using 18G 1270 press the bearing sleeve from the bearing.

Refitting

5 Grease the sleeve and bearing.

6 Stand the sleeve on the bed of the press, position the bearing, and using 18G 1270, press the bearing onto the sleeve.

CAUTION: The bearing must not be assembled to the sleeve by applying load to the outer race.

7 Position the bearing assembly in the operating lever and insert the sleeve locating plugs.

8 Press in each Mills pin to retain the plugs.

9 Refit the operating lever, see 33.25.10.

CLUTCH PEDAL —
U.K. Specification   33.30.02

Remove and refit

Removing

1 Disconnect the return springs from the clutch and brake pedals.

2 Remove the four screws to release the cover plate.

3 Disconnect the stop light switch wiring.

4 Jack up the front of the car and support with stands.

5 Attach a tube to the bleed nipples of the clutch slave cylinder and a front brake, slacken the bleed nipples and pump the clutch and brake fluid into containers – similar to the bleeding procedure in 33.15.01.

6 Disconnect the fluid pipe from the clutch master cylinder and plug the pipe.

7 Disconnect the fluid pipes from the brake master cylinder and plug the pipes.

NOTE: Brake and clutch fluid can have a detrimental effect on paintwork; ensure that fluid is not allowed to contact painted surfaces.

8 Withdraw the split pin and washer, and withdraw the clutch pedal clevis pin.

continued

CLUTCH

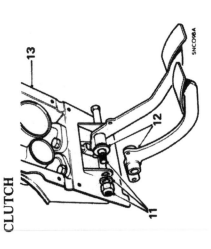

9 Remove the two screws and six bolts and spring washers retaining the pedal box to the body, noting the position of the bolts which secure the oil pressure pipe clips.
10 Raise the pedal box as far as possible.
11 Unscrew the nut and spring washer and withdraw the pivot bolt sufficiently to permit removal of the clutch pedal.
12 Remove the clutch pedal and spacer washer.
13 Remove the pedal box.
14 Remove the clutch pedal pad.

Refitting
15 Reverse the procedure in 1 to 14.
16 Bleed the clutch hydraulic system, see 33.15.01.
17 Bleed the brake hydraulic system, see 70.25.02.

CLUTCH PEDAL — U.S.A. Specification

Remove and refit 33.30.02

Removing
1 Disconnect the return springs from the clutch and brake pedals.
2 Disconnect the battery.
3 Remove the H.T. lead from the ignition coil and the white and blue lead from the ballast resistor.

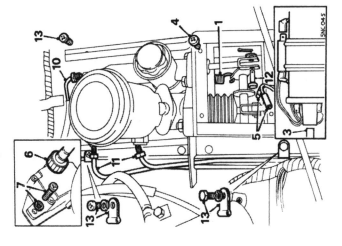

4 Remove the four screws to release the cover plate complete with ignition coil.
5 Disconnect the stop light switch wiring.
6 Disconnect the gearbox drive cable from the service interval counter (if fitted).
7 Remove the two screws retaining the service interval counter to the bracket and swing the counter aside (if fitted).
8 Jack up the front of the car and support with stands.
9 Attach a tube to the bleed nipples of the clutch slave cylinder and a front brake, slacken the bleed nipples and pump the clutch and brake fluid into containers — similar to the bleeding procedure in 33.15.01.
10 Disconnect the fluid pipe from the clutch master cylinder and plug the pipe.
11 Disconnect the fluid pipe from the brake master cylinder and plug the pipes.

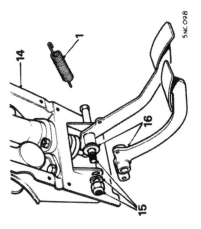

NOTE: Brake and clutch fluid can have a detrimental effect on paintwork; ensure that fluid is not allowed to contact painted surfaces.
12 Withdraw the split pin and washer, and withdraw the clutch pedal clevis pin.
13 Remove the four screws and four bolts and spring washers retaining the pedal box to the body, noting the position of the bolts which secure the oil pressure pipe clips.
14 Raise the pedal box as far as possible.
15 Unscrew the nut and spring washer and withdraw the pivot bolt sufficiently to permit removal of the clutch pedal.
16 Remove the clutch pedal and spacer washer.
17 Remove the pedal box.
18 Remove the clutch pedal pad.

Refitting
19 Reverse the procedure in 1 to 18.
20 Bleed the clutch hydraulic system, see 33.15.01.
21 Bleed the brake hydraulic system, see 70.25.02.

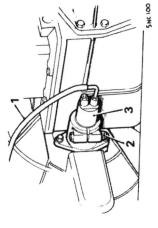

SLAVE CYLINDER

Remove and refit 33.35.01

Removing
1 Disconnect the hydraulic pipe from the slave cylinder.
2 Remove the locating bolt, nut and washer.
3 Withdraw the slave cylinder from the housing.

Refitting
4 Centralize the push rod in the housing.
5 Fit the slave cylinder to the housing.
6 Align the groove in the slave cylinder with the bolt hole in the housing.
7 Fit the locating bolt and nut.
8 Re-connect the hydraulic pipe.
9 Bleed the clutch hydraulic system, see 33.15.01.

33.25.10

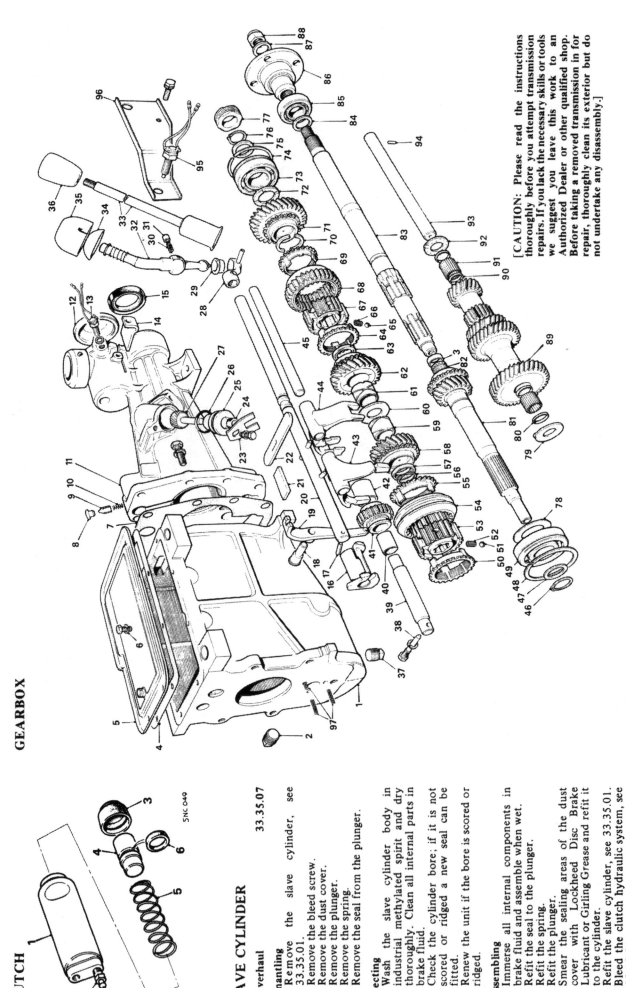

5NC 049

[CAUTION: Please read the instructions thoroughly before you attempt transmission repairs. If you lack the necessary skills or tools we suggest you leave this work to an Authorized Dealer or other qualified shop. Before taking a removed transmission in for repair, thoroughly clean its exterior but do not undertake any disassembly.]

CLUTCH

SLAVE CYLINDER

Overhaul   33.35.07

Dismantling

1. Remove the slave cylinder, see 33.35.01.
2. Remove the bleed screw.
3. Remove the dust cover.
4. Remove the plunger.
5. Remove the spring.
6. Remove the seal from the plunger.

Inspecting

7. Wash the slave cylinder body in industrial methylated spirit and dry thoroughly. Clean all internal parts in brake fluid.
8. Check the cylinder bore; if it is not scored or ridged a new seal can be fitted.
   Renew the unit if the bore is scored or ridged.

Reassembling

9. Immerse all internal components in brake fluid and assemble when wet.
10. Refit the seal to the plunger.
11. Refit the spring.
12. Refit the plunger.
13. Smear the sealing areas of the dust cover with Lockheed Disc Brake Lubricant or Girling Grease and refit it to the cylinder.
14. Refit the slave cylinder, see 33.35.01.
15. Bleed the clutch hydraulic system, see 33.15.01.

GEARBOX

KEY TO THE GEARBOX COMPONENTS

1 Gearbox case
2 Oil filler level plug
3 Spacer
4 Joint gaskets
5 Top cover
6 Top cover bolt
7 Joint gasket
8 Plug
9 Detent plunger
10 Detent spring
11 Rear extension
12 End cover
13 Reverse light switch
14 Reverse lift plate
15 Oil seal
16 Interlock spool
17 Selector shaft roll pin
18 Reverse operating lever pin
19 Reverse operating lever
20 Gear selector shaft
21 Magnet
22 Interlock spool plate
23 Retaining clip
24 Seal

25 Housing
26 'O' ring
27 Speedometer pinion
28 Gear lever yoke
29 Seat
30 Spring
31 Anti-rattle plunger
32 Lower gear-change lever
33 Upper gear-change lever
34 Dust cover washer
35 Dust cover
36 Knob
37 Drain plug
38 Reverse idler spindle locating screw
39 Reverse idler spindle
40 Reverse idler gear bush
41 Reverse idler gear
42 Reverse idler distance piece
43 3rd and 4th speed selector forks
44 1st and 2nd speed selector forks
45 Selector fork shaft
46 Circlip
47 Backing washer
48 Snap-ring

49 Ball bearing
50 Synchromesh cup
51 Ball
52 Spring
53 3rd and 4th speed synchromesh hub
54 3rd and 4th speed operating sleeve
55 Synchromesh cup
56 Mainshaft circlip
57 3rd speed gear thrust washer
58 3rd speed gear
59 Gear bush
60 Selective washer
61 Gear bush
62 2nd speed gear
63 Thrust washer
64 Synchromesh cup
65 Ball
66 Spring
67 1st and 2nd speed operating sleeve
68 Mainshaft reverse gear
69 Synchromesh cup
70 Split collar
71 1st speed gear
72 Thrust washer

73 Mainshaft centre bearing
74 Snap-ring
75 Selective washer
76 Circlip
77 Speedometer wheel
78 Oil flinger
79 Front thrust washer
80 Bearing outer retaining ring
81 1st motion shaft
82 Needle-roller bearing
83 Mainshaft
84 Washer
85 Ball bearing
86 Drive flange
87 Washer
88 Self-locking nut
89 Laygear gear cluster
90 Bearing inner retaining ring
91 Needle-rollers
92 Rear thrust washer
93 Layshaft
94 Layshaft dowel
95 Seat belt switch (if fitted)
96 Bracket (if fitted)
97 Laygear pre-load springs

37.00.02

INCO48E

SECTION THROUGH THE GEARBOX

1 1st motion shaft
2 Circlip
3 Front ball bearing
4 Snap-ring
5 Gear selector shaft
6 Gearbox top extension
7 Top cover
8 Spacer
9 Top cover bolt
10 3rd and 4th speed synchromesh hub
11 Spring
12 Ball
13 3rd and 4th speed operating sleeve
14 Selector shaft pin
15 Interlock spool plate
16 Selective washer
17 Interlock spool
18 Reverse operating lever
19 Selector shaft roll pin
20 Mainshaft reverse gear
21 Synchromesh cup
22 1st speed gear
23 Thrust washer
24 Detent plunger
25 Sealing plug
26 Selector shaft 'O' ring
27 Yoke pin
28 Gear lever yoke
29 Seat
30 Dust cover
31 Lower gear-change lever
32 Dust cover seal
33 Upper gear-change lever
34 Bush
35 Spring

36 Anti rattle plunger
37 End cover
38 Self-locking nut
39 Flange washer
40 Flange and stoneguard assembly
41 Seal
42 End ball bearing
43 Thrust washer
44 Mainshaft
45 Gearbox rear extension
46 Speedometer wheel
47 Circlip
48 Selective washer
49 Snap-ring
50 Centre ball bearing
51 Layshaft dowel
52 Bearing outer retaining ring
53 Rear thrust washer
54 Split collar
55 Thrust washer
56 Gear bush
57 2nd speed gear
58 Gear bush
59 3rd speed gear
60 Thrust washer
61 Circlip
62 Drain plug
63 Synchromesh cup
64 Bearing inner retaining ring
65 Needle rollers
66 Laygear pre-load spring
67 Layshaft
68 Front thrust washer
69 Needle-roller bearing
70 Circlip backing washer

37.00.04

GEARBOX

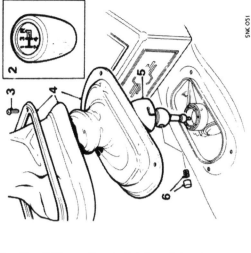

e Use new seals and gaskets.
f Before refitting the rear extension and flywheel housing smear the retaining bolts with Hylomar or equivalent jointing compound.
g Tighten the rear extension to gearbox bolts to 18 to 20 lbf ft (2.4 to 2.7 kgf m).
h Tighten the drive flange nut to 90 to 100 lbf ft (12.4 to 13.8 kgf m).

16 Pull the rear extension from the gearbox using 18G 2, ensuring that the pin of the gear selector rod does not foul the gearbox case.
17 Remove the rear extension to gearbox gasket.
18 Remove the distance piece from the mainshaft.
19 Remove the interlock spool.
20 Remove the reverse idler gear distance piece.
21 Disconnect the reverse light wiring and unscrew the reverse light switch.
22 Remove the gear selector rod and cover by tapping the selector rod rearwards.
23 Push the selector rod rearwards and expose the gear lever yoke.
24 Note the fitted position, and remove the gear lever yoke roll pin, and remove the gear lever yoke.
25 Remove the detent plunger plug.
26 Remove the gear selector rod forwards from the rear extension.
27 Remove the detent plunger and spring.
28 Remove the screw and spring washer, and remove the reverse gear lift plate.
29 Drift the oil seal and bearing from the rear extension.
30 Remove the two bolts, two nuts, spacers, spring and flat washers to release the rear engine mounting and gearbox steady assembly from the rear extension.
31 Unscrew the mounting from the rear extension.

Refitting
32 Reverse the procedure in 1 to 31 noting the following:
a Use tool 18G 134 with 18G 134 DR to refit the oil seal.
b Renew the selector shaft roll pins retaining the gear lever yoke.
c The distance washer on the mainshaft should be greased and located on the inner face of the bearing prior to refitting the rear extension.
d When refitting the gear selector shaft roll pin ensure that it is centrally positioned in the shaft to prevent difficulty when fitting the flywheel housing.

GEAR CHANGE LEVER

Remove and refit   37.16.04

Removing
1 Remove the front carpet around the tunnel.
2 Unscrew and remove the gear-change lever knob.
3 Remove the screws securing the gaiter retaining plate.
4 Remove the retaining plate, gaiter and draught excluder over the gear-change lever.

continued

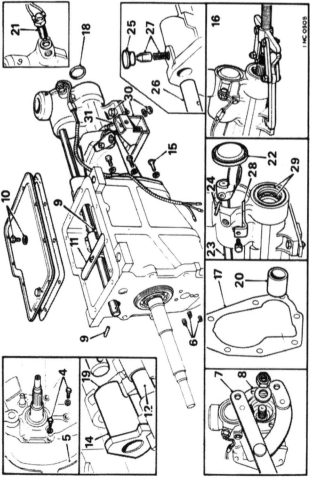

REAR EXTENSION

Remove and refit   37.12.01

Service tools: 18G 2, 18G 134, 18G 134 DR, 18G 1205

Removing
1 Remove the gearbox assembly, see 37.20.01.
2 Remove the speedometer pinion assembly, see 37.25.05.
3 Support the gearbox in a vice clamping the drain plug and using a piece of wood as a spacer.
4 Remove the five bolts and washers securing the flywheel housing to the gearbox, noting the bottom bolt is fitted with a sealing washer.
5 Remove the flywheel housing and gasket.
6 Remove the three laygear pre-load springs.
7 Using tool 18G 1205 retain the gearbox flange and remove the locknut and plain washer.
8 Remove the drive flange.
9 Remove the roll pin from the gear selector shaft.
10 Remove the eight bolts and spring washers retaining the top cover and remove the top cover and gasket, noting one bolt is removed in 1.
11 Remove the interlock spool plate.
12 Remove the selector fork shaft forwards.
13 Turn the gear selector rod until the pin engages in the reverse operating lever.
14 Slide the interlock spool forwards along the gear selector rod, then turn the gear selector rod out of engagement with the reverse operating lever.
15 Remove the bolts and spring washers securing the rear extension to the gearbox, noting the bolt which secures the harness clip for the reverse light switch.

GEARBOX

5   Ensure that the gear-change lever is in neutral position, press and turn the lever retaining cover and lift the assembly from the gearbox.

6   Collect the plunger and spring.

Refitting

7   Reverse the procedure in 1 to 6. On final assembly brush the spherical surfaces of the gear change lever stub with Duckhams Laminoid 'O' Grease or in cold climates use Duckhams Q 5848 Grease.

GEARBOX ASSEMBLY   37.20.01

Remove and refit
Service tool: 18G 1196

Removing

1   Remove the engine and gearbox, see 12.37.01.

2   Remove the bolt securing the fuel pipe clip to the gearbox top cover.

3   Slacken the clip and disconnect the fuel pipe hose from the fuel pump.

4   Remove nuts, spring and star washers, and bolts, to release the starter motor.

5   If the gearbox is to be dismantled, drain the gearbox.

6   Note that the bolt that retains the engine steady wire bracket has already been removed, see 12.37.01.

7   Remove the large locating bolt, its spring washer and nut.

8   Remove the remaining nuts and bolts and spring washers.

9   Remove the gearbox.

Refitting

10   Reverse the procedure in 1 to 9 noting:

   a   Check that the clutch driven plate is centralized using tool 18G 1196.

   b   Ensure the weight of the gearbox is not taken by the driven plate when refitting the gearbox.

   c   Fit all the nuts and bolts, and tighten finger tight.

   d   Tighten the large bolt and its nut first, then tighten the remaining nuts and bolts.

GEARBOX ASSEMBLY   37.20.04

Overhaul
Service tools: 18G 47 BF, 18G 47 BP, 18G 47 C, 18G 47 CZ, 18G 1004, 18G 1197, 18G 1198 A, 18G 1199, 18G 1208, 18G 1209

Dismantling

1   Remove the gearbox assembly, see 37.20.01.

2   Remove the rear extension, see 37.12.01.

3   Remove the 1st motion shaft, see 37.20.16.

4   Remove the selector forks.

5   Fit 18G 47 BP to the gearbox casing using two clutch housing retaining screws and washers; ensure that the centre screw and locknut are fully released before fitting the tool.

6   Tighten the centre screw of 18G 47 BP to locate and support the mainshaft spigot end, and tighten the locknut.

7   Remove the mainshaft centre bearing snap-ring.

8   Using 18G 1004 release the centre bearing mainshaft circlip from its locating groove.

9   Remove the dowel bolt and spring washer retaining the reverse idler gear spindle.

continued

37.12.01

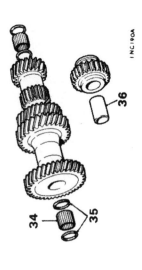

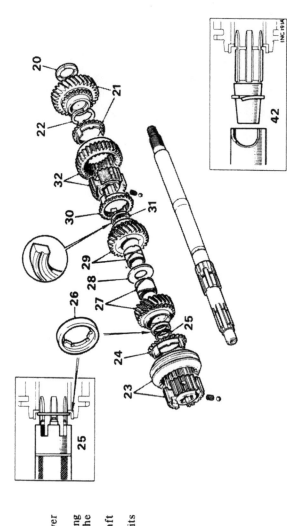

GEARBOX

10 Remove the reverse idler gear spindle.
11 Fit 18G 47 BP detail 3 using 18G 47 C and 18G 47 CZ and 18G 47 BF to the centre bearing.
12 Pull the centre bearing selective washer, circlip and speedometer pinion from the mainshaft.
13 Remove 18G 47 BP detail 1 from the gearbox case. Do not alter the centre screw or locknut setting prior to reassembling.
14 Tilt the mainshaft and remove it from the gearbox.

15 Remove the laygear assembly.
16 Remove the reverse idler gear.
17 Remove the reverse operating lever.
18 Remove the reverse operating lever pivot pin.
19 Remove the magnet from its housing in the gearbox case, or from the bottom of the gearbox case.
20 Remove the 1st speed gear mainshaft washer.
21 Remove the 1st speed gear and its synchromesh cup.
22 Remove the two split collars.

23 Remove the 3rd and 4th speed synchromesh hub and operating sleeve assembly, noting the grooved face is towards the front of the mainshaft.
24 Remove the 3rd gear synchromesh cup.
25 Using 18G 1199, the three long prongs of the tool inserted in the splines between the thrust washer tabs, remove the 3rd gear mainshaft circlip.
26 Remove the 3rd gear thrust washer.
27 Remove the 3rd gear and its bush.
28 Remove the 3rd-2nd gear SELECTIVE washer.
29 Remove the 2nd gear and its bush.
30 Remove the 2nd gear synchromesh cup.
31 Note the fitted position of the oil-grooved face of the 2nd gear washer and remove the washer.
32 Remove the 1st and 2nd speed synchromesh hub and reverse gear sleeve.

33 Remove tool 18G 1208 from the laygear.
34 Remove the 25 needle rollers from each end of the laygear cluster.
35 Remove the needle roller retaining rings from the laygear.
36 Press out the reverse idler gear bush.

140

GEARBOX

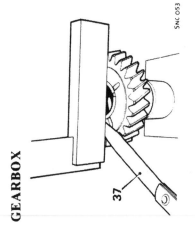

the 3rd gear mainshaft circlip. Measure the end-float of the bushes on the mainshaft and refer to the figure quoted in **DATA**. Fit the required SELECTIVE washer to obtain the correct end-float. Dismantle the mainshaft.
NOTE: Ensure that the bushes are kept with their respective gears.

39 Fit the bush to the reverse idler gear to the dimensions given in **DATA**.

40 Fit the laygear needle-roller retaining rings using 18G 1209 to the dimensions given in **DATA**.

41 Fit tool 18G 1208 to the layshaft to retain the needle-rollers.

42 Reverse the dismantling procedure in 16 to 32. Fit the 3rd gear mainshaft circlip using 18G 1198 A.

43 Fit the reverse idler spindle to the reverse gear and locate in the gearbox casing.

Reassembling

37 Measure the end-float of the 2nd and 3rd gears on their respective bushes. Stand the gear on a surface plate, insert the bush and check the end-float with a straight-edge and feeler gauge. The end-float should be within the figure quoted in **DATA**. Fit a new bush, if required, to increase the end-float.

38 Fit the 2nd gear washer, oil-grooved face away from the mainshaft shoulder, to the mainshaft. Assemble to the mainshaft the 3rd gear bush, SELECTIVE washer, 2nd gear bush, 3rd gear thrust washer with its oil-grooved face to the bush, and fit

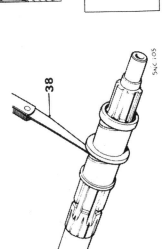

44 Fit the dowel bolt and spring washer to secure the reverse gear spindle.

45 Fit the laygear with its thrust washers in the bottom of the gearbox.

46 Tilt the mainshaft and fit it to the casing.

47 Fit 18G 47 BP detail 1 using two clutch housing retaining screws and washers.

48 Using the original setting of 18G 47 BP, locate and support the mainshaft spigot end.

49 Fit the centre bearing snap-ring to the bearing and locate the bearing on the mainshaft.

50 Fit the bearing using 18G 1197.

51 Fit the SELECTIVE washer and circlip.

52 Measure the gap between the SELECTIVE washer and circlip and refer to the figure quoted in **DATA**. Fit the required SELECTIVE washer to obtain the correct clearance.

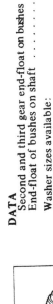

52

53 Fit the speedometer pinion.

54 Remove tool 18G 47 BP from the gearbox case.

55 Refit the selector forks.

56 Fit the first motion shaft, see 37.12.16.

57 Fit the rear extension, see 37.20.16.

58 Fit the gearbox assembly, see 37.20.01.

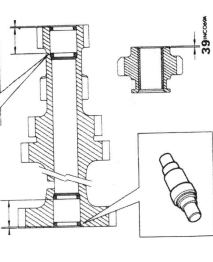

DATA

Second and third gear end-float on bushes	0.002 to 0.006 in (0.050 to 0.152 mm)
End-float of bushes on shaft	0.004 to 0.006 in (0.101 to 0.152 mm)

Washer sizes available:
Colour Code Plain . . . . 0.152 to 0.154 in (3.860 to 3.911 mm)
Green . . . . 0.156 to 0.158 in (3.962 to 4.013 mm)
Blue . . . . 0.161 to 0.163 in (4.089 to 4.140 mm)
Orange . . . . 0.165 to 0.167 in (4.191 to 4.241 mm)
Yellow . . . . 0.169 to 0.171 in (4.293 to 4.343 mm)

Laygear needle roller retaining rings:
Fitted depth: Inner . . . . 0.840 to 0.850 in (21.336 to 21.590 mm)
Outer . . . . 0.010 to 0.015 in (0.254 to 0.381 mm)
Centre bearing to circlip end-float . . . . 0.000 to 0.004 in (0.000 to 0.050 mm)
Washer sizes available:
Colour Code: Plain . . . . 0.119 to 0.121 in (3.022 to 3.073 mm)
Green . . . . 0.122 to 0.124 in (3.123 to 3.173 mm)
Blue . . . . 0.125 to 0.127 in (3.198 to 3.248 mm)
Orange . . . . 0.128 to 0.130 in (3.273 to 3.323 mm)
Reverse idler gear bush—fitted depth . . . . . . Flush, with to 0.010 in (0.254 mm) below gear face

37.20.04

GEARBOX

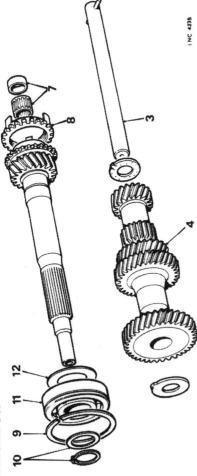

INC 428B

FIRST MOTION SHAFT 37.20.16

Remove and refit

Service tools: 18G 47 BF, 18G 47 C, 18G 47 BP, 18G 47 CZ, 18G 284, 18G 284 AA, 18G 284 AW 'A' points, 18G 1004, 18G 1208

Removing

1 Remove the gearbox assembly, see 37.20.01.
2 Remove the rear extension, see 37.12.01.
3 Using tool 18G 1208 push out the layshaft rearwards and retain the tool in the laygear.
4 Allow the laygear to drop to the bottom of the gearbox case.
5 Fit 18G 284 and 18G 284 AW to 18G 284 AA and locate and tighten onto the 1st motion shaft.

6 Extract the 1st motion shaft assembly from the gearbox.
7 Remove the mainshaft spigot roller bearing and spacer.
8 Remove the 4th gear synchromesh cup.
9 Remove the bearing snap-ring.

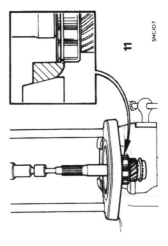

SNC107

10 Using 18G 1004, remove the bearing circlip and backing washer.
11 Using 18G 47 C, 18G 47 BF and 18G 47 BP pull the bearing from the shaft.
12 Remove the oil flinger.

INC 028A

Refitting

13 Reverse the procedure in 1 to 13, noting:

a Locate the oil flinger on the gear face with grease to prevent it falling free during replacement of the bearing.
b Ensure the laygear thrust washers are in place.
c Refit the first motion shaft bearing, using tools 18G 47 C, 18G 47 BP and 18G 47 CZ.

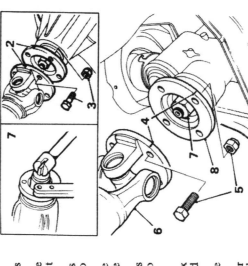

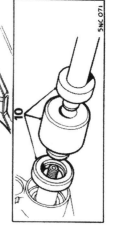

SNC 071

REAR OIL SEAL 37.23.01

Remove and refit

Service tools: 18G 134 DR, 18G 389, 18G 389 A, 18G 1205

Removing

1 Raise the car, and support with stands placed underneath the rear axle.
2 Mark the propeller shaft rear flange and the pinion flange to ensure correct alignment.
3 Remove the four nuts and bolts retaining the propeller shaft flange to the rear axle.
4 Mark the propeller shaft front flange and the gearbox flange to ensure correct alignment.
5 Remove the four nuts and bolts retaining the propeller shaft flange to the gearbox.
6 Remove the propeller shaft.
7 Using 18G 1205, retain the gearbox flange and remove the flange nut and plain washer.
8 Remove the flange from the mainshaft.
9 Extract the oil seal from the rear extension, using tools 18G 389 and 18G 389 A.

Refitting

10 Dip the new seal in oil, and fit using tool 18G 134 DR.
11 Reverse the procedure in 1 to 8, tightening the gearbox flange retaining nut to 90 to 100 lbf ft (12.4 to 13.8 kgf m).

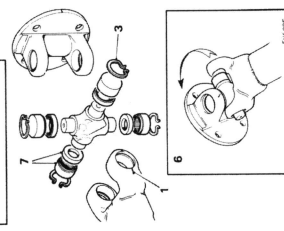

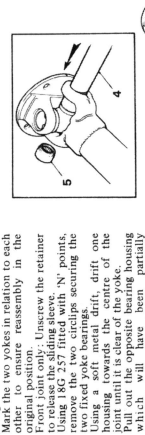

GEARBOX

SPEEDOMETER DRIVE PINION 37.25.05

Remove and refit

Removing

1 Raise the car, and support with stands placed underneath the rear axle.
2 Remove the screw and spring washer to release the locking flange and pull the speedometer cable from the drive pinion.
3 Remove the speedometer pinion assembly.
4 Remove the pinion assembly from the housing.
5 Remove the 'O' ring seals from the housing.

Refitting

6 Reverse the procedure in 1 to 5, using new 'O' ring seals if necessary.

PROPELLER SHAFT

PROPELLER SHAFT ASSEMBLY 47.15.01

Remove and refit

Removing

1 Jack up the car, and support with stands placed underneath the rear axle.
2 Mark the propeller shaft rear flange and the rear axle flange to ensure correct alignment.
3 Remove the four nuts and bolts retaining the propeller shaft flange to the rear axle.
4 Mark the propeller shaft front flange and the gearbox flange to ensure correct alignment.
5 Remove the four nuts and bolts retaining the propeller shaft flange to the gearbox flange.
6 Remove the propeller shaft.

Refitting

7 Reverse the procedure in 1 to 6, ensuring that the sliding spline flange is fitted to the gearbox.

UNIVERSAL JOINT 47.15.18

Remove and refit

Service tool: 18G 257

Removing

1 Mark the two yokes in relation to each other to ensure reassembly in the original position.
2 Front joint only: Unscrew the retainer to release the sliding sleeve.
3 Using 18G 257 fitted with 'N' points, remove the two circlips securing the two fixed yoke bearings.
4 Using a soft metal drift, drift one housing towards the centre of the joint until it is clear of the yoke.
5 Pull out the opposite bearing housing which will have been partially exposed.
6 Position the flange or shaft as shown and turn the spider clear of the fixed yoke. On front joints fitted with a grease nipple housing some leverage may be necessary.
7 Remove the bearing housing, oil seal and needle rollers.
8 Repeat 3 to 7 for the flange or shaft bearings.

Refitting

9 Reverse the procedure in 1 to 7, noting:
   a Check the splines of the sliding sleeve.
   b Smear the walls of the bearing races with grease and assemble the needle rollers to the bearing races and fill each bearing with grease to a depth of $\frac{1}{8}$ in (3 mm).
   c Fill the reservoir holes in the spider journals with a recommended grease.
   d Fit new seals to the spider journals.

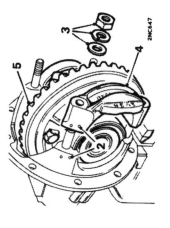

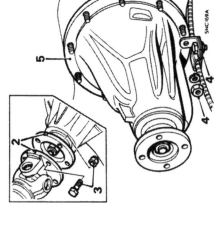

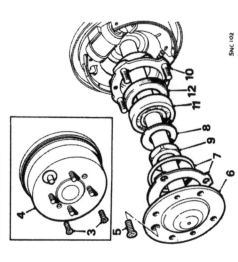

REAR AXLE

HALF-SHAFT, BEARING AND OIL SEAL

Remove and refit   51.10.02
Half-shaft   51.10.01

Service tools: 18G 134, 18G 134 Q, 18G 152, 18G 304, 18G 304 F, 18G 304 H

Removing

1 Raise and support the rear of the car under the rear axle.
2 Remove the road wheel.
3 Remove the two countersunk screws or nuts retaining the brake drum.
4 Remove the brake drum, it may be necessary to slacken off the brake adjustment if the brake shoes hold the drum.
5 Remove the countersunk screw retaining the half-shaft flange.

6 Remove the half-shaft.
7 Remove the gasket and 'O' ring seal.
8 Knock back the lock tab of the hub nut washer.
9 Unscrew the hub nut using tool 18G 152.
NOTE: Left-hand side:
     The nut is a L.H. thread.
   Right-hand side:
     The nut is a R.H. thread.
10 Remove the hub from the axle casing using tool 18G 304 with adaptors 18G 304 F and 18G 304 H.
11 Press the bearing from the hub.
12 Remove the oil seal.

Refitting

13 Pack the bearing with lithium based grease, and dip the new seal in light oil before reassembling.
14 Fit a new oil seal, using 18G 134 with adaptor 18G 134 Q, ensuring the lip of the seal is towards the bearing.
15 Press the bearing into the hub.
16 Drift the hub into the axle casing using tool 18G 134 and adaptor 18G 134 Q.
17 Reverse the procedure in 1 to 9 noting:
a. Renew the hub nut lockwasher.
b. Renew the gasket and 'O' ring seal.
18 Check the brake adjustment, see 'MAINTENANCE'.
19 Check the rear axle oil level and top up if necessary, see 'MAINTENANCE'.

DIFFERENTIAL ASSEMBLY

Remove and refit   51.15.01

Removing

1 Remove both axle half-shafts, see 51.10.01.
2 Mark the propeller shaft and pinion flanges for correct re-alignment.
3 Remove the four nuts and bolts from the pinion flange and disconnect the propeller shaft. Drain the rear axle.
4 Note the position of the hand brake cable bracket (1977 and later cars only) and remove the nuts and spring washers retaining the differential assembly unit to the axle casing.
5 Withdraw the differential assembly and gasket.

Refitting

6 Reverse the procedure in 1 to 5, noting:
a. Use a new sealing gasket if necessary.
b. Refill the axle with a Service oil.

DIFFERENTIAL ASSEMBLY

Overhaul   51.15.07
Differential cage bearings — 1 to 6 and 44 to 50   51.15.13
Differential pinion bearing — 1 to 5 and 14 to 38   51.15.19

Service tools: 18G 47 C, 18G 47 CZ or 18G 285, 18G 47 M, 18G 191, 18G 191 A, 18G 207, 18G 264, 18G 264 AB, 18G 1205, S4221A-17

[CAUTION: Precision measurements using special tools will be necessary for reassembling the differential. Please read the instructions thoroughly before you remove any component. If you lack the special tools, the skills, or a clean workshop, we suggest that you leave differential repairs to an Authorized Dealer or other qualified shop. A differential that has been assembled without the required precision measurements and adjustments will be noisy and wear rapidly. Before taking a removed differential assembly in for repair, thoroughly clean its exterior but do not undertake any disassembly.]

Dismantling

1 Remove the differential assembly, see 51.15.01.
2 Mark the location of one differential bearing cap for reassembly.
3 Remove the two nuts, plain and spring washers retaining each cap.
4 Remove the bearing caps.
5 Withdraw the differential from its housing.

continued

REAR AXLE

6 Withdraw the bearings and shims from the differential carrier, using 18G 47 C and 18G 47 M, ensuring that the pair numbers of the adaptor segments mate correctly.

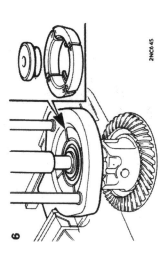

7 Turn back the lock washers locking the crown wheel retaining bolts.

8 Remove the bolts and lock washers retaining the crown wheel.

9 Remove the crown wheel.

10 Tap out the locking pin retaining the differential gear pin.

11 Remove the differential gear pin from the crown wheel side.

12 Turn the differential gears and remove the differential pinions and their thrust washers as they come free.

13 Remove the differential gear wheels and their Tufnol washers.

14 Remove the differential drive flange, see 51.15.36.

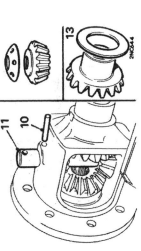
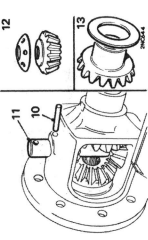

15 Drift out the pinion and remove the distance piece.

16 Remove the oil seal and outer tapered bearing cone.

17 Remove the front bearing cup from the case by drifting.

18 Remove the rear bearing cup from the case by drifting.

19 Remove the bearing cone from the pinion, using 18G 285 or 18G 47 C, 18G 47 CZ and S4221A-17.

20 Remove the pinion head washer.

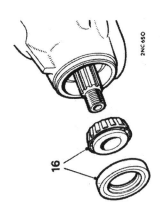

Reassembling
Setting the pinion position

21 Fit the inner and outer pinion bearing cups to the case using 18G 264, 18G 264 AB and S4221A-17.

22 Smooth off the pinion head using an oil-stone; do not erase any markings etched on the pinion head.

23 Fit a pinion head washer, recessed side towards the pinion head, of known size to the pinion.

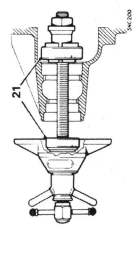

continued

51.10.01

REAR AXLE

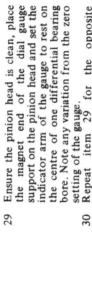
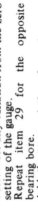

24 Fit the inner bearing cone to the pinion, using 18G 47 C and 18G 47 CZ and S4221A-17.

25 Refit the pinion and outer bearing cone to the case, omitting the bearing spacer, and the front oil seal.

26 Refit the drive flange spring washer and nut.

27 Using 18G 1205, retain the drive flange and tighten the nut until a bearing pre-load of 8 to 10 lbf in (0.09 to 0.12 kgf m) using 18G 207 is obtained.

28 Using 18G 191 and 18G 191 A, zero the gauge on the 'A' step of 18G 191 A (the pinion setting gauge).

29 Ensure the pinion head is clean, place the magnet end of the dial gauge support on the pinion head and set the indicator arm of the gauge to rest on the centre of one differential bearing bore. Note any variation from the zero setting of the gauge.

30 Repeat item 29 for the opposite bearing bore.

31 Add the two variations from the zero setting of the gauge together and divide by two to obtain the average gauge reading.

32 From the pinion, note the unbracketed figure etched on the head. If no unbracketed figure is shown the pinion is 'standard' and has no variation from its specified thickness: substitute '0' in the following calculations.

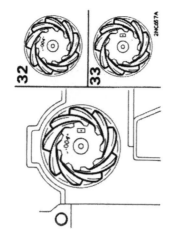

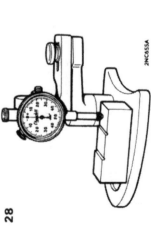

Calculating pinion head washer size

Example A
If the average gauge reading is minus:
Add the unbracketed figure etched on the pinion to . . . . −0.005 in (−0.127 mm)
the average gauge reading . . . . . . −0.002 in (−0.051 mm)

Reduce the pinion head spacer by the total amount . . . . **−0.007 in** **(−0.178 mm)**

Example B
If the average gauge reading is plus, but numerically less than the unbracketed pinion figure:
Subtract from the unbracketed figure etched on the pinion . . . . −0.005 in (−0.127 mm)
the average gauge reading . . . . . . +0.003 in (+0.076 mm)

Reduce the washer thickness by the figure obtained . . . . **−0.002 in** **(−0.051 mm)**

continued

146

REAR AXLE

Example C

If the average gauge reading is plus and numerically greater than the unbracketed pinion figure:

Subtract from the average gauge reading the unbracketed figure etched on the pinion	+0.008 in	(+0.203 mm)
	−0.003 in	(−0.076 mm)
Increase the washer thickness by the figure obtained	**+ 0.005 in**	**(+0.127 mm)**

No alteration to the pinion head washer size is required if the average gauge reading is plus and numerically equal to the unbracketed figure etched on the pinion head, or if the average gauge reading is zero and the pinion is of 'standard' thickness.

33 From the pinion, note the bracketed figure etched on the head.
  a If the figure is plus: reduce the pinion washer thickness by the amount marked.
  b If the figure is minus: increase the pinion washer thickness by the amount marked.
  A tolerance of 0.001 in (0.025 mm) is allowed in the thickness of the washer finally fitted.
  Eight pinion head washers are available ranging in 0.002 in (0.051 mm) steps from 0.116 in (2.94 mm) to 0.130 in (3.30 mm).

34 Remove the drive flange nut, washer and drive flange; extract the pinion; remove the pinion bearing and pinion head washer.

35 Fit the correct size pinion head washer as calculated in 27 to 33; refit the inner bearing cone to the pinion.

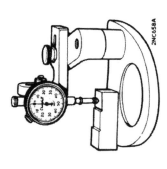

39

Setting the crown wheel position

39 Mount on 18G 191 A one differential bearing, thrust face downwards, ensuring the inner race is over the recess on the surface plate.

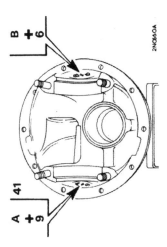

40

40 Mount 18G 191 A on the surface plate and zero the gauge on the 'A' step of the differential bearing gauge.

41 Settle the inner bearing race by pressing down against the inner ring and rotating it. Take a gauge reading on the plain inner ring. Note the reading obtained for each bearing.

36 Assemble the pinion to the carrier and fit a new distance spacer.
  CAUTION: The pinion bearing distance piece is of the collapsible type. That is to say, when the pinion nut is tightened to the correct torque spanner reading of 135 to 140 lbf ft (18.69 to 19.4 kg m) the distance piece collapses to give the correct bearing pre-load of 11 to 13 lbf in (0.126 to 0.149 kgf m). It will only perform this function once. Thus, when the pinion is reassembled a new distance piece must be fitted.

37 Fit the outer bearing cone, oil seal, drive flange, spring washer and nut.

38 Gradually tighten the drive flange nut to 135 to 140 lbf ft (18.69 to 19.35 kgf m), checking pre-load frequently during the tightening using 18G 207, and ensuring that the correct pre-load of 11 to 13 lbf in (0.126 to 0.149 kgf m) is obtained at 140 lbf ft (19.35 kgf m).

continued

147

51.15.07

REAR AXLE

42 Machining variations from the standard dimensions of the gear carrier, dimension 'A' and 'B' and the differential case, dimensions 'C' and 'D' are marked on the components in the positions illustrated.

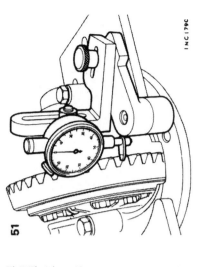

42

Machining variations: stamped individually as illustrated.

Example

A	+0.009 in	+0.127 mm
B	+0.006 in	+0.152 mm
C	+0.002 in	+0.051 mm
D	+0.002 in	+0.051 mm

Bearing variations: As measured in operations 39 to 41

Crown wheel side bearing . . . . +0.002 in (+0.127 mm)
Opposite crown wheel side . . . . +0.001 in (+0.051 mm)

CALCULATE DIFFERENTIAL SIDE BEARING SHIMS as follows:

A+D–C+0.002 in (0.178 mm) + or – the bearing variation

A+D	+0.011 in	+0.279 mm
–C	–0.002 in	–0.051 mm
	+0.009 in	+0.229 mm
+0.002	+0.002 in	+0.051 mm
	+0.011 in	+0.279 mm
Bearing variation add	+0.002 in	+0.051 mm

SHIM PACK REQUIRED +0.013 in +0.330 mm

CALCULATE SHIMS REQUIRED FOR BEARING OPPOSITE CROWN WHEEL as follows:

B–D+0.006 in (0.152 mm) + or – the bearing variation

B–D	+0.004 in	+0.102 mm
+0.006	+0.006 in	+0.152 mm
	+0.010 in	+0.254 mm
Bearing variation add	+0.001 in	+0.025 mm

SHIM PACK REQUIRED +0.011 in +0.279 mm

43 Refit the differential pinion pin, pinions and thrust washers to the differential case.

44 Fit the pinion locking peg and secure by preening the metal of the differential carrier.

45 Bolt the crown wheel to the differential case and torque tighten the bolts to 60 lbf ft (8.30 kgf m).

46 Fit the shim packs and bearings to the differential case.

47 Refit the differential assembly to the carrier.

48 Refit the bearing caps, plain washers, spring washers and nuts.

49 Tighten the nuts.

50 Using 18G 191, measure the amount of crown wheel run-out during rotation of the assembly. Maximum permissible run-out 0.002 in (0.05 mm). If the run-out is incorrect, refit the crown wheel in a different position on the case until the run-out obtained is within the figure given.

51 Mount 18G 191 on the differential carrier flange and measure the backlash between the crown wheel and pinion. The figure must correspond to that etched on the rear face of the crown wheel.

52 Decrease the backlash by increasing the thickness of the shim pack on the crown wheel side and decreasing the thickness of the shim pack on the other side by an equal amount. Reverse this procedure to increase the backlash. A movement of 0.002 in (0.05 mm) shim thickness from one side of the differential to the other side will produce a variation in backlash of approximately 0.002 in (0.05 mm).

DATA

Crown wheel backlash . . . . Etched on rear face of crown wheel

Differential bearing shim sizes . . . . 0.002 in (0.05 mm)
0.003 in (0.07 mm)
0.004 in (0.10 mm)
0.010 in (0.25 mm)

Pinion head washer sizes . . . . 0.116 in (2.94 mm)
0.118 in (2.99 mm)
0.120 in (3.04 mm)
0.122 in (3.09 mm)
0.124 in (3.14 mm)
0.126 in (3.20 mm)
0.128 in (3.25 mm)
0.130 in (3.30 mm)

Crown wheel run-out . . . . 0.002 in (0.05 mm)

Pinion bearing pre-load . . . . 8 to 10 lbf in (0.09 to 0.12 kgf m) for pinion setting only
11 to 13 lbf in (0.127 to 0.15 kgf m) for final assembly

REAR AXLE

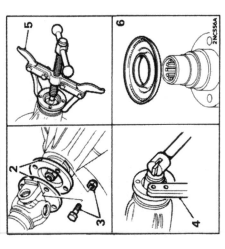

DIFFERENTIAL DRIVE FLANGE 51.15.36

Remove and refit

Service tools: 18G 1205, 18G 2

Removing

1 Raise and support the rear of the vehicle.
2 Mark the propeller shaft and pinion flanges for correct re-alignment.
3 Remove the four nuts and bolts from the pinion flange.
4 Retain the drive flange, using 18G 1205, and remove the nut and spring washer.
5 Remove the drive flange, using 18G 2.
6 Remove the drive flange stone guard.

Refitting

7 Reverse the procedure 1 to 6, noting:
  a Tighten the pinion flange nut to 140 lbf ft (19.34 kgf m).
  b Check the rear axle oil level and top up if necessary.

PINION OIL SEAL 51.20.01

Remove and refit

Removing

1 Remove the differential drive flange, see 51.15.36.
2 Extract the oil seal from the casing.

Refitting

3 Reverse the procedure 1 and 2, noting:
  a Fit the new oil seal with the lip of the seal facing inwards.
  b Tighten the drive flange retaining nut to 140 lbf ft (19.34 kgf m).
  c Check the rear axle oil level, and top up if necessary.

REAR AXLE ASSEMBLY — All U.K. and 1975-1976 U.S.A. 51.25.01

Remove and refit

Removing

1 Raise the rear of the car and support just forward of the rear spring front shackle pin.
2 Remove the road wheels.
3 Remove the rear exhaust pipe and silencers, see 30.10.22.
4 Mark the pinion and propeller drive flanges to ensure correct re-alignment.
5 Remove the four nuts and bolts retaining the propeller shaft rear flange to the pinion flange and release the propeller shaft.
6 Unscrew the union nut on the brake feed pipe at the flexible hose.

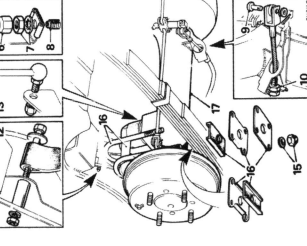

7 Remove the locknut and washer from the flexible hose.
8 Remove the flexible hose from the bracket.
9 Remove the hand brake cable clevis pin from the compensating lever.
10 Unscrew the nut and slide the nut and washer along the hand brake cable to release the cable from the compensating lever bracket.
11 Support the axle with a jack to relieve the tension on the rear axle rebound straps.
12 Remove the nut, bolt, washer and spacer to release each rebound strap complete with spacer.
13 Remove the shock absorber link securing nut, and release the link from the 'U' bolt base plate.
14 Lower the jack until the full weight of the rear axle is on the rear springs.
15 Remove the 'U' bolt nuts.
16 Remove the 'U' bolts, axle cap, mounting rubbers, brackets and base

plate.
17 Lift the axle over the L.H. spring and lower onto the floor.

Refitting

18 Reverse the procedure in 1 to 17, noting:
  a Use new rear spring mounting rubbers if necessary.
  b Do not fully tighten the spring 'U' bolts until the car has been lowered to the ground and the car weight (normal working load) has been applied to the springs.
19 Bleed the brake hydraulic system, see 70.25.02.

REAR AXLE ASSEMBLY — 1977 and later U.S.A.

Remove and refit 51.25.01

Removing

1 Raise the rear of the car and support just forward of the rear spring front shackle pin.

51.15.36

REAR AXLE

2   Remove the road wheels.
3   Remove the rear exhaust pipe and silencers, see 30.10.22.
4   Mark the pinion and propeller drive flanges to ensure correct re-alignment.
5   Remove the four nuts and bolts retaining the propeller shaft rear flange to the pinion flange and release the propeller shaft.
6   Unscrew the union nut on the brake feed pipe at the flexible hose.
7   Remove the locknut and washer from the flexible hose.
8   Remove the flexible hose from the bracket.
9   Slacken the hand brake cable adjustment nuts.
10 Remove the hand brake cable clevis pin from each wheel cylinder lever.
11 Remove the nut and screw securing the cable clip to the differential.
12 Remove the nuts and bolts securing the hand brake cable mounting strap to the rear axle casing.
13 Support the axle with a jack to relieve the tension on the rear axle rebound straps.
14 Remove the nut, bolt, washer and spacer to release each rebound strap complete with spacer.
15 Remove the shock absorber link securing nut, and release the link from the 'U' bolt base plate.
16 Lower the jack until the full weight of the rear axle is on the rear springs.
17 Remove the 'U' bolt nuts.
18 Remove the 'U' bolts, axle cap, mounting rubbers, brackets and base plate.
19 Lift the axle over the L.H. spring and lower onto the floor.

Refitting

20 Reverse the procedure in 1 to 17, noting:

a   Use new rear spring mounting rubbers if necessary.

b   Do not fully tighten the spring 'U' bolts until the car has been lowered to the ground and the car weight (normal working load) has been applied to the springs.

c   Renew the hand brake cable securing clip if damaged.

d   Renew the hand brake mounting strap if damaged or showing signs of deterioration.

21 Adjust the hand brake cable, see 70.35.10.

22 Bleed the brake hydraulic system, see 70.25.02.

STEERING – RIGHT-HAND STEER

5NC167A

5NC609

STEERING RACK

Remove and refit   57.25.01

Service tool: 18G 1063

Removing

CAUTION: Should a seal become damaged, with a subsequent loss of lubricant, it is necessary to remove the steering rack assembly for dismantling and inspection of the components. If a seal has been damaged in the workshop and dirt has not entered the steering rack assembly, a new seal may be fitted and the inner ball joint and rack lubricated with a service grease, see 57.25.03.

If the vehicle is hoisted with its front wheels clear of the ground, care should be taken to avoid forceful movement of the wheels from lock to lock as damage may occur within the steering mechanism.

1 Remove the radiator, see 26.40.01.
2 Turn the steering to the straight-ahead position.
3 Jack up and support the front of the car and remove the road wheels.
4 Remove the nuts from the tie-rod end assemblies.
5 Using tool 18G 1063, detach the tie-rod end assemblies from the steering levers.
6 Remove the steering-column pinch bolt.
7 Remove the two bolts securing the column upper fixing to the body, and collect the shim.
8 Pull back the column sufficiently to disengage the column sleeve from the pinion. Support the column.
9 Mark the steering rack housing in relation to the mounting bracket to assist when refitting.
10 Remove the clamp bolts and clamps from the mounting brackets.
11 Withdraw the steering rack assembly.

Refitting

12 Position the rack into the mounting brackets and fit the clamps but do not tighten the clamp fixing bolts.
13 Check that the rack is in the straight-ahead position with the pinch bolt flat on the pinion shaft uppermost.
14 Check that the steering-column is in the straight-ahead position with the slot of the clamp uppermost.
15 Slide the column over the pinion shaft as far as it will go.
16 Tighten the steering-column upper fixing bolts.
17 Fit and tighten the three toe-plate bolts.
18 Turn the steering-wheel one complete turn to the left and back, then one complete turn to the right and back.
19 Check that the marks made on the steering-rack housing and mounting bracket are aligned and tighten the clamp fixing bolts to 20 to 22 lbf ft (2.77 to 3.04 kgf m).

CAUTION: If the marks are not aligned or new mounting brackets are being fitted, the steering-rack must be aligned, see 57.35.04.

20 Tighten the steering-column pinch bolt to 9 to 12 lbf ft (1.24 to 1.66 kgf m).
21 Reverse the procedure in 1 to 5 noting:
  a Tighten the tie-rod end assembly ball joint nut to 28 to 32 lbf ft (3.87 to 4.48 kgf m).
  b Check the front wheel alignment, see 'MAINTENANCE'.

STEERING-RACK SEALS

Remove and refit   57.25.03

Service tool: 18G 1063

Removing

CAUTION: If the vehicle is hoisted with its front wheels clear of the ground, care should be taken to avoid forceful movement of the wheels from lock to lock as damage may occur within the steering mechanism.

1 Jack up and support the front of the car and remove the road wheel.
2 Mark the position of the tie-rod end assembly locknut, for re-assembly.
3 Slacken the tie-rod end assembly locknut.
4 Remove the nut securing the tie-rod end assembly to the steering lever.
5 Using tool 18G 1063, detach the tie-rod end assembly from the steering lever.
6 Remove the tie-rod end assembly and locknut from the tie-rod.
7 Slacken the seal retaining clips/wire.
8 Detach the large clip from the seal and allow it to hang on the end of the rack housing. Withdraw the seal from the rack housing and the tie-rod.
9 Remove the small clip and protective shield from the seal.

Inspection

10 Examine the existing grease around the inner ball joint and the rack for ingress of water or dirt; if this is evident, the steering rack must be removed for dismantling and inspection of the components, see 57.25.07.
11 If the inner ball joint and the rack are in a satisfactory condition, apply approximately 2 oz (57 gm) of a service grease around each inner ball joint and the rack including the teeth.

Refitting

12 Fit a new seal.
13 Secure the seal to the rack housing with the clip or wire.
14 Fit the protective shield and small clip to the outer end of the seal.
15 Reverse the procedure in 1 to 6.
16 Check the front wheel alignment, see 'MAINTENANCE'.

STEERING — RIGHT-HAND STEER

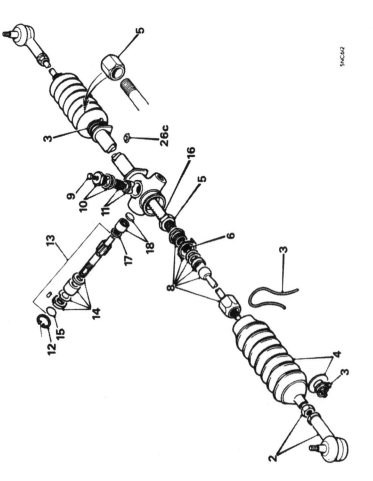

5NC62

STEERING RACK AND PINION

Overhaul   57.25.07

Dismantling

1. Remove the steering rack, see 57.25.01.

2. Slacken the locknuts and remove the tie-rod end assemblies and locknuts from the tie-rods.

3. Slacken the seal retaining clips and remove the seal retaining wire from the pinion end of the steering rack.

4. Remove the seals together with their protective shields fitted behind the outer retaining clips.

5. Slacken the locknuts and unscrew the tie-rod inner ball joint assemblies.

6. Withdraw the coil springs and unscrew the locknuts from each end of the rack.

7. Remove the seal retaining clip from the rack housing.

8. Unlock the tab washer and unscrew the sleeved nut from the cup nut and remove the tab washer, shims and cup to dismantle the tie-rod inner ball joint assembly.

9. Remove the grease plug from the screwed cap.

10. Remove the screwed cap and shims.

11. Withdraw the spring and plunger from the rack housing.

12. Remove the circlip retaining the pinion assembly.

13. Withdraw the pinion assembly and dowel.

CAUTION: Take care not to lose the dowel.

14. Remove the retaining ring, shims, the pinion shaft bush and thrust washer from the pinion shaft.

15. Remove the 'O' ring from the annular groove in the retaining ring.

16. Withdraw the rack from the pinion end of the housing.

17. Remove the thrust washer from the pinion housing bore.

18. Turn the rack housing over and, with the base of the pinion bore uppermost, drift out the lower bush and end plug.

Inspection

19. Thoroughly clean all components.

20. Inspect the rack and pinion for wear, cracks or damage, with particular attention to the condition of the teeth.

21. Thoroughly examine the seals for cracks, splits or signs of deterioration.

22. Renew all damaged or excessively worn components.

Reassembling

23. Immerse the pinion bushes and the plunger in S.A.E. 20 engine oil, and heat the oil to 100°C. (212°F.) for two hours, then allow the oil to cool before removing the bushes and plunger from the oil and fitting to the rack; this allows the pores of the bushes and plunger to be filled with lubricant.

24. Fit the bottom bush into the pinion housing as follows:

   a. Fit the large bush on the pinion shaft and then stand the splined end of the shaft on the press base-plate.

   b. Place the end plug into the recess in the lower bush and position the bush on the pinion spigot.

   c. Position the pinion housing over the pinion, and press the housing over the bush, ensuring that the splined pinion shaft is centralized in the pinion housing bore with its bush.

25. Fit the thrust washer, chamfered bore uppermost, into the pinion housing.

26. Insert the rack into the housing from the pinion end, noting the following:

   a. Liberally smear the rack and its teeth with grease.

   b. Insert the rack into the housing with 3½ in (88.90 mm) ('A') of the teeth end protruding from the 'travel' abutment face of the pinion housing.

   c. The flat on the rack registers against the locating plug (which must be taped in position), noting that the plug will be retained in position by the mounting bracket when the rack is fitted.

   d. When the rack is in the straight-ahead position the flat on the pinion must be positioned within 30° either side of the pinion housing centre line on the plunger cap side.

continued

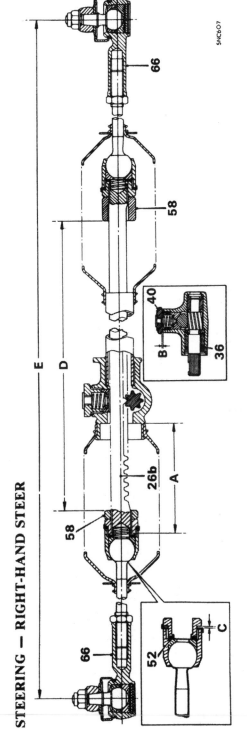

SNC607

Pinion end-float

27 Assemble the thrust washer, bush and retaining ring to the splined end of the pinion shaft, ensuring that the face of the bush with the lubricating groove butts against the thrust washer.

28 Insert the pinion assembly into the pinion housing, ensuring that the flat on the pinion is facing towards the plunger boss.

29 Fit the retaining circlip.

30 Mount a dial gauge on the rack housing.

31 Push the pinion down and zero the dial gauge.

32 Lift the pinion until the retaining ring contacts the circlip and note the dial gauge reading which represents the pinion shaft end-float.

33 Remove the dial gauge.

34 Remove the circlip and withdraw the pinion assembly.

35 Withdraw the retaining ring and fit a new 'O' ring to its annular groove.

36 From the reading obtained in 32 select shims that will give a maximum of 0.010 in (0.25 mm) end-float.
Shims are available in the following thicknesses:
0.005 in (0.13 mm).
0.010 in (0.25 mm)

37 Fit the shims and retainer to the pinion shaft.

38 Insert the pinion assembly into the pinion housing (with the pinch bolt flat towards the plunger boss), ensuring that the cut-away on the shims and retaining ring are aligned with the dowel hole in the pinion housing.

39 Fit the dowel and retaining circlip, with the points of the circlip opposite the dowel to prevent the circlip becoming dislodged.

Plunger pre-load

40 Fit the plunger and screwed cap to the rack housing, tightening the screwed cap until all end-float has been eliminated.

41 Measure the clearance ('B') between the screwed cap and the rack housing using a feeler gauge. Ensure that the housing is free from burrs.

42 Remove the screwed cap and plunger.

43 Smear the plunger with grease and fit the plunger and spring into the rack housing.

44 Make up a shim pack equal to that measured in 41 plus an additional 0.004 in (0.1 mm).

CAUTION: It is important that at least one .004 in (.1 mm) shim is used.
Shims are available in the following thicknesses:
0.002 in (0.05 mm).
0.004 in (0.1 mm).
0.010 in (0.25 mm).

45 Assemble the shims to the screwed cap; fit and tighten the cap.

46 Fit a grease nipple to the screwed cap and inject ½ to ¾ oz (14 to 21 gm) of a service grease into the unit; remove the grease nipple.

47 Fit the grease plug to the screwed cap.

48 Check that the screwed cap is correctly adjusted. If correct a force of 2 lbf (.91 kgf) acting at a radius of 8 in (20.3 cm) will rotate the pinion shaft through three-quarters of a turn in either direction of the rack centre tooth position.
Re-adjust if necessary by adding or subtracting shims beneath the screwed cap.

Tie-rod inner ball joint

49 Smear the tie-rod ball with graphite grease.

50 Slide the cup nut over the tie-rod and position the cup over the tie-rod ball.

51 Position a new tab washer on the sleeve nut followed by a shim pack of known thickness and screw the sleeve nut into the cup nut.
Shims are available in the following thicknesses:
0.002 in (0.05 mm).
0.010 in (0.25 mm).

52 Measure the clearance between the tab washer and the cap nut ('C'), using a feeler gauge. This dimension plus 0.002 in (0.05 mm) is the amount by which the shim pack must be reduced to give the correct ball end movement.

53 Dismantle the ball joint and reassemble it with the correct shim pack as determined in 52.

54 Check the pre-load on the tie-rod ball spheres. When the adjustment is correct the following torque is required on a tie-rod to produce articulation 35 degrees either side of the centre plane.
Steel cup: Articulation torque 40 lbf in (.46 kgf m).
Nylon cup: Articulation torque 15 to 50 lbf in (.17 to .57 kgf m).

CAUTION: If a nylon cup is replacing a steel cup the thrust spring must be discarded.

55 Lock the tab washer over the cup nut and sleeve nut.

56 Repeat 49 to 55 for the remaining tie-rod inner ball joint assembly.

57 Position the bellows retaining clip on the rack housing at the bearing end.

58 Screw the locknuts on to each end of the rack, ensuring that there is 23.20 in (589.28 mm) ('D') between their inside faces.

CAUTION: The locknut at the pinion end of the rack is smaller than the locknut at the bearing end of the rack.

59 Insert the thrust springs into the ends of the rack if steel cups are used in the inner ball joint assemblies.

60 Screw each tie-rod assembly as far as possible up to the locknut.

61 Tighten each locknut to 80 lbf ft (11.06 kgf m).

continued

STEERING — RIGHT-HAND STEER

62 Push the bellows onto the tie-rods, ensuring that the protective shields are fitted on the outer end of the bellows behind the small clips.

63 Lubricate around each inner ball joint and the rack including the teeth with approximately 2 oz (57 gm) of a service grease.

64 Secure the bellows to the rack housing and tie-rods with the clips and wire.

65 Screw the tie-rod end assembly locknuts onto the tie-rods.

66 Screw the tie-rod end assemblies onto the tie-rods, ensuring there is 42.68 in (1084.1 mm) ('E') between the ball pin centres.

67 Tighten the locknuts to 30 to 35 lbf ft (4.15 to 4.84 kgf m).

STEERING RACK MOUNTING BRACKETS

Remove and refit   57.33.04

Removing
1 Remove the radiator, see 26.40.01.
2 Remove the two bolts and washers securing each steering rack clamp to the mounting brackets.
3 Remove the three bolts and washers securing each mounting bracket to the chassis cross-member.
4 Remove the mounting brackets and any packing washers fitted at the pinion end of the rack between the mounting bracket and the chassis cross-member.

CAUTION: It is important that this packing is retained for refitting the mounting bracket.

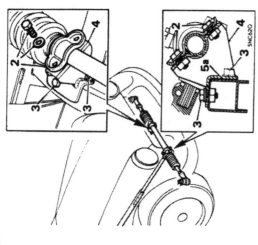

Refitting
5 Reverse the procedure in 1 to 4 noting:
a The thickness of packing removed from between the mounting bracket on the pinion end of the rack and the chassis cross-member is refitted.
b The mounting bracket fixing bolts are tightened to 17 to 18 lbf ft (2.35 to 2.4 kgf m).
c The steering rack clamp fixing bolts are tightened to 20 to 22 lbf ft (2.77 to 3.04 kgf m).

STEERING COLUMN

Remove and refit   57.40.01
Steering column lock and ignition starter switch
1 to 5 and 16 to 20   57.40.31

Removing
1 Turn the steering to the straight ahead position.
2 Remove the pinch bolt and nut securing the steering column to the steering rack pinion.

3 Disconnect the steering column switch wiring at the multi-snap connector below the fascia, and the wiring from the ignition switch.
4 Remove the two bolts securing the column upper fixing to the body, and collect the shim.
5 Withdraw the steering-column complete with steering-wheel.
6 Support the steering-column in a vice.
7 Remove the steering-wheel and hub, see 57.60.01.
8 Remove the four screws securing the upper and lower cowls.
9 Remove the upper and lower cowls.
10 Note the position of the direction indicator trip striker for correct refitment.
11 Remove the direction indicator trip striker.
12 Slacken the clip to release the wiring harness.
13 Remove the two screws securing the direction indicator/headlamp/low-high beam switch assembly, and lift the switch assembly from the column.
14 Remove the two screws to release the mounting bracket and cap from the column.
15 Withdraw the mounting bracket seating.
16 Turn the ignition key to position 1 to ensure that the steering-lock is disengaged.
17 Drill out or remove with a proprietary tool the retaining shear bolts.
18 Remove the steering-lock and ignition switch.
19 Remove the footwell seal from the steering-column.

Refitting
20 Reverse the procedure in 1 to 19 noting:
a Tighten the new shear bolts to 70 lbf in (0.8 kgf m).
b Check the operation of the steering-lock.
c Tighten the new shear bolts until the bolt heads shear off at the waisted point.

STEERING — RIGHT-HAND STEER

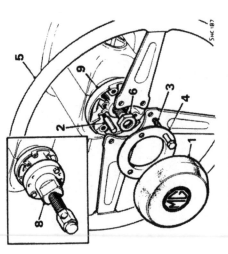

S NC 187

STEERING WHEEL

Remove and refit   **57.60.01**
Steering-wheel hub   **57.60.02**

Service tool: 18G 1181

Removing
1   Remove the steering-wheel motif assembly.
2   Remove the horn contact.
3   Remove the six bolts securing the lock ring and steering-wheel to the hub.
4   Remove the lock ring.

5   Remove the steering-wheel.
6   Slacken the nut securing the hub to the steering-column.
7   Mark the hub and column to assist correct realignment.
8   Fit 18G 1181 to the hub and pull the hub until it is a loose fit on the steering-column.
9   Remove 18G 1181, the nut and the hub.

Refitting
10   Refit the hub in its original position on the steering-column.
11   Fit the nut and tighten to 37 lbf ft (5.11 kgf m).
12   Reverse the procedure in 1 to 5.

155

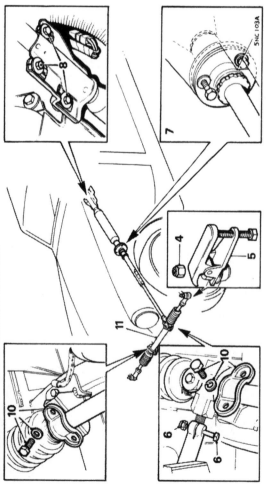

STEERING RACK 57.25.01

Service tool: 18G 1063

Removing

CAUTION: Should a seal become damaged, with a subsequent loss of lubricant, it is necessary to remove the steering rack assembly for dismantling and inspection of the components. If a seal has not entered the steering rack assembly, a new seal may be fitted and the inner ball joint and rack lubricated with a service grease, see 57.25.03.

If the vehicle is hoisted with its front wheels clear of the ground, care should be taken to avoid forceful movement of the wheels from lock to lock as damage may occur within the steering mechanism.

1 Remove the radiator, see 26.40.01.
2 Turn the steering to the straight-ahead position.
3 Jack up and support the front of the car and remove the road wheels.
4 Remove the nuts from the tie-rod end assemblies.

5 Using tool 18G 1063, detach the tie-rod end assemblies from the steering levers.
6 Remove the steering-column pinch bolt.
7 Remove the three toe-plate bolts.
8 Slacken the three steering-column upper fixing bolts and pull back the column sufficiently to disengage the column sleeve from the pinion.
9 Mark the steering rack housing in relation to the mounting bracket to assist when refitting.
10 Remove the clamp bolts and clamps from the mounting brackets.
11 Withdraw the steering rack assembly.

Refitting

12 Position the rack into the mounting brackets and fit the clamps but do not tighten the clamp fixing bolts.
13 Check that the rack is in the straight-ahead position with the pinch bolt flat on the pinion shaft uppermost.
14 Check that the steering-column is in the straight-ahead position with the slot of the clamp uppermost.

15 Slide the column over the pinion shaft as far as it will go.
16 Tighten the steering-column upper fixing bolts.
17 Fit and tighten the three toe-plate bolts.
18 Turn the steering-wheel one complete turn to the left and back, then one complete turn to the right and back.
19 Check that the marks made on the steering-rack housing and mounting bracket are aligned and tighten the clamp fixing bolts to 20 to 22 lbf ft (2.77 to 3.04 kgf m).

CAUTION: If the marks are not aligned or new mounting brackets are being fitted, the steering-rack must be aligned, see 57.35.04.

20 Tighten the steering-column pinch bolt to 9 to 12 lbf ft (1.24 to 1.66 kgf m).
21 Reverse the procedure in 1 to 5 noting:
a Tighten the tie-rod end assembly ball joint nut to 28 to 32 lbf ft (3.87 to 4.48 kgf m).
b Check the front wheel alignment, see 'MAINTENANCE'.

4 Remove the nut securing the tie-rod end assembly to the steering lever.
5 Using tool 18G 1063, detach the tie-rod end assembly from the steering lever.
6 Remove the tie-rod end assembly and locknut from the tie-rod.
7 Slacken the seal retaining clips/wire.
8 Detach the large clip from the seal and allow it to hang on the end of the rack housing. Withdraw the seal from the rack housing and the tie-rod.
9 Remove the small clip and protective shield from the seal.

Inspection

10 Examine the existing grease around the inner ball joint and the rack for ingress of water or dirt; if this is evident, the steering rack must be removed for dismantling and inspection of the components, see 57.25.07.
11 If the inner ball joint and the rack are in a satisfactory condition, apply approximately 2 oz (57 gm) of a service grease around each inner ball joint and the rack including the teeth.

Refitting

12 Fit a new seal.
13 Secure the seal to the rack housing with the clip or wire.
14 Fit the protective shield and small clip to the outer end of the seal.
15 Reverse the procedure in 1 to 6.
16 Check the front wheel alignment, see 'MAINTENANCE'.

STEERING-RACK SEALS 57.25.03

Remove and refit
Service tool: 18G 1063

Removing

CAUTION: If the vehicle is hoisted with its front wheels clear of the ground, care should be taken to avoid forceful movement of the wheels from lock to lock as damage may occur within the steering mechanism.

1 Jack up and support the front of the car and remove the road wheel.
2 Mark the position of the tie-rod end assembly locknut, for re-assembly.
3 Slacken the tie-rod end assembly locknut.

STEERING – LEFT-HAND STEER

5NC210

STEERING RACK AND PINION

Overhaul   57.25.07

Dismantling

1 Remove the steering rack, see 57.25.01.

2 Slacken the tie-rod end assembly locknuts and remove the tie-rod end assemblies and locknuts from the tie-rods.

3 Slacken the seal retaining clips and remove the seal retaining wire from the pinion end of the steering rack.

4 Remove the seals together with their protective shields fitted behind the outer retaining clips.

5 Slacken the locknuts and unscrew the tie-rod inner ball joint assemblies.

6 Withdraw the coil springs and unscrew the locknuts from each end of the rack.

7 Remove the seal retaining clip from the rack housing.

8 Unlock the tab washer and unscrew the sleeved nut from the cup nut and remove the tab washer, shims and cup to dismantle the tie-rod inner ball joint assembly.

9 Remove the grease plug from the screwed cap.

10 Remove the screwed cap and shims.

11 Withdraw the spring and plunger from the rack housing.

12 Remove the circlip retaining the pinion assembly.

13 Withdraw the pinion assembly and dowel.

CAUTION: Take care not to lose the dowel.

14 Remove the retaining ring, shims, the pinion shaft bush and thrust washer from the pinion shaft.

15 Remove the 'O' ring from the annular groove in the retaining ring.

16 Withdraw the rack from the pinion end of the housing.

17 Remove the thrust washer from the pinion housing bore.

18 Turn the rack housing over and, with the base of the pinion bore uppermost, drift out the lower bush and end plug.

Inspection

19 Thoroughly clean all components.

20 Inspect the rack and pinion for wear, cracks or damage, with particular attention to the condition of the teeth.

21 Thoroughly examine the seals for cracks, splits or signs of deterioration.

22 Renew all damaged or excessively worn components.

Reassembling

23 Immerse the pinion bushes and the plunger in S.A.E. 20 engine oil, and heat the oil to 100°C. (212°F.) for two hours, then allow the oil to cool before removing the bushes and plunger from the oil and fitting to the rack; this allows the pores of the bushes and plunger to be filled with lubricant.

24 Fit the bottom bush into the pinion housing as follows:

a Fit the large bush on the pinion shaft and then stand the splined end of the shaft on the press base-plate.

b Place the end plug into the recess in the lower bush and position the bush on the pinion spigot.

c Position the pinion housing over the pinion, and press the housing over the bush, ensuring that the splined pinion shaft is centralized in the pinion housing bore with its bush.

25 Fit the thrust washer, chamfered bore uppermost, into the pinion housing.

26 Insert the rack into the housing from the pinion end, noting the following:

a Liberally smear the rack and its teeth with grease.

b Insert the rack into the housing with 3½ in (88.90 mm) ('A') of the teeth end protruding from the 'travel' abutment face of the pinion housing.

c The flat on the rack registers against the locating plug (which must be taped in position), noting that the plug will be retained in position by the mounting bracket when the rack is fitted.

d When the rack is in the straight-ahead position the flat on the pinion must be positioned within 30° either side of the pinion housing centre line on the plunger cap side.

continued

157

STEERING — LEFT-HAND STEER

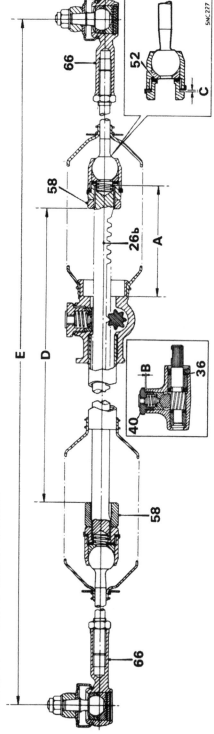

SNC 227

Pinion end-float

27 Assemble the thrust washer, bush and retaining ring to the splined end of the pinion shaft, ensuring that the face of the bush with the lubricating groove butts against the thrust washer.

28 Insert the pinion assembly into the pinion housing, ensuring that the flat on the pinion is facing towards the plunger boss.

29 Fit the retaining circlip.

30 Mount a dial gauge on the rack housing.

31 Push the pinion down and zero the dial gauge.

32 Lift the pinion until the retaining ring contacts the circlip and note the dial gauge reading which represents the pinion shaft end-float.

33 Remove the dial gauge.

34 Remove the circlip and withdraw the pinion assembly.

35 Withdraw the retaining ring and fit a new 'O' ring to its annular groove.

36 From the reading obtained in 32 select shims that will give a maximum of 0.010 in (0.25 mm) end-float.

Shims are available in the following thicknesses:

0.005 in (0.13 mm).
0.010 in (0.25 mm).

37 Fit the shims and retainer to the pinion shaft.

38 Insert the pinion assembly into the pinion housing (with the pinch bolt flat towards the plunger boss), ensuring that the cut-away on the shims and retaining ring are aligned with the dowel hole in the pinion housing.

39 Fit the dowel and retaining circlip, with the points of the circlip opposite the dowel to prevent the circlip becoming dislodged.

Plunger pre-load

40 Fit the plunger and screwed cap to the rack housing, tightening the screwed cap until all end-float has been eliminated.

41 Measure the clearance ('B') between the screwed cap and the rack housing using a feeler gauge. Ensure that the housing is free from burrs.

42 Remove the screwed cap and plunger.

43 Smear the plunger with grease and fit the plunger and spring into the rack housing.

44 Make up a shim pack equal to that measured in 41 plus an additional 0.004 in (0.1 mm).

CAUTION: It is important that at least one .004 in (.1 mm) shim is used.

Shims are available in the following thicknesses:

0.002 in (0.05 mm).
0.004 in (0.1 mm).
0.010 in (0.25 mm).

45 Assemble the shims to the screwed cap; fit and tighten the cap.

46 Fit a grease nipple to the screwed cap and inject ½ to ¾ oz (14 to 21 gm) of a service grease into the unit; remove the grease nipple.

47 Fit the grease plug to the screwed cap.

48 Check that the screwed cap is correctly adjusted. If correct a force of 2 lbf (.91 kgf) acting at a radius of 8 in (20.3 cm) will rotate the pinion shaft through three-quarters of a turn in (589.28 mm) ('D') between their inside faces.

Re-adjust if necessary by adding or subtracting shims beneath the screwed cap.

Tie-rod inner ball joint

49 Smear the tie-rod ball with graphite grease.

50 Slide the cup nut over the tie-rod and position the cup over the tie-rod ball.

51 Position a new tab washer on the sleeve nut followed by a shim pack of known thickness and screw the sleeve nut into the cup nut.

Shims are available in the following thicknesses:

0.002 in (0.05 mm).
0.010 in (0.25 mm).

52 Measure the clearance between the tab washer and the cap nut ('C'), using a feeler gauge. This dimension plus 0.002 in (0.05 mm) is the amount by which the shim pack must be reduced to give the correct ball end movement.

53 Dismantle the ball joint and reassemble it with the correct shim pack as determined in 52.

54 Check the pre-load on the tie-rod ball spheres. When the adjustment is correct the following torque is required on a tie-rod to produce articulation 35 degrees either side of the centre plane.

Steel cup: Articulation torque 40 lbf in (.46 kgf m).

Nylon cup: Articulation torque 15 to 50 lbf in (.17 to .57 kgf m).

CAUTION: If a nylon cup is replacing a steel cup the thrust spring must be discarded.

55 Lock the tab washer over the cup nut and sleeve nut.

56 Repeat 49 to 55 for the remaining tie-rod inner ball joint assembly.

57 Position the bellows retaining clip on the rack housing at the bearing end.

58 Screw the locknuts on to each end of the rack, ensuring that there is 23.20 in (589.28 mm) ('D') between their inside faces.

CAUTION: The locknut at the pinion end of the rack is smaller than the locknut at the bearing end of the rack.

59 Insert the thrust springs into the ends of the rack if steel cups are used in the inner ball joint assemblies.

60 Screw each tie-rod assembly as far as possible up to the locknut.

61 Tighten each locknut to 80 lbf ft (11.06 kgf m).

continued

158

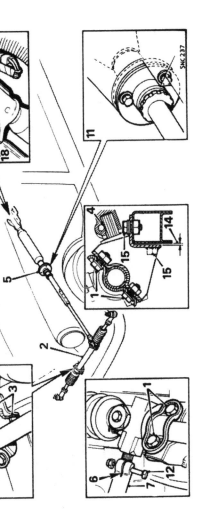

SMC.237

SMC.173

STEERING — LEFT-HAND STEER

62 Push the bellows onto the tie-rods, ensuring that the protective shields are fitted on the outer end of the bellows behind the small clips.

63 Lubricate around each inner ball joint and the rack including the teeth with approximately 2 oz (57 gm) of a service grease.

64 Secure the bellows to the rack housing and tie-rods with the clips and wire.

65 Screw the tie-rod end assembly locknuts onto the tie-rods.

66 Screw the tie-rod end assemblies onto the tie-rods, ensuring there is 42.68 in (1084.1 mm) ('E') between the ball pin centres.

67 Tighten the locknuts to 30 to 35 lbf ft (4.15 to 4.84 kgf m).

STEERING RACK MOUNTING BRACKETS   57.33.04

Remove and refit

Removing

1 Remove the radiator, see 26.40.01.

2 Remove the two bolts and washers securing each steering rack clamp to the mounting brackets.

3 Remove the three bolts and washers securing each mounting bracket to the chassis cross-member.

4 Remove the mounting brackets and any packing washers fitted at the pinion end of the rack between the mounting bracket and the chassis cross-member.

CAUTION: It is important that this packing is retained for refitting the mounting bracket. If it is mislaid or its thickness not recorded, the steering rack must be realigned, see 57.35.04.

Refitting

CAUTION: If new mounting brackets are being fitted or the steering rack is being fitted after an accident damage repair to the front end, the steering rack must be aligned, see 57.35.04.

5 Reverse the procedure in 1 to 4 noting:

a The thickness of packing removed from between the mounting bracket on the pinion end of the rack and the chassis cross-member is refitted.

b The mounting bracket fixing bolts are tightened to 17 to 18 lbf ft (2.35 to 2.4 kgf m).

c The steering rack clamp fixing bolts are tightened to 20 to 22 lbf ft (2.77 to 3.04 kgf m).

STEERING RACK AND COLUMN ALIGNMENT

Check and adjust   57.35.04

When fitting new steering-column and steering gear:

1 Fit the mounting brackets to the rack assembly, tightening the clamp bolts and then slackening off one full turn.

2 Fit the rack assembly into the car.

3 Screw in the two front bolts and the top bolt securing the mounting bracket furthest from the steering pinion to the cross-member. DO NOT tighten the bolts.

4 Check that the rack is in the straight-ahead position with the pinch bolt flat on the pinion shaft uppermost.

5 Fit the steering-column into the car, slide the fixing plate and sealing washer into the column.

6 Turn the column to the straight-ahead position with the slot of the clamp uppermost.

7 Slide the steering-column sleeve over the pinion shaft as far as it will go.

8 Fit the two top bolts and nuts into the upper fixing brackets; tighten them by hand until the weight of the column is just taken and the column fixing flanges and body brackets are parallel to each other with the spaces between them equal at both points; check that the column passes through the toe-plate approximately central in the hole.

9 Measure the spaces between the column flanges and the brackets.

continued

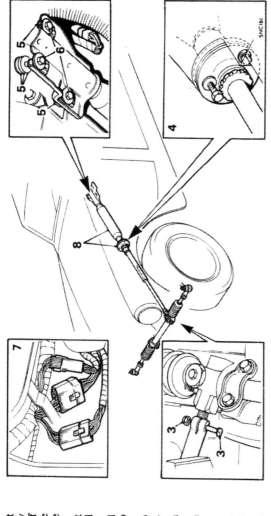

10 Remove the two fixing bolts, fit packing washers equal in thickness to the spaces, refit the bolts tightening them by hand until the washers are just pinched.

11 Fit the fixing ring and sealing washer then screw in and tighten the three toe-plate bolts.

12 Fit and tighten the pinion pinch bolt.

13 Turn the steering one complete turn to the left and back, then one complete turn to the right and back, noting any movement of the rack assembly in relation to the body cross-member; slowly turn the steering in both directions until the neutral point (i.e. where no movement of the rack assembly is visible) is found.

14 Measure the gap between the rack mounting bracket at the pinion end of the rack and the front face of the body cross-member; fit packing to the thickness of the gap.

15 Insert the two front bolts and the top bolt securing the pinion end mounting bracket to the cross-member.

16 Tighten the mounting brackets top and front securing bolts to 23 to 25 lbf ft (2.77 to 3.04 kgf m).

17 Tighten the fixing bracket clamp bolts commencing with those on the pinion end bracket.

18 Measure the gap between the upper column mounting flange and fixing bracket at the third bolt position.

19 Fit packing washers to the thickness of the gap then fit and tighten the bolt until the washers are just pinched.

20 Remove the pinion pinch bolts and the three toe-plate bolts.

21 Check, by pulling and pushing, that the steering-column slides reasonably freely up and down on the pinion; if the column is tight on the pinion the rack assembly alignment must be re-checked.

22 If the steering-column alignment check in 21 is satisfactory, refit and tighten the three toe-plate bolts.

23 Refit the pinion pinch bolt and tighten it to 9 to 12 lbf ft (1.24 to 1.66 kgf m).

24 Tighten the three top fixing bolts to 12 to 17 lbf ft (1.66 to 2.35 kgf m).

When fitting a new rack assembly to an existing column

25 Remove the rack assembly, see 57.25.01.

26 Carry out operations 1 to 3.

27 Push the steering-column forward and enter the pinion into the column sleeve as far as it will go.

28 Screw in and tighten the three toe-plate bolts.

29 Tighten the three column upper securing bolts.

30 Fit and tighten the pinion pinch bolt.

31 Carry out operations 13 to 17 and 20 to 24.

When fitting a new column to an existing rack

32 Carry out operations 4 to 12 and 20 to 24.

When fitting new mounting brackets to an existing rack

33 Carry out operations 25 to 31.

8 Withdraw the steering-column complete with steering-wheel and switches and remove the toe-plate fixing ring and sealing washer.

STEERING-COLUMN

Remove and refit   57.40.01

Removing

1 Disconnect the battery.

2 Remove the car heater air intake hose.

3 Remove the pinion pinch bolt and nut.

4 Remove the three bolts and washer securing the toe-plate fixing ring to the steering-column.

5 Note the location, quantity and thickness of the packing washers between the column upper fixing flanges and the body bracket.

6 Remove the three nuts, bolts and washers securing the column upper fixing to the body bracket and collect the packing washers.

CAUTION: If the packing washers are mislaid or their fitting positions are not recorded the steering-column must be aligned, see 57.35.04.

7 Disconnect the steering-column switch wiring at the multi-snap connectors below the fascia.

Refitting

CAUTION: If a new steering-column is being fitted it must be aligned, see 57.35.04.

9 Fit the column assembly.

10 Fit the toe-plate sealing washer and fixing ring to the steering-column.

11 Slide the steering-column over the pinion shaft.

12 Fit the packing washers to their original positions between the column upper fixing flanges and the body bracket.

13 Fit the three nuts, bolts and washers securing the column upper fixing, tightening until the packing washers are just pinched.

14 Fit the sealing washer and fixing ring to the toe-plate.

continued

STEERING WHEEL - 1978 and later

Remove and refit   57.60.01

Service tool: 18G 1317

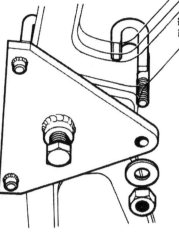
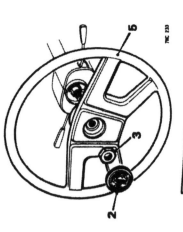

Removing

1 Set the steering-wheel in the straight-ahead position.
2 Raise the hub cover from the centre of the steering-wheel.
3 Remove the wheel retaining nut.
4 Mark the wheel hub and inner column for refitting reference.
5 Using tool 18G 1317, pull the steering wheel from the inner column.

Refitting

6 Reverse the procedure in 1 to 5, noting:

STEERING WHEEL – 1975–1977

Remove and refit   57.60.01
Steering-wheel hub   57.60.02

Service tool: 18G 1181

Removing

1 Remove the steering-wheel motif assembly.
2 Remove the horn contact.
3 Remove the six bolts securing the lock ring and steering-wheel to the hub.
4 Remove the lock ring.
5 Remove the steering-wheel.
6 Slacken the nut securing the hub to the steering-column.
7 Mark the hub and column to assist correct realignment.
8 Fit 18G 1181 to the hub and pull the hub until it is a loose fit on the steering-column.
9 Remove 18G 1181, the nut and the hub.

Refitting

10 Refit the hub in its original position on the steering-column.
11 Fit the nut and tighten to 37 lbf ft (5.11 kgf m).
12 Reverse the procedure in 1 to 5.

STEERING-COLUMN LOCK AND IGNITION STARTER SWITCH

Remove and refit   57.40.31

Removing

1 Remove the steering-column, see 57.40.01.
2 Remove the four screws securing the L.H. and R.H. cowls.
3 Remove the L.H. and R.H. cowls.
4 Turn the ignition key to position 1 to ensure that the steering-lock is disengaged.
5 Drill out or remove with a suitable proprietary tool, the retaining shear bolts.
6 Remove the steering-lock and ignition switch.

Refitting

7 Reverse the procedure in 1 to 4 noting:
a Tighten the new shear bolts to 70 lbf in (0.8 kgf m).

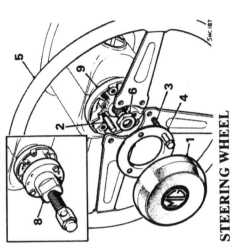

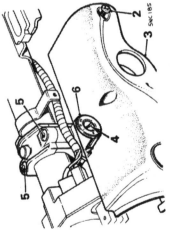

STEERING – LEFT-HAND STEER

15 Tighten the three upper fixing nuts and bolts to 12 to 17 lbf ft (1.66 to 2.35 kgf m).
16 Fit the pinion pinch bolt and nut and tighten to 9 to 12 lbf ft (1.24 to 1.66 kgf m).
17 Reconnect the wiring and fit the car heater air intake hose.

STEERING-COLUMN

Overhaul   57.40.10

Dismantling

1 Remove the steering-column assembly, see 57.40.01.
2 Remove the steering wheel and hub, see 57.60.01.
3 Remove the four screws securing the L.H. and R.H. cowls.
4 Remove the L.H. and R.H. cowls.
5 Remove the two screws securing the windscreen wiper/washer switch assembly and lift the switch assembly from the column.
6 Remove the two screws securing the direction indicator/headlamp/low–high beam switch assembly to the column.
7 Disconnect the horn slip ring lead and lift the switch assembly from the column.

8 Remove the screw securing the ignition switch to the steering column lock.
9 Disconnect the warning buzzer lead from the steering column lock and remove the ignition switch assembly.
10 Note the position of the direction indicator trip striker for correct refitment.
11 Remove the direction indicator trip striker.

Reassembling

12 Reverse the procedure in 1 to 12.

b Check the operation of the steering-lock.
c Tighten the new shear bolts until the bolt heads shear at the waisted point.

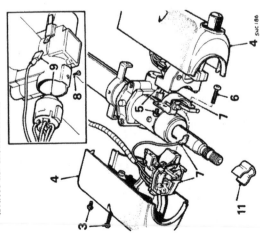

57.40.01 [LH]

FRONT SUSPENSION

a Ensure the road wheels are set in the straight-ahead position.

b Set the cancelling trip with the formed ridge facing the direction indicator switch.

c Fit the steering-wheel ensuring the tongues engage in the slots of the cancelling trip.

d Fit the nut and tighten to 37 lbf ft (5.11 kgf m).

5 Withdraw the bearings from the anti-roll bar.

Refitting

6 Reverse the procedure in 1 to 5.

7 Unscrew the centre screw of tool 18G 153, or progressively slacken the two long slave bolts, to allow the spring to expand.

8 Remove the tool 18G 153 or slave bolts to release the spring seat and spring.

Inspection

9 Check the spring length against the figures given in DATA, renew the spring if it is not within the limits.

Refitting

10 Reverse the procedure in 1 to 8, noting:

   a Ensure when refitting the tool 18G 153 or slave bolts that the guide rods of the tool or the slave bolts use diametrically opposite holes.

   b Do not omit to remove the hardwood block after the spring has been refitted.

FRONT HUB ASSEMBLY 60.25.01

Remove and refit

Service tools: 18G 134, 18G 304 F, 18G 1032

Removing

1 Raise the front of the car and support with stands under the body.

2 Remove the road wheel.

3 Depress the friction pads retaining spring and remove the split pins.

4 Remove the retaining spring.

5 Manoeuvre the friction pads to remove them, and detach the friction and anti-squeak shims.

6 Unlock and unscrew the bolts securing the supply hose support bracket and calliper and release the calliper.

7 Support the calliper on the body.

8 Remove the grease cap.

9 Remove the split pin, nut and special washer.

10 PRESSED WHEELS. Using tool 18G 304 with adaptors 18G 304 F withdraw the hub complete with brake disc.
WIRE WHEELS. Using tool 18G 1032 withdraw the hub complete with brake disc.

continued

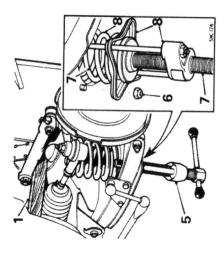

ANTI-ROLL BAR 60.10.01

Remove and refit

Removing

1 Raise the front of the car and position supports beneath the front suspension.

2 Remove the four screws and nuts to release the end stops from the anti-roll bar.

3 Remove the four screws to release the anti-roll bar bearing straps.

4 Remove the two nuts to release the links from the anti-roll bar.

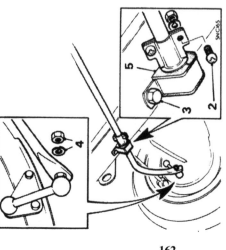

FRONT SPRING 60.20.01

Remove and refit

Service tool: 18G 153

Removing

1 Place a hardwood block 1.125 in (28.57 mm) thick under the hydraulic damper arm to keep the arm off its rubber rebound buffer.

2 Raise the front of the car and support with stands under the body.

3 Remove the road wheel.

4 Remove two diametrically opposite spring seat securing nuts and bolts.

5 Using tool 18G 153 or two long slave bolts, compress the spring.

6 Remove the remaining spring seat nuts and bolts.

DATA

Front spring

Free length of coil spring	9.85 in (25 cm)
Fitted length at load of:	
750±15 lb (337±6.8 kg)	7.08 in (18 cm)
No. of effective coils	7
Spring rate	271 lbf in (3.127 kgf m)

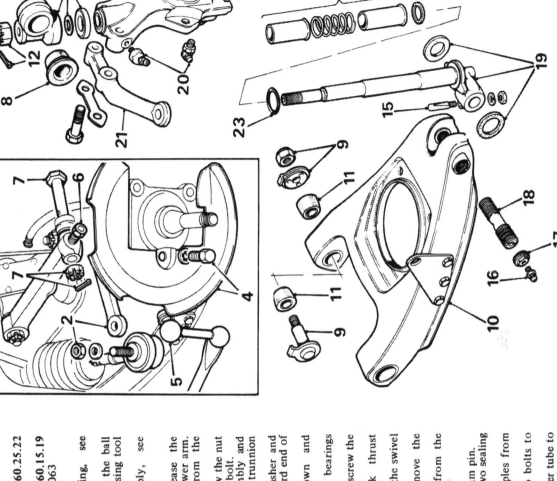

5NC179

FRONT SUSPENSION

11 Remove the brake disc retaining bolts and remove the brake disc.
12 Press the outer bearing from the hub.
13 Remove the tapered sleeve.
14 Remove the inner bearing and oil seal from the hub.

Inspection

15 Check the oil seal journal on the stub axle for signs of damage.

Refitting

16 Pack the bearings with one of the service greases, allowing the grease to protrude slightly from the bearing.
17 Fit the inner bearing, tapered sleeve and outer bearing noting:
  a The side of the bearings marked THRUST must be adjacent to the tapered bearing spacer.
  b Fit the bearing spacer with the taper towards the outer bearing.
18 Dip the new oil seal in oil before fitting.
19 Press the new oil seal into the hub using tool 18G 134.
20 Reverse the procedure in 1 to 11, noting:
  a After refitting the hub, remove any surplus grease; the grease cap should not be packed with grease.
  b Check the run-out at the outer periphery of the disc braking surface; if this exceeds 0.006 in (0.152 mm) remove and reposition the disc on the hub.
  c Tighten the disc securing bolts to 43 lbf ft (6 kgf m).
  d Tighten the hub nut to 46 lbf ft (6.9 kgf m); if necessary tighten to the next split pin hole.

FRONT HUB STUB AXLE

Remove and refit 60.25.22
Swivel pin 1 to 18 and 29 to 38 60.15.19

Service tools: 18G 1006 A, 18G 1063

Removing

1 Remove the front spring, see 60.20.01.
2 Remove the nut and release the ball joint from the steering arm using tool 18G 1063.
3 Remove the hub assembly, see 60.25.01.
4 Remove the disc dust shield.
5 Remove the nut and release the anti-roll bar link from the lower arm.
6 Remove the clamp bolt from the hydraulic damper arm.
7 Remove the split pin, unscrew the nut and remove the trunnion link bolt.
8 Lower the swivel axle assembly and remove the bushes from the trunnion link.
9 Remove the nut, special washer and fulcrum pin from each inboard end of the lower link.
10 Swing the lower link down and withdraw it from the body.
11 Remove the rubber bush bearings from the lower link.
12 Remove the split pin, and unscrew the swivel pin nut.
13 Remove the trunnion link thrust washer and shims.
14 Remove the stub axle from the swivel pin.
15 Unscrew the nut and remove the fulcrum pin cotter pin.
16 Remove the grease nipple from the screwed plug.
17 Unscrew the plug.
18 Unscrew the swivel pin fulcrum pin.
19 Remove the swivel pin and two sealing washers.
20 Remove the two grease nipples from the swivel axle.
21 Unlock and remove the two bolts to release the steering arm.
22 Lift the bottom dust excluder tube to compress the spring and withdraw the dust excluder assembly. *continued*

163

FRONT SUSPENSION

23 Remove the 'O' ring seal from the swivel pin.

24 Remove the top and bottom swivel pin bushes.

Refitting

25 Fit new bushes, noting:

a The hole in the bushes must be aligned with the lubricating holes in the swivel axle.

b The bushes have a lead at one end, enabling them to easily enter their housings.

c The bottom bush must be flush with the recessed housing and protrude approximately ⅛ in (3.2 mm) above the lower housing upper face.

26 Using tool 18G 1006 A ream the bushes to their correct size.

27 Fit the dust excluder assembly.

28 Fit the steering arm, and lock the two bolts using a new lock washer, tightening the bolts to 39 lbf ft (5.4 kgf m).

29 Fit the grease nipples to the swivel axle.

30 Assemble the swivel pin to the lower link by screwing the fulcrum pin into the lower link and using new sealing washers.

31 Fit a new cotter pin to secure the fulcrum pin.

32 Soak a new sealing washer in oil and fit it in the bottom of the swivel axle.

33 Assemble the stub axle on the swivel pin.

34 Fit the thrust washer over the swivel pin.

35 Fit a 0.008 in (0.2 mm) and a 0.012 in (0.3 mm) shim on the swivel pin.

36 Fit the trunnion with its bore towards the swivel axle and tighten the nut to 40 lbf ft (5.5 kgf m); if necessary tighten to the next split pin hole.

37 Check the movement of the swivel axle, slight resistance should be felt when the swivel axle is moved from lock to lock. There should be no vertical movement of the swivel axle. Add or remove shims to reduce or increase the resistance.

38 Fit a split pin to lock the swivel pin nut.

39 Reverse the procedure in 1 to 11.

BRAKES — RIGHT-HAND STEER
REAR BRAKE BACK PLATE

Remove and refit   70.10.26

Removing

1. Remove the rear hub, see 51.10.02.
2. Remove the rear brake shoes, see 70.40.03.
3. Remove the rear wheel cylinder, see 70.60.18.
4. Unscrew the brake shoe adjuster and remove the wedges.
5. Remove the bolts, nuts and spring washer securing the back plate to the rear axle tube.
6. Detach the back-plate.

Refitting

7. Reverse the procedure in 1 to 6 and bleed the brake hydraulic system, see 70.25.02.

HOSES

Remove and refit	
Front	70.15.02
Rear	70.15.17

CONNECTOR

Remove and refit	
Front three-way	70.15.33
Rear three-way	70.15.34

PIPES

Remove and refit	
Feed to front three-way connector	70.20.01
Feed to front left-hand hose	70.20.02
Feed to front right-hand hose	70.20.03
Feed to rear hose	70.20.13
Feed to rear left-hand wheel cylinder	70.20.17
Feed to rear right-hand wheel cylinder	70.20.18

NOTE: The operation numbers given above are included on the illustration of the braking system to facilitate identification of the individual pipes and hoses.

Removing

1. Disconnect the pipe or hose nearest to the master cylinder and plug it to prevent further loss of fluid.
2. Unscrew the pipe union.
3. Remove the locknut and lock washer.
4. Pull the hose from the body or bracket and remove the lock washer.
5. Release the body clips.
6. Remove the hose or pipe.

Refitting

7. Reverse the procedure in 1 to 7 noting:
   a. Ensure the hoses are not twisted; hold the hose hexagon ensuring it is correctly located in the body while tightening the locknut.
   b. Do not overtighten the pipe unions.
   c. Check all connections for signs of leakage after the system has been bled.
8. Bleed the brake hydraulic system, see 70.25.02.

70.10.26 [RH]

BRAKES — RIGHT-HAND STEER

BLEEDING THE SYSTEM   70.25.02

Bleed — all round

Preparation
Absolute cleanliness must be maintained throughout the entire bleeding operation, ensure that no dirt or grit enters the system. All equipment to be used must be free from fuel, paraffin, or any form of mineral oil.

1 Check that all connections are tight and that the bleed screws are closed.
2 Release the hand brake.
3 Top up the master cylinder with a recommended brake fluid.

CAUTION:
a Never re-use brake fluid which has been bled from the system.
b Keep brake fluid away from all paintwork.
c Do not allow the fluid level to fall so low that air can enter the system during bleeding; always top up the level.

Bleeding
4 Attach a bleed tube to the bleed screw on one of the rear brakes.
5 Submerge the open end of the tube in a small quantity of clean brake fluid in a transparent container.
6 Open the bleed screw half a turn.
7 Depress the brake pedal, slowly, allowing it to return unassisted.
8 Repeat this pumping action with a slight pause between each stroke.
9 When clear fluid free of air bubbles flows from the tube, tighten the bleed screw whilst the pedal is fully depressed.
10 Transfer the bleed tube to the bleed screw on the other rear brake and repeat operations 5 to 9.
11 Attach the bleed tube to the bleed screw on the L.H. front brake.
12 Repeat operations 5 to 9.
13 Transfer the bleed tube to the bleed screw on the other R.H. front brake and repeat operations 5 to 9.
14 Apply pressure to the brake pedal several times.
15 Carefully check the brake hydraulic system for leaks.
16 Drive the car and test the brakes. Pedal travel should be short and feel solid with no indication of 'sponginess'.

MASTER CYLINDER
Remove and refit   70.30.08

Removing
1 Remove the four screws to release the cover plate.
2 Withdraw the split pin and washer and remove the clevis pin.

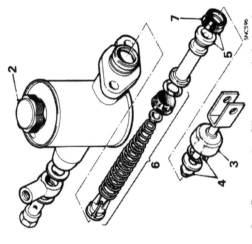

3 Unscrew the pipe unions from the master cylinder. Plug the pipes and the master cylinder.
NOTE: Brake and clutch fluid can have a detrimental effect on paintwork, ensure that fluid is not allowed to contact painted surfaces.
4 Remove the two screws, washers, and nuts securing the reservoir mounting bracket to the pedal bracket.
5 Remove the nuts, and spring washers securing the master cylinder to the pedal box.
6 Remove the master cylinder.

Refitting
7 Reverse the procedure in 1 to 6.
8 Bleed the brake hydraulic system, see 70.25.02.

MASTER CYLINDER 1975-1977
Overhaul   70.30.09

Dismantling
1 Remove the master cylinder, see 70.30.08.

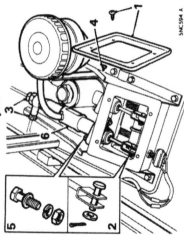

2 Remove the filler cap and drain the fluid.
3 Detach the rubber boot from the body and slide the boot along the push rod.
4 Release the circlip retaining the push rod and withdraw the push rod complete with circlip, dished washer and rubber boot.
5 Remove the piston with its secondary cup seal.
6 Remove the piston washer, main cup seal, spring, spring retainer and valve.
7 Remove the secondary cup seal from the piston by carefully stretching it over the end of the piston.

[CAUTION: Wash hydraulic cylinder components in brake fluid only. Never use gasoline or other petroleum-based solvents since they are damaging to rubber parts in the system.]

Inspection
8 Wash the master cylinder body in industrial methylated spirit and dry thoroughly. Clean all internal parts in brake fluid.
9 Check the master cylinder bore; if it is not scored or ridged new seals can be fitted. Renew the unit if the bore is scored or ridged.

Reassembling
10 Immerse all internal components in brake fluid and assemble when wet.
11 Stretch the new secondary cup seal over the piston with the lip of the seal facing towards the head of the piston.
12 Fit the valve to the large diameter end of the spring and the retainer to the small diameter end of the spring.
13 Fit the spring, valve end first into the body.
14 Fit the main cup seal, cup seal washer, piston and push rod.
CAUTION: When fitting the cup seals carefully enter the lip edge of the cup seals into the barrel first.
15 Smear the sealing areas of the rubber boot with Lockheed disc brake lubricant or Girling rubber grease.
16 Refit the circlip and rubber boot.
17 Refit the master cylinder, see 70.30.08.

MASTER CYLINDER - 1978 and later
Overhaul   70.30.09
Service tool: 18G 1112

Dismantling
1 Remove the master cylinder, see 70.30.08.
2 Remove the filler cap and drain the fluid. Refit the filler cap.
3 Plug the pipe connections and thoroughly clean the exterior of the assembly.
4 Detach the rubber boot and withdraw the push rod.
5 Grip the cylinder body in a soft-jawed vice, with the mouth of the bore uppermost.
6 Compress the return spring and remove the 'Spirolox' ring from its groove in the primary piston, taking care not to distort the coils of the spring or score the bore of the cylinder.
7 Remove the retainer and spring.
8 Using tool 18G 1112 remove the piston seal retaining circlip.
9 Move the piston up and down in the bore to free the nylon guide bearing and seal; remove the guide bearing and seal.
10 Remove the plain washer.
11 Using tool 18G 1112 remove the inner circlip retaining the piston assembly.   *continued*

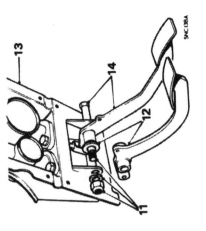

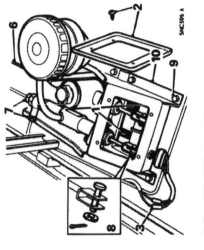

BRAKES — RIGHT-HAND STEER

12 Withdraw the primary and secondary piston assembly complete with stop washer.
13 Remove the stop washer.
14 Compress the spring separating the two pistons and drift out the secondary piston roll pin retaining the piston link.
15 Separate the pistons and remove the spring and retainer.
16 Observe the positions of the cup seals on the pistons by their indentations, and remove the cup seals and washers from the pistons.
17 Unscrew the four screws to release the plastic reservoir from the body.
18 Remove the reservoir sealing rings.
19 Unscrew the connection adaptors and discard the copper washers.
20 Remove the springs and trap valves.

Inspection
21 Thoroughly clean all the components using denatured alcohol (methylated spirit) or brake fluid and dry.
22 Check the master cylinder bore; if the bore is not scored or ridged new rubber cup seals can be fitted. Renew the unit if the bore is scored or ridged.
23 Check that the inlet and outlet ports are free of obstruction.

Reassembling
CAUTION: Immerse all internal components in brake fluid and assemble when wet.
24 Locate the piston washer on the head of the secondary piston, convex surface first.
25 Stretch the indented main cup seal, lip last, over the end of the secondary piston, and seat it correctly in its groove adjacent to the washer.
26 Stretch the plain cup seal, lip last, over the front end of the secondary piston, seating it correctly in its groove.
27 Locate the piston washer on the primary piston, convex surface first.
28 Reverse the dismantling procedure in 2 to 15 and 17 to 20 noting:
  a Use new connection adaptor copper washers.
  b Renew the secondary piston roll pin if necessary.
29 Refit the master cylinder, see 70.30.08.

sufficiently to permit removal of the clutch pedal.
12 Remove the clutch pedal and spacer washer.
13 Remove the pedal box.
14 Remove the pivot bolt and brake pedal.
15 Remove the brake pedal pad.

Refitting
16 Reverse the procedure in 1 to 8, and 10 to 19.
17 Bleed the clutch hydraulic system, see 33.15.01.
18 Bleed the brake hydraulic system, see 70.25.02.

BRAKE PEDAL ASSEMBLY   70.35.01
Remove and refit

Removing
1 Disconnect the return springs from the clutch and brake pedals.
2 Release the four screws to release the cover plate.
3 Disconnect the stop light switch wiring.
4 Jack up the front of the car and support with stands.
5 Attach a tube to the bleed nipples of the clutch slave cylinder and a front brake, slacken the bleed nipples and pump the clutch and brake fluid into containers — similar to the bleeding procedure in 33.15.01 and 70.25.02.
6 Disconnect the fluid pipe from the clutch master cylinder and plug the pipe.
7 Disconnect the fluid pipes from the brake master cylinder and plug the pipes.
Note: Brake and clutch fluid can have a detrimental effect on paintwork, ensure that fluid is not allowed to contact painted surfaces.
8 Remove the split pins and washers, and withdraw the clutch and brake pedal clevis pins.
9 Remove the two screws and six bolts and spring washers retaining the pedal box to the body.
10 Raise the pedal box as far as possible.
11 Unscrew the nut and spring washer and withdraw the pivot bolt

PEDAL BOX   70.35.03
Remove and refit

Removing
1 Remove the brake pedal, see 70 35 01.
2 Remove the clutch master cylinder from the pedal box, see 33.20.01.
3 Remove the brake master cylinder from the pedal box, see 70.30.08.
4 Remove the locknut and unscrew the stop light switch.

Refitting
5 Reverse the procedure in 1 to 4, and adjust the stop light switch, see instruction 9, 86.65.51.
6 Bleed the clutch hydraulic system, see 33.15.01.
7 Bleed the brake hydraulic system, see 70.25.02.

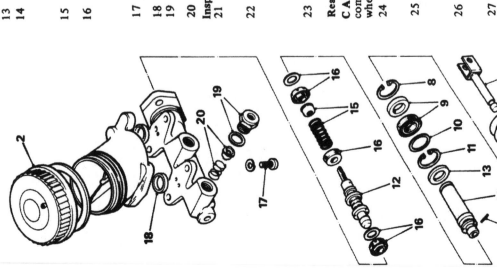

BRAKES — RIGHT-HAND STEER

HAND BRAKE LEVER ASSEMBLY 70.35.08

Remove and refit

Removing

1 Remove the L.H. front seat, see 76.70.01.
2 Remove the two screws securing the hand brake to the mounting plate.
3 Pull back the carpet and remove the three set screws securing the mounting plate to the tunnel.
4 Rotate the mounting plate 180 degrees.
5 Pull the handbrake lever away from the tunnel, remove the split pin and washer, and withdraw the clevis pin.
6 Remove the hand brake lever and separate the mounting plate from the hand brake.

Refitting

7 Assemble the mounting plate to the hand brake lever in its fitted position.
8 Rotate the mounting plate 180 degrees.
9 Reverse the procedure in 1 to 5 using a new split pin.
10 Check the hand brake operation and adjust the cable if necessary, see 70.35.10.

HAND BRAKE LEVER, PAWL AND RATCHET 70.35.09

Remove and refit

Removing

1 Remove the hand brake lever, see 70.35.08.

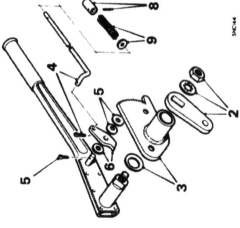

2 Remove the nut, withdraw the lockwasher, and remove the cable lever from the hand brake lever.
3 Remove the ratchet plate and spring washer from the hand brake lever.
4 Withdraw the split pin and release the catch rod from the pawl.
5 Withdraw the split pin, flat and spring washers retaining the pawl to its pivot.
6 Remove the pawl and flat washer.
7 Slide the catch rod up the hand brake lever.
8 Drift the Mills pin from the catch rod to release the thumb button.
9 Remove the catch rod, spring and washer from the hand brake lever.

Refitting

10 Lubricate the pivot points with grease.
11 Reverse the procedure in 2 to 8 noting:
  a Fit a new Mills pin if necessary.
  b Fit a pawl spring washer concave face first.
  c Fit the ratchet plate spring washer convex face first.
12 Check that the hand brake operates freely and the handle pivots.
13 Refit the hand brake lever. see 70.35.08.

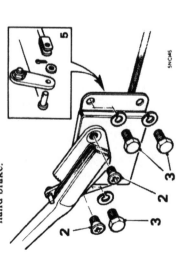

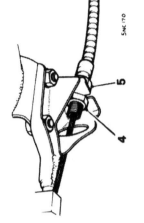

HAND BRAKE CABLE — 1975–1976 70.35.10

Adjust

1 Adjust the rear brakes, see 'Maintenance'.
2 Apply the hand brake so that the pawl engages on the third notch of the ratchet.
3 Check the braking effect on the rear wheels. The wheels should be held or tending to bind.
Adjust the cable if braking effect is inadequate.
4 Slacken the cable front adjustment nut.
5 Screw the rear adjustment nut in the required direction to adjust the position of the threaded sleeve, and tighten the front nut. Adjustment is correct when the road wheels can just be rotated. Both wheels must offer equal braking resistance.
6 Check the hand brake action. Release the hand brake and check that the rear wheels rotate freely.
7 Lower the car.

HAND BRAKE CABLE 1977 and later 70.35.10

Adjust

1 Adjust the rear brakes, see 'MAINTENANCE'.
2 Apply the hand brake so that the pawl engages on the third notch of the ratchet.
3 Check the braking effect on the rear wheels. The wheels should be held or tending to bind.
Adjust the cable if braking effect is inadequate.

4 Slacken the cable rear adjustment nut.
5 Screw the front adjustment nut in the required direction to adjust the position of the threaded sleeve, and tighten the rear nut. Adjustment is correct when the road wheels can just be rotated. Both wheels must offer equal braking resistance.
6 Check the hand brake action. Release the hand brake and check that the rear wheels rotate freely.
7 Lower the car.

HAND BRAKE COMPENSATOR — 1975–1976 only 70.35.11

Remove and refit

Removing

1 Chock the front wheels, jack up the rear of the car and support on stands beneath the rear axle.
2 Release the hand brake.
3 Remove the split pin and washer and withdraw the hand brake cable clevis pin.
4 Unscrew the rear adjustment nut, and slide the nut along the cable.
5 Detach the threaded sleeve from the abutment and withdraw the cable from the compensator mechanism.
6 Remove the split pins and withdraw the clevis pins retaining the brake rods to the balance lever.
7 Detach the brake rods and their felt pads from the balance lever.
8 Remove the two bolts and nuts to release the compensator support from the rear axle.

9 Unscrew the balance lever carrier from the compensator support.
10 Unscrew the balance lever from the carrier.
11 Remove the felt pad from the balance lever.
12 Remove the grease nipple.

Refitting
13 Fit new parts as necessary.
14 Soak the felt pads in oil.
15 Fit the grease nipple to the balance carrier.
16 Locate the large felt pad in its recess in the bottom of the balance lever.
17 Screw the balance lever to the carrier and then unscrew one full turn, ensuring the threaded hole in the carrier is in the same plane as the brake rod forks on the balance carrier.
18 Screw the carrier to the compensator support ensuring that the carrier is started on the threaded spigot with the balance lever uppermost.
19 Unscrew the carrier one full turn.
20 Grease the compensator.
21 Ensure that the balance lever swivels freely on the carrier.
22 With the balance lever upright fit the brake rods with felt pads either side of the rods in the forks.
23 Fit the clevis pins to retain the brake rods and secure using new split pins.
24 Fit the hand brake cable to the compensator, passing the fork through the hole in the bracket, locating the threaded sleeve on the abutment and positioning the relieved face of the

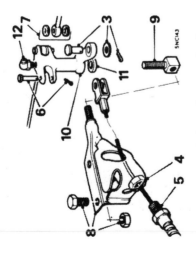

SNC143

fork towards the compensating mechanism.
25 Fit the cable clevis pin and secure with a new split pin.
26 Adjust the hand brake cable, see 70.35.10.

HAND BRAKE CABLE ASSEMBLY – 1975-1976   70.35.16
Remove and refit

Removing
1 Chock the front wheels, jack up the rear of the car and place supports beneath the rear axle.
2 Remove the hand brake lever, see 70.35.08.
3 Remove the split pin and washer, and withdraw the clevis pin from the compensating lever.
4 Unscrew the cable rear adjustment nut and slide the nut along the cable.
5 Detach the threaded sleeve from the abutment and withdraw the cable from the compensating lever mechanism.
6 Unscrew the cable front abutment nut and slide the nut along the cable.
7 Detach the cable from the front abutment bracket and withdraw the cable from the tunnel.

Refitting
8 Reverse the procedure in 2 to 6 noting:
a Renew the split pins.

b Fit the rear fork through the hole in the compensating bracket and assemble with the relieved face of the fork towards the compensating mechanism.
9 Refit the hand brake lever, see 70.35.08.
10 Check the hand brake operation and adjust if necessary, see 70.35.10.
11 Lower the car, and remove the front wheel chocks.

HAND BRAKE CABLE ASSEMBLY – 1977 and later
Remove and refit   70.35.16

Removing
1 Chock the front wheels, raise the rear of the car and place supports beneath the rear axle.
2 Remove the hand brake lever, see 70.35.08.
3 Unscrew the cable front adjustment nut and slide the nut along the cable.
4 Detach the cable from the front abutment bracket and withdraw the

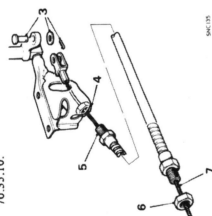

SNC135

cable from the tunnel.
5 Remove the nut and screw securing the cable clip to the differential housing and separate the clip from the cable.
6 Remove the nut and bolt securing the cable to the mounting strap.
7 Remove the split pin and washer, and withdraw the clevis pin from each backplate lever.
8 Remove the hand brake cable assembly.

Refitting
9 Reverse the procedure in 3 to 8, noting:
a Renew the clip if worn or damaged.
b Renew the mounting strap if damaged or showing signs of deterioration.
10 Refit the hand brake lever, see 70.35.08.
11 Check the hand brake operation, and adjust if necessary, see 70.35.10.
12 Lower the car, and remove the front wheel chocks.

REAR BRAKE SHOES

Remove and refit   70.40.03
Brake drum 1 to 4, 15 and 70.10.03
17 to 20

Removing
1 Chock the front wheels and release the hand brake.
2 Slacken the rear road wheel fastenings, jack up and place supports beneath the rear axle. Remove the road wheels.
3 Slacken off the brake shoe adjuster fully.
4 Remove the brake drum.
5 Lever the trailing shoe from its wheel cylinder and adjuster abutment.
6 Remove both brake shoes and shoe return springs.
Note: Retain the wheel cylinder pistons with an elastic band if new shoes are not to be fitted immediately.
7 Repeat the procedure in 3 to 6 on the other rear brake shoes.

Refitting
8 Wash all dust from the back-plate

BRAKES — RIGHT-HAND STEER

assembly and drum with denatured alcohol (methylated spirit), allow to dry.

Warning: Do not use an air line to blow dust from the brake assemblies — asbestos dust can be dangerous if inhaled.

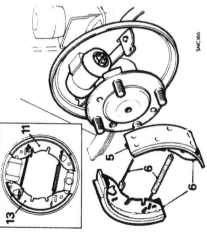

SNC165

9   Check the adjuster for easy working; lubricate moving parts if necessary.

10   Check the wheel cylinders for signs of leakage — refer to 70.60.18/26.

11   Fit the return springs into the correct holes in the trailing shoe ensuring that the clip of the largest spring is located in the slotted hole at the top of the shoe.

12   Position the trailing shoe and springs against the back plate.

13   Fit the leading shoe, locating the springs into the correct holes.

14   Locate the leading and trailing shoes over the hand brake lever, and lever the shoes onto their wheel cylinder and adjuster abutments.

15   Refit the brake drum.

16   Repeat the procedures in 11 to 15 for the other rear brake shoes.

17   Apply the foot brake several times to centralize the brake shoes.

18   Adjust the brake shoes, see MAINTENANCE.

19   Check the hand brake operation, adjust if necessary, see 70.35.10.

20   Refit the road wheels and lower the car.

FRONT BRAKE CALLIPER

Remove and refit	
Friction pads 1 to 10 and 12 to 32	**70.55.02**
	70.40.02

Service tool: 18G 590

Removing

1   Raise and support the front of the car.

2   Remove the road wheel.

3   Depress the friction pads retaining spring and withdraw the split pins.

4   Remove the retaining spring.

5   Manoeuvre the friction pads and remove the friction pads and anti-squeal shims.

6   Remove the banjo bolt and two sealing washers to release the hydraulic supply hose from the calliper.

7   Unlock and unscrew the bolts securing the hydraulic supply hose support bracket and calliper to release the calliper.

Inspection

8   Examine the lining material of the pads for wear, if the material has worn down to the minimum thickness of 1/16 in (1.6 mm), or if they will have done so before the next check is called for they must be renewed.

9   Examine the friction pad retaining spring for damage or loss of tension, renew if necessary.

10   Examine the disc; if worn on one side, one of the pistons may be seized. Overhaul the calliper if necessary. Rotate the disc by hand, and remove all scale and rust from around the edge using a scraper.

Refitting

11   Fit the calliper and supply hose support bracket using a new locking tab washer, and tighten the retaining bolts to 48 lbf ft (6.7 kgf m). Lock the bolts.

12   Check that the exposed surfaces of each piston is clean and the recesses in the calliper are free from rust and grit.

13   Check that the relieved face of each piston is correctly positioned downwards.

14   If necessary use tool 18G 590 to press each piston into the bore.

15   Fit the friction pads to the calliper, and check that the friction pads are free to move easily in the calliper recess.

16   Fit the anti-squeal shims between the pistons and friction pad pressure plates.

17   Fit the friction pad retaining spring and secure with split pins. Lock the split pins.

18   Fit the supply hose and secure with the banjo bolt and two sealing washers.

19   Bleed the brake hydraulic system, see 70.25.02.

20   Pump the brake pedal several times to position the pads against the disc.

21   Top up the master cylinder with a recommended brake fluid.

22   Lower the car.

23   Drive the car forwards and test the brakes.

FRONT BRAKE CALLIPER

Overhaul   **70.55.13**

Service tool: 18G 590

Dismantling

1   Remove the front brake calliper, see 70.55.02.

2   Clean the outside of the calliper, ensuring that all dirt and cleaning fluid are completely removed.

3   Note the position of the relieved portion of the piston face.

4   Using tool 18G 590 clamp the piston in the mounting half of the calliper.

5   Hold the cylinder on the bench and eject the outer-half piston with compressed air applied at the inlet port.

[CAUTION: Wash hydraulic cylinder components in brake fluid only. Never use gasoline or other petroleum-based solvents since they are damaging to rubber parts in the system.]

SNC134

SNC132

BRAKES — RIGHT-HAND STEER

6 Gently prise the dust seal retainer from the mouth of the calliper bore and remove the dust seal, taking care not to damage the bore of the calliper or the seal groove.

7 Remove the fluid seal from its groove in the calliper bore taking great care not to damage the bore of the calliper at the seal groove.

8 Remove the clamping tool.

9 Refit the outer-half piston only into its bore in the calliper.

10 Using tool 18G 590 clamp the outer half piston.

11 Remove the mounting-half piston dust seal retainer, dust seal, and fluid seal by repeating the procedure in 5 to 7.

12 Remove the clamping tool and outer-half piston.

13 Remove the bleed screw.

CAUTION: Do not separate the two halves of the unit.

Inspection

14 Clean all components in denatured alcohol (methylated spirit) or unused brake fluid.

15 Examine the cylinder bores and pistons; if scored or damaged, renew the unit.

16 Blow through the fluid passages with compressed air.

Reassembling

17 Lubricate the pistons and new seals in unused brake fluid.

18 Fit the fluid seals into their grooves in the cylinder bores.

19 Fit the dust seals and their retainers.

20 Fit the pistons in the bores, ensuring the relieved face is uppermost (toward the bleed screw).

21 Refit the bleed screw.

22 Refit the front brake calliper, see 70.55.02.

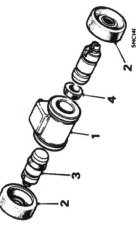

SNC140

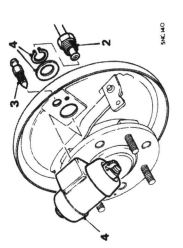

SNC144

Inspecting

5 Clean all components in denatured alcohol (methylated spirit) or unused brake fluid and dry.

6 Examine the wheel cylinder bore; if scored or damaged, fit a new unit.

7 Thoroughly clean the bleed screw and blow through with an air pressure line.

Reassembling

CAUTION: Immerse all components and new seals in a recommended brake fluid and assemble when wet.

8 Fit new seals to the pistons, with the flat surface of the seals towards the slotted end of the piston.

9 Fit the new pistons into the wheel cylinder bore, plain end first.

10 Fit new dust seals.

11 Refit the wheel cylinder, see 70.60.18.

REAR WHEEL CYLINDERS

Overhaul   70.60.26

Dismantling

1 Remove the rear wheel cylinder, see 70.60.18.

2 Remove the dust seals from the ends of the wheel cylinder.

3 Withdraw both pistons complete with their seals.

4 Remove the seals from the pistons.

[**CAUTION: Wash hydraulic cylinder components in brake fluid only. Never use gasoline or other petroleum-based solvents since they are damaging to rubber parts in the system.**]

REAR WHEEL CYLINDER

Remove and refit   70.60.18

Removing

1 Remove the rear brake-shoes from the side to be worked on, see 70.40.03.

2 Disconnect the brake pipe at the wheel cylinder and plug the pipe.

3 Remove the bleed screw.

4 Remove the circlip and washer retaining the wheel cylinder to the backplate and withdraw the cylinder assembly.

Refitting

5 Reverse the procedure in 1 to 4.

6 Bleed the hydraulic brake system, see 70.25.02.

DATA

Rear wheel cylinder bore diameter . . . .   0.687 in (17.46 mm)

SNK 163

BRAKES — LEFT-HAND STEER

REAR BRAKE BACK PLATE

Remove and refit   70.10.26

Removing
1. Remove the rear hub, see 51.10.02.
2. Remove the rear brake shoes, see 70.40.03.
3. Remove the rear wheel cylinder, see 70.60.18.
4. Unscrew the brake shoe adjuster and remove the wedges.
5. Remove the bolts, nuts and spring washer securing the back plate to the rear axle tube.
6. Detach the back-plate.

Refitting
7. Reverse the procedure in 1 to 6 and bleed the brake hydraulic system, see 70.25.02.

HOSES

Remove and refit
Front   70.15.02
Rear   70.15.17

CONNECTOR

Remove and refit
Rear three-way   70.15.34

PIPES

Remove and refit
Feed to front left-hand hose   70.20.02
Feed to front right-hand hose   70.20.03
Feed to rear hose   70.20.13
Feed to rear left-hand wheel cylinder   70.20.17
Feed to rear right-hand wheel cylinder   70.20.18
Feed to pressure differential warning actuator – primary   70.20.46
Feed to pressure differential warning actuator – secondary   70.20.47

NOTE: The operation numbers given above are included on the illustration of the braking system to facilitate identification of the individual pipes and hoses.

Removing
1. Disconnect the pipe or hose nearest to the master cylinder and plug it to prevent further loss of fluid.
2. Unscrew the pipe union.
3. Remove the locknut and lock washer.
4. Pull the hose from the body or bracket and remove the lock washer.
5. Release the body clips.
6. Remove the hose or pipe.

Refitting
7. Reverse the procedure in 1 to 7 noting:
   a. Ensure the hoses are not twisted; hold the hose hexagon ensuring it is correctly located in the body while tightening the locknut.
   b. Do not overtighten the pipe unions.
   c. Check all connections for signs of leakage after the system has been bled.
8. Bleed the brake hydraulic system, see 70.25.02.

172

BRAKES – LEFT-HAND STEER

BLEEDING THE SYSTEM

Bleed – all round   70.25.02

Preparation

Absolute cleanliness must be maintained throughout the entire bleeding operation, ensure that no dirt or grit enters the system. All equipment to be used must be free from fuel, paraffin, or any form of mineral oil.

1 Check that all connections are tight and that the bleed screws are closed.
2 Release the hand brake.
3 Top up the master cylinder with a recommended brake fluid.

CAUTION:

a Never re-use brake fluid which has been bled from the system.
b Keep brake fluid away from all paintwork.
c Do not allow the fluid level to fall so low that air can enter the system during bleeding; always top up the level.

Bleeding

4 Attach bleeder tubes to the bleed screw on the R.H. front and R.H. rear brakes and submerge the free end of each tube in a small quantity of brake fluid in a clean glass jar.
5 Open the bleed screws about half a turn.
6 Commence bleeding with very light strokes of the pedal.
DO NOT push the pedal through its entire stroke.
DO NOT test the pedal until all the air has been expelled from the system and the system fully bled.
If during the bleeding operation the warning light should glow continue bleeding until all the air is expelled from the system.
7 Repeat procedure 6 until the fluid flowing into each glass jar is free of air bubbles and then close the bleed screws during the next (last) pedal application.
Top up the reservoir after tightening the bleed screws.
8 Bleed the L.H. front and L.H. rear brakes in the manner described in procedures 4 to 7.

9 If the warning light glows attach a bleed tube to the L.H. rear brake (see procedure 4). Open the bleed screw half a turn and slowly depress the brake pedal, immediately the light goes out release the brake pedal and tighten the bleed screw. If the light fails to go out transfer the bleed tube to the R.H. front brake (see procedure 4). Slowly depress the brake pedal, immediately the light goes out release the brake pedal and tighten the bleed screw.

CAUTION: Failure to release the brake pedal immediately the light goes out will cause the piston to move too far in the opposite direction and the resetting procedure will have to be recommenced.

5 Test the brake pedal action and, if springy, re-bleed the brakes, see 70.25.02.
6 Press the brake pedal to check that the front and rear hydraulic pressure is equal: the warning light should not glow.

PRESSURE DIFFERENTIAL WARNING ACTUATOR (P.D.W.A.) VALVE

Reset   70.25.08

The hydraulic brake system has two independent circuits. If hydraulic pressure fails in one circuit, the remaining circuit will provide an emergency brake on two wheels and allow the car to be brought to rest by normal brake pedal application. A circuit failure causes the P.D.W.A. valve piston to be displaced, and when displaced the piston operates the valve switch which, in turn, causes the warning lamp on the fascia panel to illuminate.

Warning: One circuit only is inadequate as a normal service brake and the car should **not be driven until the fault has been rectified by carrying out the complete resetting procedure, operations 1 to 6.**

1 Check that there is sufficient brake fluid in the reservoir.
2 Check the brake system for leaks and correct operation, and rectify any faults.
3 Bleed the brakes, ensuring all the air has been expelled from the system, see 70.25.02.
4 Bleed the brakes on one of the wheels at the opposite end of the car to the one which had proved faulty. Slowly depress the pedal; immediately the light goes out release the pedal and close the bleed screw.

Refitting

5 Reverse the procedure in 2 to 4, taking care to seat the hydraulic pipes squarely in their connections; do not overtighten the unions. Ensure the unit is approximately horizontal.
6 Bleed the brake hydraulic system, see 70.25.02.

PRESSURE DIFFERENTIAL WARNING ACTUATOR (P.D.W.A.)

Remove and refit   70.25.13

Removing

1 Clean the switch assembly and its adjacent surroundings particularly the pipe union connections.
2 Disconnect the wiring plug from the switch.
3 Disconnect and plug the hydraulic pipes.
   a From master cylinder-primary.
   b From master cylinder-secondary.
   c To L.H. front brake.
   d To R.H. front brake
   e To rear brakes.
4 Unscrew the retaining bolts and remove the P.D.W.A. assembly.

PRESSURE DIFFERENTIAL WARNING ACTUATOR (P.D.W.A.) VALVE

Overhaul   70.25.14

Dismantling

1 Remove the P.D.W.A. valve, see 70.25.13.
2 Remove the end plug and discard the copper washer.
3 Unscrew the nylon switch.
4 Withdraw the shuttle valve piston assembly from the bore; use a low pressure air line to free the piston if necessary.
5 Remove and discard the two piston seals.

continued

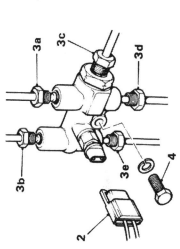

BRAKES — LEFT-HAND STEER

Inspection

6 Thoroughly clean all the components using denatured alcohol (methylated spirit) or brake fluid, and dry.

7 Check the bore of the casing, if it is not scored or ridged new seals can be fitted.
Renew the unit if the bore is scored or ridged.

8 Reconnect the wiring to the switch, and actuate the switch plunger, with the ignition switched on, to test the switch operation and warning light circuit. Disconnect the wiring from the switch.

Reassembling

CAUTION: Immerse the piston and new seals in brake fluid and assemble when wet.

9 Fit two new seals, lips facing outwards from the piston centre.

10 Lubricate the piston assembly with Lockheed Disc Brake Lubricant, and fit the piston into the bore, taking care that the lip of the leading seal is not turned back.

11 Fit a new copper washer to the end plug, screw in and tighten the end plug to 400 lbf in (2.3 kgf m).

12 Screw in the nylon switch and carefully tighten it to 15 lbf in (0.173 kgf m).

13 Refit the P.D.W.A. valve, see 70.25.13.

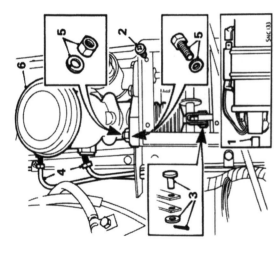

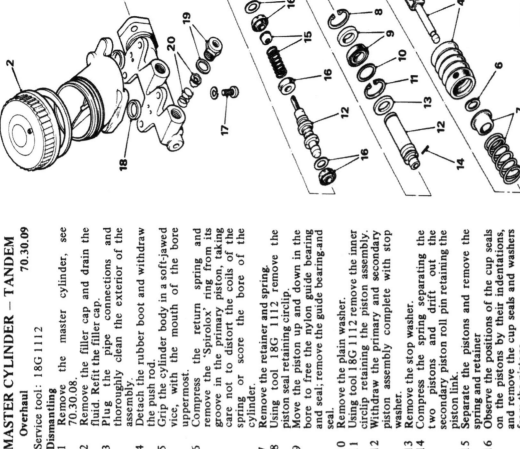

SNC49

MASTER CYLINDER — TANDEM

Overhaul   70.30.09

Service tool: 18G 1112

Dismantling

1 Remove the master cylinder, see 70.30.08.

2 Remove the filler cap and drain the fluid. Refit the filler cap.

3 Plug the pipe connections and thoroughly clean the exterior of the assembly.

4 Detach the rubber boot and withdraw the push rod.

5 Grip the cylinder body in a soft-jawed vice, with the mouth of the bore uppermost.

6 Compress the return spring and remove the 'Spirolox' ring from its groove in the primary piston, taking care not to distort the coils of the spring or score the bore of the cylinder.

7 Remove the retainer and spring.

8 Using tool 18G 1112 remove the piston seal retaining circlip.

9 Move the piston up and down in the bore to free the nylon guide bearing and seal; remove the guide bearing and seal.

10 Remove the plain washer.

11 Using tool 18G 1112 remove the inner circlip retaining the piston assembly.

12 Withdraw the primary and secondary piston assembly complete with stop washer.

13 Remove the stop washer.

14 Compress the spring separating the two pistons and drift out the secondary piston roll pin retaining the piston link.

15 Separate the pistons and remove the spring and retainer

16 Observe the positions of the cup seals on the pistons by their indentations, and remove the cup seals and washers from the pistons.

17 Unscrew the four screws to release the plastic reservoir from the body.

18 Remove the reservoir sealing rings.

19 Unscrew the connection adaptors and discard the copper washers.

20 Remove the springs and trap valves.

continued

MASTER CYLINDER — TANDEM

Remove and refit   70.30.08

Removing

1 Remove the H.T. lead from the ignition coil, and the white/blue lead from the resistor.

2 Remove the four screws to release the cover plate complete with ignition coil.

3 Withdraw the split pin and washer and remove the clevis pin.

4 Unscrew the pipe unions from the master cylinder. Plug the pipes and the master cylinder.
NOTE: Brake and clutch fluid can have a detrimental effect on paintwork, ensure that fluid is not allowed to contact painted surfaces.

5 Remove the bolts, nuts, and spring washers securing the master cylinder to the pedal box.

6 Remove the master cylinder.

Refitting

7 Reverse the procedure in 1 to 6.

8 Bleed the brake hydraulic system, see 70.25.02.

[CAUTION: Wash hydraulic cylinder components in brake fluid only. Never use gasoline or other petroleum-based solvents since they are damaging to rubber parts in the system.]

174

BRAKES — LEFT-HAND STEER

Inspection

21 Thoroughly clean all the components using denatured alcohol (methylated spirit) or brake fluid and dry.

22 Check the master cylinder bore; if the bore is not scored or ridged new rubber cup seals can be fitted. Renew the unit if the bore is scored or ridged.

23 Check that the inlet and outlet ports are free of obstruction.

Reassembling

CAUTION: Immerse all internal components in brake fluid and assemble when wet.

24 Locate the piston washer on the head of the secondary piston, convex surface first.

25 Stretch the indented main cup seal, lip last, over the end of the secondary piston, and seat it correctly in its groove adjacent to the washer.

26 Stretch the plain cup seal, lip last, over the front end of the secondary piston, seating it correctly in its groove.

27 Locate the piston washer on the primary piston, convex surface first.

28 Reverse the dismantling procedure in 2 to 15 and 17 to 20 noting:

  a Use new connection adaptor copper washers.

  b Renew the secondary piston roll pin if necessary.

29 Refit the master cylinder, see 70.30.08.

BRAKE PEDAL ASSEMBLY   70.35.01

Remove and refit

Removing

1 Disconnect the return springs from the clutch and brake pedals.

2 Disconnect the battery.

3 Remove the H.T. lead from the ignition coil and the white/blue lead from the ballast resistor.

4 Release the four screws to release the cover plate complete with ignition coil.

5 Disconnect the stop light switch wiring.

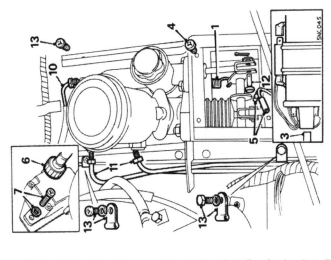

12 Remove the split pins and washers, and withdraw the clutch and brake pedal clevis pins.

13 Remove the four screws and four bolts and spring washers retaining the pedal box to the body, noting the position of the bolts that secure the oil pressure pipe clips.

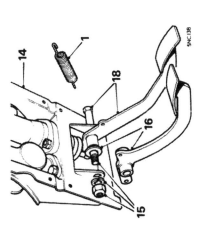

6 Disconnect the gearbox drive cable from the service interval counter.

7 Remove the two screws retaining the service interval counter to the bracket and swing the counter aside.

8 Jack up the front of the car and support with stands.

9 Attach a tube to the bleed nipples of the clutch slave cylinder and a front brake, slacken the bleed nipples and pump the clutch and brake fluid into containers — similar to the bleeding procedure in 33.15.01 and 70.25.02.

10 Disconnect the fluid pipe from the clutch master cylinder and plug the pipe.

11 Disconnect the fluid pipes from the brake master cylinder and plug the pipes.

Note: Brake and clutch fluid can have a detrimental effect on paintwork, ensure that fluid is not allowed to contact painted surfaces.

PEDAL BOX   70.35.03

Remove and refit

Removing

1 Remove the brake pedal, see 70 35 01.

2 Remove the clutch master cylinder from the pedal box, see 33.20.01.

3 Remove the brake master cylinder from the pedal box, see 70.30.08.

4 Remove the locknut and unscrew the stop light switch.

Refitting

5 Reverse the procedure in 1 to 4, and adjust the stop light switch, see instruction 9, 86.65.51.

6 Bleed the clutch hydraulic system, see 33.15.01.

7 Bleed the brake hydraulic system, see 70.25.01.

14 Raise the pedal box as far as possible.

15 Unscrew the nut and spring washer and withdraw the pivot bolt sufficiently to permit removal of the clutch pedal.

16 Remove the clutch pedal and spacer washer.

17 Remove the pedal box.

18 Remove the pivot bolt and brake pedal.

19 Remove the brake pedal pad.

Refitting

20 Reverse the procedure in 1 to 8, and 10 to 19.

21 Bleed the clutch hydraulic system, see 33.15.01.

22 Bleed the brake hydraulic system, see 70.25.02.

BRAKES — LEFT-HAND STEER

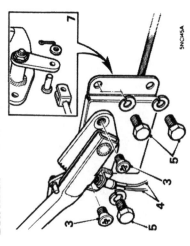

HAND BRAKE LEVER ASSEMBLY
Remove and refit   70.35.08

Removing
1 Disconnect the battery.
2 Remove the L.H. front seat, see 76.70.01.
3 Remove the two screws securing the hand brake to the mounting plate.
4 Disconnect the wiring from the handbrake warning switch.
5 Pull back the carpet and remove the three set screws securing the mounting plate to the tunnel.
6 Rotate the mounting plate 180 degrees.
7 Pull the handbrake lever away from the tunnel, remove the split pin and washer, and withdraw the clevis pin.
8 Remove the hand brake lever and separate the mounting plate from the hand brake.
9 Unscrew the locknut and remove the handbrake warning switch from its bracket.

Refitting
10 Assemble the mounting plate to the hand brake lever in its fitted position.
11 Rotate the mounting plate 180 degrees.
12 Reverse the procedure in 1 to 5 using a new split pin.
13 Check the hand brake operation and adjust the cable if necessary, see 70.35.10.
14 Adjust the hand brake warning switch see 86.65.46.

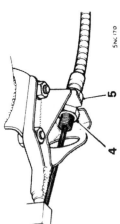

HAND BRAKE LEVER, PAWL AND RATCHET
Remove and refit   70.35.09

Removing
1 Remove the hand brake lever, see 70.35.08.
2 Remove the nut, withdraw the lockwasher, and remove the cable lever from the hand brake lever.
3 Remove the ratchet plate and spring washer from the hand brake lever.
4 Withdraw the split pin and release the catch rod from the pawl.
5 Withdraw the split pin, flat and spring washers retaining the pawl to its pivot.
6 Remove the pawl and flat washer.
7 Slide the catch rod up the hand brake lever.
8 Drift the Mills pin from the catch rod to release the thumb button.
9 Remove the catch rod, spring and washer from the hand brake lever.

Refitting
10 Lubricate the pivot points with grease.
11 Reverse the procedure in 2 to 8 noting:
  a Fit a new Mills pin if necessary.
  b Fit a pawl spring washer concave face first.
  c Fit the ratchet plate spring washer convex face first.
12 Check that the pawl operates freely and the handle pivots.
13 Refit the hand brake lever, see 70.35.08.

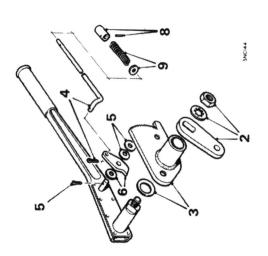

HAND BRAKE CABLE — 1975-1976
Adjust   70.35.10
1 Adjust the rear brakes, see 'Maintenance'.
2 Apply the hand brake so that the pawl engages on the third notch of the ratchet.
3 Check the braking effect on the rear wheels. The wheels should be held or tending to bind.
Adjust the cable if braking effect is inadequate.
4 Slacken the cable front adjustment nut.
5 Screw the rear adjustment nut in the required direction to adjust the position of the threaded sleeve, and tighten the front nut. Adjustment is correct when the road wheels can just be rotated. Both wheels must offer equal braking resistance.
6 Check the hand brake action. Release the hand brake and check that the rear wheels rotate freely.
7 Lower the car.

HAND BRAKE CABLE — 1977 and later
Adjust   70.35.10
1 Adjust the rear brakes, see 'Maintenance'.
2 Apply the hand brake so that the pawl engages on the third notch of the ratchet.
3 Check the braking effect on the rear wheels. The wheels should be held or tending to bind.
Adjust the cable if braking effect is inadequate.
4 Slacken the cable rear adjustment nut.
5 Screw the front adjustment nut in the required direction to adjust the position of the threaded sleeve, and tighten the rear nut. Adjustment is correct when the road wheels can just be rotated. Both wheels must offer equal braking resistance.
6 Check the hand brake action. Release the hand brake and check that the rear wheels rotate freely.
7 Lower the car.

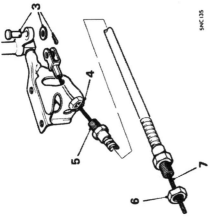

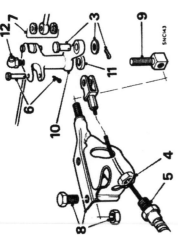

BRAKES — LEFT-HAND STEER

HAND BRAKE COMPENSATOR — 1975-1976 only   70.35.11

Remove and refit

Removing
1 Chock the front wheels, jack up the rear of the car and support on stands beneath the rear axle.
2 Release the hand brake.
3 Remove the split pin and washer and withdraw the hand brake cable clevis pin.
4 Unscrew the rear adjustment nut, and slide the nut along the cable.
5 Detach the threaded sleeve from the abutment and withdraw the cable from the compensator mechanism.
6 Remove the split pins and withdraw the clevis pins retaining the brake rods to the balance lever.
7 Detach the brake rods and their felt pads from the balance lever.
8 Remove the two bolts and nuts to release the compensator support from the rear axle.
9 Unscrew the balance lever carrier from the compensator support.
10 Unscrew the balance lever from the carrier.
11 Remove the felt pad from the balance lever.
12 Remove the grease nipple.

Refitting
13 Fit new parts as necessary.
14 Soak the felt pads in oil.
15 Fit the grease nipple to the balance carrier.

16 Locate the large felt pad in its recess in the bottom of the balance lever.
17 Screw the balance lever to the carrier and then unscrew one full turn, ensuring the threaded hole in the carrier is in the same plane as the brake rod forks on the balance carrier.
18 Screw the carrier to the compensator support ensuring that the carrier is started on the threaded spigot with the balance lever uppermost.
19 Unscrew the carrier one full turn.
20 Grease the compensator.
21 Ensure that the balance lever swivels freely on the carrier.
22 With the balance lever upright fit the brake rods with felt pads either side of the rods in the forks.
23 Fit the clevis pins to retain the brake rods and secure using new split pins.
24 Fit the hand brake cable to the compensator, passing the fork through the hole in the bracket, locating the threaded sleeve on the abutment and positioning the relieved face of the fork towards the compensating mechanism.
25 Fit the cable clevis pin and secure with a new split pin.
26 Adjust the hand brake cable, see 70.35.10.

HAND BRAKE CABLE ASSEMBLY — 1975-1976   70.35.16

Remove and refit   70.35.16

Removing
1 Chock the front wheels, jack up the rear of the car and place supports beneath the rear axle.
2 Remove the hand brake lever, see 70.35.08.
3 Remove the split pin and washer, and withdraw the clevis pin from the compensating lever.
4 Unscrew the cable rear adjustment nut and slide the nut along the cable.
5 Detach the threaded sleeve from the abutment and withdraw the cable from the compensating lever mechanism.
6 Unscrew the cable front abutment nut and slide the nut along the cable.

7 Detach the cable from the front abutment bracket and withdraw the cable from the tunnel.

Refitting
8 Reverse the procedure in 2 to 6 noting:
a Renew the split pins.
b Fit the rear fork through the hole in the compensating bracket and assemble with the relieved face of the fork towards the compensating mechanism.
9 Refit the hand brake lever, see 70.35.08.
10 Check the hand brake operation and adjust if necessary, see 70.35.10.
11 Lower the car, and remove the front wheel chocks.

HAND BRAKE CABLE ASSEMBLY — 1977 and later   70.35.16

Remove and refit   70.35.16

Removing
1 Chock the front wheels, raise the rear of the car and place supports beneath the rear axle.
2 Remove the hand brake lever, see 70.35.08.
3 Unscrew the cable front adjustment nut and slide the nut along the cable.
4 Detach the cable from the front abutment bracket and withdraw the cable from the tunnel.
5 Remove the nut and screw securing the cable clip to the differential housing and separate the clip from the cable.
6 Remove the nut and bolt securing the cable to the mounting strap.
7 Remove the split pin and washer, and withdraw the clevis pin from each backplate lever.
8 Remove the hand brake cable assembly.

Refitting
9 Reverse the procedure in 3 to 8, noting:
a Renew the clip if worn or damaged.
b Renew the mounting strap if damaged or showing signs of deterioration.
10 Refit the hand brake lever, see 70.35.08.
11 Check the hand brake operation, and adjust if necessary, see 70.35.10.
12 Lower the car, and remove the front wheel chocks.

BRAKES – LEFT-HAND STEER

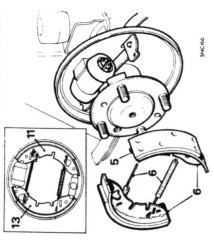

SNC 60

REAR BRAKE SHOES

Remove and refit
Brake drum 1 to 4, 15 and   70.40.03
17 to 20   70.10.03

Removing
1 Chock the front wheels and release the hand brake.
2 Slacken the rear road wheel fastenings, jack up and place supports beneath the rear axle. Remove the road wheels.
3 Slacken off the brake shoe adjuster fully.
4 Remove the brake drum.
5 Lever the trailing shoe from its wheel cylinder and adjuster abutment.
6 Remove both brake shoes and shoe return springs.
Note: Retain the wheel cylinder pistons with an elastic band if new shoes are not to be fitted immediately.
7 Repeat the procedure in 3 to 6 on the other rear brake shoes.

Refitting
8 Wash all dust from the back-plate assembly and drum with denatured alcohol (methylated spirit), allow to dry.
Warning: Do not use an air line to blow dust from the brake assemblies — asbestos dust can be dangerous if inhaled.

9 Check the adjuster for easy working; lubricate moving parts if necessary.
10 Check the wheel cylinders for signs of leakage – refer to 70.60.18/26.
11 Fit the return springs into the correct holes in the trailing shoe ensuring that the clip of the largest spring is located in the slotted hole at the top of the shoe.
12 Position the trailing shoe and springs against the back plate.
13 Fit the leading shoe, locating the springs into the correct holes.
14 Locate the leading and trailing shoes over the hand brake lever, and lever the shoes onto their wheel cylinder and adjuster abutments.
15 Refit the brake drum.
16 Repeat the procedures in 11 to 15 for the other rear brake shoes.
17 Apply the foot brake several times to centralize the brake shoes.
18 Adjust the brake shoes, see 70.35.10.
Maintenance.
19 Check the hand brake operation, adjust if necessary, see 70.35.10.
20 Refit the road wheels and lower the car.

FRONT BRAKE CALLIPER

Remove and refit   70.55.02
Friction pads 1 to 10 and 12 to 32   70.40.02

Service tool: 18G 590

Removing
1 Raise and support the front of the car.
2 Remove the road wheel.
3 Depress the friction pads retaining spring and withdraw the split pins.
4 Remove the retaining spring.
5 Manoeuvre the friction pads and remove the friction pads and anti-squeal shims.
6 Remove the banjo bolt and two sealing washers to release the hydraulic supply hose from the calliper.
7 Unlock and unscrew the bolts securing the hydraulic supply hose support bracket and calliper to release the calliper.

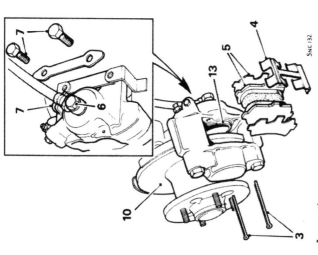

SNC 132

Inspection
8 Examine the lining material of the pads for wear, if the material has worn down to 1/16 in (1.6 mm), or if they will have done so before the next check is called for they must be renewed.
9 Examine the friction pad retaining spring for damage or loss of tension, renew if necessary.
10 Examine the disc; if worn on one side, one of the pistons may be seized. Overhaul the calliper if necessary. Rotate the disc by hand, and remove all scale and rust from around the edge using a scraper.

Refitting
11 Fit the calliper and supply hose support bracket using a new locking tab washer, and tighten the retaining bolts to 48 lbf ft (6.7 kgf m). Lock the bolts.
12 Check that the exposed surfaces of each piston is clean and the recesses in the calliper are free from rust and grit.

13 Check that the relieved face of each piston is correctly positioned downwards.
14 If necessary use tool 18G 590 to press each piston into the bore.
15 Fit the friction pads to the calliper, and check that the friction pads are free to move easily in the calliper recess.
16 Fit the anti-squeal shims between the pistons and friction pad pressure plates.
17 Fit the friction pad retaining spring and secure with split pins. Lock the split pins.
18 Fit the supply hose and secure with the banjo bolt and two sealing washers.
19 Bleed the brake hydraulic system, see 70.25.02.
20 Pump the brake pedal several times to position the pads against the disc.
21 Top up the master cylinder with a recommended brake fluid.
22 Lower the car.
23 Drive the car forwards and test the brakes.

FRONT BRAKE CALLIPER

Overhaul   70.55.13

Service tool: 18G 590

Dismantling
1 Remove the front brake calliper, see 70.55.02.
2 Clean the outside of the calliper, ensuring that all dirt and cleaning fluid are completely removed.
3 Note the position of the relieved portion of the piston face.
4 Using tool 18G 590 clamp the piston in the mounting half of the calliper.
5 Hold the cylinder on the bench and eject the outer-half piston with compressed air applied at the inlet port.

[CAUTION: Wash hydraulic cylinder components in brake fluid only Never use gasoline or other petroleum-based solvents since they are damaging to rubber parts in the system.]

BRAKES — LEFT-HAND STEER

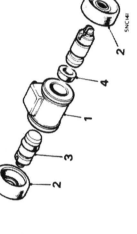

pistons; if scored or damaged, renew the unit.

16 Blow through the fluid passages with compressed air.

Reassembling

17 Lubricate the pistons and new seals in unused brake fluid.
18 Fit the fluid seals into their grooves in the cylinder bores.
19 Fit the dust seals and their retainers.
20 Fit the pistons in the bores, ensuring the relieved face is uppermost (toward the bleed screw).
21 Refit the bleed screw.
22 Refit the front brake calliper, see 70.55.02.

6 Gently prise the dust seal retainer from the mouth of the calliper bore and remove the dust seal, taking care not to damage the bore of the calliper or the seal groove.
7 Remove the fluid seal from its groove in the calliper bore taking great care not to damage the bore of the calliper at the seal groove.
8 Remove the clamping tool.
9 Refit the outer-half piston only into its bore in the calliper.
10 Using tool 18G 590 clamp the outer half piston.
11 Remove the mounting-half piston dust seal retainer, dust seal, and fluid seal by repeating the procedure in 5 to 7.
12 Remove the clamping tool and outer-half piston.
13 Remove the bleed screw.

CAUTION: Do not separate the two halves of the calliper.

Inspection

14 Clean all components in denatured alcohol (methylated spirit) or unused brake fluid.
15 Examine the cylinder bores and

Inspecting

5 Clean all components in denatured alcohol (methylated spirit) or unused brake fluid and dry.
6 Examine the wheel cylinder bore; if scored or damaged, fit a new unit.
7 Thoroughly clean the bleed screw and blow through with an air pressure line.

Reassembling

Caution: Immerse all components and new seals in a recommended brake fluid and assemble when wet.

8 Fit new seals to the pistons, with the flat surface of the seals towards the slotted end of the piston.
9 Fit the new pistons into the wheel cylinder bore, plain end first.
10 Fit new dust seals.
11 Refit the wheel cylinder, see 70.60.18.

REAR WHEEL CYLINDERS 70.60.26

Overhaul

Dismantling

1 Remove the rear wheel cylinder, see 70.60.18.
2 Remove the dust seals from the ends of the wheel cylinder.
3 Withdraw both pistons complete with their seals.
4 Remove the seals from the pistons.

[CAUTION: Wash hydraulic cylinder components in brake fluid only. Never use gasoline or other petroleum-based solvents since they are damaging to rubber parts in the system.]

DATA

Rear wheel cylinder bore diameter . . . . 0.687 in (17.46 mm)

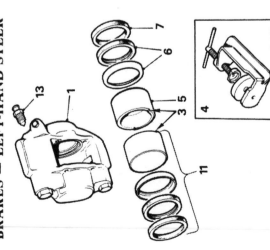

REAR WHEEL CYLINDER 70.60.18

Remove and refit

Removing

1 Remove the rear brake-shoes from the side to be worked on, see 70.40.03.
2 Disconnect the brake pipe at the wheel cylinder and plug the pipe.
3 Remove the bleed screw.
4 Remove the circlip and washer retaining the wheel cylinder to the backplate and withdraw the cylinder assembly.

Refitting

5 Reverse the procedure in 1 to 4.
6 Bleed the hydraulic brake system, see 70.25.02.

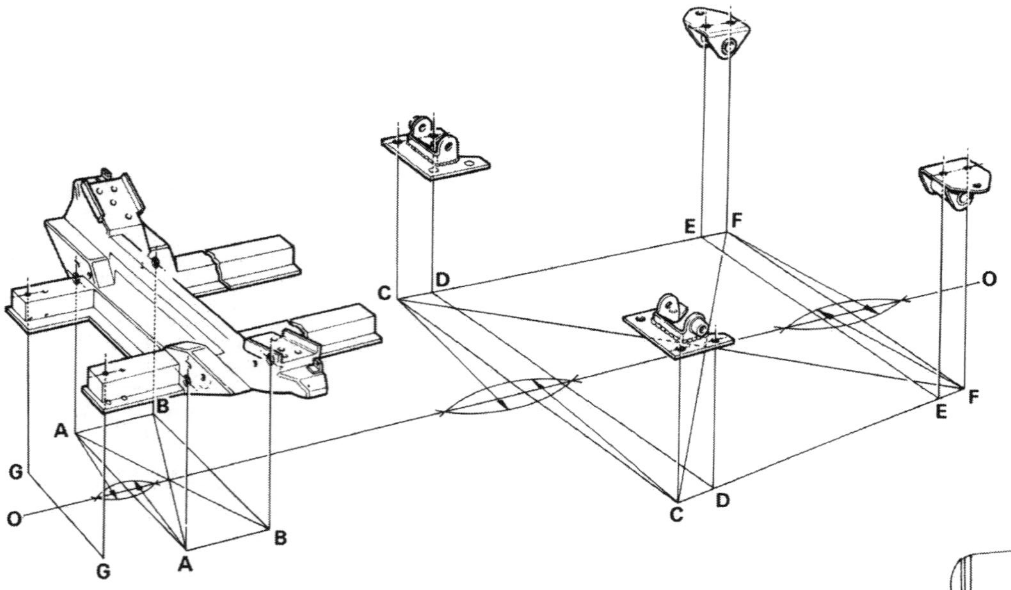

Key to the Horizontal Alignment Check

Code	Dimension	Location
0–0		Datum
A–A	18 21/32 to 18 21/32 in (446.32 to 467.11 mm)	Front fulcrum pin centre — eye to eye
B–B	18 21/32 to 18 21/32 in (446.32 to 467.11 mm)	Rear fulcrum pin centre — eye to eye
C–C	39.969 to 40.031 in (1015.21 to 1016.79 mm)	Rear spring front mounting — front outer bolt — hole to hole
D–D	39.969 to 40.031 in (1015.21 to 1016.79 mm)	Rear spring front mounting — rear outer bolt — hole to hole
E–E	35¾ in (908 mm)	Rear spring rear mounting — front bolt — hole to hole
F–F	35¾ in (908 mm)	Rear spring rear mounting — rear bolt — hole to hole
G–G	13¼ in (336.5 mm)	Radiator duct panel fixing — beam to beam

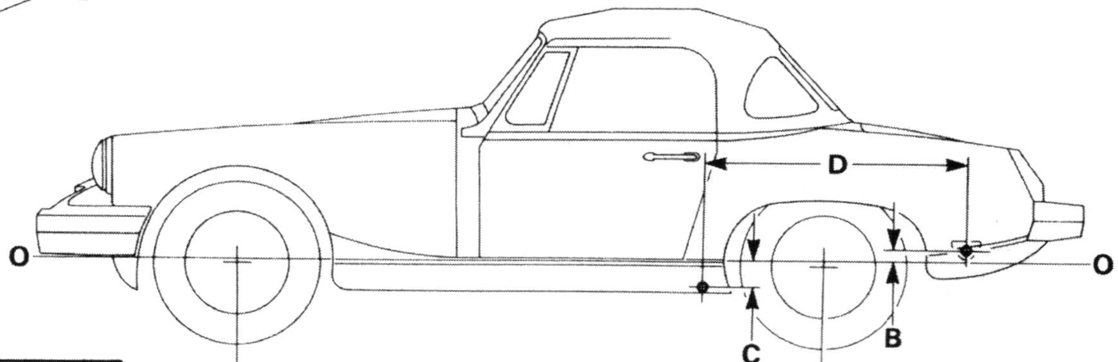

VERTICAL ALIGNMENT CHECK

6NB 006

Code	Dimension	Location
0–0		Datum
A	80 in (2.03 m)	Wheelbase
B	0.47 in (12 mm)	Datum to rear spring — rear shackle
C	3.944 in (100.2 mm)	Datum to rear spring — front mounting
D	35.48 in (901.2 mm)	Rear spring centres — edge to edge

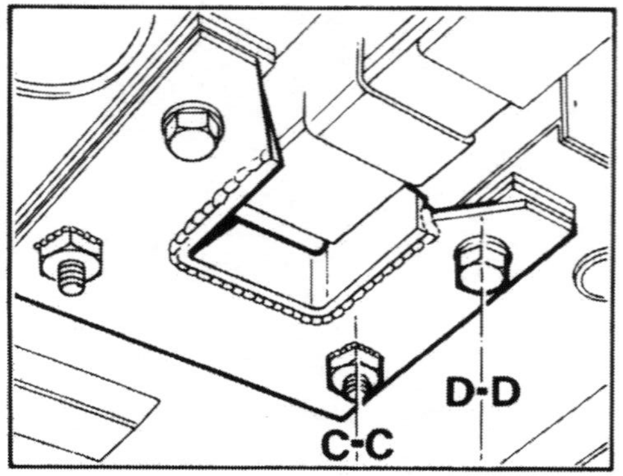

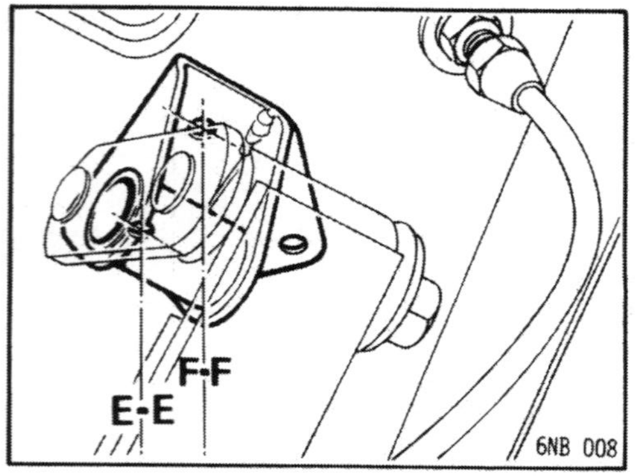

6NB 008

BODY

BOOT LID LOCK   76.19.11

Remove and refit

Removing

1 Disconnect the battery.
2 Remove the two nuts securing the handle assembly to the boot lid.
3 Remove the two bolts, nuts and washers securing the lock assembly to the boot lid.
4 Withdraw the handle and remove the lock.

Refitting

5 Reverse the procedure in 1 to 4.
NOTE: Rotation is restricted to 90° on both the handle and the lock, when fitting the handle ensure that it is correctly positioned to permit operation.

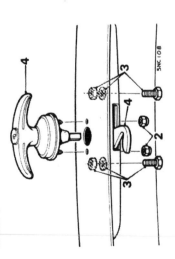

BUMPER ASSEMBLY

Overhaul – Front   76.22.09
          Rear   76.22.18

NOTE: To ensure sufficient flexibility the rubber bumper bar should be at a temperature of about 21°C (70°F) or higher during dismantling and assembling.

Dismantling

1 Remove the bumper assembly see 76.22.08 or 76.22.15.
2 Front bumper:
  a Remove the two bolts and washers to release the number-plate assembly.
  b Remove the front parking lamp assemblies, see 86.40.26.
  c Remove the MG motif.
  d Mark for location and remove the mounting brackets from the armature.
  e Drill the heads off the four rivets and remove the support tube.
3 Drill the heads off the rivets securing the rubber bumper bar to the armature, levering the rubber clear of the top rivets as necessary.
4 Punch the rivets through into the armature and remove the clamping plates.
5 Remove the armature from the rubber.

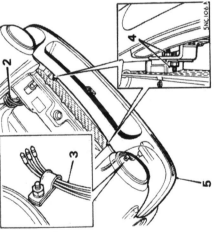
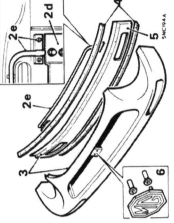
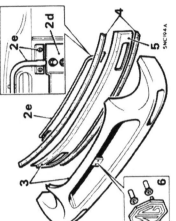

FRONT BUMPER ASSEMBLY   76.22.08

Remove and refit

Removing

1 Disconnect the battery.
2 Disconnect the parking lamp cables at the connectors in the engine compartment.
3 Withdraw the cables from the clip behind the head lamp.
4 Remove the four nuts and eight washers securing the bumper inner springs to the car.
5 Remove the bumper assembly.
6 Remove the number plate and its brackets.
7 Remove the two parking lamp lenses.
8 Remove the two parking lamp assemblies.

Refitting

9 Reverse the procedure in 1 to 8,
  a Fit the lamp lenses with their drain slots downwards.
  b Fit the inner springs with their studs uppermost.

Reassembling

6 Front bumper:
Ensure that the 'MG' motif is secured to the rubber bumper bar.
7 Ensure that the new rivets fit all the holes in the rubber; if necessary clear the holes with a drill.
8 Fit the armature into the rubber, noting:
  a Front bumper: Ensure that the number plate bracket holes are towards the bottom of the assembly.
  b Rear bumper: Ensure that the lashing brackets are towards the bottom of the assembly.
9 Fit the bottom clamping plate and insert the centre rivet and both end rivets.
10 Secure the three fitted rivets.
11 Fit and secure the remainder of the bottom rivets.
12 Fit the top clamping plate and insert the centre rivet and both end rivets.
13 Clamp the rubber to the armature with 'G' clamps.
14 Lever back the rubber as necessary and secure the three fitted rivets.
15 Lever back the rubber as necessary and fit and secure the remainder of the top rivets.
NOTE: It may be necessary to move the clamps so that they are close to the area being levered.
16 Front bumper: Rivet on the support tube.
17 Fit the bumper assembly see 76.22.08 or 76.22.15.

REAR BUMPER ASSEMBLY   76.22.15

Remove and refit

Removing

1 Disconnect the battery.
2 Remove, from inside the boot, the four nuts and eight washers securing the bumper assembly.
3 Remove the bumper assembly.

Refitting

4 Reverse the procedure in 1 to 3.

continued

BODY

CENTRE CONSOLE   76.25.01

Remove and refit

Removing

1 Disconnect the battery.
2 Release and remove the gearbox tunnel carpet.
3 Remove the screws securing the centre console.
4 Pull the centre console away and move aside (towards the steering-column).
5 Remove the hazard flasher unit from its clip.
6 Disconnect the wiring from the hazard switch, cigar-lighter, seat belt warning light, interior light, and 'CATALYST' warning light (if fitted).
7 Remove the console.
8 Remove the hazard flasher unit clip.
9 Remove the hazard flasher switch.
10 Remove the 'FASTEN BELTS' warning lamp.
11 Remove the 'CATALYST' warning lamp (if fitted).
12 Remove the courtesy lamp.
13 Remove the 'MG' motif.
14 Remove the bezel.

Refitting

15 Reverse the procedure in 1 to 14, connecting the wiring as shown in the wiring diagram, see 86.00.01/03.

DOOR GLASS REGULATOR   76.31.44
                              76.31.01

Remove and refit

Door glass

Removing

1 Disconnect the battery.
2 Remove the door trim pad and moulding, see 76.34.15
3 Fit the regulator handle.
4 Remove the regulator arm stop.
5 Remove the two bolts securing the ventilator assembly to the front edge of the door.
6 Remove the two nuts and washers securing the ventilator assembly to the top of the door.
7 Remove the two bolts securing the bottom of the door glass front channel.
8 Tilt the ventilator assembly forward and remove the bracket from the bottom of the door glass front channel.
9 Remove the eight bolts securing the regulator mechanism.
10 Wind the regulator mechanism to the rear of the door glass, tilt the glass rearwards and disengage the mechanism from the glass lower channel.
11 Push the door glass inner weather strip down into the door and remove it and its retaining clips.
12 Pull the door glass up and remove it by tilting it inwards.
13 Lift out the ventilator assembly.
14 Remove the regulator handle and withdraw the regulator mechanism from the door.

Refitting

15 Reverse the procedure in 1 to 14.

VENTILATOR ASSEMBLY

Remove and refit   76.31.28

Removing

1 Disconnect the battery.
2 Remove the door trim pad and moulding, see 76.34.15.
3 Fit the regulator handle.
4 Remove the regulator arm stop.
5 Remove the two bolts securing the ventilator assembly to the front edge of the door.
6 Remove the two nuts and washers securing the ventilator assembly to the top of the door.
7 Remove the two bolts securing the bottom of the door glass front channel.
8 Tilt the ventilator assembly forward and remove the bracket from the bottom of the door glass front channel.
9 Pull out the ventilator assembly.

Refitting

15 Reverse the procedure in 1 to 14.

DOOR MOULDING

Remove and refit   76.34.15
Door trim pad   76.34.01

Removing

1 Disconnect the battery.
2 Remove the screw and remote control handle and plastic washer.
3 Remove the two screws and lift off the escutcheon.
4 Remove the screw and lift off the regulator handle and its escutcheon.
5 Lever the end caps off the door pull, remove the two screws and detach the door pull.
6 Lever the door trim pad away from the door to release its clips and pull the trim pad down to disengage it from the top moulding.
7 Remove the adhesive tape from the apertures in the door.

continued

Refitting

10 Fit the ventilator assembly to the door, springing the front projection into its aperture.
11 Reverse the procedure in 1 to 8.

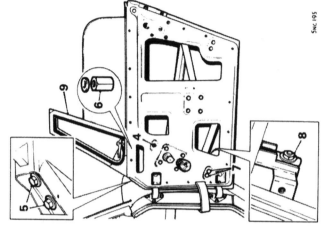

76.19.11

BODY

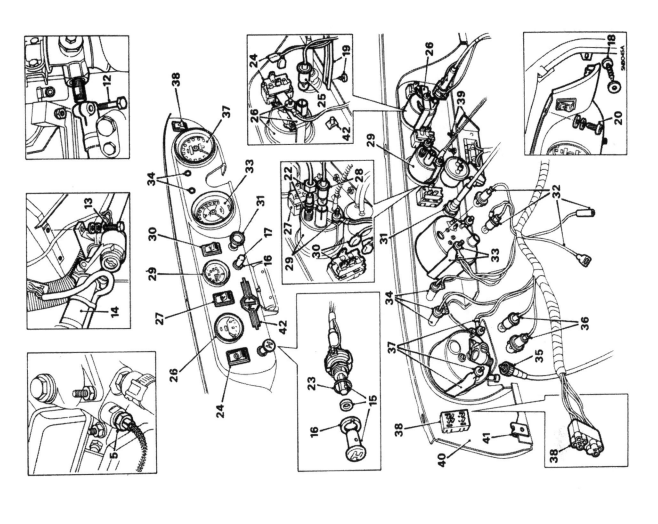

8 Remove the two nuts and washers from inside the door and lift off the top moulding.

Refitting

9 Reverse the procedure in 1 to 8.
   NOTE: When fitting the remote control escutcheon, ensure that the interior lock lever engages the hole in the link.

DOOR LOCK

Remove and refit   76.37.12

Removing

1 Disconnect the battery.
2 Remove the door trim pad, see 76.34.01.
3 Remove the adhesive tape covering the rear aperture in the door.
4 Remove the three screws and lift out the remote control mechanism.
5 Remove the three screws and lift out the door lock.

Refitting

6 Reverse the procedure in 1 to 5, noting:
   a When fitting the door lock, ensure that the link engages the fork on the private lock.
   b When fitting the remote control mechanism, ensure that its stud engages the operating lever.

FASCIA — Right-hand steer (1975-1977)

Remove and refit   76.46.01

Service tool: 18G 671

Removing

1 Disconnect the battery.
2 Disconnect the radiator bottom hose to drain the cooling system.
3 Remove the four screws securing the flasher switch top and bottom cowls.
4 Remove the top and bottom cowls.
5 Remove the temperature transmitter from its adaptor in the thermostat and water pump housing.
6 Release the clips securing the capillary tube to the inlet manifold water pipe and to the bulkhead.

7 Straighten out the capillary tube and remove the securing clips.
8 Push in the capillary tube grommet in the bulkhead.
9 Disconnect the choke cable from the cam lever on the carburetter and collect the cable pin and screw.
10 Release rubber strap securing the choke cable to the spring clip on the heater body.
11 Withdraw the rubber cover from the choke cable.
12 Remove the pinch bolt and nut securing the steering-column to the steering rack pinion.
13 Remove the two bolts, plain and spring washers securing the outer column mounting bracket to the footwell and collect the shim(s) if fitted.
14 Pull the steering-column clear of the pinion and allow the steering wheel to rest on the driver's seat.
15 Depress the heater control knob plunger and remove the knob and rubber washer.
16 Unscrew the locking rings from the heater and windscreen washer controls, using 18G 671.
17 Remove the windscreen washer plunger from the pump.
18 Remove the two screws and plain washers securing the lower ends of the fascia.
19 Remove the two screws securing the fascia support stays to the fascia.
20 Remove the three screws, plain and spring washers securing the top of the fascia.
21 Lower the fascia assembly and tilt it forward to give access to the rear of the fascia.
22 Unscrew the oil pressure pipe nut from the gauge.
    NOTE: Be careful not to lose the oil pressure pipe sealing washer.
23 Remove the spring washer from the heater switch.
24 Disconnect the wiring harness from the panel lamp switch and remove the switch.
25 Disconnect the wiring harness and pull out the bulb holder from the fuel gauge.
                                        continued

183

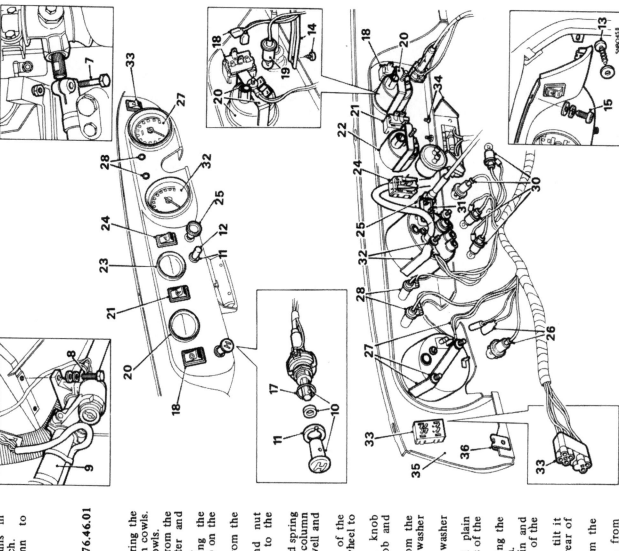

BODY

26 Remove the knurled retaining nut, washer, earthing wires, bridge piece and remove the fuel gauge.

27 Disconnect the wiring harness from the windscreen wiper switch and remove the switch.

28 Pull out the bulb holder from the oil pressure and water temperature gauge.

29 Remove the two knurled retaining nuts, washers, earthing wires, bridge piece and remove the gauge, complete with capillary tube.

30 Disconnect the wiring harness from the lighting switch and remove the switch.

31 Unscrew the choke cable securing nut, withdraw the cable from the fascia and bulkhead, and collect the nut and washer.

32 Disconnect the wiring harness and pull out the bulb holder from the tachometer.

33 Remove the two knurled nuts, washers, earthing wires, clamps and remove the tachometer.

34 Remove the direction indicator warning lights from the fascia.

35 Disconnect the speedometer cable from the angle drive on the speedometer.

36 Pull out the two bulb holders from the speedometer.

37 Remove the two knurled nuts, washers, earthing wires, clamps, and remove the speedometer.

38 Disconnect the multi-connector plug from the hazard warning switch and remove the switch.

39 Remove the three screws to release the interior lamp from the fascia.

40 Remove the fascia panel from the car.

41 Remove the spring nuts from the ends of the fascia panel.

42 Release the spire nuts and remove the 'MG' motif from the fascia panel.

Refitting

43 Reverse the procedure in 1 to 42, noting:

a Connect the wiring harness to the instruments and switches as shown in the wiring diagram (86).

b Adjust the position of the steering-column on the pinion so

that the slip ring remains in contact with the horn switch.

c Refit the steering-column to toeboard seal, if necessary.

FASCIA — Right-hand steer (1978 and later)

Remove and refit   76.46.01

Service tool: 18G 671

Removing

1 Disconnect the battery.

2 Remove the four screws securing the flasher switch top and bottom cowls.

3 Remove the top and bottom cowls.

4 Disconnect the choke cable from the cam lever on the carburetter and collect the cable pin and screw.

5 Release rubber strap securing the choke cable to the spring clip on the heater body.

6 Withdraw the rubber cover from the choke cable.

7 Remove the pinch bolt and nut securing the steering-column to the steering rack pinion.

8 Remove the two bolts, plain and spring washers securing the outer column mounting bracket to the footwell and collect the shim(s) if fitted.

9 Pull the steering-column clear of the pinion and allow the steering wheel to rest on the driver's seat.

10 Depress the heater control knob plunger and remove the knob and rubber washer.

11 Unscrew the locking rings from the heater and windscreen washer controls, using 18G 671.

12 Remove the windscreen washer plunger from the pump.

13 Remove the two screws and plain washers securing the lower ends of the fascia.

14 Remove the two screws securing the fascia support stays to the fascia.

15 Remove the three screws, plain and spring washers securing the top of the fascia.

16 Lower the fascia assembly and tilt it forward to give access to the rear of the fascia.

17 Remove the spring washer from the heater switch.

18 Disconnect the wiring harness from

BODY

the panel lamp switch and remove the switch.

19 Disconnect the wiring harness and pull out the bulb holder from the fuel gauge.

20 Remove the knurled retaining nut, washer, earthing wires, bridge piece and remove the fuel gauge.

21 Disconnect the wiring harness from the windscreen wiper switch and remove the switch.

22 Disconnect the wires and pull out the bulb holder from the coolant temperature gauge.

23 Remove the knurled retaining nut, washer, earthing wires, bridge piece and remove the gauge.

24 Disconnect the wiring harness from the lighting switch and remove the switch.

25 Unscrew the choke cable securing nut, withdraw the cable from the fascia and bulkhead, and collect the nut and washer.

26 Disconnect the wiring harness and pull out the bulb holder from the tachometer.

27 Remove the two knurled nuts, washers, earthing wires, bridge piece and remove the tachometer.

28 Remove the direction indicator warning lights from the fascia.

29 Disconnect the speedometer cable from the speedometer.

30 Pull out the bulb holders from the speedometer.

31 Disconnect the wires from the voltage stabilizer.

32 Remove the two knurled nuts, washers, earthing wires, clamps, and remove the speedometer.

33 Disconnect the multi-connector plug from the hazard warning switch and remove the switch.

34 Remove the three screws to release the interior lamp from the fascia.

35 Remove the fascia panel from the car.

36 Remove the spring nuts from the ends of the fascia panel.

Refitting

37 Reverse the procedure in 1 to 30, noting:

a Connect the wiring harness to the instruments and switches as shown in the wiring diagram (86).

b Adjust the position of the steering-column on the pinion so that the slip ring remains in contact with the horn switch.

c Refit the steering-column to toeboard seal, if necessary.

FASCIA — Left-hand steer (manual choke)

Remove and refit   76.46.01

Removing

1 Disconnect the battery.

2 Disconnect the radiator bottom hose to drain the cooling system.

3 Remove the temperature transmitter from its adaptor in the thermostat and water pump housing.

4 Remove the clips securing the capillary tube to the air manifold and to the bulkhead.

5 Disconnect the choke cable from the carburetter.

6 Release the oil pressure gauge pipe clips from the pedal box.

7 Disconnect the speedometer upper cable from the service interval counter.

8 Remove the screws retaining the centre console and move it aside.

9 Remove the three screws securing the fascia support plates to the bulkhead.

10 Press the retaining plunger and remove the heater control knob.

11 Remove the nut and two washers securing the heater control, withdraw the control from the back of the fascia and allow it to hang.

12 Remove the two knurled retaining nuts, washers, and the bridge piece from behind the oil pressure gauge.

13 Partially withdraw the gauge from the fascia and unscrew the oil pressure pipe nut.
NOTE: Be careful not to lose the oil pressure pipe sealing washer.

14 Remove the two knurled retaining nuts, the washers, the earthing cables and the clamps from behind the tachometer.

15 Withdraw the tachometer from the fascia and disconnect the wiring.

16 Remove the four nuts and the washers securing the top of the fascia.

continued

FASCIA — Left-hand steer (automatic choke through 1977)

Remove and refit   76.46.01

Removing

1   Disconnect the battery.
2   Disconnect the radiator bottom hose to drain the cooling system.
3   Remove the temperature transmitter from its adaptor in the thermostat and water pump housing.
4   Disconnect the capillary tube from the clips on the rocker cover.

[NOTE: Attachments to the engine may be slightly different on 1976 cars.]

5   Remove the clips securing the capillary tube to the bulkhead.
6   Disconnect the oil pressure pipe from the oil switch connector.
7   Release the oil pressure gauge pipe clips from the pedal box.
8   Release and remove the gearbox tunnel carpet, remove the screws retaining the centre console and move the console aside (towards the steering-column).
9   Disconnect the speedometer cable from the speedometer.
10   Remove the three screws securing the fascia support plates to the bulkhead.
11   Press the retaining plunger and remove the heater control knob.
12   Remove the nut and two washers securing the heater control, withdraw the control from the back of the fascia and allow it to hang.
13   Remove the two knurled retaining nuts, the washers, the earthing cables and the clamps from behind the tachometer.
14   Withdraw the tachometer from the fascia and disconnect the wiring.
15   Remove the two knurled retaining nuts, washers, and the bridge piece from behind the oil pressure gauge.
16   Thread the oil pipe complete with its grommet through the bulkhead sufficient to unscrew the oil pressure pipe nut from the oil gauge.
NOTE: Be careful not to lose the oil pressure pipe sealing washer.
17   Disconnect the bulb from the oil gauge, thread the capillary tube complete with its grommet through the bulkhead and remove the gauge from the fascia.
18   Remove the four nuts and the washers securing the top of the fascia.
19   Partly withdraw the fascia and disconnect the two multi-pin plugs

continued

17   Pull the fascia away and disconnect the two multi-pin plugs and the earth lead.
18   Pull the choke cable and speedometer cable through the bulkhead and remove the fascia assembly from the car.
19   Disconnect and remove the wiring harness from the fascia.
20   Remove the securing nut and washer and withdraw the choke cable assembly from the fascia.
21   Disconnect the trip remote control from its bracket.
22   Remove the knurled nuts, washers and clamps and remove the speedometer.
23   Remove the knurled nut, washer, and bridge piece and remove the fuel gauge.
24   Remove the three nuts and washers and remove the heater control dial and light box from the front and rear faces of the fascia.
25   Remove the retainer from the heater blower switch and remove the switch.
26   Remove the retainer from the light switch and remove the switch.
27   Remove the retaining clip from the brake test switch and remove the switch.
28   Press the pin in the rheostat knob and remove the knob.
29   Unscrew the locking ring and remove the rheostat.
30   Remove the direction indicator warning lamps.
31   Remove the ignition warning lamp.
32   Remove the main beam warning lamp.
33   Remove the three fascia support plates.
34   Remove the trip remote control bracket.
35   Remove the cubby box lock striker.

Refitting

36   Reverse the procedure in 1 to 35, connecting the wiring harness to the instruments and switches as shown in the wiring diagram (86).

20 and remove the fascia.

20 Disconnect and remove the wiring harness from the fascia.

21 Disconnect the trip remote control from its bracket.

22 Remove the knurled nuts, washers and clamps and remove the speedometer.

23 Remove the knurled nut, washer, and bridge piece and remove the fuel gauge.

24 Remove the three nuts and washers and remove the heater control dial and light box from the front and rear faces of the fascia.

25 Remove the retainer from the heater blower switch and remove the switch.

26 Remove the retainer from the light switch and remove the switch.

27 Remove the retaining clip from the brake warning light and remove the warning light.

28 Press the pin in the rheostat knob and remove the knob.

29 Unscrew the locking ring and remove the rheostat.

30 Remove the direction indicator warning lamps.

31 Remove the ignition warning lamp.

32 Remove the main beam warning lamp.

33 Remove the blank from the fascia.

34 Remove the three fascia support plates.

35 Remove the trip remote control bracket.

36 Remove the cubby box lock striker.

Refitting

37 Reverse the procedure in 1 to 36, connecting the wiring harness to the instruments and switches as shown in the wiring diagram (86.00.01/03).

FASCIA — Left-hand steer (automatic choke from 1978)

Remove and refit   76.46.01

Removing

1 Disconnect the battery.

2 Remove the screws retaining the centre console and move the console aside (towards the steering-column).

3 Remove the three screws securing the fascia support plates to the bulkhead.

4 Press the retaining plunger and remove the heater control knob.

5 Remove the nut and two washers securing the heater control, withdraw the control from the back of the fascia and allow it to hang.

6 Remove the two knurled retaining nuts, the washers, the earthing cables and the clamps from behind the tachometer.

7 Withdraw the tachometer from the fascia and disconnect the wiring.

8 Remove the four nuts and the washers securing the top of the fascia.

9 Partly withdraw the fascia and disconnect the two multi-pin plugs and single snap connector.

10 Disconnect the speedometer cable from the speedometer and remove the fascia.

11 Disconnect and remove the wiring harness from the fascia.

12 Disconnect the trip remote control from its bracket.

13 Remove the knurled nuts, washers and clamps and remove the speedometer.

14 Remove the knurled nut, washer, and bridge piece and remove the fuel gauge.

15 Remove the knurled nut, washer, and bridge piece and remove the coolant temperature gauge.

16 Remove the three nuts and washers and remove the heater control dial and light box from the front and rear faces of the fascia.

17 Remove the retainer from the heater blower switch and remove the switch.

18 Remove the retainer from the light switch and remove the switch.

19 Remove the retaining clip from the brake warning light and remove the warning light.

20 Press the pin in the rheostat knob and remove the knob.

21 Unscrew the locking ring and remove the rheostat.

22 Remove the direction indicator warning lamps.

23 Remove the ignition warning lamp.

24 Remove the main beam warning lamp.

25 Remove the oil pressure warning lamp.

26 Remove the three fascia support plates.

27 Remove the trip remote control bracket.

28 Remove the cubby box lock striker.

Refitting

29 Reverse the procedure in 1 to 28, connecting the wiring harness to the instruments and switches as shown in the wiring diagram (86.00.01/03).

DOOR HANDLE (OUTSIDE)

Remove and refit   76.58.01

Removing

1 Disconnect the battery.

2 Remove the door trim pad and moulding, see 76.34.15.

3 Remove the door glass, see 76.31.01.

4 Remove the nut, screw, and four washers securing the handle to the door and remove the handle.

Refitting

5 Position the handle on the door with its seating washers fitted and check the clearance between the plunger bolt on the handle and the lock contactor on the lock. If necessary adjust the position of the plunger bolt to obtain a maximum clearance of 0.030 in (0.79 mm).

6 Reverse the procedure in 1 to 4.

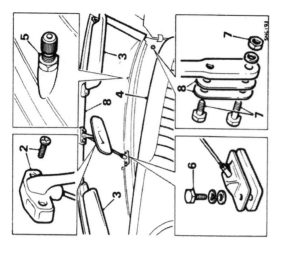

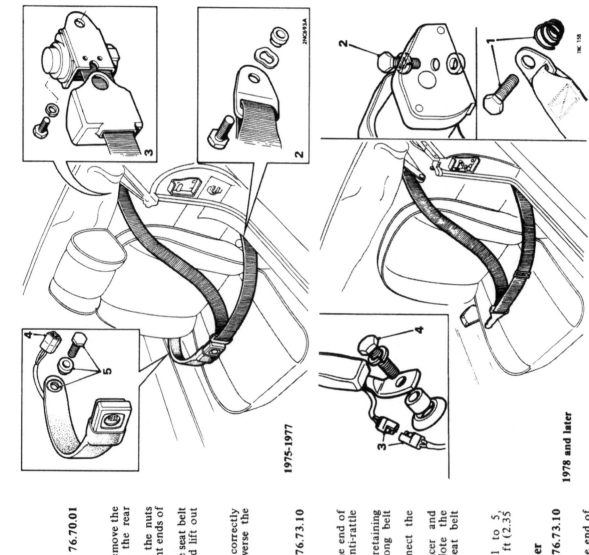

BODY

SEATS

Remove and refit   76.70.01

Removing
1. Disconnect the battery.
2. Move the seat forward and remove the bolts and washers securing the rear ends of the seat runners.
3. From under the car remove the nuts and washers securing the front ends of the seat runners.
4. Raise the seat, disconnect the seat belt warning cables (if fitted) and lift out the seat.

Refitting
5. Ensure that the runners are correctly located on the seat and reverse the procedure in 1 to 4.

SEAT BELTS — 1975–1977

Remove and refit   76.73.10

Removing
1. Disconnect the battery.
2. Remove the bolt retaining the end of the long belt and collect the anti-rattle washer and spacer.
3. Remove the bolt and washer retaining the reel and remove the long belt assembly.
4. Lift the carpet and disconnect the wiring from the short belt.
5. Remove the bolt and spacer and remove the short belt. Note the anti-rattle washer in the seat belt sleeve.

Refitting
6. Reverse the procedure in 1 to 5, tightening the bolts to 17 lbf ft (2.35 kgf m).

SEAT BELTS — 1978 and later

Remove and refit   76.73.10

Removing
1. Remove the bolt retaining the end of the long belt to the sill and collect the anti-rattle washer spring.
2. Lift the reel cover and remove the bolt retaining the reel to the mounting bracket.

3. USA and Canada: Lift the carpet and disconnect the wiring from the locking device.
4. Remove the bolt, spacer and anti-rattle washer and remove the locking device.

Refitting
5. Reverse the procedure in 1 to 4, tightening the bolts to 17 lbf ft (2.35 kgf m).

1975-1977

1978 and later

WINDSCREEN ASSEMBLY

Remove and refit   76.81.02

Removing
1. Disconnect the battery.
2. Remove the mirror from the windscreen.
3. Remove the sun visors from the windscreen.
4. Move the fascia, see 76.46.01, sufficiently to obtain access to the bolts securing the windscreen side pillars to the 'A' posts.
5. Slacken the nuts on the windscreen wiper wheelboxes to release the bottom seal.
6. Remove the two bolts securing the windscreen centre stay to the body.
7. Remove the two nuts and four bolts securing the windscreen side pillars to the 'A' posts.
8. Remove the shims from between the side pillars and 'A' posts and lift off the windscreen assembly.

Refitting
9. Reverse the procedure in 1 to 8, ensuring that the hood fits correctly before final tightening of the side pillar bolts.

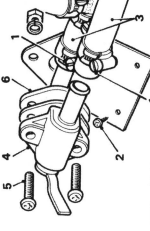

1975–1976

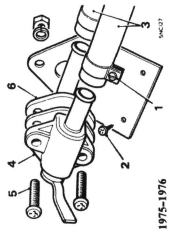

HEATING AND VENTILATING

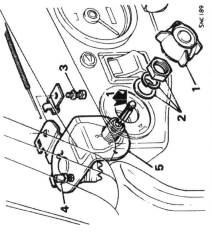

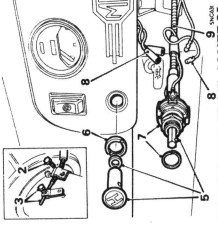

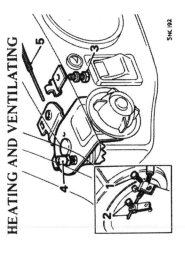

HEATER AIR FLOW CONTROL CABLE — Left-hand steer

Remove and refit 80.10.06

Removing

1 Remove the screw to release the outer cable from the bracket on the heater air intake tube.
2 Slacken the screw and release the inner cable from the lever on the heater air intake tube.
3 Remove the screw to release the outer cable from the control mechanism.
4 Slacken the screw and release the inner cable from the control mechanism.
5 Remove the inner and outer cable assembly.
6 Remove the rubber sleeve from the cable assembly.

Refitting

7 Reverse the procedure in 1 to 6 noting:
  a Check the operation of the air intake valve and adjust if necessary by altering the positions of the inner and outer control cables on the air intake tube.

HEATER AIR FLOW CONTROL — Right-hand steer

Remove and refit 80.10.09
Heater fan switch 80.10.22

Service tool: 18G 671

Removing

1 Disconnect the battery.
2 Remove the screw to release the heater control cable from the bracket on the heater air intake tube.
3 Slacken the screw and release the heater control inner cable from the lever on the heater air intake tube.
4 Detach the grommet from the bulkhead and the control cable.
5 Depress the heater control knob plunger and remove the knob and rubber washer.
6 Unscrew the heater control locking ring, using 18G 671.
7 Remove the heater control from the fascia and collect the spring washer.
8 Disconnect the heater fan switch wires at the snap connectors.
9 Withdraw the heater control cable from the bulkhead.

Refitting

10 Reverse the procedure in 1 to 9, noting:
  a Check the operation of the air intake valve and adjust if necessary by altering the positions of the inner and outer cables on the air intake tube.

HEATER AIR FLOW CONTROL — Left-hand steer

Remove and refit 80.10.09

Removing

1 Depress the retaining plunger and withdraw the heater air flow control knob.
2 Remove the nut and two washers securing the control mechanism to the fascia.
3 Remove the screw to release the outer cable from the control assembly.
4 Slacken the screw and release the inner cable from the control assembly.
5 Remove the control assembly.

Refitting

6 Reverse the procedure in 1 to 5, noting:
  a Check the operations of the air intake valve and adjust if necessary by altering the positions of the inner and outer cables on the air intake tube.

HEATER WATER VALVE

Remove and refit 80.10.10

Removing

WARNING: If the cooling system is hot remove the expansion filler cap slowly to release the pressure gradually from the cooling system.

1977 and later

1 Slacken the two clips securing the water hoses to the valve assembly.
2 Remove the two screws securing the valve assembly bracket to the bulkhead.
3 Detach the two hoses from the valve and position them to prevent excessive loss of coolant.
4 Remove the heater water valve assembly from the car.
5 Remove the two screws, nuts and washers securing the valve to the bracket.
6 Remove the valve, gasket and inlet pipe flange from the bracket.

Refitting

7 Reverse the procedure in 1 to 6.
8 Check the engine coolant level, see MAINTENANCE.

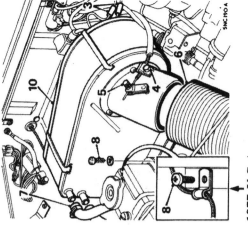

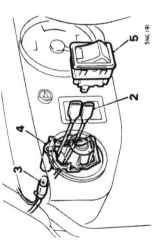

HEATER FAN SWITCH — Left-hand steer

Remove and refit   80.10.22

Removing

1 Disconnect the battery.
2 Disconnect the two leads from the heater blower switch.
3 Detach the bulb from the switch retainer.
4 Detach the switch retainer from the switch.
5 Remove the switch from the fascia.

Refitting

6 Reverse the procedure in 1 to 5.

WINDSCREEN DEMISTER DUCTS — Right-hand steer

Remove and refit   80.15.02

Removing

1 Remove the four screws securing the flasher switch top and bottom cowls.
2 Remove the top and bottom cowls.
3 Remove the two bolts securing the steering-column mounting bracket to the footwell and collect the shim(s), if fitted.
4 Remove the steering-column to pinion pinch bolt and nut.
5 Withdraw the steering-column from the pinion.
6 Remove the seven screws securing the fascia and pull the fascia rearward to allow access to the demister ducts.
7 Detach the air hose from each demister duct.

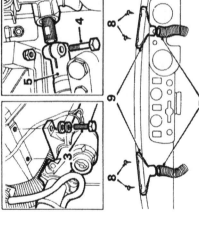

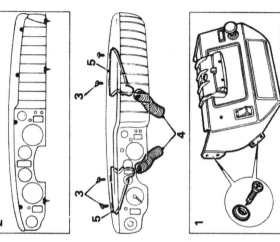

8 Remove the two screws securing each demister duct.
9 Remove the demister ducts.

Refitting

10 Reverse the procedure in 1 to 9 noting:

   a Adjust the position of the steering-column on the pinion so that the slip ring remains in contact with the horn switch.

   b Refit the steering-column to toeboard seal, if necessary.

WINDSCREEN DEMISTER DUCTS — Left-hand steer

Remove and refit   80.15.02

Removing

1 Remove the eight screws and washers securing the centre console and move the console aside.
2 Remove the three screws and the four nuts and washers securing the fascia and pull the fascia forward to allow access to the demister ducts.

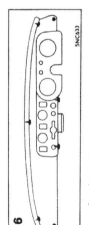

3 Remove the two screws securing each demister duct.
4 Detach the air hose from each demister duct.
5 Remove the demister ducts.

Refitting

6 Reverse the procedure in 1 to 5.

HEATER UNIT

Remove and refit   80.20.01

Removing

1 Disconnect and remove the battery and remove the battery tray.
2 Disconnect the bottom hose from the radiator to drain the cooling system.
3 Disconnect the heater fan motor wires at the snap connectors.
4 Remove the bolt to release the heater control cable from the bracket on the heater air intake tube.
5 Slacken the bolt and release the heater control inner cable from the lever on the heater air intake tube.
6 Disconnect the air vent hose from the heater air intake tube.
7 Slacken the clips and remove the two water hoses from the heater unit.
8 Remove the six screws securing the heater unit to the bulkhead, noting the position of the screw which also locates the capillary tube clip.
9 Place the clip securing the water temperature capillary tube aside.
10 Remove the heater unit from the car.

Refitting

11 Reverse the procedure in 1 to 10, noting:

   a Check the operation of the air intake valve and adjust if necessary by altering the positions of the inner and outer control cables on the air intake tube.

   b Refill the cooling system, see 'MAINTENANCE'.

HEATING AND VENTILATION

HEATER UNIT

Overhaul	**80.20.08**
Heater fan and motor, 1 to 4, 6 to 10	**80.20.15**
Heater matrix, 1 to 5	**80.20.29**

Dismantling

1　Remove the heater unit, see 80.20.01.
2　Drain the heater unit.
3　Remove the five spring clips securing the heater cover to the heater body.
4　Remove the heater cover taking care not to damage the heater seal.
5　Remove the heater matrix.

6　Remove the three screws securing the fan and motor assembly to the heater body.
7　Remove the fan and motor assembly.
8　Note the position of the fan on the motor spindle.
9　Remove the clip securing the fan to the motor spindle.
10　Tap the motor spindle out of the fan to release the fan from the motor.

Reassembling

11　Reverse the procedure in 1 to 10, applying a coat of a suitable adhesive to fix the heater body seal to the heater cover flange.

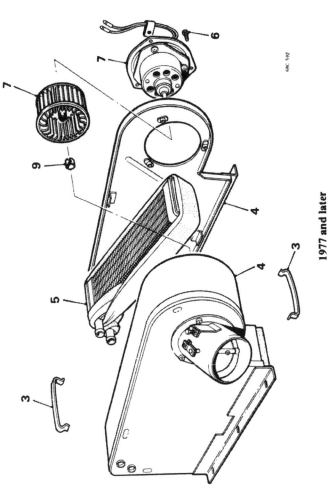

1977 and later

6NC 592

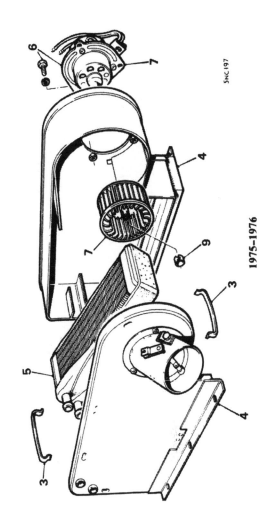

1975-1976

SNC 197

WINDSCREEN WIPERS AND WASHERS

SNC23

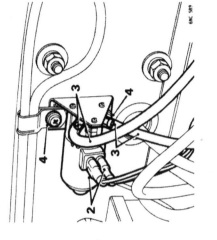

6NC 589

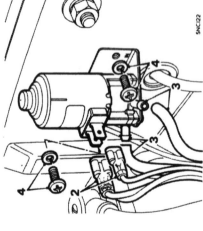

SNC122

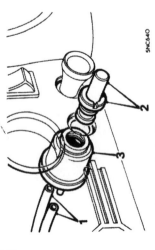

SNC640

WASHER PUMP —
U.K. Specification

Remove and refit   84.10.21

Removing

1 Disconnect the two tubes from the pump.
2 Unscrew the bezel to detach the bezel and plunger.
3 Remove the pump from the fascia.

Refitting

4 Reverse the procedure in 1 to 3.

WASHER PUMP — 1975-76 U.S.A.

Remove and refit   84.10.21

Removing

1 Disconnect the battery.
2 Disconnect the two cables from the terminal blades on the pump.
3 Disconnect the two tubes from the pump.
4 Remove the two screws and washers to release the pump from the bulkhead.

Refitting

5 Reverse the procedure in 1 to 4, ensuring that the tube from the reservoir is connected to the pump intake and the tube to the washer jets is connected to the pump outlet.

WASHER PUMP
— 1977 and later U.S.A.

Remove and refit   84.10.21

Removing

1 Disconnect the battery.
2 Disconnect the two cables from the terminal blades on the pump.
3 Disconnect the two tubes from the pump.
4 Remove the two screws and washers to release the pump from the bulkhead, noting the top screw also locates the clip for the vapour pipes.

Refitting

5 Reverse the procedure in 1 to 4, ensuring that the tube from the reservoir is connected to the pump intake and the tube to the washer jets is connected to the pump outlet.

WINDSCREEN WIPER MOTOR
AND DRIVE

Remove and refit   84.15.09

Removing

1 Disconnect the battery.
2 Remove the wiper arms and blades.
3 Unscrew the nut securing the drive tube to the motor assembly.
4 Disconnect the wiring plug from the motor.
5 Remove the two bolts and washers securing the wiper motor clamp band to the wheel arch.
6 Remove the wiper motor clamp band, the wiper motor complete with inner cable, the mounting rubber and the mounting plate.

Refitting

7 Reverse the procedure in 1 to 6 ensuring that the inner cable is lubricated with Ragosine Listate Grease or equivalent.

WINDSCREEN WIPERS AND WASHERS

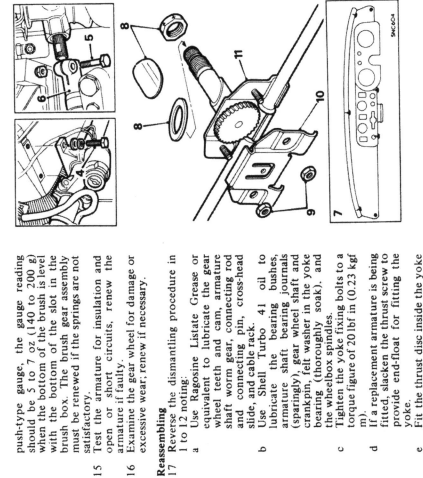

WINDSCREEN WIPER MOTOR

Overhaul   84.15.18

Dismantling

1 Remove the motor and drive, see 84.15.09.
2 Remove the four wiper motor gearbox cover retaining screws.
3 Remove the gearbox cover.
4 Remove the circlip and flat washer securing the connecting rod to the crankpin.
5 Withdraw the connecting rod taking care not to lose the flat washer fitted under it.
6 Remove the inner cable assembly.
7 Remove the cross-head slide.
8 Remove the circlip and washer securing the shaft and gear.
9 Clean any burrs from the gear shaft and withdraw the gear, taking care not to lose the dished washer fitted under it.
10 Note the alignment marks on the yoke and gearbox for reassembly.
11 Unscrew the two fixing bolts from the motor yoke and remove the yoke assembly and armature. The yoke assembly must be kept clear of metallic particles which will be attracted to the pole piece.
12 Remove the screws to release the brushgear and detach the terminal and switch assembly.

Inspection

13 Examine the brushes for excessive wear, if the main brushes (diametrically opposite) are worn to $\frac{3}{16}$ in (4.8 mm) or if the narrow section of the third brush is worn to the full width of the brush the brush gear assembly must be renewed.
14 Check the brush spring pressure with a push-type gauge, the gauge reading should be 5 to 7 oz (140 to 200 g) when the bottom of the brush is level with the bottom of the slot in the brush box. The brush gear assembly must be renewed if the springs are not satisfactory.
15 Test the armature for insulation and open or short circuits, renew the armature if faulty.
16 Examine the gear wheel for damage or excessive wear; renew if necessary.

Reassembling

17 Reverse the dismantling procedure in 1 to 12 noting:
a Use Ragosine Listate Grease or equivalent to lubricate the gear wheel teeth and cam, armature shaft worm gear, connecting rod and connecting pin, cross-head slide, and cable rack.
b Use Shell Turbo 41 oil to lubricate the bearing bushes, armature shaft bearing journals (sparingly), gear wheel shaft and crankpin, felt washer in the yoke bearing (thoroughly soak). and the wheelbox spindles.
c Tighten the yoke fixing bolts to a torque figure of 20lbf in (0.23 kgf m).
d If a replacement armature is being fitted, slacken the thrust screw to provide end-float for fitting the yoke.
e Fit the thrust disc inside the yoke bearing with its concave side towards the end face of the bearing.
f Fit the dished washer beneath the gear wheel with its concave side towards the gear wheel.
g When fitting the connecting rod to the crankpin ensure that the larger of the two flat washers is fitted under the connecting rod with the smaller one on top beneath the circlip.
h Fit the thrust screw and locknut supplied with the armature and adjust the screw, an end-float of 0.004 to 0.008 in (0.1 to 0.21 mm) should exist on the armature. Tighten the thrust screw locknut.

WINDSCREEN WIPER WHEELBOX L.H. — Right-hand steer

Remove and refit   84.15.28

Removing

1 Remove the wiper motor and drive, see 84.15.09.
2 Remove the four screws securing the flasher switch top and bottom cowls.
3 Remove the top and bottom cowls.
4 Remove the two bolts securing the steering-column mounting bracket to the footwell and collect the shim(s), if fitted.
5 Remove the steering-column to pinion pinch bolt and nut.
6 Withdraw the steering-column from the pinion.

WINDSCREEN WIPERS AND WASHERS

7 Remove the seven screws securing the fascia and pull the fascia rearwards to allow access to the L.H. wheelbox.
8 Remove the left hand wiper spindle retaining nut, the bush and the washer.
9 Remove the two nuts securing the wheelbox cover plate.
10 Remove the cover plate.
11 Remove the wheelbox assembly.

Refitting
12 Lubricate the wheelbox gear and spindle with Ragosine Listate Grease or equivalent and place the wheelbox assembly in position on the car.
13 Fit the wheelbox spindle retaining nut. Do not tighten.
14 Fit the drive cable tubes to the wheelbox.
15 Fit the wheelbox cover plate. Do not tighten the two retaining nuts.
16 Remove the spindle retaining nut and fit the rubber washer, sealing with a suitable rubber putty.
17 Fit the spindle bush and refit the retaining nut.
18 Tighten the wheelbox cover plate retaining nuts.
19 Refit the wiper arm and blade.
20 Reverse the procedure in 1 to 19 noting:
  a Adjust the position of the steering-column on the pinion, so that the slip ring remains in contact with the horn switch.
  b Refit the steering-column to toeboard seal, if necessary.

WINDSCREEN WIPER WHEELBOX L.H. — Left-hand steer

Remove and refit   84.15.28

Removing
1 Remove the wiper motor and drive, see 84.15.09.
2 Remove the left hand wiper spindle retaining nut, the bush and the washer.
3 Remove the two nuts securing the wheelbox cover plate.
4 Remove the cover plate.
5 Remove the wheelbox assembly.

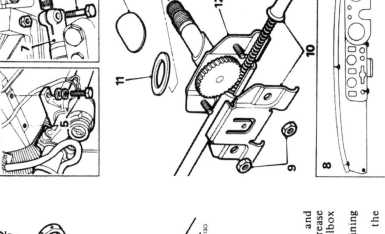

Refitting
6 Lubricate the wheelbox gear and spindle with Ragosine Listate Grease or equivalent and place the wheelbox assembly in position on the car.
7 Fit the wheelbox spindle retaining nut. Do not tighten.
8 Fit the drive cable tubes to the wheelbox.
9 Fit the wheelbox cover plate. Do not tighten the two retaining nuts.
10 Remove the spindle retaining nut and fit the rubber washer, sealing with a suitable rubber putty.
11 Fit the spindle bush and refit the retaining nut.
12 Tighten the wheelbox cover retaining nuts.
13 Refit the wiper arm and blade.
14 Refit the wiper motor and drive, see 84.15.09.

WINDSCREEN WIPER WHEELBOX R.H. — Right-hand steer

Remove and refit   84.15.29

Removing
1 Disconnect the battery.
2 Remove the right hand wiper arm and blade.
3 Remove the four screws securing the flasher switch top and bottom cowls.
4 Remove the top and bottom cowls.
5 Remove the two bolts securing the steering-column mounting bracket to the footwell and collect the shim(s), if fitted.

6 Remove the steering-column to pinion bolt and nut.
7 Withdraw the steering-column from the pinion.
8 Remove the seven screws securing the fascia and pull the fascia rearwards to allow access to the R.H. wheelbox.
9 Remove the two nuts securing the wheelbox cover plate
10 Remove the cover plate and slide the tube from the drive cable.
11 Remove the wiper spindle retaining nut.
12 Remove the wheelbox assembly.

Refitting
13 Lubricate the wheelbox gear and spindle with Ragosine Listate Grease or equivalent and place the wheelbox assembly in position on the car.
14 Fit the wheelbox spindle retaining nut. Do not tighten.
15 Fit the drive cable tubes to the wheelbox.
16 Fit the wheelbox cover plate. Do not tighten the two retaining nuts.
17 Remove the spindle retaining nut and fit the rubber washer, sealing with a suitable rubber putty.
18 Fit the spindle bush and refit the retaining nut.
19 Tighten the wheelbox cover retaining nuts.
20 Refit the wiper arm and blade.
21 Reverse the procedure 1 to 8 noting:
  a Adjust the position of the steering-column on the pinion so that the slip ring remains in contact with the horn switch.
  b Refit the steering-column to toeboard seal, if necessary.

WINDSCREEN WIPERS AND WASHERS

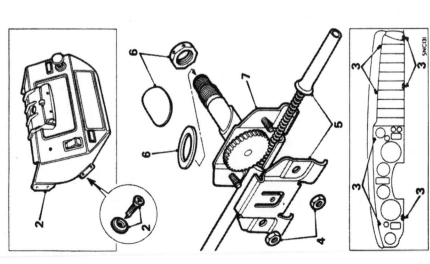

and pull the fascia forward to allow access to the right hand wheelbox.

4 Remove the two nuts securing the wheelbox cover plate.
5 Remove the cover plate and slide the tube from the drive cable.
6 Remove the wiper spindle retaining nut.
7 Remove the wheelbox assembly.

Refitting
8 Reverse the procedure in 1 to 7 ensuring that the wheelbox gear and spindle are lubricated with Ragosine Listate Grease or equivalent.

WINDSCREEN WIPER
WHEELBOX CENTRE POSITION

Remove and refit   84.15.31

Removing
1 Remove the right hand wheelbox, see 84.15.29.
2 Remove the two nuts securing the wheelbox cover plate.
3 Remove the cover plate.
4 Slide the tube from the drive cable.
5 Remove the wiper arm and blade.
6 Remove the wiper spindle securing nut.
7 Remove the wheelbox.

Refitting
8 Reverse the procedure in 1 to 7 ensuring that the wheelbox spindle and gear are lubricated with Ragosine Listate Grease or equivalent.

WINDSCREEN WIPER WHEELBOX
R.H. — Left-hand steer

Remove and refit   84.15.29

Removing
1 Remove the right hand wiper arm and blade.
2 Remove the eight screws and washers securing the centre console and move the console aside.
3 Remove the three screws and the four nuts and washers securing the fascia

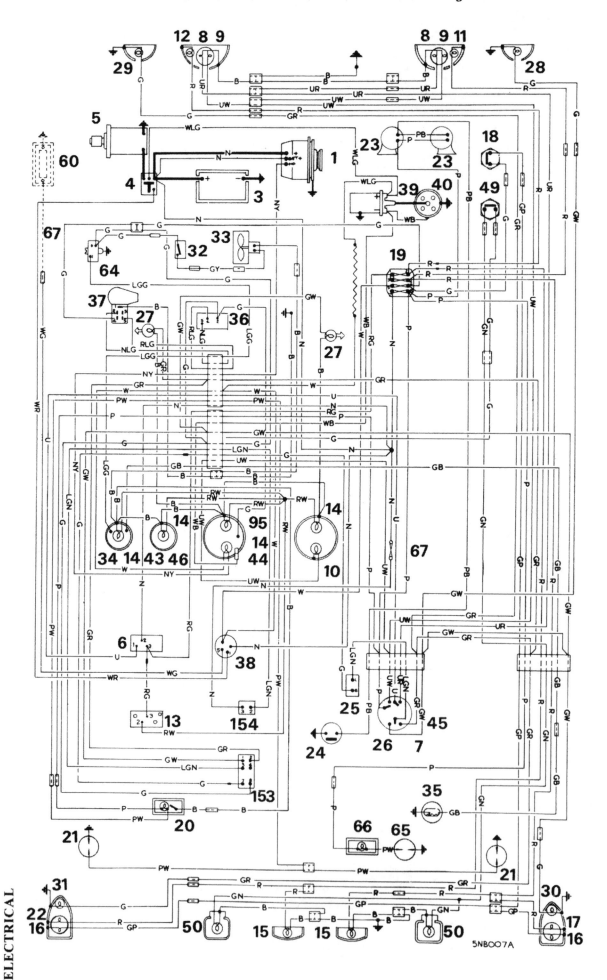

5NBOO7A

KEY TO THE WIRING DIAGRAM:
1975-1977 U.K. Specification — Right-hand Steer

1	Alternator	29	L.H. front direction indicator lamp
3	Battery (12-volt)	30	R.H. rear direction indicator lamp
4	Starter solenoid	31	L.H. rear direction indicator lamp
5	Starter motor	32	Heater or fresh-air motor switch
6	Lighting switch	33	Heater or fresh-air motor
7	Headlamp dip switch	34	Fuel gauge
8	Headlamp dip beam	35	Fuel gauge tank unit
9	Headlamp main beam	36	Windscreen wiper switch
10	Headlamp main beam warning lamp	37	Windscreen wiper motor
11	R.H. sidelamp	38	Ignition/starter switch
12	L.H. sidelamp	39	Ignition coil
13	Panel lamp switch	40	Distributor
14	Panel lamp	43	Oil pressure gauge
15	Number-plate illumination lamp	44	Ignition warning lamp
16	Stop lamps	45	Headlamp flasher switch
17	R.H. tail lamp	46	Coolant temperature gauge
18	Stop lamp switch	49	Reverse lamp switch
19	Fuse unit (4-way)	50	Reverse lamps
20	Interior courtesy lamp	60	Radio (if fitted)*
21	Interior lamp door switches	64	Instrument voltage stabilizer
22	L.H. tail lamp	65	Luggage compartment switch
23	Horn	66	Luggage compartment lamp
24	Horn-push	67	Line fuse for radio*
25	Flasher unit	95	Tachometer
26	Direction indicator switch	153	Hazard warning switch
27	Direction indicator warning lamps	154	Hazard warning flasher unit.
28	R.H. front direction indicator lamp		

*Optional fitment circuits shown dotted

CABLE COLOUR CODE

N	Brown	P	Purple	W	White
U	Blue	G	Green	Y	Yellow
R	Red	LG	Light Green	B	Black

When a cable has two colour code letters the first denotes the main
colour and the second denotes the tracer colour.

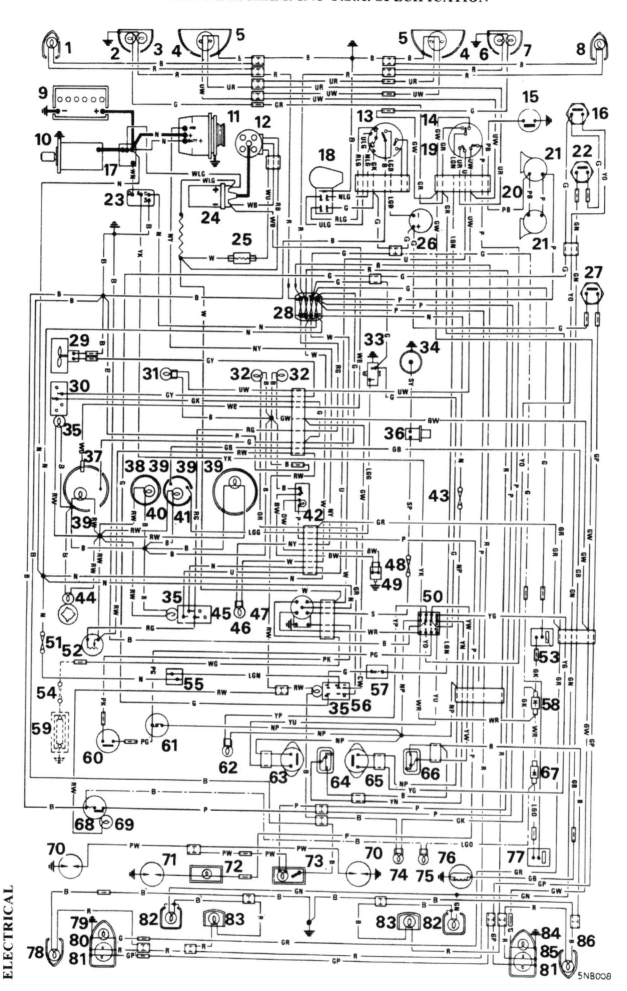

ELECTRICAL

5NB008

KEY TO THE WIRING DIAGRAM:
1975 U.S.A. Specification

Several of the components listed in this key may not be included in the specification of all models.

1. L.H. front side marker lamp
2. L.H. front flasher lamp
3. L.H. parking lamp
4. Headlamp main beam
5. Headlamp dip beam
6. R.H. parking lamp
7. R.H. front flasher lamp
8. R.H. front side-marker lamp
9. Battery
10. Starter motor
11. Alternator
12. Distributor
13. Combined windscreen washer and wiper switch
14. Direction indicator switch
15. Horn push
16. Seat belt warning gearbox switch – if fitted
17. Starter solenoid
18. Windscreen wiper motor
19. Headlamp dip switch
20. Headlamp flasher switch
21. Horn
22. Reverse lamp switch
23. Starter solenoid relay – if fitted
24. Ignition coil
25. Resistor – distributor
26. Windscreen washer pump
27. Stop lamp switch
28. Fuse unit
29. Heater motor
30. Heater motor switch
31. Headlamp main beam warning lamp
32. Direction indicator warning lamp
33. Instrument voltage stabilizer
34. Running-on control valve oil pressure switch
35. Switch illumination lamp
36. Running-on control valve
37. Tachometer
38. Oil pressure gauge
39. Panel lamp
40. Coolant temperature gauge
41. Fuel gauge
42. Brake pressure warning lamp and lamp test push
43. Line fuse for seat belt warning
44. Heater control illumination lamp
45. Lighting switch
46. Ignition warning lamp
47. Ignition/starter switch
48. Line fuse for running-on control valve
49. Brake pressure failure switch
50. Sequential seat belt control unit – if fitted
51. Line fuse for hazard warning
52. Panel lamp switch
53. Service interval counter for E G R valve
54. Line fuse for radio*
55. Hazard warning flasher unit
56. Hazard warning switch
57. Flasher unit
58. Diode for E G R valve service interval counter
59. Radio*
60. Ignition key audible warning door switch
61. Audible warning buzzer – if fitted
62. 'Fasten belts' warning light
63. Driver's seat switch – if fitted
64. Driver's seat belt buckle switch
65. Passenger's seat switch – if fitted
66. Passenger's seat belt buckle switch – if fitted
67. Diode for catalytic converter service interval counter – if fitted
68. Cigar lighter
69. Cigar lighter illumination lamp
70. Interior courtesy lamp door switch
71. Luggage compartment lamp switch
72. Luggage compartment lamp
73. Interior courtesy lamp
74. E G R warning light
75. CATALYST warning light – if fitted
76. Fuel gauge tank unit
77. Service interval counter for catalytic converter – if fitted
78. L.H. rear side marker lamp
79. L.H. rear flasher lamp
80. L.H. tail lamp
81. Stop lamp
82. Reverse lamp
83. Number plate illumination lamp
84. R.H. rear flasher lamp
85. R.H. tail lamp
86. R.H. rear side marker lamp

* Optional fitment circuits shown dotted

CABLE COLOUR CODE

N.	Brown.	P.	Purple.	W.	White.	K.	Pink.
U.	Blue.	G.	Green.	Y.	Yellow.	O.	Orange.
R.	Red.	LG.	Light Green.	B.	Black.	S.	Slate.

When a cable has two colour code letters the first denotes the main colour and the second denotes the tracer colour.

86.00.04

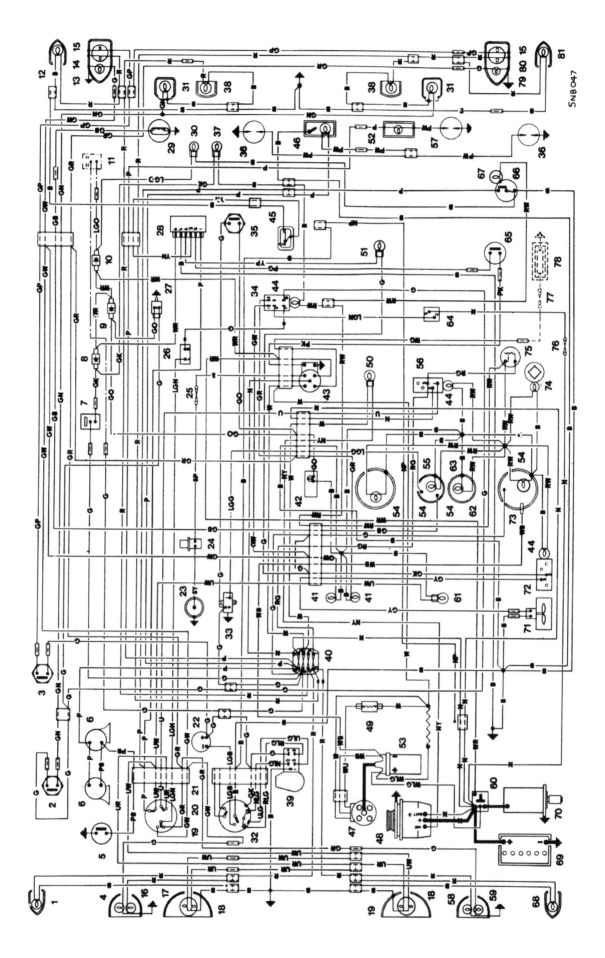

WIRING DIAGRAM: 1976 U.S.A. SPECIFICATION

ELECTRICAL

86.00.05

5NB047

KEY TO THE WIRING DIAGRAM:
1976 U.S.A. Specification

Several of the components listed in this key may not be included in the specification of all models.

1 R.H. front side-marker lamp
2 Reverse lamp switch
3 Stop lamp switch
4 R.H. front flasher lamp
5 Horn push
6 Horn
7 Service interval counter for E G R valve
8 Diode for E G R valve service interval counter
9 Diode for brake warning
10 Diode for catalytic converter service interval counter – if fitted
11 Service interval counter for catalytic converter – if fitted
12 R.H. rear side-marker lamp
13 R.H. rear flasher lamp
14 R.H. tail lamp
15 Stop lamp
16 R.H. parking lamp
17 Headlamp main beam
18 Headlamp dip beam

19 Direction indicator switch
20 Headlamp dip switch
21 Headlamp flasher switch
22 Windscreen washer pump
23 Running-on control valve oil pressure switch
24 Running-on control valve
25 Line fuse for running-on control valve
26 Flasher unit
27 Brake pressure failure switch
28 Time delay buzzer
29 Fuel gauge tank unit
30 'CATALYST' warning light – if fitted
31 Reverse lamp
32 Combined windscreen washer and wiper switch
33 Instrument voltage stabilizer
34 Hazard warning switch
35 Handbrake switch
36 Interior courtesy lamp door switch
37 E G R warning light
38 Number plate illumination lamp

39 Windscreen wiper motor
40 Fuse unit
41 Direction indicator warning lamp
42 Handbrake warning lamp
43 Ignition starter switch
44 Switch illumination lamp
45 Driver's seat belt buckle switch
46 Interior courtesy lamp
47 Distributor
48 Alternator
49 Resistor – distributor
50 Ignition warning lamp
51 'FASTEN BELTS' warning lamp
52 Luggage compartment lamp
53 Ignition coil
54 Panel lamp
55 Fuel gauge
56 Lighting switch
57 Luggage compartment lamp switch
58 L.H. parking lamp
59 L.H. front flasher lamp
60 Starter solenoid

61 Headlamp main beam warning lamp
62 Oil pressure gauge
63 Coolant temperature gauge
64 Hazard warning flasher unit
65 Ignition key audible warning door switch
66 Cigar lighter
67 Cigar lighter illumination lamp
68 L.H. front side-marker lamp
69 Battery
70 Starter motor
71 Heater motor
72 Heater motor switch
73 Tachometer
74 Heater control illumination lamp
75 Panel lamp switch
76 Line fuse for hazard warning
77 Line fuse for radio*
78 Radio*
79 L.H. rear flasher lamp
80 L.H. tail lamp
81 L.H. rear side-marker lamp

* Optional fitment circuits shown dotted

CABLE COLOUR CODE

N. Brown.	P. Purple.	W. White.	K. Pink.
U. Blue.	G. Green.	Y. Yellow.	O. Orange.
R. Red.	LG. Light Green.	B. Black.	S. Slate.

When a cable has two colour code letters the first denotes the main colour and the second denotes the tracer colour.

86.00.06

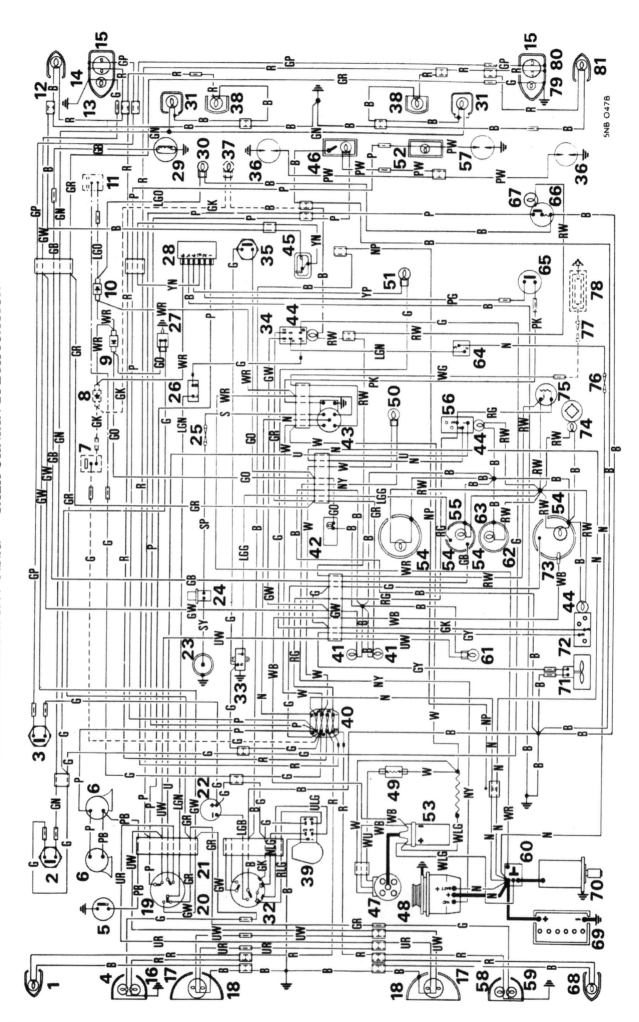

WIRING DIAGRAM: 1977 U.S.A. — CALIFORNIAN SPECIFICATION

ELECTRICAL

KEY TO THE WIRING DIAGRAM:
1977 U.S.A. — Californian Specification

Several of the components listed in this key may not be included in the specification of all models.

1 R.H. front side marker lamp
2 Reverse lamp switch
3 Stop lamp switch
4 R.H. front flasher lamp
5 Horn push
6 Horn
7 Service interval counter for E G R valve.*
8 Diode for E G R valve service interval counter
9 Diode for brake warning
10 Diode for catalytic converter service interval counter — if fitted
11 Service interval counter for catalytic converter — if fitted
12 R.H. rear side-marker lamp
13 R.H. rear flasher lamp
14 R.H. tail lamp
15 Stop lamp
16 R.H. parking lamp
17 Headlamp main beam
18 Headlamp dip beam
19 Direction indicator switch
20 Headlamp dip switch
21 Headlamp flasher switch
22 Windscreen washer pump
23 Running-on control valve oil pressure switch
24 Running-on control valve
25 Line fuse for running-on control valve
26 Flasher unit
27 Brake pressure failure switch
28 Time delay buzzer
29 Fuel gauge tank unit
30 'CATALYST' warning light — if fitted
31 Reverse lamp
32 Combined windscreen washer and wiper switch
33 Instrument voltage stabilizer
34 Hazard warning switch
35 Handbrake switch
36 Interior courtesy lamp door switch
37 E.G.R. valve warning light*
38 Number plate illumination lamp
39 Windscreen wiper motor
40 Fuse unit

41 Direction indicator warning lamp
42 Handbrake warning lamp
43 Ignition starter switch
44 Switch illumination lamp
45 Driver's seat belt buckle switch
46 Interior courtesy lamp
47 Distributor
48 Alternator
49 Resistor — distributor
50 Ignition warning lamp
51 'FASTEN BELTS' warning lamp
52 Luggage compartment lamp
53 Ignition coil
54 Panel lamp
55 Fuel gauge
56 Lighting switch
57 Luggage compartment lamp switch
58 L.H. parking lamp
59 L.H. front flasher lamp
60 Starter solenoid
61 Headlamp main beam warning lamp
62 Oil pressure gauge

63 Coolant temperature gauge
64 Hazard warning flasher unit
65 Ignition key audible warning door switch
66 Cigar lighter
67 Cigar lighter illumination lamp
68 L.H. front side-marker lamp
69 Battery
70 Starter motor
71 Heater motor
72 Heater motor switch
73 Tachometer
74 Heater control illumination lamp
75 Panel lamp switch
76 Line fuse for hazard warning
77 Line fuse for radio*
78 Radio*
79 L.H. rear flasher lamp
80 L.H. tail lamp
81 L.H. rear side-marker lamp

* Optional fitment circuits shown dotted

CABLE COLOUR CODE

N.	Brown.	P.	Purple.	W.	White.	K.	Pink.
U.	Blue.	G.	Green.	Y.	Yellow.	O.	Orange.
R.	Red.	LG.	Light Green.	B.	Black.	S.	Slate.

When a cable has two colour code letters the first denotes the main colour and the second denotes the tracer colour.

86.00.08

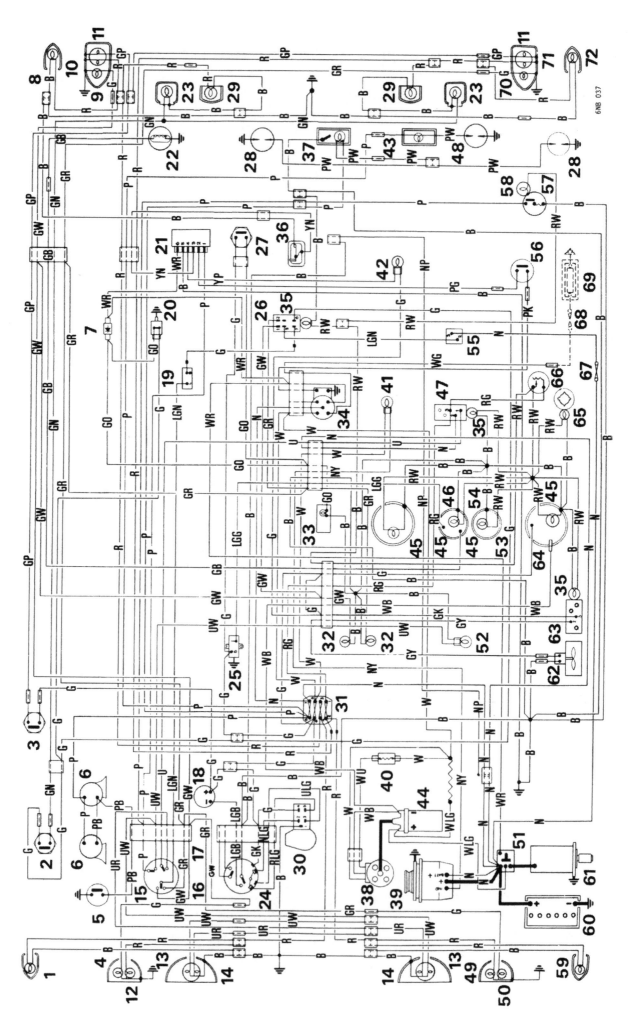

WIRING DIAGRAM: 1977 U.S.A. — FEDERAL & CANADIAN SPECIFICATION

ELECTRICAL

86.00.09

204

KEY TO THE WIRING DIAGRAM—
1977 U.S.A. — Federal & Canadian Specification

Several of the components listed in this key may not be included in the specification of all models.

1 R.H. front side-marker lamp
2 Reverse lamp switch
3 Stop lamp switch
4 R.H. front flasher lamp
5 Horn-push
6 Horn
7 Diode for brake warning
8 R.H. rear side-marker lamp
9 R.H. rear flasher lamp
10 R.H. tail lamp
11 Stop lamp
12 R.H. parking lamp
13 Headlamp main beam
14 Headlamp dip beam
15 Direction indicator switch
16 Headlamp dip switch
17 Headlamp flasher switch
18 Windscreen washer pump

19 Flasher unit
20 Brake pressure failure switch
21 Time delay buzzer
22 Fuel gauge tank unit
23 Reverse lamp
24 Combined windscreen washer and wiper switch
25 Instrument voltage stabilizer
26 Hazard warning switch
27 Hand brake switch
28 Interior courtesy lamp door switch
29 Number-plate illumination lamp
30 Windscreen wiper motor
31 Fuse unit
32 Direction indicator warning lamp
33 Hand brake warning lamp
34 Ignition starter switch
35 Switch illumination lamp
36 Driver's seat belt buckle switch

37 Interior courtesy lamp
38 Distributor
39 Alternator
40 Resistor – distributor
41 Ignition warning lamp
42 'FASTEN BELTS' warning lamp
43 Luggage compartment lamp
44 Ignition coil
45 Panel lamp
46 Fuel gauge
47 Lighting switch
48 Luggage compartment lamp switch
49 L.H. parking lamp
50 L.H. front flasher lamp
51 Starter solenoid
52 Headlamp main beam warning lamp
53 Oil pressure gauge
54 Coolant temperature gauge
55 Hazard warning flasher unit

56 Ignition key audible warning door switch
57 Cigar-lighter
58 Cigar-lighter illumination lamp
59 L.H. front side-marker lamp
60 Battery
61 Starter motor
62 Heater motor
63 Heater motor switch
64 Tachometer
65 Heater control illumination lamp
66 Panel lamp switch
67 Line fuse for hazard warning
68 Line fuse for radio*
69 Radio*
70 L.H. rear flasher lamp
71 L.H. tail lamp
72 L.H. rear side-marker lamp

* Optional fitment circuits shown dotted

CABLE COLOUR CODE

N.	Brown	P.	Purple	W.	White	K.	Pink
U.	Blue	G.	Green	Y.	Yellow	O.	Orange
R.	Red	LG.	Light Green	B.	Black	S.	Slate

When a cable has two colour code letters the first denotes the main colour and the second denotes the tracer colour.

86.00.10

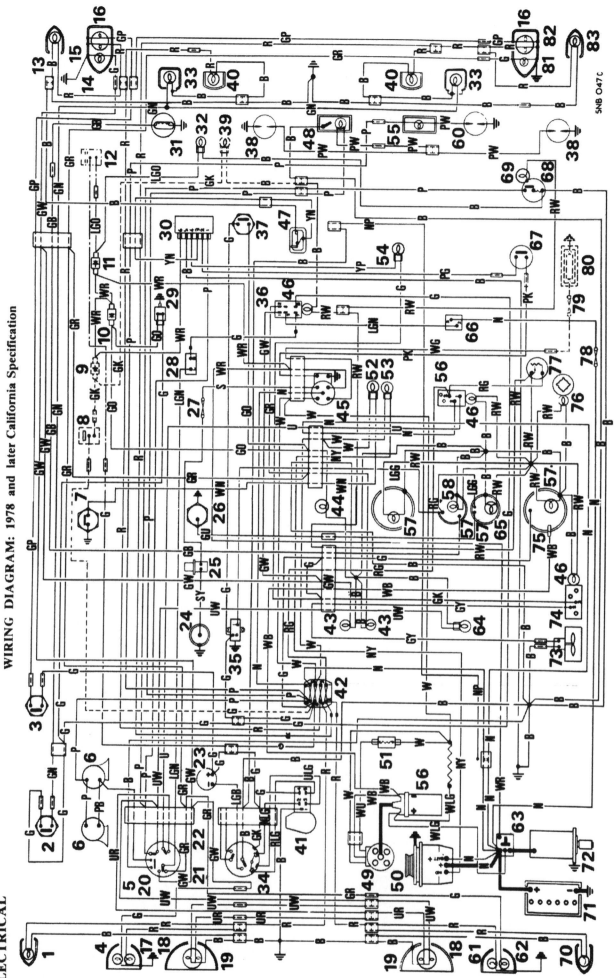

WIRING DIAGRAM: 1978 and later California Specification

5NB O47C

ELECTRICAL

KEY TO THE WIRING DIAGRAM:
1978 and later California Specification

Several of the components listed in this key may not be included in the specification of all models.

1 R.H. front side marker lamp
2 Reverse lamp switch
3 Stop lamp switch
4 R.H. front flasher lamp
5 Horn push
6 Horn
7 Oil pressure switch
8 Service interval counter for E.G.R. valve.
9 Diode for E.G.R. valve service interval counter.
10 Diode for brake warning
11 Diode for catalytic converter service interval counter — if fitted
12 Service interval counter for catalytic converter — if fitted
13 R.H. rear side-marker lamp
14 R.H. rear flasher lamp
15 R.H. tail lamp
16 Stop lamp
17 R.H. parking lamp
18 Headlamp main beam
19 Headlamp dip beam

20 Direction indicator switch
21 Headlamp dip switch
22 Headlamp flasher switch
23 Windscreen washer pump
24 Running-on control valve oil pressure switch
25 Running-on control valve
26 Coolant temperature transmitter
27 Line fuse for running-on control valve
28 Flasher unit
29 Brake pressure failure switch
30 Time delay buzzer
31 Fuel gauge tank unit
32 'CATALYST' warning light — if fitted
33 Reverse lamp
34 Combined windscreen washer and wiper switch
35 Instrument voltage stabilizer
36 Hazard warning switch
37 Handbrake switch
38 Interior courtesy lamp door switch
39 E.G.R. valve warning light
40 Number plate illumination lamp

41 Windscreen wiper motor
42 Fuse unit
43 Direction indicator warning lamp
44 Handbrake warning lamp
45 Ignition starter switch
46 Switch illumination lamp
47 Driver's seat belt buckle switch
48 Interior courtesy lamp
49 Distributor
50 Alternator
51 Resistor — distributor
52 Oil pressure warning light
53 Ignition warning lamp
54 'FASTEN BELTS' warning lamp
55 Luggage compartment lamp
56 Ignition coil
57 Panel lamp
58 Fuel gauge
59 Lighting switch
60 Luggage compartment lamp switch
61 L.H. parking lamp
62 L.H. front flasher lamp

63 Starter solenoid
64 Headlamp main beam warning lamp
65 Oil pressure gauge
66 Hazard warning flasher unit
67 Ignition key audible warning door switch
68 Cigar lighter
69 Cigar lighter illumination lamp
70 L.H. front side-marker lamp
71 Battery
72 Starter motor
73 Heater motor
74 Heater motor switch
75 Tachometer
76 Heater control illumination lamp
77 Panel lamp switch
78 Line fuse for hazard warning
79 Line fuse for radio*
80 Radio*
81 L.H. rear flasher lamp
82 L.H. tail lamp
83 L.H. rear side-marker lamp

* Optional fitment circuits shown dotted

CABLE COLOUR CODE

N.	Brown.	P.	Purple.	W.	White.	K.	Pink.
U.	Blue.	G.	Green.	Y.	Yellow.	O.	Orange.
R.	Red.	LG.	Light Green.	B.	Black.	S.	Slate.

When a cable has two colour code letters the first denotes the main colour and the second denotes the tracer colour.

86.00.12

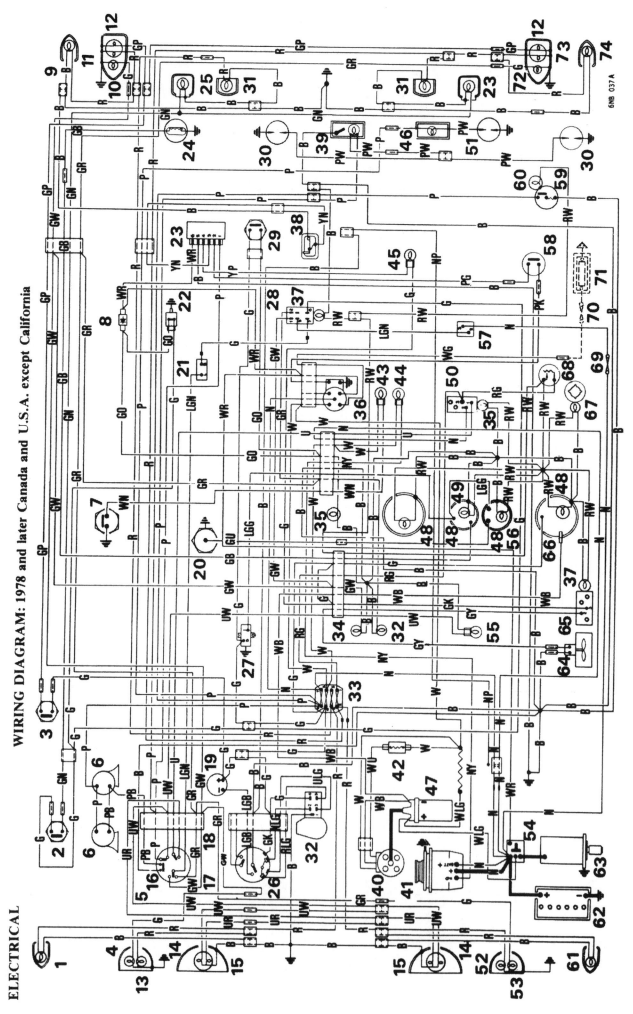

WIRING DIAGRAM: 1978 and later Canada and U.S.A. except California

ELECTRICAL

ELECTRICAL

KEY TO THE WIRING DIAGRAM:
1978 and later Canada and U.S.A. except California

Several of the components listed in this key may not be included in the specification of all models.

1   R.H. front side-marker lamp
2   Reverse lamp switch
3   Stop lamp switch
4   R.H. front flasher lamp
5   Horn-push
6   Horn
7   Oil pressure switch
8   Diode for brake warning
9   R.H. rear side-marker lamp
10 R.H. rear flasher lamp
11 R.H. tail lamp
12 Stop lamp
13 R.H. parking lamp
14 Headlamp main beam
15 Headlamp dip beam
16 Direction indicator switch
17 Headlamp dip switch
18 Headlamp flasher switch
19 Windscreen washer pump

20 Coolant temperature transmitter
21 Flasher unit
22 Brake pressure failure switch
23 Time delay buzzer
24 Fuel gauge tank unit
25 Reverse lamp
26 Combined windscreen washer and wiper switch
27 Instrument voltage stabilizer
28 Hazard warning switch
29 Hand brake switch
30 Interior courtesy lamp door switch
31 Number-plate illumination lamp
32 Windscreen wiper motor
33 Fuse unit
34 Direction indicator warning lamp
35 Hand brake warning lamp
36 Ignition starter switch
37 Switch illumination lamp

38 Driver's seat belt buckle switch
39 Interior courtesy lamp
40 Distributor
41 Alternator
42 Resistor — distributor
43 Oil pressure warning light
44 Ignition warning lamp
45 'FASTEN BELTS' warning lamp
46 Luggage compartment lamp
47 Ignition coil
48 Panel lamp
49 Fuel gauge
50 Lighting switch
51 Luggage compartment lamp switch
52 L.H. parking lamp
53 L.H. front flasher lamp
54 Starter solenoid
55 Headlamp main beam warning lamp
56 Coolant temperature gauge

57 Hazard warning flasher unit
58 Ignition key audible warning door switch
59 Cigar-lighter
60 Cigar-lighter illumination lamp
61 L.H. front side-marker lamp
62 Battery
63 Starter motor
64 Heater motor
65 Heater motor switch
66 Tachometer
67 Heater control illumination lamp
68 Panel lamp switch
69 Line fuse for hazard warning
70 Line fuse for radio*
71 Radio*
72 L.H. rear flasher lamp
73 L.H. tail lamp
74 L.H. rear side-marker lamp

* Optional fitment circuits shown dotted

CABLE COLOUR CODE

N.	Brown	P.	Purple	W.	White	K.	Pink
U.	Blue	G.	Green	Y.	Yellow	O.	Orange
R.	Red	LG.	Light Green	B.	Black	S.	Slate

When a cable has two colour code letters the first denotes the main colour and the second denotes the tracer colour.

86.00.14

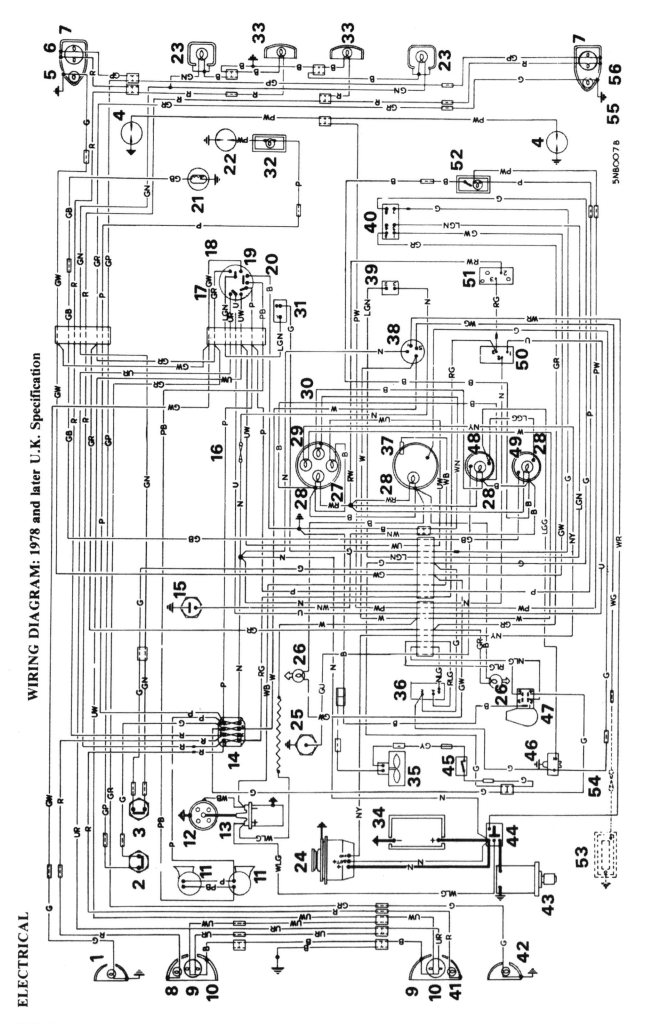

ELECTRICAL

WIRING DIAGRAM: 1978 and later U.K. Specification

ELECTRICAL

KEY TO THE WIRING DIAGRAM:
1978 and later U.K. Specification

Several of the components listed in this key may not be included in the specification of all models.

1 R.H. front direction indicator lamp
2 Stop lamp switch
3 Reverse lamp switch
4 Interior lamp door switches
5 R.H. rear direction indicator lamp
6 R.H. tail lamp
7 Stop lamps
8 R.H. sidelamp
9 Headlamp main beam
10 Headlamp dip beam
11 Horn
12 Distributor
13 Ignition coil
14 Fuse unit (4-way)

15 Oil pressure switch
16 Line fuse for hazard warning
17 Headlamp flasher switch
18 Direction indicator switch
19 Horn push
20 Headlamp dip switch
21 Fuel gauge tank unit
22 Luggage compartment lamp
23 Reverse lamps
24 Alternator
25 Coolant temperature transmitter
26 Direction indicator warning lamps
27 Main beam warning light
28 Panel lamp

29 Ignition warning light
30 Oil pressure warning light
31 Flasher unit
32 Luggage compartment lamps
33 Number plate illumination lamp
34 Battery (12 volt)
35 Heater or fresh air motor
36 Windscreen wiper switch
37 Tachometer
38 Ignition/starter switch
39 Hazard warning flasher unit
40 Hazard warning switch
41 L.H. sidelamp
42 L.H. front direction indicator

43 Starter motor
44 Starter solenoid
45 Heater or fresh air motor
46 Instrument voltage stabilizer
47 Windscreen wiper motor
48 Coolant temperature gauge
49 Fuel gauge
50 Lighting switch
51 Panel lamp switch
52 Interior courtesy lamp
53 Radio*
54 Line fuse for radio*
55 L.H. rear direction indicator lamp
56 L.H. tail lamp

* Optional fitment circuits shown dotted

CABLE COLOUR CODE

N.	Brown	P.	Purple	W.	White	K.	Pink
U.	Blue	G.	Green	Y.	Yellow	O.	Orange
R.	Red	LG.	Light Green	B.	Black	S.	Slate

When a cable has two colour code letters the first denotes the main colour and the second denotes the tracer colour.

86.00.16

ELECTRICAL

REPLACEMENT BULBS (U.S.A.)

	Watts	Part No.
Sidelamp (with flasher)	5/21	GLB 380
Stop/tail	5/21	GLB 380
Reverse	18	BFS 273
Number-plate lamp (1977 and later)	6	GLB 501
Number-plate lamp (1977)	6	BFS 254
Direction indicator	21	GLB 382
Side marker lamp, front and rear	5	BFS 501
Ignition warning lamp	2	GLB 281
Main beam warning lamp	2	GLB 281
Direction indicator warning lamp (1976 and later)	2	GLB 987
Direction indicator warning lamp (1976-1977)	2	GLB 281
Brake warning lamp	1.5	GLB 280
EGR valve warning lamp (if fitted)	1.5	GLB 280
'CATALYST' warning lamp (if fitted)	2	GLB 281
Panel illumination lamp	2.2	GLB 987
Cigar-lighter illumination	2.2	BFS 643
Luggage compartment lamp	6	GLB 254
Courtesy lamp	6	GLB 254
'FASTEN BELTS' warning lamp	2	GLB 281
Switch illumination	2	GLB 281
Heater rotary control illumination	2	GLB 281

SEALED BEAM UNITS

	Watts	Part No.
Headlamp — sealed beam (1975)	50/40	BHA 5315
Headlamp — sealed beam (1976 and later)	60/50	BHA 5382

REPLACEMENT BULBS (Right-hand steer)

	Watts	Part No.
Pilot lamp (capless bulb)	5	GLB 501
Stop/tail	5/21	GLB 380
Reverse	18	BFS 273
Number-plate lamp	6	GLB 989
Direction indicator	21	GLB 382
Ignition warning lamp	2	GLB 281
Main beam warning lamp	2	GLB 281
Direction indicator warning lamp	2	GLB 281
Panel illumination lamp	2.2	GLB 987
Luggage compartment lamp	6	GLB 254
Courtesy lamp	6	GLB 254

SEALED BEAM UNIT

	Watts	Part No.
Headlamp	50/40	GLU 104

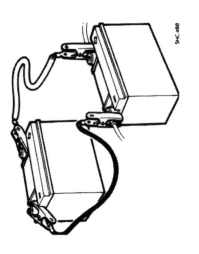

SAC 488

SERVICE PRECAUTIONS 86.01.01

Polarity
Ensure that the correct battery polarity is maintained at all times: reversed battery or charger connections will damage the alternator rectifiers.

Battery connections
The battery must never be disconnected while the engine is running.

Testing semi-conductor devices
Never use an ohmmeter of the type incorporating a hand-driven generator for checking the rectifiers or the transistors.

Battery boosting and charging
CAUTION: The following precautions must be observed to avoid the possibility of serious damage to the charging system or electrical components of the vehicle.

Battery boosting: When connecting an additional battery to boost a discharged battery in the vehicle, ensure that:

— the booster battery is of the same nominal voltage as the vehicle battery.

— the interconnecting cables are of sufficient capacity to carry starting current.

— the cables are inter-connected one at a time and to the booster battery first.

— the cables are connected between the battery terminals in the following order:

First, + (Positive) to + (Positive) and then — (Negative) to — (Negative).

— the engine speed is reduced to 1000 rev/min or below before disconnecting the boost battery. The vehicle battery must never be disconnected while the engine is running.

Battery charging: When charging the battery in the vehicle from an outside source such as a trickle charger ensure that:

— the charger voltage is the same as the nominal voltage of the battery.

— the charger positive (+) lead is connected to the positive (+) terminal of the battery.

— the charger negative (—) lead is connected to the negative (—) terminal of the battery.

ELECTRICAL
TESTING THE CHARGING CIRCUIT   86.01.02

Test conditions: Alternator drive belt adjusted correctly, battery terminals clean and tight, battery in good condition (electrolyte specific gravity readings consistent), and cables and terminal connections in the charging circuit in good condition.

	Test	Procedure		Remarks
1.	To check that battery voltage is reaching the alternator	Remove the cable connector from the alternator. Connect the negative side of a voltmeter to earth. Switch on the ignition. Connect the positive side of the voltmeter to each of the alternator cable connectors in turn.	a	If battery voltage is not available at the 'IND' cable connector, check the no-charge warning lamp, bulb and the warning lamp circuit for continuity.
			b	If battery voltage is not available at the main charging cable connector, check the circuit between the battery and the alternator for continuity.
			c	If battery voltage is available at the cable connectors mentioned in 'a' and 'b' proceed with test 2.
2.	Alternator test	Reconnect the cable connector to the alternator. Disconnect the brown cable with eyelet from the terminal on the starter motor solenoid. Connect an ammeter between the brown cable and the terminal on the starter motor solenoid. Connect a voltmeter across the battery terminals. Run the engine at 6,000 alternator rev/min and wait until the ammeter reading is stable.	a	If a zero ammeter reading is obtained, remove the end cover and disconnect the surge protection device lead from its terminal on the alternator. If the alternator output is normal, renew the surge protection device. If the reading is still zero, remove and overhaul the alternator.
			b	If an ammeter reading below 10 amps. and a voltmeter reading between 13.6 and 14.4 volts is obtained, and the battery is in a low state of charge, check the alternator performance on a test bench. The alternator output should be 34 amperes at 14 volts, at 6,000 r.p.m.
			c	If an ammeter reading below 10 amps. and a voltmeter reading below 13.6 volts is obtained, remove the alternator and renew the voltage regulator.
			d	If an ammeter reading above 10 amps. and a voltmeter reading above 14.4 volts is obtained, remove the alternator and renew the voltage regulator.

213

ELECTRICAL

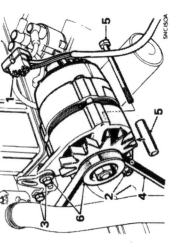

SNC150A

ALTERNATOR – U.K. Specification

Remove and refit   86.10.02

Removing

1 Disconnect the wiring plug from the alternator.
2 Slacken the alternator pivot bolt.
3 Slacken the adjusting link screws.
4 Detach the fan belt from the alternator pulley.
5 Remove the pivot bolt and spacer.
6 Remove the adjusting link screw and lift the alternator from the car.

Refitting

7 Reverse the procedure in 1 to 6 and check the fan belt tension, see 'MAINTENANCE'.

ALTERNATOR – U.S.A. Specification

Remove and refit   86.10.02

Removing

1 Disconnect the battery.
2 Disconnect the wiring plug from the alternator.
3 Remove the nut, bolt and washer securing the alternator and guard to the adjusting link.
4 Remove the nut and washer securing the alternator and guard to the air pump mounting bracket.
5 Remove the alternator guard.

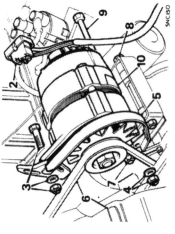

SNC150

6 Detach the fan belt from the alternator pulley.
7 Slacken the bolt securing the air pump mounting bracket to the engine front mounting plate.
8 Slacken the bolt securing the air pump to the air pump mounting bracket.
9 Remove the bolt securing the alternator to the air pump mounting bracket.
10 Remove the alternator.

Refitting

11 Reverse the procedure in 1 to 10, noting:
a Check the fan belt tension, see 'MAINTENANCE'.

ALTERNATOR

Overhaul   86.10.08

Dismantling

1 Remove the alternator, see 86.10.02.
2 Remove the two screws to release the end cover from the alternator.
3 Detach the leads from the terminal blades on the rectifier plates.
4 Remove the four screws to release the two brush assemblies and the leads from the brush holder, noting the leaf spring fitted at the side of the inner brush.
5 Remove the screw to release the surge protection device lead from the brush holder.
6 Remove the two bolts to release the brush holder complete with regulator from the slip-ring end bracket.

7 Remove the screw to release the regulator from the brush holder, noting the position of the connector link and the distance piece.
8 Remove the set bolt securing the surge protection device to the slip-ring end bracket.
9 Remove the set bolt securing the rectifier earthing link to the slip-ring end bracket.
10 Using a pair of pliers as a thermal shunt to avoid overheating the diodes, unsolder each of the three stator cables in turn from the rectifier.
11 Slacken the nut to release the rectifier assembly from the slip-ring end bracket.
12 Mark the drive-end bracket, the stator lamination pack, and the slip-ring end bracket to assist re-assembly.
13 Remove the three through-bolts and withdraw the slip-ring end bracket and the stator lamination pack.
14 Remove the 'O' ring from inside the slip-ring end bracket.
15 Remove the nut and withdraw the pulley and fan from the rotor shaft.

16 Remove the pulley key and withdraw the distance piece from the rotor shaft.
17 Press the rotor out of the drive-end bracket bearing.
18 Withdraw the distance piece from the drive end of the rotor.
19 Remove the circlip to release the bearing, bearing cover-plates, 'O' ring, and felt washer from the drive-end bracket.

Inspection

20 Check the bearings for wear and roughness; if necessary, repack the

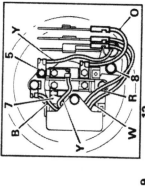

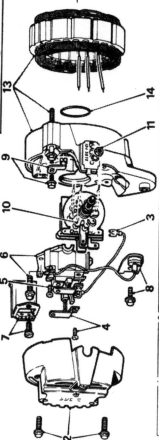

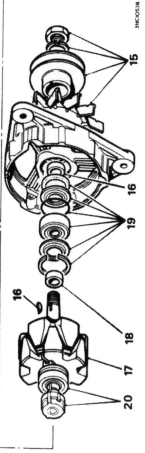

3NC053B

bearings with Shell Alvania RA grease or equivalent. To renew the slip-ring end bearing, unsolder the two field connections from the slip-ring and withdraw the slip-ring and the bearing from the rotor shaft. Reassemble ensuring that the shielded side of the bearing faces the slip-ring assembly. Use Fry's H.T. 3 solder or equivalent to remake the field connections to the slip-ring.

21 Clean the surfaces of the slip-ring removing any evidence of burning using very fine glass paper.

22 Check the field winding insulation, connecting the test equipment (see DATA) between one of the slip-rings and a rotor lobe.

23 Check the field windings against the specification given in DATA, connecting the test equipment between the slip-rings.

24 Check the stator windings for continuity, connecting the test equipment (see DATA) between any two of the stator cables, then repeating the test using the third cable in place of one of the first two.

25 Check the stator winding insulation, connecting the test equipment (see DATA) between any one of the three stator cables and the stator lamination pack.

26 Check the nine rectifying diodes, connecting the test equipment (see DATA) between each diode pin and its associated heatsink in the rectifier pack in turn, and then reverse the test equipment connections. Current should flow in one direction only. Renew the rectifier assembly if a diode is faulty.

27 Check the brush spring pressure and the brush length against the specification given in DATA.

Reassembling
28 Reverse the procedure in 1 to 19, noting:
a Support the inner track of the bearing when refitting the rotor to the drive-end bracket.
b Use 'M' grade 45-55 tin-lead solder to remake the stator to rectifier pack connections, using a pair of pliers as a thermal shunt to avoid overheating of the diodes.
c Tighten the alternator pulley nut to 25 lbf ft (3.46 kgf m).

DATA

Field winding:
Resistance at 20°C (68°F) . . . . 3.3 ohms ± 5%
Current flow at 12 volts . . . . 3 amperes
Insulation test equipment . . . . 110-volt a.c. supply and 15-watt test lamp

Stator windings:
Continuity test equipment . . . . 12-volt d.c. supply and 36-watt test lamp
Insulation test equipment . . . . 110-volt a.c. supply and 15-watt test lamp
Diode current test equipment . . . . 12-volt d.c. supply and 1.5-watt test lamp
Alternator output at 14 volts . . . . 34 amp at 6000 alternator rev/min
Brush length—new . . . . 0.5 in (12.6 mm)
Brush length—minimum . . . . 0.2 in (5 mm) protruding beyond brush box moulding
Brush spring pressure . . . . 9 to 13 oz (255 to 369 gm) when brush is pushed in flush with brush box face

HORN

Remove and refit   86.30.09

Removing
1 Disconnect the battery.
2 Remove the six screws and washers securing the radiator grille to the body.
3 Remove the radiator grille.
4 Disconnect the wiring from the horn.
5 Remove the nut securing the horn to the mounting bracket.
6 Remove the horn.

Refitting
7 Reverse the procedure in 1 to 6.

DISTRIBUTOR — Conventional

Remove and refit   86.35.20

Removing
1 Disconnect the battery.
2 Detach the air intake hose from the heater and place aside.
3 Remove the distributor cap and leads.
4 Disconnect the low tension distributor lead.
5 Detach the vacuum pipe from the vacuum retard unit.
6 Turn the engine until the timing notches on the crankshaft pulley are aligned with the 10° B.T.D.C. point on the timing indicator. The distributor rotor arm should be in the firing position for No. 1 sparking plug.
7 Slacken the nut and bolt to release the distributor clamp.
8 Withdraw the distributor assembly.

Refitting
9 Set the engine and distributor rotor arm as in instruction 6 and fit the distributor.
10 Tighten the distributor clamp nut and bolt.
11 Reverse the procedure in 1 to 5.
12 Check the ignition timing, see 'MAINTENANCE'.

DISTRIBUTOR — Conventional

Overhaul   86.35.26

Dismantling
1 Note the relative position of the offset drive dog to the rotor arm lobe. The centre line of the drive dog is parallel with and offset to the centre line of the rotor arm.
2 Remove the rotor arm.
3 Remove the cam oiling pad.
4 Remove the two screws retaining the vacuum unit.
(Early cars: Note that two prongs protrude downwards from the base plate and straddle one of the retaining screws.)
5 Disengage the operating arm from the movable plate and remove the assembly.
6 Push the grommet and low tension lead through the body towards the inside of the housing.
7 Remove the base plate retaining screws.
8 Remove the base and bearing plate assembly.
(Early cars. Lever the base plate from its retaining groove in the body.)
9 Drive out the parallel pin retaining the drive dog.

continued

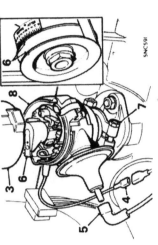

ELECTRICAL

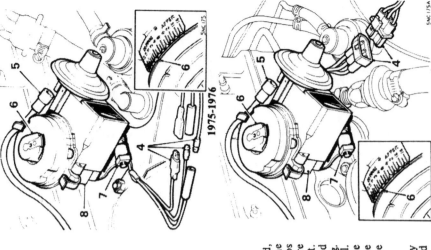

1975-1976

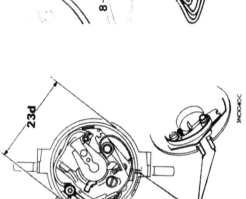

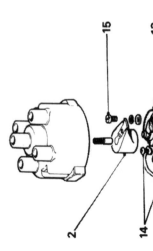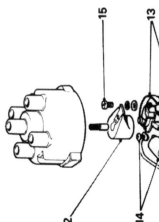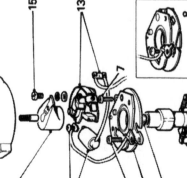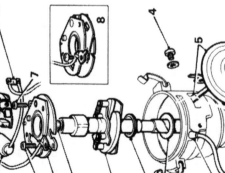

11 Remove the centre spindle complete with the automatic advance weights and springs.

12 Remove the steel washer and nylon spacer from the spindle.

13 Push the moving contact spring inwards and unclip the low tension lead.

14 Remove the screw retaining the earth lead tag and the capacitor.

15 Remove the screw, spring and plain washer retaining the fixed contact and remove the contact assembly.

Inspection

16 Examine the fit of the drive spindle in its bush, and the spindle cam for wear. The automatic advance mechanism should not be dismantled other than to remove the control springs. If any of the moving parts are excessively worn or damaged, the complete spindle assembly must be renewed. If the spindle bearing is worn allowing excessive side play, the complete distributor must be replaced.

17 Check the spring between the fixed and movable plates. Operate the plate and examine for freedom of movement and excessive wear. Renew as an assembly.

18 Examine the distributor and cap for cracks and signs of tracking. Examine the pick-up brush for wear and freedom of movement in its holder. Renew as necessary.

19 Check the rotor for damage, electrode security, and burning or tracking. Renew as necessary.

Reassembling

20 During reassembly grease the pivots of the weights and springs and the spindle bearing area with Rocol MP (Molypad).

21 Grease the outside of the contact breaker hollow pivot post and lightly smear the spindle cam, using Retinax 'A' grease.

22 Apply one or two drops of clean engine oil to the oiling pad.

23 Reverse the procedure in 1 to 15, noting:

    a Set the contact points gap to 0.014 to 0.016 in (0.36 to 0.40 mm).

b If a new drive spindle is fitted, tap the drive end of the distributor dog to flatten the pips on the thrust washer and ensure the correct amount of end-float. The new spindle should be drilled through the hole in the drive dog. Use a 3/16 in (4.76 mm) drill. During drilling, push the spindle from the cam end, pressing the drive dog and washer against the body shank.

EARLY CARS

c Position the base plate assembly so that the two downward pointing prongs will straddle the screw hole below the cap clip. Ensure the base plate is pressed against the register in the body of the distributor so that the chamfered edge engages the undercut.

d Measure across the centre of the distributor at a right angle to the slot in the base plate. Tighten the securing screw and re-measure the distance across the body. Unless the measurement has increased by at least 0.006 in (0.152 mm) the contact breaker base plate must be renewed.

1977 and later

DISTRIBUTOR — Lucas Opus

Remove and refit   86.35.20

Removing

1 Disconnect the battery.

2 Detach the car heater air intake hose from the heater air intake and place aside.

3 Remove the distributor cap and leads.

4 Disconnect the three low tension distributor leads.

5 Detach the vacuum pipe from the vacuum retard unit.

23d

23d 23d

23c

10 Remove the drive dog and thrust washer, noting that the raised pips on the washer face the drive dog.

6 Turn the engine until the timing notches on the crankshaft pulley are aligned with the 10° B.T.D.C. point on the timing indicator. The distributor rotor arm should be in the firing position for No. 1 sparking plug.
7 Slacken the nut and bolt to release the distributor clamp.
8 Withdraw the distributor assembly.

Refitting
9 Set the engine and distributor rotor arm as in instruction 6 and fit the distributor.
10 Tighten the distributor clamp nut and bolt.
11 Reverse the procedure in 1 to 5.
12 Check the ignition timing, see 'MAINTENANCE'.

DISTRIBUTOR — Lucas Opus

Overhaul   86.35.26

Dismantling
1 Remove the distributor, see 86.35.20.
2 Remove the rotor arm.
3 Remove the anti-flash shield.
4 Remove the felt pad.
5 Remove the two screws, spring washers and plain washers securing the pick-up to the moving plate.
6 Remove the three screws and washers securing the amplifier module to the distributor body.
7 Detach the retard unit link from the pin on the moving plate.
8 Detach the pick-up wiring grommet from the distributor body and remove the amplifier module complete with pick-up and leads.
9 Remove the two spring clips from the distributor body.
10 Drive out the pin securing the retard unit to the amplifier module and withdraw the unit.
11 Remove the circlip and washer securing the timing rotor.
12 Remove the timing rotor and rubber 'O' ring.
13 Remove the two screws securing the base plate to the distributor body.
14 Remove the base plate.
15 Drive out the pin securing the driving dog to the distributor spindle.
16 Remove the driving dog and thrust washer.
17 Ensure that the spindle is free of burrs and withdraw it from the distributor body.
18 Remove the shim.
19 Remove the two return springs.

Reassembling
20 Reverse the procedure in 1 to 19, noting:
a Lubricate the centrifugal weights assembly, the distributor spindle and the moving plate pin with Rocol 'Moly pad' or equivalent.
b Fit the timing rotor with the large locating lug in the corresponding slot.

c All 1975, 1976, and California cars from 1977: Ensure that the vacuum unit fitted is a Retard Unit; see 'ENGINE TUNING DATA'.
d Remaining 1977 and later U.S.A. Federal States and Canada: Ensure that the vacuum unit fitted is an Advance Unit, see 'ENGINE TUNING DATA'.
e Ensure that the amplifier module and the wiring grommet are correctly seated before the three securing screws are tightened.
f Adjust the pick up air gap, see 86.35.31.
g Lubricate the distributor, see 'MAINTENANCE'.

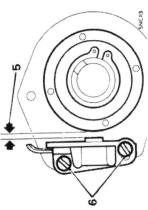

DISTRIBUTOR

Pick-up air gap—adjust   86.35.31

CAUTION: Do not insert a feeler gauge into the pick-up air gap, when the ignition circuit is energised.

1 Disconnect the battery.
2 Remove the distributor cap and leads.
3 Remove the distributor rotor arm.
4 Remove the anti-flash shield.
5 Check the air gap: it should be 0.014 to 0.016 in (0.35 to 0.40 mm).
6 If adjustment is required, slacken the two screws securing the pick-up, and move the pick-up about the pivot screw to give the correct setting.
7 Tighten the two screws and check the air gap.
CAUTION: Ensure that this checking operation is carried out as the air gap may alter substantially when the two screws are tightened.

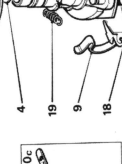

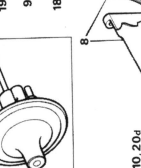

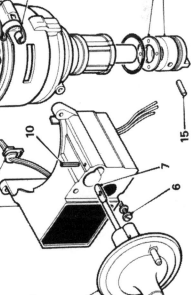

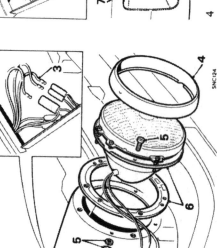

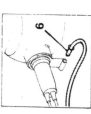
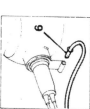
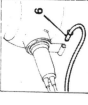
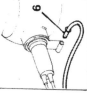

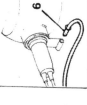
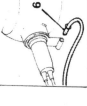
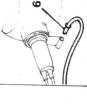
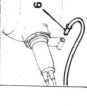

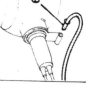
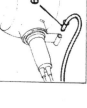
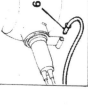
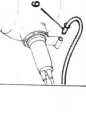
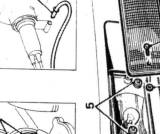
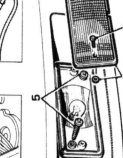

HEADLAMP ASSEMBLY — except U.S.A.

Remove and refit   86.40.02

Removing

1 Disconnect the battery.
2 Remove the screw and nut to release the wiring clip from the body in the front corner of the engine compartment.
3 Disconnect the headlamp wiring at the connectors in the front corner of the engine compartment.
4 Ease the bottom of the outer rim forwards and lift it off the retaining lugs at the top of the lamp.
5 Remove the four screws, nuts and washers securing the headlamp assembly to the body and detach the flasher lamp wiring clip.
6 Remove the headlamp assembly and rubber seal.

Refitting

7 Reverse the procedure in 1 to 6.

HEADLAMP ASSEMBLY — U.S.A.

Remove and refit   86.40.02

Removing

1 Disconnect the battery.
2 Remove the screws and nuts to release the wiring clips from the body in the engine compartment and under the wing.
3 Disconnect the wiring at the snap connectors in the engine compartment.
4 Remove the outer rim.
5 Remove the four screws, nuts and washers securing the headlamp unit to the body.
6 Remove the headlamp unit and rubber seal from the body.

Refitting

7 Reverse the procedure in 1 to 6.

FRONT PARKING/FLASHER LAMP ASSEMBLY — U.S.A.

Remove and refit   86.40.26

Removing

1 Disconnect the battery. Remove the screws and nuts to release the wiring clips from the body in the engine compartment and under the wing.
2 Disconnect the two feed cables at the snap connectors in the engine compartment.
3 Remove the two screws securing the lens to the lamp unit.

4 Remove the lens and rubber washers from the lamp unit.
5 Remove the two screws securing the lamp unit to the bumper.
6 Pull the unit forward and disconnect the earth lead.
7 Remove the lamp unit.

Refitting

8 Reverse the procedure in 1 to 7 noting:
    a The lens is marked 'TOP' to ensure correct refitment.

FRONT FLASHER LAMP ASSEMBLY — except U.S.A.

Remove and refit   86.40.42

Removing

1 Disconnect the battery.
2 Remove the screw and nut to release the wiring clip from the body in the front of the engine compartment.
3 Disconnect the flasher lamp feed cable at the connector in the front of the engine compartment.
4 Remove the two screws securing the lens to the lamp unit.
5 Remove the lens and rubber washers.
6 Remove the two screws securing the lamp unit to the bumper.
7 Detach the unit from the bumper and disconnect the earth cable.
8 Remove the lamp unit.

Refitting

9 Reverse the procedure in 1 to 8 noting that the lens is marked 'TOP' to ensure correct refitment.

SIDE FRONT MARKER LAMP ASSEMBLY

Remove and refit   86.40.59

Removing

1 Disconnect the battery.
2 Remove the screws and nuts to release the wiring clips from the body in the engine compartment and under the wing.
3 Disconnect the earth cable from the lamp unit and the feed cable at the snap connector in the engine compartment.
4 Remove the two nuts, washers and rubber seals securing the unit to the body.
5 Remove the lamp unit complete with mounting plate and seal.

Refitting

6 Reverse the procedure in 1 to 5.

ELECTRICAL

TAIL, STOP AND FLASHER LAMP ASSEMBLY
86.40.70

Remove and refit

Removing

1. Disconnect the battery.
2. Disconnect the wiring at the snap connectors in the luggage compartment.
3. Remove the nut securing the harness clip.
4. Remove the three nuts securing the lamp assembly to the body.
5. Remove the lamp assembly complete with seal.

Refitting

6. Reverse the procedure in 1 to 5.

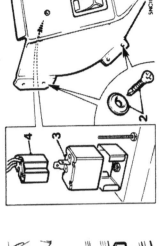

NUMBER-PLATE LAMP
86.40.86

Remove and refit

Removing

1. Disconnect the battery.
2. Remove the two nuts and washers securing the lamp assembly to the number plate.
3. Detach the lamp assembly from the number plate and disconnect the wiring at the terminals on the lamp assembly.

Refitting

4. Reverse the procedure in 1 to 3.

COURTESY LAMP ASSEMBLY — U.S.A. only
86.45.10

Remove and refit

Removing

1. Disconnect the battery.
2. Remove the eight screws and washers securing the centre console.
3. Manoeuvre the console forward to allow access to the wiring harness.
4. Disconnect the courtesy lamp wiring at the snap connectors on the harness.
5. Remove the two screws securing the lamp lens and withdraw the lens.

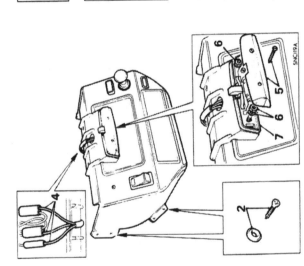

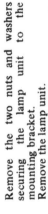

6. Remove the two nuts and washers securing the lamp unit to the mounting bracket.
7. Remove the lamp unit.

Refitting

8. Reverse the procedure in 1 to 7.

SERVICE INTERVAL WARNING LAMP EGR VALVE/CATALYST — U.S.A. only

Remove and refit	86.45.84
Bulb 2 to 3	86.45.85

Removing

1. Disconnect the battery.
2. Remove the eight screws and washers securing the centre console to the body and move the console to give access to the back of the warning lamp.
3. Detach the bulb holder from the warning lamp and remove the bulb.

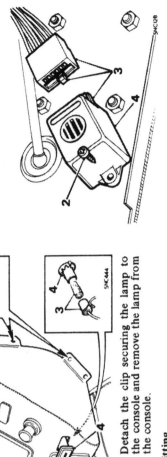

4. Disconnect the wiring plug from the flasher unit.

Refitting

5. Reverse the procedure in 1 to 4.

4. Detach the clip securing the lamp to the console and remove the lamp from the console.

Refitting

5. Reverse the procedure in 1 to 4.

HAZARD WARNING FLASHER UNIT — U.S.A. only
86.55.12

Remove and refit

Removing

1. Disconnect the battery.
2. Remove the eight screws and washers securing the console to the body and move the console to allow access to the flasher unit.
3. Detach the flasher unit from its retaining clip on the console.

SEAT BELT WARNING BUZZER / TIMER MODULE — U.S.A. only
86.57.08

Remove and refit

Removing

1. Disconnect the battery.
2. Remove the screw securing the module to the bulkhead behind the L.H. side of the facia.
3. Depress the retaining lever and withdraw the wiring plug from the multi connector on the module.
4. Remove the warning buzzer/timer module from the car.

Refitting

5. Reverse the procedure in 1 to 4.

86.40.02

ELECTRICAL

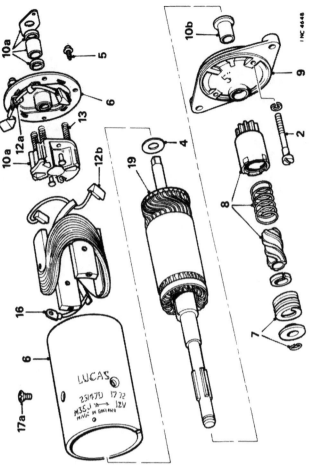

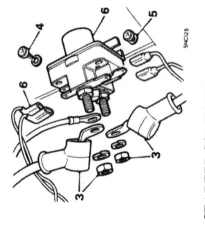

STARTER MOTOR
Remove and refit   86.60.01

Removing
1 Disconnect the battery.
2 Remove the air vent hose.
3 Disconnect the inlet hose from the fuel pump (U.S.A. only).
4 Remove the two nuts and washers securing the fuel pump to the engine (U.S.A. only).
5 Detach the pump from the engine and place aside (U.S.A. only).
6 Remove the nut and washer securing the lead to the starter motor and move the lead aside.
7 Remove the two nuts and washers securing the starter motor assembly to the engine and gearbox housing.
8 Detach the starter motor from the two securing bolts, the shim and the adaptor plate.
9 Remove the starter motor from the car.

Refitting
10 Fit the starter motor with the lead terminal uppermost.
11 Reverse the procedure in 1 to 7, fitting a new fuel pump gasket to U.S.A. cars.

STARTER SOLENOID
Remove and refit   86.60.08

Removing
1 Disconnect the battery.
2 Detach the car heater air intake hose from the heater air intake and place aside.
3 Pull back the rubber covers, remove the securing nuts and washers and detach the leads from the main terminals on the solenoid.
4 Remove the R.H. screw and washer securing the solenoid to the body.
5 Slacken the L.H. screw securing the solenoid to the body using a crosshead screw bit on a flexible lead.
6 Slide out the solenoid and disconnect the L.T. leads from the terminals on the solenoid, noting their positions for correct refitment.

Refitting
7 Reverse the procedure in 1 to 6.

STARTER MOTOR
Overhaul   86.60.13

Dismantling
1 Remove the starter motor, see 86.60.01.
2 Remove the two screws to release the drive-end bracket.
3 Withdraw the drive-end bracket complete with the armature and drive.

4 Remove the thrust washer from the commutator end of the armature.
5 Remove the four screws retaining the commutator end bracket.
6 Detach the bracket from the yoke, disengage the field brushes from the brush holder and remove the bracket.
7 Compress the spring of the inertia drive and remove the retaining ring from the armature shaft.
8 Withdraw the drive assembly from the armature shaft.
9 Withdraw the drive-end bracket from the armature shaft.

Inspection
10 Check for excessive side-play of the armature shaft in the bushes, renewing the bushes if necessary, noting:
  a. To remove the commutator end bracket bush, unrivet the end plate and detach the plate, felt seal, and brush box moulding. Screw a ½ in. tap part-way into the bush and withdraw the bush from the bracket.

  b. Support the drive-end bracket and press out the bush.
  c. Prior to fitting, new bushes must either be immersed in new engine oil for a period of 24 hours, or immersed in new engine oil maintained at a temperature of 100°C (212°F) for two hours, allowing the oil to cool before removing the bush.
  d. Press new bushes into position, using a polished shouldered mandrel the same diameter as the bearing surface of the armature shaft. Do not ream the bushes after fitting.

11 Examine the drive components for wear or damage. Renew as necessary.
12 Check that the brushes move freely in the brush box moulding. Renew brushes that are worn to the dimension given in DATA, noting:
  a. Cut the end bracket brush flexibles from the terminal post. Make a groove in the head of the post sufficiently deep to

accommodate the new brush flexibles. Solder the long and short brush flexibles into the terminal groove.

b. Cut the field winding brush flexibles about a ¼ in (6.4 mm) from the joint of the field winding. Solder the new brush flexibles to the ends of the old brush flexibles. Ensure that the joint is adequately insulated.

13 Using a new brush, check the pressure of each brush spring in turn against the specification given in DATA, renewing the springs if necessary, noting:

a. Extract the old springs using long-nosed pliers.

b. Fully compress the new springs between first finger and thumb.

c. Insert the spring horizontally in the brushbox moulding and finally locate in position.

14 Check the insulation of the brush springs and terminal post by connecting the test equipment (see DATA) between each spring in turn and the commutator end bracket and then between the bracket and the terminal post.

15 Check the field winding continuity, connecting the test equipment (see DATA) between each field brush in turn and the yoke.

16 Remove the rivet securing the field winding connection to the yoke. Ensure that the connection is clear of the yoke and check the field winding insulation, connecting the test equipment (see DATA) between each brush in turn and the yoke.

17 If the field windings are still suspect, prove them by substitution:

a. Slacken the four pole-shoe retaining screws. Remove the screws from one pair of diametrically opposite pole-shoes and remove the pole-shoes from the yoke. Slide the windings from beneath the remaining pole-shoes and withdraw them from the yoke.

b. Loosely fit the new windings and position the pole-shoes and insulation piece between the yoke and the brush connection to the windings. Tighten the pole-shoe screws evenly.

c. Rivet the field winding connection to the yoke.

18 Check the armature shaft. If the shaft is bent or distorted, the armature must be renewed.

19 Examine the commutator brush surface for burrs, pitting and wear. If necessary, skim the commutator in a lathe, ensuring that the finished thickness of the commutator copper is not less than the dimension given in DATA. After skimming, polish the commutator brush surface with a flat surface of very fine glass-paper. Do not undercut the insulation slots.

20. Check the armature insulation, connecting the test equipment (see DATA) between one of the commutator segments and the armature shaft.

21 Check the armature for short-circuited windings, using specialized armature testing (Growler) equipment. In the absence of this equipment a suspect armature should be checked by substitution.

Reassembling

22 Reverse the procedure in 2 to 9.

23 Mount the starter motor on a test bench and check its performance against the specification in DATA.

24 Refit the starter motor, see 86.60.01.

DATA

Armature:

Commutator copper minimum thickness	0.08 in (2.03 mm)
Insulation test equipment	110-volt a.c. supply and 15-watt test lamp
Minimum brush length	⅜ in (10 mm)
Brush spring pressure	28 ozf (0.8 kgf) when a brush protrudes ⅟₁₆ in (1.5 mm) from the brush box moulding

Brush spring and terminal post insulation test equipment	110-volt a.c. supply and 15-watt test lamp

Field windings:

Continuity test equipment	12-volt d.c. supply and 12-watt test lamp
Insulation test equipment	110-watt a.c. supply and 15-watt test lamp

Starter motor performance (obtained with a 12-volt 43Ah (20-hour rate) battery in a 70 per cent charged condition at 20°C (68°F):

Lock torque	7 lbf ft (0.97 kgf m) with 350 to 375 amp
Torque at 1,000 rev/min	4.4 lbf ft (0.64 kgf m) with 260 to 275 amp
Light running current	65 amp at 8,000 to 10,000 rev/min

86.60.01

5 Note the location, quantity and thickness of the packing washers between the column upper fixing flanges and the body bracket.

6 Remove the three nuts bolts and washers securing the column upper fixing to the body bracket and collect the packing washers.
CAUTION: If the packing washers are mislaid or their fitting positions are not recorded, the steering column must be aligned on refitting, see 57.35.04.

7 Pull the steering column back sufficiently for the switch cowl to clear the fascia.

8 Remove the four screws securing the L.H. and R.H. cowls to the column.

9 Remove the L.H. and R.H. cowls.

10 Remove the two screws to detach the windscreen wiper/washer switch from the bracket on the column.

11 Disconnect the wiring plug and remove the switch assembly from the car.

12 Remove the two screws securing the direction indicator/headlight switch to the bracket on the column.

13 Disconnect the lead from the horn slip ring terminal.

14 Disconnect the wiring plug and remove the switch assembly from the car.

15 Remove the screw securing the ignition/starter switch to the steering lock assembly.

16 Disconnect the warning buzzer lead from the terminal on the steering lock.

17 Disconnect the wiring plug and remove the switch assembly from the car.

Refitting

18 Reverse the procedure as necessary in 8 to 17.

19 Refit the column assembly, see 11 to 16, 57.40.01.

20 Reconnect the battery.

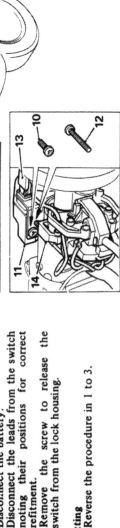

IGNITION/STARTER/STEERING LOCK SWITCH — U.S.A. SPECIFICATION

Remove and refit	86.65.03
1 to 9, 15 to 19	
Windscreen wiper/washer switch	86.65.41
1 to 11, 18, 19	
Direction indicator/headlight switch	86.65.55
1 to 9, 12 to 14, 18, 19	

Removing

1 Disconnect the battery.

2 Remove the car heater air intake hose.

3 Remove the steering column pinion pinch-bolt and nut.

4 Remove the three bolts and washers securing the toe-plate fixing ring to the steering column.

ELECTRICAL

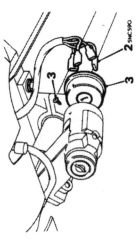

IGNITION/STARTER/STEERING LOCK SWITCH — Right-hand steer

Remove and refit   86.65.03

Removing

1 Disconnect the battery.

2 Disconnect the leads from the switch noting their positions for correct refitment.

3 Remove the screw to release the switch from the lock housing.

Refitting

4 Reverse the procedure in 1 to 3.

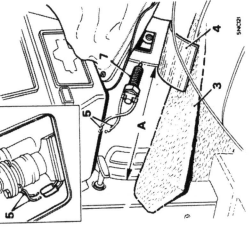

SNC 643

HAND BRAKE WARNING SWITCH – U.S.A. only   86.65.45

Remove and refit

Removing

1 Disconnect the battery.
2 Remove the L.H. front seat, see 76.70.01.
3 Apply the handbrake.
4 Disconnect the switch wiring.
5 Unscrew the lock nut and remove the switch.

Refitting

6 Reverse the procedure in 1 to 5.
7 Reconnect the battery.
8 Adjust the switch, see 86.65.46.
9 Refit the L.H. front seat, see 76.70.01.

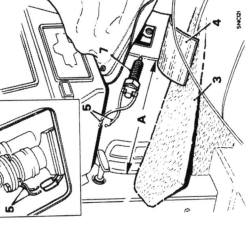

SNC21

REVERSE LAMP SWITCH   86.65.20

Remove and refit

Removing

1 Disconnect the battery.
2 Remove the carpet from the front of the gearbox tunnel.
3 Peel back the felt from the top half of the left hand side of the gearbox tunnel.
4 Carefully peel back a 2½ in wide by 3½ in long strip of sound insulation material from the top half of the left hand side of the gearbox tunnel at a point 8½ in ('A') from the front of the tunnel.
5 Disconnect the reverse lamp switch cables from the wiring harness at the connectors on the harness.
6 Withdraw the switch cables through the aperture in the gearbox tunnel.
7 Unscrew the reverse lamp switch, complete with spacing washer (if fitted), from the gearbox.

Refitting

8 Reverse the procedure in 1 to 7.

HAND BRAKE WARNING SWITCH – U.S.A. only   86.65.46

Check and adjust

1 Switch on the ignition.
2 Position the handbrake in the off position.
3 Slacken the locknuts and adjust the switch until the warning light goes out.
4 Tighten the locknuts.
5 Apply the handbrake and check that the warning light operates.
6 Switch off the ignition.

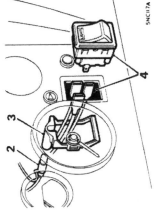

SNC17A

LIGHTING SWITCH – U.S.A. only   86.65.10

Remove and refit

Removing

1 Disconnect the battery.
2 Remove the bulb from the switch retainer.
3 Remove the retainer from the switch.
4 Withdraw the switch and disconnect the leads, noting their positions for correct refitment.

Refitting

5 Reverse the procedure in 1 to 4.

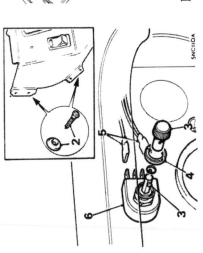

SNC10A

RHEOSTAT SWITCH – U.S.A. only   86.65.07

Remove and refit

Removing

1 Disconnect the battery.
2 Remove the eight screws and washers securing the console to the body and move the console aside.
3 Depress the retaining plunger in the switch knob and withdraw the knob.
4 Remove the switch retainer using 18G 671.
5 Disconnect the wiring from the switch.
6 Remove the switch from the fascia.

Refitting

7 Reverse the procedure in 1 to 6.

86.65.03

BRAKE WARNING LAMP — 1977 and later U.S.A. [86.65.45]

Remove and refit

Removing
1. Disconnect the battery.
2. Remove the car heater air intake hose.
3. Disconnect the oil pressure gauge pipe from the 'T' piece on the wheel arch.
4. Release the oil pressure gauge pipe clips from the pedal box assembly.
5. Remove the screws to release the clips securing the capillary tube to the bulkhead.
6. Carefully feed the slack length of capillary tube in the engine compartment through the grommet in the bulkhead.
7. Remove the knurled nuts and the bridge piece from behind the oil pressure and water temperature gauge.
8. Withdraw the gauge from the fascia, detach the bulb holder and remove the gauge aside.
9. Remove the retaining clip from the brake warning lamp.
10. Withdraw the lamp from the fascia.
11. Disconnect the leads from the lamp.

Refitting
12. Reverse the procedure in 1 to 11.

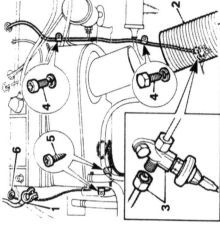
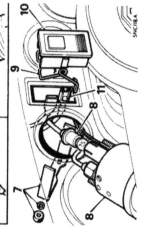

7. Remove the knurled nuts and the bridge piece from behind the oil pressure and water temperature gauge.
8. Withdraw the gauge from the fascia, detach the bulb holder and remove the gauge aside.
9. Remove the retaining switch from the brake warning test switch.
10. Withdraw the switch from the fascia.
11. Disconnect the leads from the switch noting their positions for correct refitment.

Refitting
12. Reverse the procedure in 1 to 11.

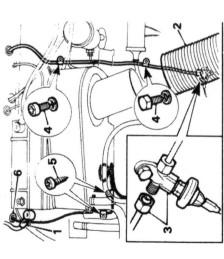

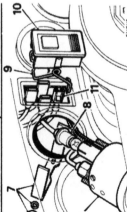

BRAKE WARNING SWITCH — 1975-1976 U.S.A. 86.65.49

Remove and refit

Removing
1. Disconnect the battery.
2. Remove the car heater air intake hose.
3. Disconnect the oil pressure gauge pipe from the 'T' piece on the wheel arch.
4. Release the oil pressure gauge pipe clips from the pedal box assembly.
5. Remove the screws to release the clips securing the capillary tube to the bulkhead.
6. Carefully feed the slack length of capillary tube in the engine compartment through the grommet in the bulkhead.

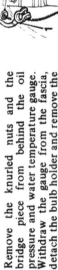

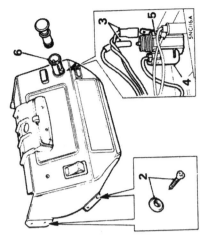

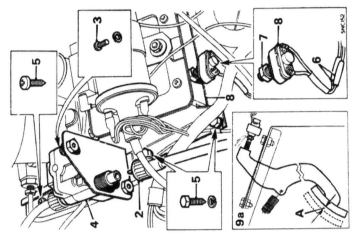

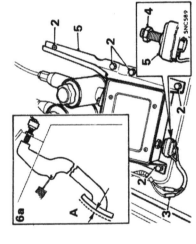

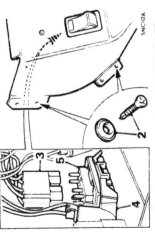

HAZARD WARNING SWITCH — U.S.A. only

Remove and refit　　86.65.50

Service tool: 18G 1145

Removing

1　Disconnect the battery.
2　Remove the eight screws and washers securing the console to the body and move the console to allow access to the warning switch.
3　Disconnect the wiring plug from the warning switch.
4　Detach the bulb holder complete with bulb and place aside.
5　Using 18G 1145/2, remove the switch from the console.

Refitting

6　Reverse the procedure in 1 to 5.

STOP LIGHT SWITCH — U.K. Specification

Remove and refit　　86.65.51

Removing

1　Disconnect the battery.
2　Slacken the eight set screws securing the pedal box to the body.
3　Disconnect the stop light switch wiring at the connectors on the harness.
4　Unscrew the stop light switch lock nut.
5　Lift the pedal box assembly and unscrew the switch from the pedal box.

Refitting

6　Reverse the procedure in 1 to 5 noting:
　a　Screw in the stop light switch until there is a free movement of ⅛ in ('A') on the brake pedal.
　b　Recheck this measurement after tightening the pedal box securing screws.

STOP LIGHT SWITCH — U.S.A. Specification

Remove and refit　　86.65.51

Removing

1　Disconnect the battery.
2　Disconnect the gearbox drive cable from the service interval counter (if fitted).
3　Remove the two screws securing the service interval counter to the mounting bracket (if fitted).
4　Detach the counter if fitted, and place aside.
5　Slacken the eight set screws securing the pedal box to the body.
6　Disconnect the stop light switch wiring at the connectors on the harness.
7　Unscrew the stop light switch lock nut.
8　Lift the pedal box assembly and unscrew the switch from the pedal box.

Refitting

9　Reverse the procedure in 1 to 8 noting:
　a　Screw in the stop light switch until there is a free movement of ⅛ in ('A') on the brake pedal.
　b　Recheck this measurement after tightening the pedal box securing screws.

CIGAR LIGHTER — U.S.A. only

Remove and refit　　86.65.60

Removing

1　Disconnect the battery.
2　Remove the eight screws and washers securing the console to the body and move the console to allow access to the cigar lighter body.
3　Disconnect the wiring from the cigar lighter.
4　Detach the bulb holder from the cigar lighter body.
5　Unscrew the outer shell from the cigar lighter body.
6　Withdraw the cigar lighter body from the front of the console.

Refitting

7　Reverse the procedure in 1 to 6.

MAIN WIRING HARNESS — Right-hand steer only

Remove and refit　　86.70.07

Removing

1　Disconnect the battery.
2　Disconnect the wiring harness from the R.H. headlamp, sidelamp and flasher lamp cables at the connectors in the front corner of the engine compartment.

225

86.65.45

ELECTRICAL

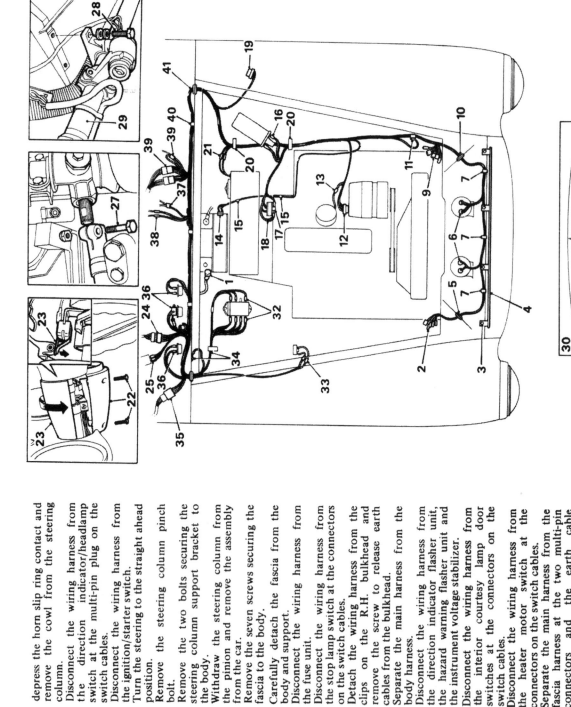

SNB043

3 Remove the six screws and washers securing the radiator grille to the body.

4 Remove the radiator grille.

5 Withdraw the wiring harness from the engine compartment through the front valance.

6 Disconnect the wiring harness from the horns.

7 Detach the wiring harness from the clips on the bonnet lock platform.

8 Remove the heater air intake hose.

9 Disconnect the wiring harness from the L.H. headlamp, sidelamp and flasher lamp cables at the connectors in the front corner of the engine compartment.

10 Withdraw the wiring harness through the front valance into the engine compartment.

11 Remove the screw to release the wiring harness retaining clip and the earth cable from the L.H. wing panel.

12 Disconnect the wiring harness from the alternator.

13 Disconnect the wiring harness from the distributor at the connector on the distributor low-tension cable.

14 Disconnect the wiring harness at the reverse lamp switch at the connector in the gearbox tunnel.

15 Detach the wiring harness from the clips in the gearbox tunnel.

16 Disconnect the wiring harness from the coil terminals.

17 Remove the nut, washer and battery cable to release the wiring harness from the main terminal on the starter solenoid.

18 Disconnect the wiring harness from the terminal blades on the starter solenoid.

19 Disconnect the wiring harness from the windscreen wiper motor.

20 Detach the wiring harness from the clips on the left hand side of the bulkhead.

21 Disconnect the wiring harness from the heater fan motor at the connectors on the motor cables.

22 Remove the four screws securing the cowls to the steering column and detach the lower cowl.

23 Rotate the upper cowl anti-clockwise,

depress the horn slip ring contact and remove the cowl from the steering column.

24 Disconnect the wiring harness from the direction indicator/headlamp switch at the multi-pin plug on the switch cables.

25 Disconnect the wiring harness from the ignition/starter switch.

26 Turn the steering to the straight ahead position.

27 Remove the steering column pinch bolt.

28 Remove the two bolts securing the steering column support bracket to the body.

29 Withdraw the steering column from the pinion and remove the assembly from the car.

30 Remove the seven screws securing the fascia to the body.

31 Carefully detach the fascia from the body and support.

32 Disconnect the wiring harness from the fuse unit.

33 Disconnect the wiring harness from the stop lamp switch at the connectors on the switch cables.

34 Detach the wiring harness from the clips on the R.H. bulkhead and remove the screw to release earth cables from the bulkhead.

35 Separate the main harness from the body harness.

36 Disconnect the wiring harness from the direction indicator flasher unit, the hazard warning flasher unit and the instrument voltage stabilizer.

37 Disconnect the wiring harness from the interior courtesy lamp door switches at the connectors on the switch cables.

38 Disconnect the wiring harness from the heater motor switch at the connectors on the switch cables.

39 Separate the main harness from the fascia harness at the two multi-pin connectors and the earth cable connector.

40 Detach the harness from the clips on the bulkhead.

41 Withdraw the wiring harness from the engine compartment and then remove the harness from the car.

Refitting

42 Reverse the procedure in 1 to 41.

226

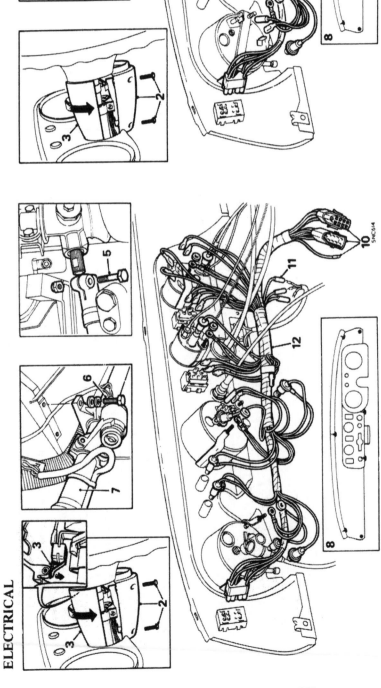

Cars with electric tachometers

Cars with cable-driven tachometers

FASCIA WIRING HARNESS —
Right-hand steer only

Remove and refit   86.70.10

Removing

1   Disconnect the battery.
2   Remove the four screws securing the cowls to the steering-column and detach the lower cowl.
3   Rotate the upper cowl anti-clockwise, depress the horn slip ring contact and remove the cowl from the steering-column.
4   Turn the steering to the straight ahead position.
5   Remove the steering-column pinch bolt.
6   Remove the two bolts securing the steering-column support bracket to the body.

7   Withdraw the steering-column from the pinion and support the column assembly in the car.
8   Remove the seven screws securing the fascia to the body.
9   Carefully detach the fascia from the body and support.
10   Separate the fascia harness from the main harness at the two multi connectors and the earth cable connector.
11   Disconnect the wiring harness from the courtesy lamp at the connectors on the lamp leads.
12   Disconnect the wiring harness from the instruments, warning lamps and switches at the rear of the fascia.
13   Remove the wiring harness from the car.

Refitting

14   Reverse the procedure in 1 to 13.

86.70.10

MAIN WIRING HARNESS
— Left-hand steer

Remove and refit   86.70.07

Removing

1 Disconnect the battery.
2 Disconnect the wiring harness from the R.H. headlamp, sidelamp, flasher lamp and side-marker lamp cables at the connectors in the front of the R.H. corner of the engine compartment.
3 Remove the six screws and washers securing the radiator grille to the body and remove the grille.
4 Disconnect the wiring harness from the horns.
5 Detach the wiring harness from the clips on the bonnet platform.
6 Remove the heater air intake hose.
7 Disconnect the wiring from the L.H. headlamp, sidelamp, flasher lamp and side-marker lamp cables at the connectors in the front of the L.H. corner of the engine compartment.
8 Withdraw the wiring harness through the front valance into the engine compartment.
9 Remove the screw to release the wiring harness retaining clip and the earth cable from the L.H. wing panel.
10 Disconnect the wiring harness from the alternator.
11 Disconnect the wiring harness from the distributor at the connector on the distributor cables.
12 Disconnect the wiring harness from the reverse lamp switch at the connector in the gearbox tunnel.
13 Detach the wiring harness from the clips in the gearbox tunnel.
14 Disconnect the wiring harness from the brake pressure failure switch.
15 Disconnect the wiring from the coil terminals and the ballast resistor terminals.
16 Disconnect the wiring from the stop light switch.
17 Remove the nut, washer and battery cable to release the wiring harness from the main terminal on the starter solenoid.

18 Disconnect the wiring harness from the terminal blades on the starter solenoid.
19 Disconnect the wiring harness from the windscreen wiper motor.
20 Detach the harness from the clips on the left-hand side of the bulkhead.
21 Disconnect the wiring harness from the heater fan motor at the connectors on the motor cables.
22 Disconnect the wiring harness from the windscreen washer pump.
23 Disconnect the wiring harness from the fuse unit.
24 Disconnect the wiring harness from the battery cut-off relay.
25 Detach the wiring harness from the clips on the R.H. side of the bulkhead and remove the screw to release the earth cables from the bulkhead.
26 Remove the three screws securing the fascia support plates to the bulkhead.
27 Release and remove the gearbox tunnel carpet, remove the screws retaining the centre console and move the console aside (towards the steering-column).
28 Disconnect the wiring harness from the cigar lighter, and at the connection on the illumination lead.
29 Disconnect the wiring harness from the courtesy lamp connections.
30 Disconnect the radio wiring from the harness.
31 Disconnect the wiring harness from the hazard warning flasher unit, leaving the flasher unit in its clip on the console.
32 Disconnect the plug and detach the bulb from the hazard warning switch.
33 Detach the bulb from the hazard warning light.
34 Remove the five screws and washers to release the L.H. scuttle trim pad from the body.
35 Remove the front screw securing the sill trim pad.
36 Remove the tape securing the seat switch and the handbrake switch harness to the body L.H. scuttle panel.
37 Carefully ease the sill trim pad away from the sill to release the wiring harness.
38 Fold back the front of the carpet

ELECTRICAL

under the L.H. seat and release the harness from the clips on the floor.

39 Disconnect the wiring harness from the handbrake switch at the connectors on the switch cable.

40 Disconnect the wiring harness from the seat switch from the connector under the R.H. seat.

41 Pull the harness from under the carpet and then away from the scuttle panel.

42 Disconnect the harness connector from the buzzer module.

43 Separate the three multi-pin connectors feeding the windscreen wiper/washer switch, direction indicator/flasher switch, and the ignition switch.

44 Disconnect the wiring harness from the audible warning switch connections.

45 Detach the rubber strap securing the wiring harness to the windscreen wiper rack tube.

46 Disconnect the wiring harness from the interior courtesy lamp door switches at the connector on the switch cable.

47 Separate the main wiring harness from the fascia harness at the two multi-pin connectors.

48 Disconnect the wiring harness from the voltage stabilizer.

49 Disconnect the wiring harness from the direction indicator flasher unit.

50 Separate the main wiring harness from the body harness at the two multi-pin connectors.

51 Detach the wiring harness from the clips on the bulkhead.

52 Withdraw the end of the wiring harness from the engine compartment into the passenger compartment through the aperture on the R.H. side of the bulkhead.

53 Carefully feed and withdraw the wiring harness from behind the fascia towards the steering-column.

54 Withdraw the wiring harness from the engine compartment through the aperture on the L.H. side of the bulkhead into the passenger compartment and then remove the wiring harness from the car.

Refitting
55 Reverse the procedure in 1 to 54.

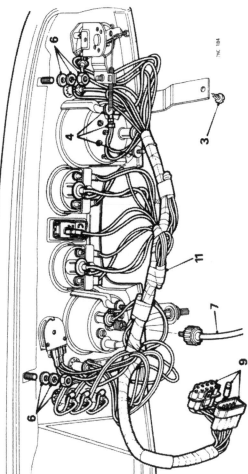

DSC 184

FASCIA WIRING HARNESS
— Left-hand steer

Remove and refit   86.70.10

1 Disconnect the battery.

2 Remove the screws retaining the centre console and move the console aside (towards the steering-column).

3 Remove the three screws securing the fascia support plates to the bulkhead.

4 Remove the two knurled nuts, washers, earth wires and clamps from the tachometer.

5 Withdraw the tachometer from the fascia and disconnect the wires and illumination bulb.

6 Remove the four nuts and washers securing the top of the fascia to the body.

7 Disconnect the speedometer cable from the speedometer.

8 Withdraw the fascia from the body and support.

9 Separate the fascia harness from the main harness at the two multi-connectors and single snap connector.

10 Disconnect the wiring harness from the instruments, warning lamps and switches at the rear of the fascia.

11 Remove the fascia wiring harness from the car.

Refitting
12 Reverse the procedure in 1 to 11.

BODY WIRING HARNESS
— Left-hand steer

Remove and refit   86.70.12

Removing
1 Disconnect the battery.

2 Remove the nine screws to release the cubby box from beneath the fascia.

3 Remove the three screws and washers to release the R.H. scuttle trim pad from the body, noting their positions as the cubby box screws also retain the trim pad.

4 Remove the R.H. seat, see 76.70.01, and remove the four screws and washers to release the R.H. sill trim pad from the body.

5 Separate the body harness from the main harness at the multi-connectors under the fascia.

6 Detach the wiring harness from the clips in the front of the passenger compartment.

7 Disconnect the wiring harness from the L.H. side-marker lamp and tail lamp assembly at the connectors on the lamp cables.

8 Remove the nut and washer to release the clip securing the wiring harness to the L.H. tail lamp assembly.

9 Disconnect the wiring harness from the number-plate lamps at the two connectors on the lamp cables.

10 Disconnect the wiring harness from the reverse lamps.

11 Remove the nut and washer to release the earth cable from the boot lid striker reinforcement bracket.

12 Disconnect the wiring harness from the R.H. side-marker lamp and tail lamp assembly at the connectors on the lamp cables.

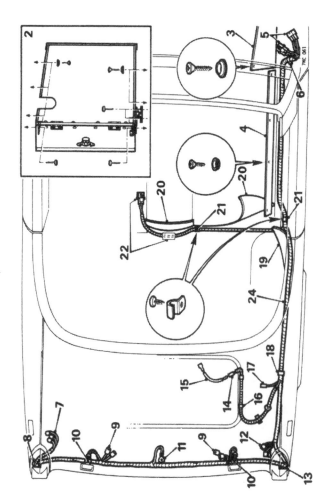

11 Disconnect the wiring harness from the R.H. tail lamp assembly at the connectors on the lamp cables.

12 Remove the nut and washer to release the clip securing the wiring harness to the R.H. tail lamp assembly.

13 Disconnect the wiring harness from the petrol gauge tank unit at the connector on the tank unit cable.

14 Detach the harness from the clips on the petrol tank and the body and pull the harness into the luggage compartment.

15 Disconnect the wiring harness from the luggage compartment lamp switch at the connector on the switch cable.

16 Detach the wiring harness from the clip on the R.H. rear wing.

17 Attach securely a draw cable to the wiring harness in the passenger compartment.

18 Carefully detach the lower portion of the R.H. rear quarter trim pad and remove the harness retaining clip.

19 Withdraw the wiring harness from the passenger compartment into the luggage compartment.

20 Detach the wiring harness from the draw cable, leaving the draw cable in position in the body panelling.

Refitting

21 Reverse the procedure in 1 to 20.

BODY WIRING HARNESS – Right-hand steer only   86.70.12
Remove and refit

Removing

1 Disconnect the battery.

2 Remove the five screws and washers to release the R.H. scuttle trim pad from the body.

3 Remove the R.H. seat, see 76.70.01 and remove the four screws and washers to release the R.H. sill trim pad from the body.

4 Separate the body harness from the main harness at the multi-connector under the fascia.

5 Detach the wiring harness from the clips in the front of the passenger compartment.

6 Disconnect the wiring harness from the L.H. tail lamp assembly at the connectors on the lamp cables.

7 Remove the nut and washer to release the clip securing the wiring harness to the L.H. tail lamp assembly.

8 Disconnect the wiring harness from the number plate lamps at the connectors on the lamp cables.

9 Disconnect the wiring harness from the reverse lamps.

10 Remove the nut and washer to release the earth cable from the boot lid striker reinforcement bracket.

21 Remove the clips securing the wiring harness to the body in the rear of the passenger compartment.

22 Detach the tape securing the harness to the top of the propeller shaft tunnel and disconnect the wiring harness from the driver's seat belt at the connector on the seat belt cable.

23 Attach securely a draw cable to the wiring harness in the passenger compartment.

24 Withdraw the wiring harness from the passenger compartment into the luggage compartment.

25 Detach the wiring harness from the draw cable, leaving the draw cable in position in the body panelling.

Refitting

26 Reverse the procedure in 1 to 25.

13 Remove the nut and washer to release the clip securing the wiring harness to the R.H. tail lamp assembly.

14 Disconnect the wiring harness from the petrol gauge tank unit at the connector on the tank unit cable.

15 Disconnect the cable from the petrol gauge tank unit.

16 Detach the harness from the clips on the petrol tank and the body and pull the harness into the luggage compartment.

17 Disconnect the wiring harness from the luggage compartment lamp switch at the connector on the switch cable.

18 Detach the wiring harness from the clip on the R.H. rear wing.

19 Carefully detach the lower portion of the R.H. rear quarter trim pad.

20 Carefully turn back the rear carpet, and the carpet at the rear of the propeller shaft tunnel.

INSTRUMENTS — RIGHT-HAND STEER
(Cars with cable-driven tachometers)

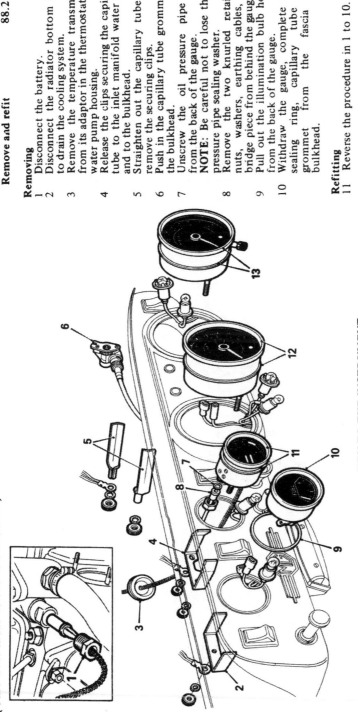

SPEEDOMETER

Remove and refit 88.30.01

Removing

1 Disconnect the battery.
2 Unscrew the angle drive from the back of the speedometer.
3 Pull out the main beam and illumination bulb holders from the back of the speedometer.
4 Remove the two knurled retaining nuts, washers, earthing cables, and clamps from behind the speedometer.
5 Hold the direction indicator switch lever down and towards the steering wheel, and withdraw the speedometer complete with sealing ring from the fascia.

Refitting

6 Reverse the procedure in 1 to 5.

TACHOMETER

Remove and refit 88.30.21

Removing

1 Disconnect the battery.
2 Pull out the ignition and illumination bulb holders from the back of the tachometer.
3 Disconnect the cables from the back of the tachometer.
4 Remove the two knurled retaining nuts, washers, earthing cables, and clamps from behind the tachometer.
5 Withdraw the tachometer and sealing ring from the fascia.

Refitting

6 Reverse the procedure in 1 to 5.

OIL PRESSURE AND WATER TEMPERATURE GAUGE

Remove and refit 88.25.11

Removing

1 Disconnect the battery.
2 Disconnect the radiator bottom hose to drain the cooling system.
3 Remove the temperature transmitter from its adaptor in the thermostat and water pump housing.
4 Release the clips securing the capillary tube to the inlet manifold water pipe and to the bulkhead.
5 Straighten out the capillary tube and remove the securing clips.
6 Push in the capillary tube grommet in the bulkhead.
7 Unscrew the oil pressure pipe nut from the back of the gauge. NOTE: Be careful not to lose the oil pressure pipe sealing washer.
8 Remove the two knurled retaining nuts, washers, earthing cables, and bridge piece from behind the gauge.
9 Pull out the illumination bulb holder from the back of the gauge.
10 Withdraw the gauge, complete with sealing ring, capillary tube and grommet from the fascia and bulkhead.

Refitting

11 Reverse the procedure in 1 to 10.

FUEL GAUGE

Remove and refit 88.25.26

Removing

1 Disconnect the battery.
2 Pull out the illumination bulb holder from the back of the fuel gauge.
3 Disconnect the cables from the back of the fuel gauge.
4 Remove the knurled retaining nut, washer, earthing cables, and bridge piece from behind the fuel gauge.
5 Withdraw the fuel gauge and sealing ring from the fascia.

Refitting

6 Reverse the procedure in 1 to 5.

KEY TO THE INSTRUMENT COMPONENTS

1 Temperature transmitter adaptor
2 Fuel gauge bridge piece
3 Capillary tube grommet
4 Oil pressure and water temperature gauge bridge piece
5 Tachometer and speedometer clamps
6 Speedometer angle drive
7 Sealing washer for oil pressure pipe
8 Oil pressure pipe
9 Sealing ring for fuel gauge
10 Fuel gauge
11 Oil pressure and water temperature gauge
12 Tachometer and sealing washer
13 Speedometer and sealing washer

INSTRUMENTS — LEFT-HAND STEER
(Cars with cable-driven tachometers)

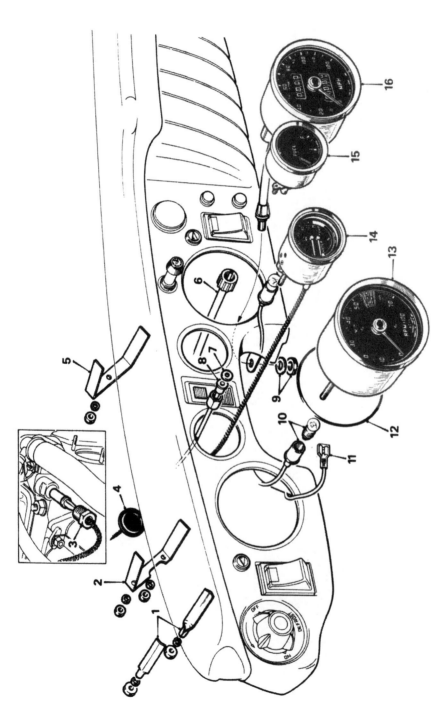

KEY TO THE INSTRUMENT COMPONENTS

1 Tachometer and speedometer clamps.
2 Oil pressure and water temperature gauge bridge piece.
3 Temperature transmitter adaptor.
4 Grommet.
5 Fuel gauge bridge piece.
6 Speedometer cable.
7 Sealing washer for oil pressure pipe.
8 Oil pressure pipe.
9 Knurled nut and flat washer securing the speedometer remote control.
10 Bulb and bulb holder.
11 Wiring.
12 Sealing ring.
13 Tachometer.
14 Oil pressure and water temperature gauge.
15 Fuel gauge.
16 Speedometer.

232

INSTRUMENTS – LEFT-HAND STEER
(Cars with cable-driven tachometers)

OIL PRESSURE AND WATER
TEMPERATURE GAUGE   88.25.11

Remove and refit

Removing
1 Disconnect the battery.
2 Disconnect the radiator bottom hose to drain the cooling system.
3 Remove the temperature transmitter from its adaptor in the thermostat and water pump housing.
4 Release the capillary tube from the clips on the rocker cover.
5 Remove the clips securing the capillary tube to the bulkhead.
6 Disconnect the oil pressure pipe from the oil switch connector.
7 Release the oil pressure gauge pipe clips from the pedal box.
8 Release and remove the gearbox tunnel carpet, remove the screws retaining the centre console and move the console back and aside (towards the steering-column).
9 Remove the two knurled retaining nuts, washers, and the bridge piece from behind the gauge.
10 Thread the oil gauge pipe and its grommet through the fascia sufficient to partially withdraw the gauge from the fascia and unscrew the oil pipe nut.

   NOTE: Be careful not to lose the oil pressure pipe sealing washer.
11 Pull the capillary tube and its grommet into the car.
12 Remove the gauge, complete with capillary tube from the fascia.

Refitting
13 Reverse the procedure in 1 to 12.

FUEL GAUGE   88.25.26

Remove and refit

Removing
1 Disconnect the battery.
2 Disconnect the speedometer cable from the speedometer.
3 Release and remove the gearbox tunnel carpet, remove the screws retaining the centre console, and move the console back and aside (towards the steering-column).
4 Remove the two knurled retaining nuts, washers, and clamps from behind the speedometer.
5 Remove the knurled nut retaining the trip remote control in its bracket.
6 Withdraw the speedometer from the fascia and pull out the bulb holder.
7 Remove the knurled retaining nut, washer, and bridge piece from behind the fuel gauge.
8 Withdraw the fuel gauge from the fascia, pull out the bulb holder and disconnect the cables.

Refitting
9 Reverse the procedure in 1 to 8.

SPEEDOMETER   88.30.01

Remove and refit

Removing
1 Disconnect the battery.
2 Disconnect the speedometer cable from the speedometer.
3 Release and remove the gearbox tunnel carpet, remove the screws retaining the centre console, and move the centre console back and aside (towards the steering-column).
4 Remove the two knurled retaining nuts, washers, and clamps from behind the speedometer.
5 Remove the knurled nut retaining the trip remote control in its bracket.
6 Withdraw the speedometer from the fascia and pull out the bulb holder.

Refitting
7 Reverse the procedure in 1 to 6.

TACHOMETER   88.30.21

Remove and refit

Removing
1 Disconnect the battery.
2 Remove the two knurled retaining nuts, the washers, the earthing cables, and the clamps from behind the tachometer.
3 Withdraw the tachometer from the fascia and disconnect the wiring.

Refitting
4 Reverse the procedure in 1 to 3.

INSTRUMENTS (All cars with electric tachometers)

COOLANT TEMPERATURE GAUGE – USA and Canada

Remove and refit   88.25.14

Removing
1 Disconnect the battery.
2 Release and remove the gearbox tunnel carpet, remove the screws retaining the centre console and move the console back and aside (towards the steering-column).
3 Remove the knurled retaining nut, washer, and the bridge piece from behind the gauge.
4 Disconnect the **wires** from the back of the gauge.
5 Pull out the illumination bulb holder from the back of the gauge.
6 Remove the gauge from the fascia.

Refitting
7 Reverse the procedure in 1 to 6.

7NC 089A

COOLANT TEMPERATURE GAUGE – UK

Remove and refit   88.25.11

Removing
1 Disconnect the battery.
2 Remove the knurled retaining nut, washer, earthing cables, and bridge piece from behind the gauge.
3 Pull out the illumination bulb holder from the back of the gauge.
4 Disconnect the wires from the back of the gauge.
5 Withdraw the gauge, complete with sealing ring from the fascia.

Refitting
6 Reverse the procedure in 1 to 5.

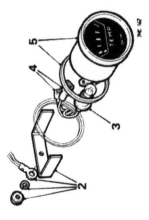

7NC 147

FUEL GAUGE – USA and Canada

Remove and refit   88.25.26

Removing
1 Disconnect the battery.
2 Disconnect the speedometer cable from the speedometer.
3 Release and remove the gearbox tunnel carpet, remove the screws retaining the centre console, and move the console back and aside (towards the steering-column).
4 Remove the two knurled retaining nuts, washers, and clamps from behind the speedometer.
5 Remove the knurled nut retaining the trip remote control in its bracket.
6 Withdraw the speedometer from the fascia and pull out the bulb holder.
7 Remove the knurled retaining nut, washer, and bridge piece from behind the fuel gauge.
8 Withdraw the fuel gauge from the fascia, pull out the bulb holder and disconnect the cables.

Refitting
9 Reverse the procedure in 1 to 8.

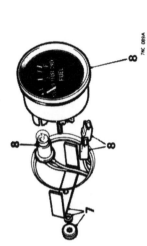

7NC 089A

FUEL GAUGE – UK

Remove and refit   88.25.26

Removing
1 Disconnect the battery.
2 Pull out the illumination bulb holder from the back of the fuel gauge.
3 Disconnect the cables from the back of the fuel gauge.
4 Remove the knurled retaining nut, washer, earthing cables, and bridge piece from behind the fuel gauge.
5 Withdraw the fuel gauge and sealing ring from the fascia.

Refitting
6 Reverse the procedure in 1 to 5.

7NC 148

INSTRUMENTS (All cars with electric tachometers)

SPEEDOMETER – USA and Canada   88.30.01

Remove and refit

Removing
1 Disconnect the battery.
2 Disconnect the speedometer cable from the speedometer.

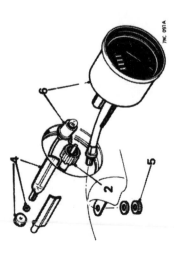

3 Release and remove the gearbox tunnel carpet, remove the screws retaining the centre console, and move the centre console back and aside (towards the steering-column).
4 Remove the two knurled retaining nuts, washers, and clamps from behind the speedometer.
5 Remove the knurled nut retaining the trip remote control in its bracket.
6 Withdraw the speedometer from the fascia and pull out the bulb holder.

Refitting
7 Reverse the procedure in 1 to 6.

SPEEDOMETER – UK   88.30.01

Remove and refit

Removing
1 Disconnect the battery.
2 Press in the clip and disconnect the speedometer cable from the speedometer.
3 Pull out the illumination bulb holders from the back of the speedometer.

4 Disconnect the wires from the voltage stabilizer.
5 Remove the knurled nut retaining the trip remote control in its bracket.
6 Remove the two knurled retaining nuts, washers, earthing cables, and clamps from behind the speedometer.
7 Hold the direction indicator switch lever down and towards the steering wheel, and withdraw the speedometer complete with sealing ring from the fascia.

Refitting
8 Reverse the procedure in 1 to 7.

TACHOMETER – USA and Canada   88.30.21

Remove and refit

Removing
1 Disconnect the battery.
2 Remove the two knurled retaining nuts, the washers, the earthing cables, and the clamps from behind the tachometer.

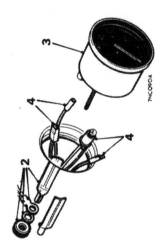

3 Withdraw the tachometer from the fascia.
4 Disconnect the wires and bulb holder from the tachometer.

Refitting
5 Reverse the procedure in 1 to 4.

TACHOMETER – UK   88.30.21

Remove and refit

Removing
1 Disconnect the battery.
2 Pull out the illumination bulb holder from the back of the tachometer.

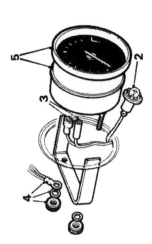

3 Disconnect the cables from the back of the tachometer.
4 Remove the two knurled retaining nuts, washers, earthing cables, and clamps from behind the tachometer.
5 Withdraw the tachometer and sealing ring from the fascia.

Refitting
6 Reverse the procedure in 1 to 5.

SERVICE TOOLS

All service tools mentioned in this Manual must be obtained direct from the tool manufacturers:

Messrs V L Churchill & Co Ltd
P O Box No 3
London Road
Daventry
Northants NN11 4NF
England

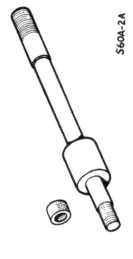

S60A-2A

S60A–2A   Valve Guide Remover Replacer Adaptor Set

MO832

18G 134   Bearings and Oil Seal Replacer — Basic Tool

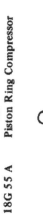

MI295

18G 134 BM   Oil Seal Replacer

18G 134 DR   Gearbox Rear Oil Seal Replacer Adaptor

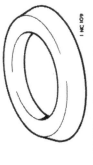

INC 109

18G 47 CZ   Bearing Remover — Basic Tool Adaptor Ring

178K

18G 47 M   Differential Bearing Remover Adaptor

MO804

18G 55 A   Piston Ring Compressor

60A

60A   Valve Guide Remover Replacer

18G 47 BF   Adaptor Set

INC 101

18G 47 BP   Adaptor Set — Remover Replacer Mainshaft Bearing and Speedometer Gear

MO786

18G 47 C   Bearing Remover — Basic Tool

MO827

18G 2   Pulley — Remover Basic Tool

18G 45   Valve Spring Compressor

99–1

18G 284 AAA First Motion Shaft Remover Adaptor

1NCO96

18G 284 AW Adaptor

1NCO77

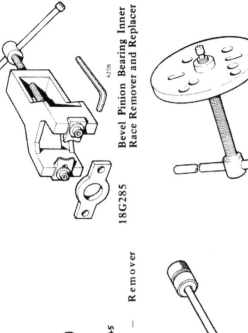

18G285 Bevel Pinion Bearing Inner Race Remover and Replacer

4228

Hub Remover — Basic Tool

18G 304

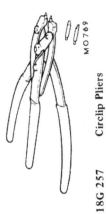

MO769

18G 257 Circlip Pliers

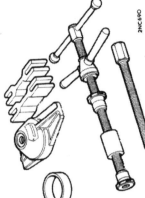

2NC690

18G 264 Basic Tool

A 1045

18G 264 AB Adaptor — Remover Replacer

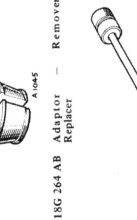

1NC112

18G 284 Impulse Extractor — Basic Tool

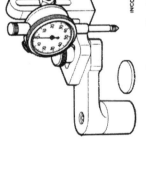

1NCO16

18G 191 Bevel Pinion Setting Gauge

4344

18G 191 A Differential Bearing Gauge

MOB35

18G 207 Bearing Pre-load Gauge

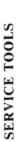

SNAO6O

18G 134 Q Rear Hub Replacer and Adaptor

466

18G 152 Rear Hub Nut Spanner

4347

18G 153 Front Suspension Spring Compressor

SERVICE TOOLS

18G 304 F   Bolt Adaptor — ⅜ in UNF

18G 304 H   Hub Remover Thrust Pad

S 353   Carburetter Adjusting Tool

18G 372   Torque Wrench — 30 to 140 lbf ft — 4 to 20 kgf m

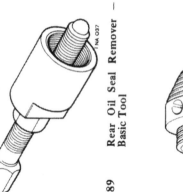

18G 389   Rear Oil Seal Remover — Basic Tool

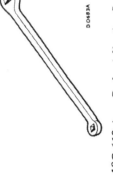

18G 389 A   Rear Oil Seal Remover Adaptor

18G 536   Torque wrench 20 to 100 lbf in — 0.3 to 1.2 kgf m

18G 536 A   Torque Wrench Socket Adaptor

18G 537   Torque Wrench — 10 to 50 lbf ft — 2 to 7 kgf m

18G 590   Disc Brake Re-setting Tool

18G 619 A   Brake Adjusting Spanner

18G 1004   Circlip Pliers

18G 1006   Swivel Axle Bush Reamer

18G 1032   Hub Remover — Wire Wheels

18G 1063   Steering Arm and Ball Joint

18G 1112   Circlip Pliers

SERVICE TOOLS

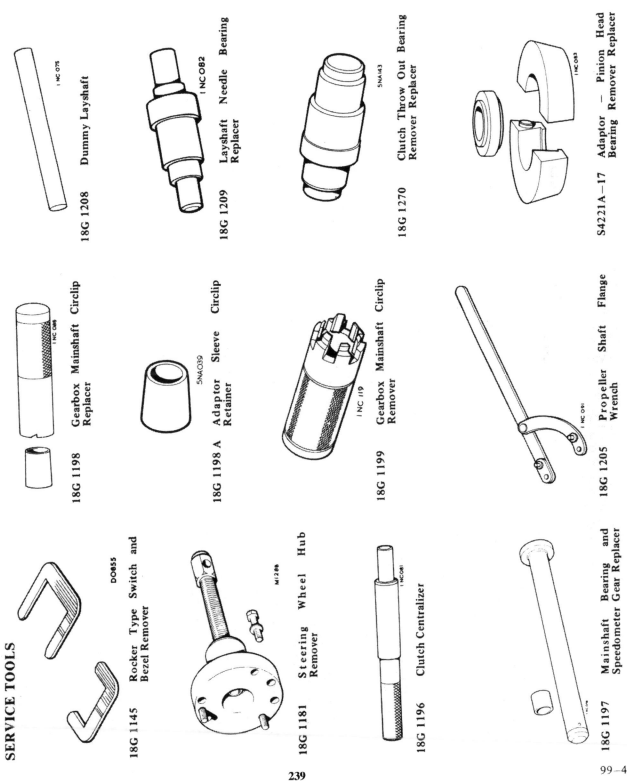

DO855

18G 1145   Rocker Type Switch and Bezel Remover

M1286

18G 1181   Steering Wheel Hub Remover

1 NC 081

18G 1196   Clutch Centralizer

1 NC 016

18G 1197   Mainshaft Bearing and Speedometer Gear Replacer

1 NC 086

18G 1198   Gearbox Mainshaft Circlip Replacer

5NA039

18G 1198 A   Adaptor Sleeve Circlip Retainer

1 NC 119

18G 1199   Gearbox Mainshaft Circlip Remover

1 NC 091

18G 1205   Propeller Shaft Flange Wrench

1 NC 078

18G 1208   Dummy Layshaft

1 NC 082

18G 1209   Layshaft Needle Bearing Replacer

5NA143

18G 1270   Clutch Throw Out Bearing Remover Replacer

1 NC 083

S4221A—17   Adaptor — Pinion Head Bearing Remover Replacer

239

99—4

ADSORPTION CANISTER SPECIAL MAINTENANCE — 1978 and later

ADSORPTION CANISTER SPECIAL MAINTENANCE — 1978 and later

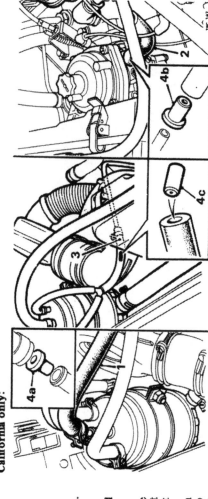

Canada and USA except California:

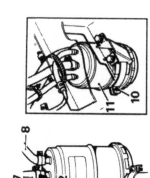

Purge and vapour line restrictors

1 Disconnect the purge line from the primary adsorption canister.
2 Disconnect the purge line from the carburetter.
3 Disconnect the hose from the vapour line.
4 Examine the orifice of the following restrictors for obstruction:
   a Primary adsorption canister restrictor.
   b Carburetter restrictor.
   c Vapour line restrictor.
5 Clear any dirt or deposit from the restrictors using a length of wire. DO NOT use air pressure.
6 Refit the restrictors.
7 Connect the purge pipe to the primary adsorption canister and the carburetter.
8 Connect the hose to the vapour pipe.

California only:

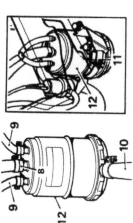

Adsorption canisters — California only

Primary canister — renewal
1 Disconnect the purge pipe.
2 Disconnect the vapour pipes.
3 Disconnect the inter-connecting pipe.
4 Remove the securing bracket nut and bolt.
5 Remove the primary canister.
6 Transfer the restrictor in the canister outlet for the purge pipe to the new canister.
7 Fit the new canister, reconnect the purge, vapour and inter-connecting pipes, and tighten the securing bracket nut and bolt.

Secondary canister — renewal
8 Disconnect the inter-connecting pipe.
9 Disconnect the vapour pipes.
10 Disconnect the air vent pipe.
11 Remove the securing bracket nut and bolt.
12 Remove the secondary canister.
13 Fit the new canister, reconnect the inter-connecting vapour and air vent pipes, and tighten the securing bracket nut and bolt.
CAUTION: Care should be taken when renewing the canister not to disturb the running-on control valve or its connections.

Adsorption canisters — Canada and USA except California

Secondary canister — renewal
1 Disconnect the two outer vent pipes from the top of the canister.
2 Disconnect the central vent pipe.
3 Disconnect the inter-connecting pipe.
4 Remove the securing bracket nut and bolt.
5 Remove the secondary canister.
6 Fit the new canister, reconnect the vent and inter-connecting pipes, and tighten the securing bracket nut and bolt.

Primary canister — renewal
7 Disconnect the purge pipe.
8 Disconnect the vapour pipes.
9 Disconnect the inter-connecting pipe.
10 Remove the securing bracket nut and bolt.
11 Remove the primary canister.
12 Transfer the restrictor in canister outlet for the purge pipe to the new canister.
13 Fit the new canister, reconnect the purge, vapour and inter-connecting pipes, and tighten the securing bracket nut and bolt.

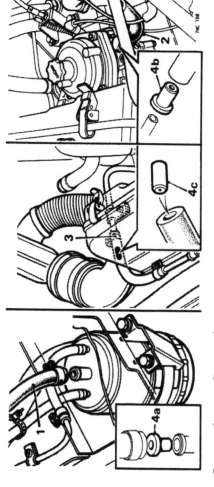

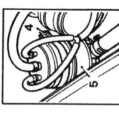

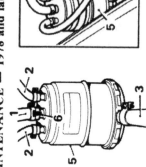

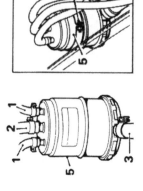

Repair Operation Manual
Supplement

Publication Part No. AKM 4071/1

To be used in conjunction with
Repair Operation Manual AKM 4071

This Supplement contains information on the servicing
and maintenance of 1979 Model Year Cars

GENERAL SPECIFICATION DATA

Gearbox

Ratios: Top	. . . .	1 : 1
Third	. . . .	1.43 : 1
Second	. . . .	2.11 : 1
First	. . . .	3.41 : 1
Reverse	. . . .	3.75 : 1
Overall ratios: Top	. . . .	3.72 : 1
Third	. . . .	5.33 : 1
Second	. . . .	7.86 : 1
First	. . . .	12.69 : 1
Reverse	. . . .	13.96 : 1

Rear axle

Ratio	. . . .	3.72 : 1

ENGINE TUNING DATA — California specification only

Carburetter

Needle	. . . .	45R

Exhaust Emission

Exhaust gas analyser reading at engine idle speed	. . . .	3 to 7% (5% nominal)
Air pump test speed	. . . .	850 rev/min

MAINTENANCE

Maintenance Summary — California only

The maintenance for 1979 model year is identical to that given in the Repair Operation Manual for 1978 except for the following which is now deleted.

At 'E' Service:
Renew catalytic converter (every 25,000 miles).

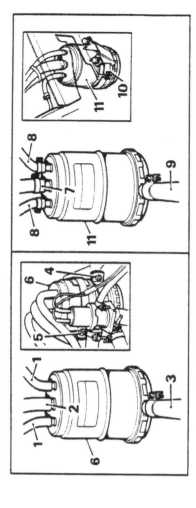

Adsorption canisters — California only

The charcoal adsorption canisters (6) and (11) must be renewed every 50,000 miles.

To remove the secondary canister
Disconnect the two outer vent pipes (1) and the central vent pipe (2) from the top of the canister. Disconnect the running-on control hose (3) from its connection on the canister. Remove the securing bracket nut and bolt (4) and the running-on control valve bracket nut and bolt (5) and remove the secondary canister (6).

CAUTION: Care should be taken when renewing the canister not to disturb the running-on control valve or its connections.

To remove the primary canister
Disconnect the purge pipe (7), vapour pipes (8) and the connecting pipe (9) from their connections on the canister. Remove the securing bracket nut and bolt (10) and remove the primary canister (11).
NOTE: Transfer the restrictor in the primary canister outlet pipe (7) to the new canister.

Refitting
When refitting, ensure that all connections to the primary and secondary canisters are secure.

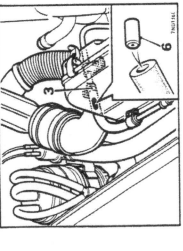

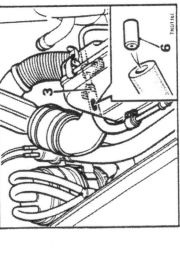

Thoroughly clean the air cleaner cover and casing. Fit a new element into the cover, ensuring the seal of the element faces the casing. To refit the cover, locate the spigots of the cover in the lower lip of the casing and secure with the two clips. Connect the hot air pipe to the air temperature control valve.

Air cleaner element renewal — USA and Canada

Disconnect the hot air pipe (1) from the air temperature control valve (2). Release the two clips (3) on the top of the casing (4). Move the cover (5) and element (6) away from the casing and then withdraw and discard the element.

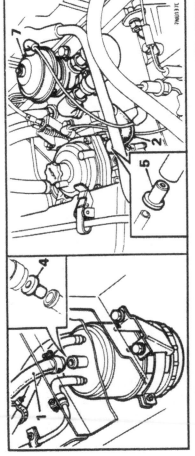

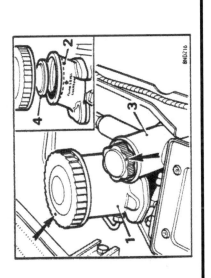

Purge and vapour line restrictors — California only

To check, disconnect the purge line (1) from the primary adsorption canister, and the purge line (2) from the carburetter, also disconnect the hose (3) from the vapour line.
Examine the orifice of the primary canister restrictor (4), the carburetter restrictor (5) and the vapour line restrictor (6) for obstruction. Clear any dirt or deposit from the restrictor orifice, using a length of wire. DO NOT use air pressure to clear any dirt.

Brake and clutch master cylinders — UK

The level of the fluid in the brake master cylinder reservoir is visible through the plastic reservoir (1); the level must be maintained up to the position marked (2) on the side of the reservoir.
To check the level of the fluid in the clutch master cylinder reservoir (3), remove the plastic filler cap. The fluid level must be maintained at the bottom of the filler neck.
Use only the recommended grade of brake fluid to top up the master cylinder, refer to 'SERVICE LUBRICANTS' on page 09—1 of the Repair Operation Manual.
Before replacing the brake filler cap separate the dome (4) from the filler cap and check that the breather hole is clear of obstruction. Snap fit the dome onto the filler cap.

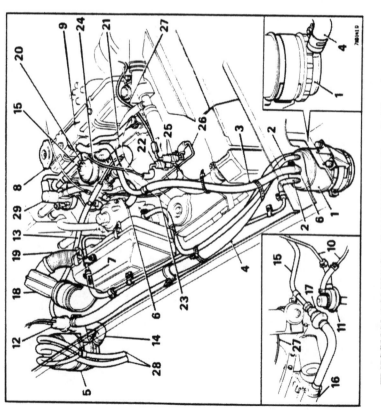

LAYOUT OF EVAPORATIVE LOSS CONTROL – California only

1 Primary charcoal adsorption canister
2 Vapour lines
3 Purge line
4 Connecting pipe
5 Secondary charcoal adsorption canister
6 Restricted connection
7 Restrictor
8 Sealed oil filler cap
9 Oil separator/flame trap (arrester)
10 Fuel pipe
11 Fuel pump

12 Running-on control valve
13 Sensing pipe
14 Running-on control hose
15 Air vent pipe
16 Fuel tank
17 Sealed fuel filler cap
18 Vapour line
19 Vapour tube
20 Capacity limiting tank
21 Separation tank

EMISSION CONTROL COMPONENTS – California only

1 Primary charcoal adsorption canister
2 Vapour lines
3 Purge line
4 Connecting pipe
5 Secondary charcoal adsorption canister
6 Restricted connection
7 Restrictor
8 Sealed oil filler cap
9 Oil separator/flame trap (arrester)
10 Fuel pipe
11 Fuel pump
12 Running-on control valve
13 Sensing pipe
14 Running-on control hose
15 Air injection pipe
16 Air pump

17 Check valve
18 Air temperature control valve
19 Hot air pipe
20 Exhaust gas recirculation valve
21 E.G.R. valve pipe
22 E.G.R. valve flame trap
23 E.G.R. valve flame trap line to carburetter
24 Flame trap line to E.G.R. valve
25 Distributor flame trap
26 Distributor flame trap line to carburetter
27 Flame trap line to distributor vacuum unit
28 Air vent pipe
29 Gulp valve

244

EXHAUST EMMISSION CONTROL

General description – California only

Air is pressure-fed from an air pump via an injection pipe to the cylinder head exhaust port of each cylinder. A check valve in the air delivery line prevents blow-back from high pressure exhaust gases.

IMPORTANT: The efficient operation of the system is dependent on the engine being correctly tuned. The ignition and spark plug settings, valve clearances, and carburetter adjustments given for a particular engine (see 'EN..NE TUNING DATA') must be strictly ...ed to at all times.

Gulp valve – California only

The gulp valve, fitted in the pump discharge line to the inlet manifold, controls the flow of air for leaning-off the rich air/fuel mixture present in the manifold immediately following throttle closure after running at full throttle opening (i.e. engine over-run).

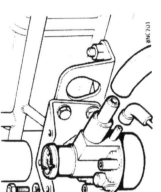

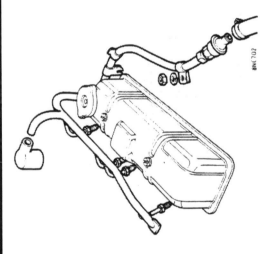

AIR INJECTION PIPE – California only

Remove and refit	17.25.20

Follow the instructions given on page 17–5 of the Repair Operation Manual, noting the following:

a It is not necessary to remove the air cleaner.

b Four unions now secure the air injection pipe to the cylinder head.

MASTER CYLINDER – TANDEM – UK

Remove and refit	70.30.08
Overhaul	70.30.09

Refer to page 70–4 of the Repair Operation Manual when information on the master cylinder is required. The procedure is the same as that described for USA and Canada.

ELECTRICAL

HANDBRAKE WARNING SWITCH – UK

Remove and refit	86.65.45
Check and adjust	86.65.46

Refer to page 86–20 of the Repair Operation Manual when information associated with the handbrake warning switch is required. The procedure is the same as that described for USA and Canada.

GULP VALVE – California only

Remove and refit	17.25.30

To remove the gulp valve, disconnect the hoses from the valve then unscrew the three screws securing the valve to the bracket.

When refitting, ensure all the hoses are secure and air-tight.

BRAKES

BLEEDING THE SYSTEM – UK

Bleed – all round	70.25.02

When bleeding the system refer to page 70–2 of the Repair Operation Manual as the procedure is the same as that described for USA and Canada.

PRESSURE DIFFERENTIAL WARNING ACTUATOR (P.D.W.A.) VALVE – UK

Reset	70.25.08
Remove and refit	70.25.13
Overhaul	70.25.14

Refer to page 70–3 of the Repair Operation Manual when information associated with the P.D.W.A. valve is required. The procedure is the same as that described for USA and Canada.

CIGAR LIGHTER – UK

Remove and refit	86.65.60

Refer to page 86–21 of the Repair Operation Manual when information on the cigar lighter is required. The procedure is the same as that described for USA and Canada.

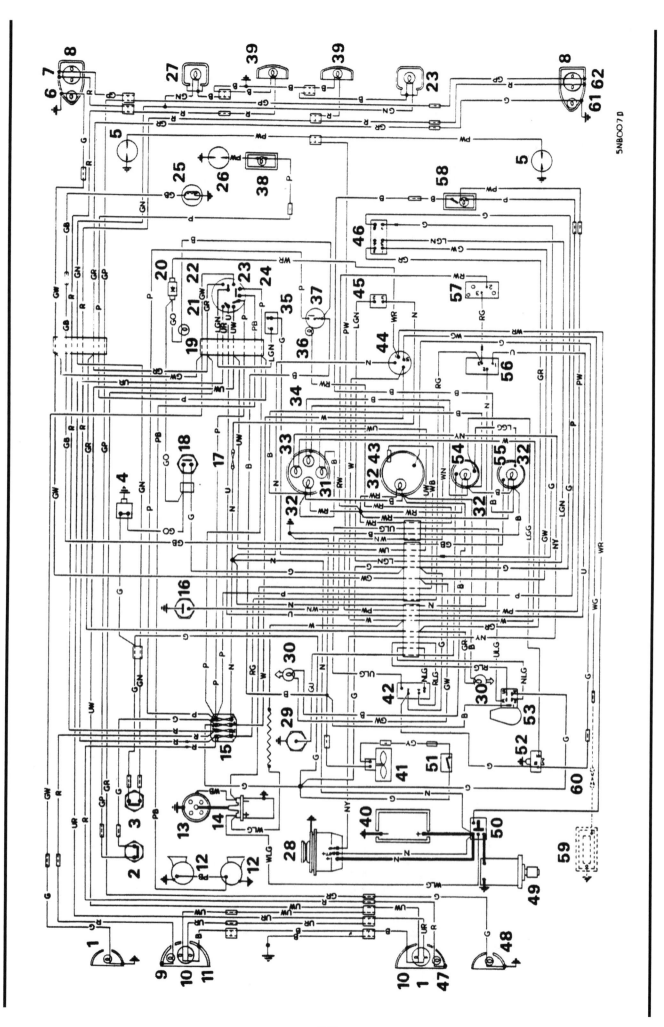

5NBOO7D

KEY TO THE WIRING DIAGRAM

UK Specification

Several of the components listed in this key may not be included in the specification of all models.

1 R.H. front direction indicator lamp
2 Stop lamp switch
3 Reverse lamp switch
4 Brake pressure failure switch
5 Interior lamp door switches
6 R.H. rear direction indicator lamp
7 R.H. tail lamp
8 Stop lamps
9 R.H. sidelamp
10 Headlamp main beam
11 Headlamp dip beam
12 Horn
13 Distributor
14 Ignition coil
15 Fuse unit (4-way)
16 Oil pressure switch

17 Line fuse for hazard warning
18 Handbrake switch
19 Brake warning lamp
20 Diode for brake warning
21 Headlamp flasher switch
22 Direction indicator switch
23 Horn-push
24 Headlamp dip switch
25 Fuel gauge tank unit
26 Luggage compartment switch
27 Reverse lamps
28 Alternator
29 Coolant temperature transmitter
30 Direction indicator warning lamps
31 Main beam warning light

32 Panel lamp
33 Ignition warning light
34 Oil pressure warning light
35 Flasher unit
36 Cigar lighter illumination lamp
37 Cigar lighter
38 Luggage compartment lamp
39 Number plate illumination lamp
40 Battery (12 volt)
41 Heater or fresh air motor
42 Windscreen wiper switch
43 Tachometer
44 Ignition/starter switch
45 Hazard warning flasher unit
46 Hazard warning switch

47 L.H. sidelamp
48 L.H. front direction indicator
49 Starter motor
50 Starter solenoid
51 Heater or fresh air motor
52 Instrument voltage stabilizer
53 Windscreen wiper motor
54 Coolant temperature gauge
55 Fuel gauge
56 Lighting switch
57 Panel lamp switch
58 Interior courtesy lamp
59 Radio
60 Line fuse for radio
61 L.H. rear direction indicator lamp
62 L.H. tail lamp

CABLE COLOUR CODE

N	Brown	P	Purple	W	White	K	Pink
U	Blue	G	Green	Y	Yellow	O	Orange
R	Red	LG	Light Green	B	Black	S	Slate

When a cable has two colour code letters the first denotes the main colour and the second denotes the tracer colour.

OFFICIAL TECHNICAL BOOKS

Brooklands Technical Books has been formed to supply owners, restorers and professional repairers with official factory literature.

Workshop Manuals

Midget Instruction Manual		9781855200739
Midget TD & TF	AKD580A	9781870642552
MGA 1500 1600 & 1600 Mk. 2	AKD600D	9781869826307
MGA Twin Cam	AKD926B	9781855208179
Austin-Healey Sprite Mk. 2, Mk. 3 & Mk. 4 and		
MG Midget Mk. 1, Mk. 2 & Mk. 3		
	AKD4021	9781855202818
Midget 1500	AKM4071B	9781855201699
MGB & MGB GT	AKD3259 & AKD4957	9781855201743
MGB GT V8 Supplement		9781855201859
MGB, MGB GT and MGB GT V8		9781783180578
MGC	AKD 7133	9781855201828
Rover 25 & MG ZR 1999-2005		
	RCL0534ENGBB	9781855208834
Rover 75 & MG ZT 1999-2005		
	RCL0536ENGBB	9781855208841
MGF - 1.6 MPi, 1.8 MPi, 1.8VVC		
RCL 0051ENG, RCL0057ENG		
& RCL0124		9781855207165
MGF Electrical Manual 1996-2000 MY		
	RCL0341	9781855209077
MG TF	RCL0493	9781855207493

Parts Catalogues

MGA 1500	AKD1055	9781870642569
MGA 1600 Mk. 1 & Mk. 2	AKD1215	9781870642613
Austin-Healey Sprite Mk. 1 & Mk. 2 and		
MG Midget Mk. 1 (Mechanical & Body Edition)		
AKD3566 & AKD3567		9781783180509
Austin-Healey Sprite Mk. 3 & Mk. 4 and		
MG Midget Mk. 2 & Mk. 3 (Mechanical & Body		
Edition 1969)	AKD3513 & AKD3514	9781783180554
Austin-Healey Sprite Mk. 3 & Mk. 4 and		
MG Midget Mk. 2 & Mk. 3 (Feb 1977 Edition)		
	AKM0036	9780948207419
MGB up to Sept 1976	AKM0039	9780948207068
MGB Sept 1976 on	AKM0037	9780948207440

Owners Handbooks

Midget Series TD		9781870642910
Midget TF and TF 1500		
Operation Manual	AKD658A	9781870642934
MGA 1500	AKD598G	9781855202924
MGA 1600	AKD1172C	9781855201668
MGA 1600 Mk. 2	AKD1958A	9781855201675
MGA Twin Cam (Operation)	AKD879	9781855207929
MGA Twin Cam (Operation)	AKD879B	9781855207936
MGA 1500 Special Tuning	AKD819A	9781783181728
MGA 1500 and 1600 Mk. 1 Special Tuning		
	AKD819B	9781783181735
Midget TF and TF 1500	AKD210A	9781855202979
Midget Mk. 3 (GB 1967-74)	AKD7596	9781855201477
Midget (Pub 1978)	AKM3229	9781855200906
Midget Mk. 3 (US 1967-74)	AKD7883	9781855206311
Midget Mk. 3 (US 1976)	AKM3436	9781855201767
Midget Mk. 3 (US 1979)	AKM4386	9781855201774
MGB Tourer (Pub 1965)	AKD3900C	9781869826741

MGB Tourer & GT (Pub 1969)	AKD3900J	9781855200609
MGB Tourer & GT (Pub 1974)	AKD7598	9781869826727
MGB Tourer & GT (Pub 1976)	AKM3661	9781869826703
MGB GT V8	AKD8423	9781869826710
MGB Tourer & GT (US 1968)	AKD7059B	9781870642514
MGB Tourer & GT (US 1971)	AKD7881	9781870642521
MGB Tourer & GT (US 1973)	AKD8155	9781870642538
MGB Tourer (US 1975)	AKD3286	9781870642545
MGB (US 1979)	AKM8098	9781855200722
MGB Tourer & GT Tuning	CAKD4034L	9780948207051
MGB Special Tuning 1800cc	AKD4034	9780948207006
MGC	AKD4887B	9781869826734
MGF (Modern shape)	RCL0332ENG	9781855208339

Owners Workshop Manuals - Autobooks

MGA & MGB & GT 1955-1968	
(Glove Box Autobooks Manual)	9781855200937
MGA & MGB & GT 1955-1968	
(Autobooks Manual)	9781783180356
Austin-Healey Sprite Mk. 1, 2, 3 & 4 and	
MG Midget Mk. 1, 2, 3 & 1500 1958-1980	
(Glove Box Autobooks Manual)	9781855201255
Austin-Healey Sprite Mk. 1, 2, 3 & 4 and	
MG Midget Mk. 1, 2, 3 & 1500 1958-1980	
(Autobooks Manual)	9781783180332
MGB & MGB GT 1968-1981	
(Glove Box Autobooks Manual)	9781855200944
MGB & MGB GT 1968-1981	
(Autobooks Manual)	9781783180325

Carburetters

SU Carburetters Tuning Tips & Techniques	
	9781855202559
Solex Carburetters Tuning Tips & Techniques	
	9781855209770
Weber Carburettors Tuning Tips and Techniques	
	9781855207592

Restoration Guide

MG T Series Restoration Guide	9781855202115
MGA Restoration Guide	9781855203020
Restoring Sprites & Midgets	9781855205987
Practical Classics On MGB Restoration	9780946489428

MG - Road Test Books

MG Gold Portfolio 1929-1939	9781855201941
MG TA & TC GOLD PORT 1936-1949	9781855203150
MG TD & TF Gold Portfolio 1949-1955	9781855203167
MG Y-Type & Magnette Road Test Portfolio	9781855208629
MGB & MGC GT V8 GP 1962-1980	9781855200715
MGA & Twin Cam Gold Portfolio 1955-1962	9781855200784
MGB Roadsters 1962-1980	9781869826109
MGC & MGB GT V8 LEX	9781855203631
MG Midget Road Test Portfolio 1961-1979	9781855208957
MGF & TF Performance Portfolio 1995-2005	9781855207073
Road & Track On MG Cars 1949-1961	9780946489398
Road & Track On MG Cars 1962-1980	9780946489817

From MG specialists, Amazon and all good motoring bookshops.

Brooklands Books Ltd., P.O. Box 146, Cobham, Surrey, KT11 1LG, England, UK

www.brooklandsbooks.com